NL ARMS

Netherlands Annual Review of Military Studies

Editor-in-Chief

Patrick Oonincx, Breda, The Netherlands

Managing Editor

Lisette Vos, Breda, The Netherlands

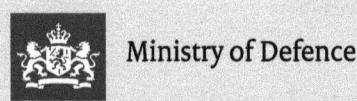 Ministry of Defence

Series Information

The series aims to create an overview of scientific research in military sciences and it shows the extent to which researchers of the Faculty of Military Sciences (FMS) of the Netherlands Defence Academy contribute to this field of expertise.

Research at the Faculty is confined to military-relevant, multi-disciplinary areas and therefore deals with issues relating, among others, to:

- Command and control in military operations
- Leadership and ethics
- Military law and history
- Operational analysis
- Navigation
- Combat systems
- Military platforms
- Cyber warfare

The series is peer-reviewed and reflects the diversity and quality of the Faculty of Military Sciences at its best. With NL ARMS the FMS hopes to serve as a trigger for more international comparative research on military sciences.

Editorial Office

E.T.M. Vos
Faculty of Military Sciences
Netherlands Defence Academy
P.O. Box 90 002
4800 PA Breda
The Netherlands

More information about this series at http://www.springer.com/series/13908

Wim Klinkert · Myriame Bollen ·
Marenne Jansen · Henk de Jong ·
Eric-Hans Kramer · Lisette Vos
Editors

NL ARMS Netherlands Annual Review of Military Studies 2019

Educating Officers: The Thinking Soldier - The NLDA and the Bologna Declaration

Editors
Wim Klinkert
Faculty of Military Sciences
Netherlands Defence Academy
Breda, The Netherlands

Marenne Jansen
Institute for Management Research
Radboud University
Nijmegen, The Netherlands

Eric-Hans Kramer
Faculty of Military Sciences
Netherlands Defence Academy
Breda, The Netherlands

Myriame Bollen
Faculty of Military Sciences
Netherlands Defence Academy
Breda, The Netherlands

Henk de Jong
Faculty of Military Sciences
Netherlands Defence Academy
Breda, The Netherlands

Lisette Vos
Faculty of Military Sciences
Netherlands Defence Academy
Breda, The Netherlands

ISSN 1387-8050   ISSN 2452-235X   (electronic)
NL ARMS
ISBN 978-94-6265-314-6   ISBN 978-94-6265-315-3   (eBook)
https://doi.org/10.1007/978-94-6265-315-3

Published by T.M.C. ASSER PRESS, The Hague, The Netherlands www.asserpress.nl
Produced and distributed for T.M.C. ASSER PRESS by Springer-Verlag Berlin Heidelberg

© T.M.C. ASSER PRESS and the authors 2019
No part of this work may be reproduced, stored in a retrieval system, or transmitted in any form or by any means, electronic, mechanical, photocopying, microfilming, recording or otherwise, without written permission from the Publisher, with the exception of any material supplied specifically for the purpose of being entered and executed on a computer system, for exclusive use by the purchaser of the work.
The use of general descriptive names, registered names, trademarks, service marks, etc. in this publication does not imply, even in the absence of a specific statement, that such names are exempt from the relevant protective laws and regulations and therefore free for general use.

This T.M.C. ASSER PRESS imprint is published by the registered company Springer-Verlag GmbH, DE, part of Springer Nature.
The registered company address is: Heidelberger Platz 3, 14197 Berlin, Germany

Foreword

The Netherlands Annual Review of Military Studies appears yearly as a volume dedicated to an emerging topic in the field of military research. Traditionally it consists of chapters written by scientists from the Faculty of Military Sciences (FMS) and their co-workers who reflect on the central topic from their specific scientific expertise. This year we have taken a slightly different approach by choosing a topic that is one of the core businesses of the faculty, namely academic officers' education.

In 2019 it has been 20 years since the Bologna Declaration was signed by a majority of European ministers. The core mission of the Bologna Process and the main objective of structural reforms in higher education have been to ensure and enhance the quality and relevance of learning and teaching. A European Higher Education Area (EHEA) has been built in which goals and policies are agreed upon at the European level, and then implemented in national education systems and higher education institutions. Academic freedom and integrity, institutional autonomy, participation of students and staff in higher education governance, and public responsibility for and of higher education form the backbone of the EHEA. This was also emphasized in last year's communique of the ministerial conference in Paris within the Bologna Process.

When reading the statement above, one may wonder not only whether it is possible to implement this in a military education environment but also what such an education system would look like. Looking at our neighbours in Germany, we see a hybrid education model that has already existed for over 40 years. There the Bundeswehr universities in Hamburg and Munich are subject to legal stipulations of the respective Bundesländer Hamburg and Bavaria. The university status as well as all regulations concerning the academic programs have to be approved by the two culture ministers. In The Netherlands, issues regarding academic freedom, governance etcetera in the military context have been addressed to a large extent by the installation of the Foundation for Scientific Education and Research of the Netherlands Defence Academy. However, discussions on these issues are ongoing and can be found throughout this volume as well.

Besides issues like academic freedom and university structures, several chapters in this volume address the way education takes place at FMS with respect to educational philosophies, challenges, and solutions within the military academic setting. We think that we have succeeded in combining academic education and preparing for the military profession in good harmony. This combination is a 'must have' in preparing modern-day officers for their future tasks in a complex and uncertain world. Within academic degree programs we look for a balance between building knowledge on military operations, technology, organisations on the one hand and critical thinking on the other. To meet the aforementioned requirements, the FMS uses the metaphor the 'Thinking Soldier', which will be a returning topic of discussion throughout this year's NL ARMS.

In this Foreword I would like to take the opportunity to thank all my colleagues that contributed to this volume, not in the last place the editors who did a great job in organising and finalising all the contributions. To the readers I can only say 'Become part of the world of the Thinking Soldier' and enjoy reading this book.

Breda/Den Helder, The Netherlands

Prof. Dr. Patrick Oonincx
Dean of Faculty Military Sciences
Netherlands Defence Academy

Preface

In 1999, 29 European ministers for Education and Science signed the Bologna Declaration, thereby agreeing to coordinate higher education across Europe by the implementation of the Bachelor's and Master's (BaMa) system. As it turned out, next to civilian universities and institutes for higher education, military academies across Europe, have also introduced the BaMa system into their programs for officers' education. This marks a transition from the old days, when officers' education took place within a national military system, under military command, grounded in principles, traditions and needs, as professed by the Ministries of Defence (MoDs) and the armed forces, in particular.

For reasons of recruitment, employability, good governance and the so-called civilian effect—resulting from the recognition of awarded degrees—in 2002, the Dutch Minister of Defence decided to merge all officers' educational programs into one institute, the Netherlands Defence Academy (NLDA). In doing so, and where applicable, the BaMa system was to be adhered to. In The Netherlands, therefore, the Bologna Declaration can be seen as crucial leverage for the development of in-house academic degree programs as a fundamental part of both initial and more advanced levels of officers' education.

Obviously, the in-house degree programs at NLDA were to remain attuned and relevant to the needs of the MoD and the military professional field. Most significantly, and contrary to previous times, however, implementation of the BaMa system meant that from now on, Dutch traditional strongholds of officers' education were obliged to submit part of their officers' education (i.e., the degree programs) to independent civilian quality control. For, similarly to other institutes for higher education in The Netherlands, the military relevant degree programs were to be assessed and validated according to frameworks devised by the Ministry for Education, Culture and Science.

In this sense, the MoD decision has instigated change processes which continue to impact academic officers' education to this day, ranging from the institutional context and governance structure to educational philosophies and insights, reflective practices and didactical solutions, needed to address specific demands from a specific target population.

Instead of implementing pre-formulated answers, such broad-ranging change requires comprehensive search processes into challenges, which are partly inherent to the introduction of academia within the walls of a military institute. For instance, it has been questioned whether cadets and midshipmen should take part in academic studies at all, instead of postponing this until later into their careers. The meaning—and necessity—of academic freedom, or the meaning of critical thinking and how this relates to socialization processes, also, have been topics of debate. Questions such as these point to challenges and controversies that, preferably, would be studied jointly to obtain answers. As of yet, no comfortable end state to "re-freeze" into after change can be expected.

The editorial board of NL ARMS 2019 strives to offer a platform to academics, military and civilian practitioners, as well as combinations of the three, to reflect and share their thoughts on officers' education 'before and after' Bologna, both in The Netherlands and abroad. To this end, controversies and challenges, affecting various aspects and systems of officers' education, have been grouped into five themes. Four themes are derived from insights and ongoing challenges in the development of the academic part of Dutch officers' education, comprising institutional settings and—change, educational philosophy, educational challenges and reflective practices, and didactical solutions. The fifth theme, international perspectives, provides insights into the strategic environments, challenges and controversies, identified at sister-academies, as well as ways to further officers' education across Europe, e.g., by making use of Erasmus programs.

Institutional Settings and Change Processes

In The Netherlands, before the implementation of the BaMa system, officers' education for Army and Air Force cadets was provided at the Royal Military Academy, in Breda, whereas, the Navy educated its midshipmen at the Royal Netherlands Navy College, in Den Helder. Next to being approximately 200 kilometers apart, geographically, both institutes could avail of their own governance structure, including their own faculties, and were placed either under Army/Air Force or Navy military command. Communication and cooperation between the institutes remained limited. In 2005, academic and administrative staff from both institutes merged into the newly established Faculty of Military Sciences (FMS) under the umbrella of the—also newly established—NLDA, and this implied more than merely 'changing umbrellas'.

Although both institutes for officers' education in Breda and Den Helder have remained intact, from 2005 onwards, Navy, Army, Air Force cadets and midshipmen, added onto by *Marechaussee* cadets, are enrolled jointly in one of three FMS Bachelor degree programs. Currently, all cadets and midshipmen studying military systems and technology are educated in Den Helder, regardless of which branch of the armed forces they belong to. Along the same line, cadets and midshipmen enrolled in war studies or military management studies are pursuing their degree program in Breda.

From 2006, the (preparation of) accreditation processes instigated further institutional change. In order to be allowed to award appropriate academic degrees, the Accreditation Organization of the Netherlands and Flanders (NVAO) demanded a change in the FMS NLDA governance structure. More particularly, to gain NVAO accreditation, all management influence, including state influence, as in exerting military command, was to be strictly excluded from the process of awarding academic degrees. For this reason, in 2011, the independent Foundation for Academic Education and Research at NLDA (SWOON) has been established.

The first two chapters in this volume pay attention to the change processes, which, although they have resulted in a firmer position of academia within a military institution, have not yet led to commonly shared views on governance. Also, the bottom-up approach that has resulted in actual educational reform is highlighted. In Chap. 1, Rijsdijk and Oonincx hold that, whereas, the need for academic officers' education to meet present day professional requirements is generally acknowledged, questions on how to best govern academic education and research within a military organisation remain under debate. The principle of academic freedom as a pre-condition for academic education and research is crucial to this debate, as it implies a level of autonomy of academics and students that is not self-evident in a military structure. Situating the institutional development at FMS in the context of university reform, the authors discuss similarities and differences that may help to reposition the FMS as a small scale academic community in both a military and broader social context.

Rothman, in Chap. 2, seeks to explain the successful reform of initial military education in The Netherlands between 1989 and 2011. The author argues, that, whereas, from a strategic perspective, it made good sense to adopt civilian education standards, the initiative to do so did not come from the Ministry of Defence, which was distracted by multiple missions overseas and budget cuts at home. Instead, reform was the outcome of processes within the institutes for military education themselves, in response to changes in education policy as well as in the strategic context.

In Chap. 3, de Bruijn and Doense, respectively, commanders of the Royal Netherlands Navy College and the Royal Military Academy put forward that, due to increasing global instability, novel warfare areas and the dominant role of technology, the Netherlands armed forces are to increase their agility and adaptiveness. Not only will this objective affect the composition of the armed forces, but, also, future officers are expected to be able to function in complex, highly technological environments, and to lead their mixed and changing teams of specialists into achieving relevant results. To prepare aspiring officers sufficiently for these novel challenges, within NLDA, improved cooperation between institutes that contribute to officers' education, is adamant. The authors are convinced that, as character building has always been at the heart of officer education, again, it will be key in providing solutions for the future. To this end, the presented framework of military virtues serves to connect all elements of officers' education offered at NLDA institutes.

Timmermans and Bertrand, in Chap. 4, open up yet another ethical discourse by taking a closer look at how oaths function in the education and training of military officers. On the one hand, officers take part in oaths and pledges as part of their own training and induction, and, on the other hand, in their future role as officers, they administer oaths themselves. Drawing on business ethics, the authors hold that understanding the performative functioning of oaths, as a means to entrench integrity within organizations and its individual members, may offer new insight into the steering of organizations towards integrity both theoretically and in practice.

Educational Philosophy

The multifaceted strategic and operational contexts, in which military professionals perform their jobs, necessitates them to think creatively when 'designing' solutions for problems in the military field as well as to reflect on—and take responsibility for the outcomes of their actions and ideas. Moreover, officers educated today will help to develop the military of the future. These considerations traditionally have had a significant effect on educational philosophies at military academies. Many contemporary Western institutes for officers' education espouse to cultivate the formation of cadets according to the *Bildung*-ideal. In terms of educational philosophy *Bildung* relates to educating broad-minded generalists and it is still being debated whether and how the intrinsic nature of the *Bildung*-ideal can be reconciled with the practice of socialization in initial officers' education. Questions that need to be studied in-depth are e.g., at what point does education turn into socialization, and, at what point does socialization, that takes place according to a tightly delineated idea, conflict with the essential nature of education as professed in the *Bildung*-ideal.

In Chap. 5, Jansen and Verweij examine the philosophical underpinnings of character education and show inherent difficulties, faced by military academies, when aiming to develop leaders of character. For, to train outstanding leaders, able to deal with the complexities of warfare in the best possible way, appears far from straightforward. The authors argue that to understand what it takes to implement military character education, one first needs to understand its preconditions. By formulating these preconditions and discussing their implications, Chap. 5 evaluates a dominant traditional paradigm in military officers' education.

In Chap. 6, van Baarle and Verweij explore the relevance of Foucault's ideas on the 'art-of-living' concept for ethics education in military organizations. Given Foucault's intellectual indebtedness to Nietzsche, the authors, first, present a theoretical analysis of *Bildung* as a concept and subsequently proceed to focus on the 'art-of-living' concept. It is proposed that, as, art-of-living fosters awareness of power dynamics in case of military moral dilemmas, Foucault's concept may support military personnel with alternative ways to deal with moral dilemmas responsibly.

In Chap. 7, Kramer and Moorkamp, argue that organizational characteristics of military taskforces confront military professionals with specific challenges. Following Schön, the authors put forward such challenges highlight the necessity of reflective practice, that is geared simultaneously towards 'self-designing' an organizational system and enacting the mission environment. In other words, while operating under dangerous and turbulent conditions, military professionals invest major effort to refine and reshape their organizations. Based on research findings over the past 20 years, the authors aim to contribute to novel ways to incorporate the reflective practice concept in military education and research.

Educational Challenges and Reflective Practices

Implementing and maintaining a viable BaMa system in officers' education has spurred re-thinking the educational philosophy and explication of objectives that military relevant academic degree programs aim to achieve. To act on the need for knowledge and strategic thinking in the military field, as well as on the need to keep attuned to the Erasmus and Bologna Processes regarding academic education, both practice based—and science based knowledge are to be integrated to achieve deeper understanding. When academic knowledge is considered relevant to practice based knowledge, cognitive understanding as well as the skills to use what is learned will improve, and, moreover, reflection and critical thinking will be enhanced. To do so, to a certain extent, the challenge is to find ways to combine, or even merge, professional military education and academic reflection and critical thinking.

In The Netherlands, at the level of exit qualifications, to all its Bachelor's graduates FMS applies the metaphor of the 'Thinking Soldier'. This metaphor locates officers in technologically sophisticated, knowledge-intensive organizations within uncertain, dangerous, and ethically challenging environments, in which they execute the state's monopoly on violence. Grounded in Schön's concept of 'reflective practitioner', the Thinking Soldier suggests that such conditions create strong intellectual as well as pragmatic challenges, requiring officers to keep a broad focus and an open mind and, most importantly, to take responsibility for their actions, as these do not only affect their own lives, but the lives and livelihoods of others as well. According to Schön, problem solving by practitioners does not—and principally cannot—resemble 'technical rationality'. Quoting Schön: "Technical rationality holds that practitioners are instrumental problem solvers who select technical means best suited to particular purposes". The problems practitioners need to solve escape the reach of technical rationality because of their indeterminateness. Characteristically, practical problems are uncertain, unique and value-laden. This does not mean that practical problem solving is beyond the reach of theory and involves an unjustifiable 'muddling through'. Instead, based on the concept of the reflective practitioner, it is argued that reflection-in-action (thinking what they are doing while they are doing it) can be used to form hypotheses on actions or interventions. According to Schön, "An overarching theory does not give a rule that can be applied to predict or control a particular event, but it supplies a language from which to construct particular descriptions and themes from which to develop particular interpretation". In this way, the concept of the reflective practitioner not only offers an alternative to technical rationality, but, also helps to demystify practice as if it were an art based on a kind of intuitive knowing that escapes conceptualization.

In the context of officers' education, the concept of reflective practitioner refers to the need for critical thinking, reflection and responsibility and accountability for one's own actions. Reflection may start by feelings of bewilderment and doubt as to the situation one finds oneself confronted with, to be followed by an urge to study, interpret and confer meaning to what is happening, and to analyze and clarify problems in order to deal with them. Reflection is not only about skills, but also about attitudes, such as open mindedness, openness, a real interest in other people and the world around you as well as a need for critical thinking. These things matter, because, as mentioned above, by their actions, military officers do not only affect their own lives, but the lives of others as well. As such, the concept of "the reflective practitioner" can be regarded as the basis for a particular view on *Bildung*.

In Chap. 8, Bijlsma elaborates on the meaning of reflectivity for operational servicemen and—women. To this end, the author introduces two concepts of reflective learning: experiential learning theory and problem based learning. With this framework, the actual situation on officers' education is explored. The author pleads for more attention to reflectivity in the curricula and in the classroom.

Van Doorn, in Chap. 9, links the need for flexibility and adaptiveness, also put forward in Chap. 3 by de Bruijn and Doense, to 'learning while working'. The latter is often referred to as reflective practice, and, in this light, coaching—as in facilitating learning—can be viewed as 'the new leadership'. To this end, the author examines how the theoretical perspective on Critical Success Factors (CSFs) in coaching may offer a practical framework for organisational learning and the education of reflective practitioners. Specific attention is paid to its appropriateness to the education of future military leaders.

Van Tilborg, Bijlsma and Muis, in Chap. 10, discuss how military, often exposed to extremely stressful situations, may benefit from the preventive effects of mindfulness training, whilst, simultaneously facilitating and deepening reflectivity. The authors have used an individual, low-dose, self-training mindfulness intervention (i.e., a 10-day mind-fitness training), conducted amongst 173 Dutch military, to explore the effects on mindfulness, stress, wellbeing, working memory capacity, and situational awareness. It was found that the intervention sorted a negative effect on stress and positive effects on mindfulness, wellbeing and (self-rated) situational awareness. In Chap. 11, Annink and van Mook ask how teachers contribute to the development of cadets from novices to experts, based on five predetermined characteristics, comprising (1) individual and collective learning, (2) military and academic education, (3) the role of teachers, (4) professional identity and (5) learning strategies. Not only do the authors find that all five characteristics are related to the development of cadets into experts, but, moreover, teachers influence this development process by stimulating the cadets' reflective ability, by granting sufficient time to practice knowledge and skills and by differentiating between individual and collective learning needs. Beeres and Bollen, in Chap. 12, look for factors, identified in literature, that influence the academic performance of undergraduate students in military management studies at FMS. To this end, over the last six years, surveys have been conducted amongst 184 cadets and midshipmen, representing all services within the Dutch armed forces. Based on statistical results, amongst others, the authors find that neither service, nor gender, nor age can be associated with academic performance.

Didactical Solutions

As a theme, 'didactical solutions' is embedded in the previous two themes. For, once an educational philosophy has been established and educational challenges and reflective practices can be addressed, it comes down to actually 'doing' education. How does one give *hands and feet* to the ideals of a 'reflective practitioner'? Inherent tensions between practice—and scientific-based knowledge, relevant to the military, continue to challenge both the providers and the receivers of military education. Academic staff in higher education need to enable their students to engage in dialogues to explore complex issues from different points of view and gain insights that cannot be achieved individually. The intention is to create an effective, productive balance of adaptive—and creative learning, where students can apply what they have learned to their relevant professional context, and where they can also use creative learning, critical thinking and reflection to generate new professional knowledge. The ability to apply professional knowledge, gained through adaptive learning, in a professional context, and to generate new professional knowledge by reflection on one's own actions and creative learning, lies at the heart of the concept of the reflective practitioner. From the perspective of the reflective practitioner, academic officers' education cannot merely be about providing the raw academic materials, and, subsequently, letting practitioners sort it out for themselves. Additionally, officers' education takes place in a very specific environment: the military organization and the boarding school, which both demand/compel certain forms of student behavior and mirror certain ideas, reflecting the 'ideal officer'. This environment is brought into the classroom and academic staff are to relate to it.

In Chap. 13, de Jong and Baudet put forward, that, as military professionals operate in complex environments characterized by confusing and contradictory visual (dis)information, academically trained officers, at least, should possess some awareness of the consequences of 'manoeuvring' in this equally allusive and persuasive domain of visual rhetoric. 'Iconic images' can transfer important (political) messages and therefore may be used to influence all those involved in conflicts. The authors argue that studying relationships between form, content and function in iconic images of war positively enhance understanding of the complex nature of conflict, war and warfare and the responsibilities of the officer therein. Therefore, 'thinking soldiers' also need critical tools from the toolbox of the (art) historian.

Klinkert, based on the metaphor of the 'thinking soldier' and rooted in the history of military education, in Chap. 14, elaborates on how battlefield tours (BFTs) support both the development of critical thinking as well as understanding the realities of war. Analyses and discussions at the location of historical military confrontations are thought to further understanding on the realities of war and improve future decision making. In many ways, BFTs constitute a very practice-orientated method of educating military professionals, increasingly being underpinned by reflection and critical thinking. The author examines efforts to create BFTs that meet academic standards, whilst still providing cadets and midshipmen with professional insights in the realities of war, and, thus remaining relevant to their future work as subaltern officers.

In Chap. 15, Brinkel, Murphy and Noll apply the concept of the reflective practitioner to staff rides. Both in Ireland and in The Netherlands, staff rides are believed to establish a learning environment that allows for maximum student involvement, a non-hierarchical exchange of views and experiences and the positioning of the teacher as coach and enabler. As noted by Klinkert in Chap. 14 regarding battlefield tours, staff rides, also, are rooted in the idea that professional military artistry cannot be learned solely through technical training and learning regulations by heart, but, instead needs to be experienced in a reflective practicum. To this end, staff rides are set up as a function of the aim to encourage reflection, ethical aspects, questions behind the questions and the confrontation of practice with values and personal convictions.

When developing didactic concepts in officers' education, one has to keep in mind that, for the most part, cadets and midshipmen will not pursue an academic career. Unique didactical solutions are required to integrate practice-based and scientific-based knowledge, some of which are presented in this volume. In officers' education, science based knowledge and creative learning serve to support the further development of the professional field, i.e., practice based knowledge, behavior and actions. This means that theories are to be relevant to the professional working field. As to practice-based knowledge, this must be underpinned by (empirical) research, instead of proven experience only. In doing so, research on military practices, challenges and controversies as a scientific base, will continue to contribute to improve education, professional competencies and the development of a common body of knowledge. Partaking in academic officers' education that is geared towards delivering reflective practitioners means that students, whether they are cadets, midshipmen, officers or civilians will be involved in research themselves and, therefore, will have to learn to reflect on military practices. Their contributions to (action) research will support the military to solve problems and will add to the development of a body of knowledge for the armed forces to draw on. This body of knowledge is based on a variety of academic disciplines, ranging from technical sciences to law, humanities and a wide range of social sciences. The authors of Chaps. 16, 17 and 18 pay attention to specific parts of curricula, that are characteristic to officers' education, either fitting in with the demands of a specific branch or service within the armed forces, or being of a more generic and even '*education permanente*' nature.

Frerks, in Chap. 16, elaborates on how, at the end of the Bachelor's degree program in war studies and the initial military training, Dutch cadets and midshipmen have to understand the political and policy environment they will operate in during their future professional life. This competence is part of the 'Thinking Soldier' concept that guides their education at FMS. The course on Netherlands Security and Defence Policy aims to achieve this. The author highlights the goals and main contents of this course and clarifies how the complicated substance of this topic is being taught at bachelor's level using a variety of educational tools. Visser-Schönbeck, in Chap. 17, discusses how to approach military law, a subject taught in various programs for officers' education. Military law covers several branches of law officers use, for instance, administrative law or disciplinary law to apply in the case of subordinates, or humanitarian law or operational law to apply in the field. Consequently, courses on military law take place throughout military careers; not only during initial education, but also at later stages. From a didactical point of view, legal education needs a very practical approach, applying the law to cases to clarify theoretical aspects, whilst, at the same time, maintaining an academic basis. The author discusses the implications for the ways such courses can be set up.

In Chap. 18, Dado, Schmets, Krosenbrink and Krabbenborg explain how the Engineers Regiment, in order to adjust to the changing military operational and organizational context, adopts new methods and techniques in the areas of military strategy, management, organization and technology. Amongst others, this requires rethinking the desired and required competences of the Regiment's—current and future—personnel and the academic education of future officers. Educational and research institutes within—or associated with the Dutch defence organization anticipate interactions between military practice, education and research, i.e., an intensified collaboration within the Golden Triangle. Within the scope of the FMS educational and research programs, the authors address both current developments and the required interaction between military practice, education and research.

International Perspectives

NLARMS 2019's fifth and last theme is dedicated to international perspectives, which provide insights into challenges and controversies, identified at sister-academies, as well as ways to further officers' education across Europe. It will appear that, due to differing security situations, demographics, national governance strategies and other impacting factors, the contexts in which military academies across Europe educate officers and, in doing so, are able to contribute to the development of military capabilities, vary considerably.

In Chap. 19, Mengelberg and Scalas discuss how, from the end of the Cold War, officers' training and education across Europe has both broadened and become strengthened by additional institutional structures due to multilateral, organizational and inter-organizational initiatives. Notably, to this effect, the authors view EU's entrance in the security and defence domain under the umbrella of the European security architecture as a milestone. Although strengthening these initiatives is met by challenges due to diversified national interests, persevering to do so is expected to offer opportunities also. The authors elaborate on developments in training, education and research in the European security and defence domain and address current challenges and opportunities.

In Chap. 20, Bileišis and Ungurytė-Ragauskienė, from an historical-institutional angle, focus on Lithuania's security situation. Resulting from both economic growth as well as demographic decline, the Lithuanian military are faced with an unfavorable recruitment environment, severely impeding the staffing of military units. Due to perceived external threats, the country feels necessitated to expand its professional officer corps, beyond the number of officers graduating from the military academy. The authors explore why security services, either resorting under the Military Statute or the Interior Service Statute, fail to coordinate the development of professional military competencies. They find three possible reasons. First, security services fit into a broader Lithuanian governance model, characterized by multi-level fragmentation and resistant to integration policies, even in instances of political salience. Furthermore, some institutions have their civilian functions 'militarized', whilst others have their military functions 'demilitarized', hampering the development of military competences. Third, and seemingly paradoxically, increased defence spending seems to drive the military and support services in the armed forces apart.

In Chap. 21, Jansen, Brænder and Moelker compare notes on educational reforms in The Netherlands and Denmark over the last decade. Regarding recruitment and educational models, the authors conclude that change in Denmark has been more radical than in The Netherlands. Denmark switched to recruiting academics and shortening the educational trajectory whilst the Dutch kept both long (Bachelor's degree program) and short (applied vocational training and skills and drills) models and mixed their recruiting strategy. Both countries also offer career possibilities for NCOs entering the officer corps. In both countries, however, tensions between the soldier's habitus and the scholar's habitus have not been resolved. The strengths and weaknesses of both countries' educational reforms in terms of "what sets the officer apart?" are discussed. The authors recommend possible escapes from the dilemma of a training that on the one hand is too scholarly and academic, or, on the other hand, emphasises too much military skills and drills. Developing the habitus of the Thinking Soldier may prove the new way ahead.

The epilogue offers a perspective on the complex position occupied by any in-house academic faculty within a military organization. It is argued that within this specific context, an academic faculty can only remain valuable when it is able to retain a certain critical distance from the environment for which it educates. This means that it should be able to resist certain pressures from within the military organization. Particularly in times of budget cuts such pressures can be experienced as quite significant. At the same time, compared to other academic institutes, a faculty within a military organization is located in an altogether different biotope. Therefore, a faculty such as FMS also needs to be able to resist trends that occur within the 'civilian' academic world that would alienate it from its biotope.

At this point, the editors would like express their deep gratitude to all contributing authors. We sincerely hope, all those interested in officers' education will enjoy many instances of critical thought, reflection and creativity while reading this volume.

Breda, The Netherlands

Wim Klinkert
Myriame Bollen
Marenne Jansen
Henk de Jong
Eric-Hans Kramer
Lisette Vos

Contents

Part I Institutional Settings and Change Processes

1 Governing Academic Education and Research in the Military in the Context of University Reforms 3
Erna Rijsdijk and Patrick Oonincx

2 Making the Academic Turn: How Bottom-up Initiatives Drove Education Reform at the Netherlands Defence Academy 17
Maarten Rothman

3 Character Is (the) Key! The Application of Virtue Ethics to Improve Officers' Education 27
Joost Doense and Jaco de Bruijn

4 A Performative Account of the Use of Oaths to Enhance Integrity Within the Military 43
Job Timmermans and Robert Bertrand

Part II Educational Philosophy

5 Officer *Bildung*: A Philosophical Investigation of Preconditions for Military Character Education 59
Marenne Jansen and Desiree Verweij

6 A Critical Appraisal of the *Bildung* Ideal in Military Ethics Education 77
Eva van Baarle and Desiree Verweij

7 Reflective Practice in Synthetic Expeditionary Task Forces 97
Eric-Hans Kramer and Matthijs Moorkamp

8 From Thinking Soldiers to Reflecting Officers—Facts and Reflections on Officers' Education 115
Tom Bijlsma

9   Five Critical Success Factors for Coaching: A Perspective
    on Educating Reflective Practitioners 133
    Ger van Doorn

10 Mindfulness in the Dutch Military – Train Your Brain 155
    Anouk van Tilborg, Tom Bijlsma and Susanne Muis

11 The Impact of Educational Characteristics on the Development
    of Cadets from Novices to Experts 181
    Charlotte Annink and Nicole van Mook

12 Determinants of Academic Performance in Bachelor Theses:
    Evidence from the Faculty of Military Sciences at the Netherlands
    Defence Academy 195
    Robert Beeres and Myriame Bollen

Part III Didactical Solutions

13 Iconic Images and Military Education: A Delicate
    Relationship 211
    Henk de Jong and Floribert Baudet

14 Bologna Meets the Battlefield – Using Historical Battlefields
    in Modern Academic Military Education 231
    Wim Klinkert

15 The Staff Ride as Reflective Practicum – Impressions
    and Experiences of the Faculty of Military Sciences
    and Maynooth University 247
    Theo Brinkel, David Murphy and Jörg Noll

16 Policy for Cadets and Midshipmen – Teaching Dutch Security
    and Defence Policy at the Netherlands Defence Academy 261
    Georg E. Frerks

17 Legal Education: A Matter of Motivation? An Overview
    of Aspects of Legal Education for Officers 273
    Kirsten Visser-Schönbeck

18 Military Engineering – Practice, Education and Research
    in The Netherlands; the Golden Triangle 285
    Edwin Dado, Alexander Schmets, Rick Krosenbrink
    and Dennis Krabbenborg

Part IV International Perspectives

19 A European Army of Thinking Soldiers – European Academic
    Officers' Education: Challenges and Opportunities 305
    Sabine Mengelberg and Riccardo Scalas

20	**Lilliputians Divided: How Service Statutes Fragment Lithuanian Security Services**............................. 321
	Mantas Bileišis and Svajūnė Ungurytė-Ragauskienė
21	**What Sets the Officer Apart? Dutch and Danish Educational Reforms Leading to the Habitus of the Thinking Soldier** 337
	Marenne Jansen, Morten Brænder and René Moelker

Epilogue.. 355

Editors and Contributors

About the Editors

Prof. Dr. Wim Klinkert holds the chair in Modern Military History at the Netherlands Defence Academy and is professor of military history at the University of Amsterdam. He is specialized in Dutch military history of the 19th–20th century and in the history of Dutch military education. His latest book in English was published in 2013: *Defending neutrality. The Netherlands prepares for War, 1900–1925* (Brill Publishers, Leiden/Boston).

Prof. Dr. Myriame Bollen is professor of Civil-Military Interaction at the Faculty of Military Sciences of the Netherlands Defence Academy, where she chairs the department of Military Management Studies and she is a visiting professor at the Baltic Defence College Estonia.

Marenne Jansen, MA works at the Advisory Council for International Affairs, while writing her Ph.D. at the Institute for Management Research of the Radboud University. Her research focuses on military leadership development, and the nexus between development and security. In addition, she is interested in educational philosophy, sustainable development and the role of international organizations. She has taught courses on these topics for bachelor and master students at various Dutch universities, international diplomats, and NGO employees.

Henk de Jong, MA is assistant professor of Military History at the Faculty of Military Sciences of the Netherlands Defence Academy. His research focusses on cultural aspect of war and warfare.

Prof. Dr. Eric-Hans Kramer is professor of Military Management and Organization at the Faculty of Military Sciences of the Netherlands Defence Academy. His research interests include integral organization theory, systems safety and the relation between organizational context and psychotrauma. His work has been published in various journals and books and he has also written a book entitled *Organizing Doubt*, which was published in 2007.

Lisette Vos, MSc is an educational specialist and secretary of the Faculty Board at the Faculty of Military Sciences of the Netherlands Defence Academy.

Contributors

Charlotte Annink Netherlands Defence Academy, Breda, The Netherlands

Floribert Baudet Faculty of Military Sciences, Netherlands Defence Academy, Breda, The Netherlands

Robert Beeres Faculty of Military Sciences, Netherlands Defence Academy, Breda, The Netherlands

Robert Bertrand Faculty of Military Sciences, Netherlands Defence Academy, Breda, The Netherlands

Tom Bijlsma Faculty of Military Sciences, Netherlands Defence Academy, Breda, The Netherlands

Mantas Bileišis Jonas Žemaitis Military Academy of Lithuania, Vilnius, Lithuania

Myriame Bollen Faculty of Military Sciences, Netherlands Defence Academy, Breda, The Netherlands

Theo Brinkel Faculty of Military Sciences, Netherlands Defence Academy, Breda, The Netherlands

Morten Brænder Aarhus University, Aarhus, Denmark

Edwin Dado Faculty of Military Sciences, Netherlands Defence Academy, Breda, The Netherlands

Jaco de Bruijn Royal Netherlands Naval College, Netherlands Defence Academy, Den Helder, The Netherlands

Henk de Jong Faculty of Military Sciences, Netherlands Defence Academy, Breda, The Netherlands

Joost Doense Royal Military Academy, Netherlands Defence Academy, Breda, The Netherlands

Georg E. Frerks Faculty of Military Sciences, Netherlands Defence Academy, Breda, The Netherlands

Marenne Jansen Radboud University, Nijmegen, The Netherlands

Wim Klinkert Faculty of Military Sciences, Netherlands Defence Academy, Breda, The Netherlands

Dennis Krabbenborg Faculty of Military Sciences, Netherlands Defence Academy, Breda, The Netherlands

Eric-Hans Kramer Faculty of Military Sciences, Netherlands Defence Academy, Breda, The Netherlands

Rick Krosenbrink Faculty of Military Sciences, Netherlands Defence Academy, Breda, The Netherlands

Sabine Mengelberg Faculty of Military Sciences, Netherlands Defence Academy, Breda, The Netherlands

René Moelker Faculty of Military Sciences, Netherlands Defence Academy, Breda, The Netherlands

Matthijs Moorkamp Institute for Management Research, Radboud University Nijmegen, Nijmegen, The Netherlands

Susanne Muis University Utrecht, Utrecht, The Netherlands

David Murphy Maynooth University, Maynooth, Ireland

Jörg Noll Faculty of Military Sciences, Netherlands Defence Academy, Breda, The Netherlands

Patrick Oonincx Faculty of Military Sciences, Netherlands Defence Academy, Breda, The Netherlands

Erna Rijsdijk Faculty of Military Sciences, Netherlands Defence Academy, Breda, The Netherlands

Maarten Rothman Faculty of Military Sciences, Netherlands Defence Academy, Breda, The Netherlands

Riccardo Scalas Netherlands Defence Academy, Breda, The Netherlands

Alexander Schmets Faculty of Military Sciences, Netherlands Defence Academy, Breda, The Netherlands

Job Timmermans Faculty of Military Sciences, Netherlands Defence Academy, Breda, The Netherlands

Svajūnė Ungurytė-Ragauskienė Mykolas Romeris University, Vilnius, Lithuania

Eva van Baarle Faculty of Military Sciences, Netherlands Defence Academy, Breda, The Netherlands

Ger van Doorn Faculty of Military Sciences, Netherlands Defence Academy, Breda, The Netherlands

Nicole van Mook Netherlands Defence Academy, Breda, The Netherlands

Anouk van Tilborg GenDx, Utrecht, The Netherlands

Desiree Verweij Faculty of Military Sciences, Netherlands Defence Academy, Breda, The Netherlands

Kirsten Visser-Schönbeck Royal Netherlands Air Force, Utrecht, The Netherlands

Part I
Institutional Settings and Change Processes

Chapter 1
Governing Academic Education and Research in the Military in the Context of University Reforms

Erna Rijsdijk and Patrick Oonincx

Contents

1.1 A Short History of the Faculty of Military Studies 4
1.2 Academic Freedom as Organizing Principle 6
1.3 The Classical University 7
1.4 The Professors' University 8
1.5 The Democratic University 9
1.6 The Managers' University 11
1.7 Conclusion 14
References 15

Abstract This chapter elaborates on the processes of institutionalisation and governance of academic education and research at the Faculty of Military Studies (FMS) at the Netherlands Defence Academy (NLDA). The need for academic officers' education to meet present day professional requirements is generally acknowledged, but questions of how to best govern academic education and research within a military organization remain under debate. The principle of academic freedom as a pre-condition for academic education and research is crucial to this debate, because it implies a level of autonomy of academics and students that is not self-evident in a military structure. Nevertheless, "civil" universities also need to guarantee academic freedom in tension with other principles that come with the organization, finance and societal demands of scholarship. Universities have

---

E. Rijsdijk (✉)
Faculty of Military Sciences, Netherlands Defence Academy, PO Box 90002
4800 PA Breda, The Netherlands
e-mail: eac.rijsdijk@mindef.nl

P. Oonincx
Faculty of Military Sciences, Netherlands Defence Academy, Breda, The Netherlands
e-mail: pj.oonincx@mindef.nl

© T.M.C. ASSER PRESS and the authors 2019
W. Klinkert et al. (eds.), *NL ARMS Netherlands Annual Review of Military Studies 2019*, NL ARMS, https://doi.org/10.1007/978-94-6265-315-3_1

struggled – and still struggle – to find a good balance between academic autonomy and its governance too. As a result universities have gone through different stages of governance reform. Situating the institutional development of the FMS in the context of university reform enables us to see parallels and differences that may serve as references for future change in the FMS governance structure. It may help to reposition the FMS more self-consciously as a small scale academic community in both a military and broader social context.

Keywords Academic freedom · Military academia · Governance · Faculty of Military Studies · Netherlands Defence Academy · University reforms

1.1 A Short History of the Faculty of Military Studies

In The Netherlands, military officers' education has been regulated by the state from 1890, when it was decided by law (WMOL)[1] that future officers of the land forces needed to be educated in specific fields, such as law and military regulations, mathematics, but also horse riding.[2] Although its content had a practical orientation, military education was meant to broaden the intellectual horizons of the future military officers and was set up separately from the military training. The need and relevance of academic education for future military officers has been debated ever since. As Wim Klinkert's study on striving for academic schooling for the Dutch military (from 1890 to 2011) demonstrates, proponents and opponents could be found both in the military and in civil society.[3] Unfortunately, this debate often narrows down to the question of the status of the officer and whether academic thinking would be counterproductive or not for the skills to beat the enemy.

After the Cold War, opinions turned in favour of academic schooling for officers because the world and the potential enemy had changed. The overall situation was perceived as increasingly complex, and for future battlefields it was obviously necessary not only to think in terms of military skills but also to understand political and economic consequences of military actions. New technologies found their ways to the modern battlefields. These evolutions required academic education for those who had to deal with it. Similar observations on academic education and the changing world were topic of a Harvard University study "Learning Peace: Attitudes of Future Officers Toward the Security Requirements of the Post-Cold War World".[4] This working paper examines whether the education system applied

---

[1] WMOL: Wet tot regeling van het Militair Onderwijs bij de Landmacht (21 juli 1890) [Act to regulate Military Education at the Army (21 July 1890) "Voor zoover daarbij de opleiding voor den officiersrang en de hoogere vorming van den officier zijn betrokken". ["As it concerns the education for the rank of officer and higher officers' training"].

[2] Klinkert 2012, p. 5.

[3] Klinkert 2012.

[4] Franke 1997.

at West Point Academy would meet future demands. Outcomes of the study include the expansion of analytical abilities to accommodate the increasing complexity of the strategic environment. Also it was mentioned that future officers have to learn to manage diversity, gender, religion, culture and have to train "beyond the battlefield". In those days, the opposition to the notion of "meeting future demands necessitates academic education" mostly stemmed from the military ranks. In the same period, European countries also addressed the issue of academic education of military officers. Although in some countries military academies were already recognised as universities, the issue whether and why the educational program for officers should be at an academic level was at the front of the debate. In 1999, the University of Vienna and the Austrian National Defence Academy organized a first international conference on academic studies for officers from a central European perspective. Contributions from ten European countries confirmed the outcome of the John M. Olin report for many of the academies involved. Furthermore, the conference made the differences in academic status of the several military institutes clearly visible.[5]

In 2002, Member of Parliament – and former spokesman of the Ministry of Defence – Mat Herben filed a motion[6] in which he urged the Minister of Defence (MoD) to merge all officers' education programs into one institute and to follow the European Bologna declaration of 1999.[7] In this declaration, European countries agreed to coordinate their higher education by the introduction of a Bachelor's and Master's (BaMa) system. For the military and maritime officers' education in The Netherlands, this motion constituted the logical step towards accredited academic degree programs. Another corollary of the motion was the creation of an academic faculty to develop, teach and maintain the degree programs, as well as to conduct academic research in relation to the program topics. It was agreed that the academic programs would be set up in close relation to military practices and training, thus as part of a military institution in which future officers live and receive their military training. Academic education at the present FMS is designed to develop reflective practitioners who approach problems in the military field in a critical way and avail of sufficient intellectual creativity to generate constructive solutions that may be of an operational, technical or organizational nature. The FMS philosophy is grounded in the expectation that the future officers operate effectively in decision making processes in environments that are both knowledge intensive and stressful.

---

[5] Albrecht 1999.

[6] M. Herben c.s., kamerstuk 28600-X-32, 2002.

[7] Bologna 1999. Joint Declaration of the European Ministers of Education convened in Bologna on 19 June 1999.

1.2 Academic Freedom as Organizing Principle

Accepting that academic education is necessary for military officers to meet present day professional requirements, this chapter addresses the debate on the institutional development of the FMS. The concept of academic freedom as a foundational principle for academic education and research plays a crucial role in this debate. There is no question about the *importance* of the principle of academic freedom, but opinions differ on how this principle guides the governance of education and research in a military organization. As we will demonstrate, some aspects of this debate are not exclusive to the organization of an academic community within the military, but play a role in governance reform of universities as well. Therefore, insight into developments in university governance may contribute to understanding governance in military academia, and, more particularly, why the question of participation of the academic community in governance continues to play a role in accredited education and research programs.

Academic freedom is not only generally acknowledged as a pre-condition to knowledge production, but also as essential for the functioning of democracy. In many states academic freedom therefore is a constitutional right. In a report on academic freedom and integrity in academic education and research, Joris Groen has analysed the legal status and developments of these concepts in The Netherlands.[8] He describes the current status of academic freedom as an "emerging constitutional right" that – in combination with academic integrity – is seen as a core norm of academic education and research.[9] The role of the state is not only to guarantee that freedom, but also to create the conditions to govern education and research according to the principles of academic freedom and integrity. In Dutch law academic freedom comprises, firstly, the freedom for the researcher to initiate research themes and to conduct research according to one's own research perspectives; secondly, the freedom for students to receive education without indoctrination and without being forced to adhere to, or to proclaim specific academic perspectives and, thirdly, the freedom for teachers to proclaim their own academic views and the teacher and to determine the content and method of education.[10] The freedom of academic staff and students regarding education and research is, however, not unrestricted. Teachers, for example, are obligated to educate students responsibly in such a way that students are enabled to make progress throughout the educational program of the institution and they are to teach in accordance with the institutional teaching and exam regulations (TERs).[11] In this respect, academic freedom also implies *responsibilities of individual academics*, and, even more so, *responsibilities of academic communities*. Thus, academic freedom cannot be

---

[8] Groen 2016. In 2017, this report was published as a chapter in Groen's Ph.D. thesis Academische vrijheid. Een juridische verkenning [Academic Freedom. A legal exploration].

[9] Groen 2016, pp. 5–8.

[10] Groen 2016, p. 26.

[11] Groen 2016, p. 27.

separated from organizational responsibilities. In Dutch law, academic freedom is therefore beheld as a *foundational* principle of university governance.[12] Consequently, academic institutions are to be autonomous to a high extent in organising their academic freedom and integrity. Over time, however, there have been considerable changes regarding the ways to provide autonomy and governance participation in academic institutions. Groen identifies four university reform stages that we will use to contextualise the institutional development of the FMS. These stages are *the classical university* (1815–1960), *the professors university* (1960–1970), *the democratic university* (1970–1997), and, last, *the managers university* (1997–present).[13] We regard these stages as periods of transition in which different of organization and governance practices reflect changing views on what are necessary pre-conditions for academic education and research.

1.3 The Classical University

In 1815, three institutions in Leiden, Utrecht and Groningen became state universities. Groen marks those institutions as *classical universities* (1815–1960). The *classical university* had a dual organization structure, which comprised a hierarchal state management of personnel and finance as well as a corporal form of academic self-government of education and research. Key academic positions such as a board of curators, the rector, and the professors were appointed by the state. The unsalaried board of curators consisted of five members who met twice a year to draw up the budget and to oversee whether the educational laws were upheld by the university, to take care of the university buildings and properties, and to allocate the education and courses among the professors. In practice, there was much freedom for professors to determine the content and form of those courses. Research was unregulated and was not seen as a legal task of universities. The professors were part of an executive body called *Senatus academicus* led by the rector whose position alternated among the professors. It was the senate's task to supervise academic discipline ["*tucht*" in Dutch] and education. Between the state and the academic senate, the board of curators, in practice, functioned as a buffer between the state and academic freedom.[14]

We note that the current FMS governance structure has much in common with the dual organization structure of this *classical university*. As was the case at the classic university, regulations are primarily directed at educational tasks commissioned by

---

[12] Groen 2016, p. 26.
[13] Groen 2016, p. 31.
[14] Groen 2016, pp. 32–33.

an unsalaried supervising body named SWOON[15] acting a buffer between the Ministry of Defence and the academic community. Personnel and finance are hierarchically managed by the Ministry of Defence, whereas FMS has executive tasks in academic education and research. The SWOON board bears final responsibility for the academic education and research programs. Because the board members only meet a few times a year, in practice, allows for a certain leeway when it comes to organization, governance and execution of education and research at the FMS.

1.4 The Professors' University

During the 1950s, the growth of universities instigated a new law on Academic Education (WWO)[16] which marks the nascence of *the professors' university (1960–1970)*. WWO conferred the status of autonomous legal subjects to universities, involving increased budgetary autonomy and a modernisation of governance. Due to the expansion of universities, academic self-governance by professors in a *Senatus Academicus* had become inefficient, and instead, WWO enabled the delegation of governing tasks to the faculties. Moreover, the faculties became involved in governance of the university as a whole and the position of the professors changed considerably. In the *classical university*, professors were approached as teachers for specific courses, while the WWO legal regime positioned them as leaders of other academic staff and as leaders and supervisors of other academic staff including their education and research. This re-positioning created a strong formal hierarchy between professors and other staff.[17]

Within the FMS, some characteristics of the *professors' university* are recognisable. In the sense that some of the professors are positioned as leaders of other academic staff. Moreover, because FMS's academic staff consists of both military and civilians, military hierarchical lines impact the organization and governance of education and research, especially when professors also hold a military rank. Among military academic personnel, military ranks, to a large extent determine whether one has a position as teacher, assistant professor or associate professor. To a certain extent this also applies to the academic "rank" of professor, albeit that, nowadays, a Ph.D. degree is one of the academic conditions for a military professorship and the appointment needs to be approved by the academic advisory council WAR[18] which is part of SWOON. WAR members are professors of Dutch

---

[15] SWOON is the Dutch acronym for *Stichting Wetenschappelijk Onderwijs en Onderzoek NLDA* [Foundation for Academic Education and Research at the NLDA] and should certainly not be confused with its meaning in English, namely 'a partial or total loss of consciousness' (Merriam Webster web dictionary).

[16] WWO is the Dutch acronym for *Wet op het Wetenschappelijk Onderwijs*, 1960 [Act on Scientific Education].

[17] Groen 2016, pp. 35–38.

[18] WAR is the Dutch acronym for *Wetenschappelijke Adviesraad* [Academic advisory council].

universities and, in that respect, the appointment of military professors can also be seen as a decision of academic peers. Allocation of research and education is not directly related to this internal hierarchy. Academic freedom in the FMS is restricted to the content of education and research, and, to a limited extent, to the organization and governance thereof.

1.5 The Democratic University

In the 1960s, as the political culture changed and the number of university students expanded, opposition rose against the strong formal hierarchy within universities. Not long after the demonstrations in Paris, in 1968, a new law (WUB, 1970)[19] prescribed a democratisation of university governance, based on equal participation across the university community. This new law marks the beginning the *democratic university* (1970–1997). Encompassing all levels, the new *democratic university*'s governance structure included students and non-academic staff to guarantee broader democratic relations to society. An elected university board [*universiteitsraad*] came to be in charge as internal "law maker", and an executive board [*college van bestuur*] whose members were still appointed by the government, became responsible for the daily management at the university. At faculty level, an executive faculty board [*faculteitsraad*] was elected. At least half of its members were academic staff. Faculty boards did not hold any management power, but were solely responsible for the coordination of education and research. As to the content and quality of academic research and education, the responsibility thereof remained the prerogative of academic staff, although the previous hierarchy between professors, academic staff and students became less formal. WUB also provided for a novel supervisory board of deans to advise on education and research policies. An interesting paradox in this system was, according to Groen, that participatory interest groups restricted the executive powers of the executive university board to such an extent that that full implementation of the democratic structure, as ordained by law, could not be achieved. In 1985, the WUB was revised and the ensuing law on academic education (WWO),[20] enabled top management to gain superiority over the democratic representatives of the university. In The Netherlands, the WWO was the first law stating academic freedom to be a fundamental governance principle, although the meaning of the concept was not stipulated in detail to avoid controversies.[21] In 1988, 388 rectors and heads of universities of the European Community confirmed this principle of academic freedom and institutional

---

[19] WUB is the Dutch acronym for *Wet op Universitaire Bestuurshervorming* [Act on university reform] of 1970.

[20] WWO is the Dutch abbreviation for Wet houdende herziening regeling van het wetenschappelijk onderwijs [a revision of the act on academic education] of 25 September 1985.

[21] Groen 2016, pp. 38–43.

autonomy as guideline for good governance and self-understanding of universities by signing the Bologna *Magna Charta Universitatum*. The document states, that freedom in research and training is the fundamental principle of university life, and governments and universities, each as far as in them lies, must ensure respect for this fundamental requirement. Rejecting intolerance and always open to dialogue, a university is an ideal meeting ground for researchers capable of imparting their knowledge and well equipped to develop it by research and innovation and for students entitled, able and willing to enrich their minds with that knowledge.[22]

The fact that academic freedom, for the first time, was expressed by law as a fundamental governance principle to which end governance participation of the academic community is key, demonstrates the emergence of a new social perspective on academic freedom, education and knowledge production.

The new perspective on academic freedom as a fundamental governance principle, turned out to be a serious obstacle for the integration of academic education in the military. In 1985, the Cabinet proposed a law (WWOK)[23] parallel to the WWO that would regulate academic education within the military. The Education Council of the Netherlands advised against it, because of insufficient guarantees for academic freedom. The Council argued that the proposed WWOK, as separate to the WWO, placed itself outside the reach of the laws on academic education. The Council also found that the implementation of academic freedom was wrongly delegated to the governing statutes and regulations of the military organization. Decisions of the institutional board [*College van Bestuur*] concerning academic education could be overruled by the MoD and the participatory council [instellingsraad] would only have an advisory position. The defence policy of the MoD would be normative, which implied that military aspects of education would be superior to academic aspects.[24] In 1986, the Council of State also expressed its doubt on the autonomy of education and research and the guarantees for academic freedom.[25] Finally, in 1990, after years of debate, Minister Ritzen of Education rejected the proposed WWOK that would have freed the way to military academic degree programs. Ritzen's main objection concerned the lack of democracy in the proposed governance structure of the military academy and the integrated approach to military and academic education.[26]

The concept of the *democratic university* did not make it into the new millennium, but the fundamental principle of autonomy as guideline for good governance of academic education and research – as stated in the Bologna Magna Charta

---

[22] Bologna 1988.
[23] WWOK is the Dutch acronym for Wet Wetenschappelijk Onderwijs Krijgsmacht [Proposed act on academic education within the military] of 1985.
[24] Education Council of the Netherlands 1985.
[25] Klinkert 2012, p. 33.
[26] Klinkert 2012, p. 34.

Universitatum declaration of 1988[27] – has not been abandoned. In contemporary university governance, staff and student participation is still required, however, their governing role has changed.

1.6 The Managers' University

In the 1990, a more business-like approach of public management – internationally known as New Public Management (NPM) – led to changing political views on university governance. In 1997, a new law (MUB), amended the WHW of 1992[28] to "modernise" the governance- and participation structures at universities.[29] The *democratic university* was to be replaced by the *managers' university* (1997–present). MUB instigated more hierarchical relations between the universities' management levels, thereby fundamentally changing the governance structure. At faculty level, decision-making powers were replaced by participatory bodies that in some matters had advisory rights and in other matters consent was needed. Faculties were granted some autonomous powers, more or less comparable to the relations between municipalities and the central government. The autonomy of faculties, dubbed academic freedom, comprised mainly the content and design of education and research.[30] Based on the governance practice of academic hospitals, the law introduced a supervisory board for universities, its members to be appointed by the Minister of Education. Thus, the powers of university managers were to be balanced by participatory bodies, a supervisory board reporting to the Minister and a rather independent position of the faculty in determining the contents of research and education.[31]

In short, MUB broke with the principle of democratic government and introduced a clear division between responsibilities of management, internal control, and staff and student participation. According to Nolen's study on the legal position of the manager in education,[32] MUB re-positioned student and staff participation, including rights to negotiate, advise and approve of management decisions, in such a way that these rights granted the representation of interests of students and staff.[33] The role of participatory bodies thus changed from democratic co-governance into a position that had more in common with "client" participation.

---

[27] The Joint Declaration of the European Ministers of Education convened in Bologna on 19 June 1999 refers to the fundamental principles of the Bologna *Magna Charta Universitatum* declaration of 1988 (Bologna 1999).

[28] WHW is the Dutch acronym of *Wet op het Hoger onderwijs en Wetenschappelijk onderzoek* [Act on higher education] of 8 October 1992.

[29] MUB is the Dutch acronym for Modernisering Universitaire Bestuursorganisatie [modernizing university governance], (27 February 1997).

[30] Groen 2016, p. 44.

[31] Groen 2016, pp. 43–47.

[32] Nolen 2017.

[33] Nolen 2017, p. 280.

Although, over the years, formal empowerment of participatory bodies increased, support of the academic community for the *managers' university* was lacking. Induced by severe budget cuts in government funding of academia, and compounded by the lack of influence as experienced by academic staff and students regarding financial management decisions that impacted education and research, in 2012, students and staff protested against the *managers university* at VU University, and in 2015 at the University of Amsterdam by occupying university's management headquarters the Maagdenhuis. Proponents for more participation in university governance see students and staff as an academic community that needs to have more autonomy in self-organization. They point to the 1970 WUB and its principle of co-governance, which, in 1997, was forsaken due to the implementation of MUB.[34] Budget cuts and a lack of influence on budget spending were not the only reasons to protest. In 2012, VU professor Lorenz published a frequently cited article "If You're So Smart, Why Are You under Surveillance? Universities, Neoliberalism, and New Public Management" in which he addressed the managerial control practices as part of a New Public Management strategy approached education and research in terms of markets, clients and efficiency.[35] The adopted discourses on efficiency, quality, accountability, transparency, flexibility, products and clients play an important role in management control practices. Although, the terminology as such represents positive values of governance, Lorenz demonstrates how their implementation by means of audit and control mechanisms result in counterproductive effects. As Lorenz notes, "combined with the ever increasing pressure of work and the abolition of the professional regime of time, this process undermines the essence of what drives academics to do what they do".[36] The problem signalled by Lorenz is not unique to present day universities. In The Netherlands, similar discussions are held about the negative effects of control processes for professionals in the health care sector. In her PhD theses *Control With Care*, Jacqueline Heeren-Bogers finds that especially in organizations with" a high degree of asymmetry of power between managers and employees and organizations with few "reality checks" of external influences" like the military, a coercive bureaucracy is advocated in which the issuing of rules and procedures tends to elicit behavioural reactions – indifference, resistance, alienation – among staff.[37]

The NPM view on education and research as "products" of which the quality could be assessed independently of the governance structure of the institution, also led to a different assessment of academic education within the military organization. In 2010, the external quality assurance organization NVAO[38] advised the accreditation of all three BA programs of the FMS. Nevertheless, this advice did not

---

[34] Nolen 2017, p. 280.
[35] Lorenz 2012.
[36] Lorenz 2012, p. 613.
[37] Heeren-Bogers 2018, pp. 47–48.
[38] NVAO: Nederlands Vlaamse Accreditatie Organisatie [Netherlands Flemish Accreditation Organization].

automatically lead to the government's approval. The government demanded an independent legal entity, not being the state, to govern academic education and research and to confer academic degrees at the FMS. It was only by means of a complex legal construction that this foundation named SWOON could be put in place. The SWOON members are senior representatives of the Ministry of Defence, public and private management, and – in an advisory position – university professors, who meet a couple of times a year. They are responsible for guaranteeing the independence of the foundation concerning the accreditation of academic education.[39] SWOON has also a task in securing the relations to the MoD. The Faculty Board is responsible for the daily governance of academic education and research. They are not responsible for the FMS budget and means. The Dean and faculty staff consist of both military and civilian staff who are paid and managed by the Defence organization. In 2011, the first acknowledged and civilian recognised academic educational BA degree programs were finally a fact. As opposed to the 1990s, when the integration of military training and academic education, was seen as an obstacle to obtain civilian recognition and acknowledgement, now, FMS graduates could obtain a BA degree, next to their officer's diploma. Decision making on the academic degrees was to be the exclusive responsibility of SWOON, that decided independently from military (or civilian) management. Since 2011, all BA programs have been successfully assessed as well as four MA degree programs and the FMS is currently preparing for its research program to get academic accreditation as well. As mentioned before, the governance structure of SWOON and the FMS resembles that of the *classical university*. There is no staff or student participation in the executive board of SWOON, except for the Dean who holds an advisory role. But like the situation at the *classical university*, daily governance is in the hands of the faculty, in which students and staff are part of the participatory bodies.

From 2011 until 2019, no major changes in the governance structure in the FMS governance structure have occurred. However, the expansion in the number of degree programs as a result of growing demands of the MoD, the ambitions of the FMS, and changing policies in higher education, including demands for better guarantees of academic integrity, have put pressure on the existing structure. As this chapter focuses on FMS governance in the context of university reforms, we need to return briefly to the developments in university governance after the protests of 2012 and 2015. At the time, Dutch government responded to the protests of the academic community by introducing a law meant to increase democracy and governability in education (WVB),[40] which became part of the WHW in 2017. This law, however, was not so much a return to the *democratic university*, but, according to Nolen, confirmed the government's interest in more practical forms of

---

[39] SWOON 2011, Article 12.11.

[40] WVB: Wet Versterking Bestuurskracht [Act to increase democracy and governability in Dutch higher education].

participation.[41] For university governance it meant, for example, that the role of participatory bodies was strengthened in the selection, appointment and dismissal of academics and managers and in the quality control of education. The external quality insurance organization NVAO also responded to the critique of increasing pressure the bureaucratic quality control procedures on the autonomy of the academic community. It states in its *NVAO Strategy 2017–2020* that "with its adapted frameworks and working methods, NVAO wants to give the institutions greater autonomy and strengthen the involvement of students and staff".[42] As a result, academic institutions gain more freedom in accounting for the quality of their education and research.

1.7 Conclusion

Neither SWOON nor the FMS are bound by law to adopt a university governance structure because the institution is not funded by the Ministry of Education. SWOON and the FMS are only bound by the WHW as far as it concerns the quality of academic education and research. Nevertheless, as we have seen, because of the fundamental principle of academic freedom, academic quality cannot be fully separated from governance. As a result, WHW's legal requirements of accountability for that academic quality, *do* push the Faculty governance in the direction of a "normal" university department. Whether or not this is a good development whilst maintaining the relevance of the FMS to the MoD remains under discussion. In the context of the development of the *managers university* as far as it results from the growth of universities, the smaller size of the FMS academic community offers good opportunities for governance participation of academic staff and students. The other challenge for FMS's academic autonomy – as well as it is for universities – are the audit and control practices becoming instruments that may undermine trust and motivation of academic professionals. As stated in NVAO's new strategy, it might be worthwhile to explore new forms of accountability that leaves room for professional academic autonomy. Having situated the institutional development of the FMS in the context of university reform enables us to see parallels and differences that may serve as references for future adaptations in the FMS governance structure. It may help to keep the balance between academic autonomy and governance and to reposition the FMS more self-consciously as a small scale academic community in both a military and broader social context.

Acknowledgement The authors would like to thank Lisette Vos for her contribution to this chapter by sharing her in-depth knowledge of the archives of the FMS and Myriame Bollen for her review and helpful editorial recommendations.

---

[41] Nolen 2017, p. 281.
[42] NVAO 2017.

References

Albrecht G (ed) (1999) Academic Studies for Officers: A Central European Perspective. Presentations of the 1st International Conference, Vienna.
Bologna (1988) Magna Charta Universitatum, Bologna.
Bologna (1999) Joint Declaration of the European Ministers of Education convened in Bologna on 19 June 1999.
Education Council of the Netherlands (1985) Voorontwerp van Wet Wetenschappelijk Onderwijs voor de Krijgsmacht van 24 September 1985 [Proposed law on academic education within the military of 24 September 1985]. The Hague.
Franke V C (1997) Learning Peace: Attitudes of Future Officer toward the Security Requirements of the Post-Cold War World. John M. Olin Institute for Strategic Studies at Harvard University.
Groen J R (2016) Academische vrijheid en wetenschappelijke integriteit: Een onderzoek naar vrijheid en verantwoordelijkheid in wetenschappelijk onderwijs en onderzoek [Academic freedom and academic integrity. A study of freedom and responsibility in academic education and research]. Academie voor overheidsjuristen, The Hague.
Groen J R (2017) Academische vrijheid. Een juridische verkenning [Academic Freedom. A legal exploration]. PhD thesis, Erasmus University, Rotterdam.
Heeren-Bogers J (2018) Control with Care. The value of soft controls in the management control system of the Dutch Defence organization. PhD thesis, Erasmus University, Rotterdam.
Klinkert W (2012) Mars naar de wetenschap: Het streven naar de wetenschappelijk opgeleide officier, 1890–2011 [Striving for the Academic Status of Officers' Education, 1890–2011]. Netherlands Defence Academy, Breda.
Lorenz C (2012) If You're So Smart, Why Are You under Surveillance? Universities, Neoliberalism, and New Public Management Critical Inquiry, 38:599–629.
Nolen M (2017) De bestuurder in het onderwijs. De juridische positie van de bestuurder in vijf onderwijssectoren [Managing directors (*bestuurders*) in education. The legal position of members of the management board in five educational sectors]. Boom Juridisch, The Hague.
NVAO (2017) NVAO Strategy 2017–2020, The Hague (17 March 2017).
SWOON (2011) Oprichtingsakte van de Stichting Wetenschappelijk Onderwijs en Onderzoek NLDA [Instrument of Incorporation and Statutes of the Foundation for Academic Education and Research NLDA].

Dr. Erna Rijsdijk is Chair of the Faculty Council and a Lecturer at the Faculty of Military Sciences of the Netherlands Defence Academy. She studied politics and critical security studies at the University of Amsterdam, the University of Newcastle (UK) and the VU University (Amsterdam), where she completed her Ph.D. dissertation *Lost in Srebrenica: Responsibility and Subjectivity in the Reconstructions of a Failed Peacekeeping Mission* in 2012. Recently, in 2018, she published *Reconstituting the Dutch State in the NIOD Srebrenica Report* in *The Palgrave Handbook of State Sponsored History After 1945* edited by B. Beverage and N. Wouters.

Prof. Dr. Patrick Oonincx is Dean of the Faculty of Military Sciences of the Netherlands Defence Academy. Before that he was a full professor in Navigation Technology and a board member of the Faculty. He holds a Ph.D. in mathematics and is an editorial board member of several international journals on Navigation and Signal Processing.

Chapter 2
Making the Academic Turn: How Bottom-up Initiatives Drove Education Reform at the Netherlands Defence Academy

Maarten Rothman

Contents

2.1	Introduction..	18
2.2	Changes in Educational Content...	19
2.3	Strategic Change, Defence Policy and Military Education.....................................	21
2.4	Academic Initiative...	23
2.5	Conclusion...	25
References...		26

Abstract This chapter seeks to explain the successful reform of primary military education in The Netherlands between 1989 and 2011. Adopting civilian education standards made good sense from a strategic perspective, but the initiative did not come from the Ministry of Defence, which was distracted by multiple missions overseas and budget cuts at home. Instead reform was the outcome of processes at a lower level of decision-making, largely within the military education institutes themselves, and in response to changes in education policy as well as in the strategic situation.

Keywords Primary military education · education reform · national security strategy · bottom-up initiative · academic freedom · Netherlands Defence Academy

---

M. Rothman (✉)
Faculty of Military Sciences, Netherlands Defence Academy, PO Box 90002, 4800 PA Breda, The Netherlands
e-mail: mgd.rothman@mindef.nl

© T.M.C. ASSER PRESS and the authors 2019
W. Klinkert et al. (eds.), *NL ARMS Netherlands Annual Review of Military Studies 2019*, NL ARMS, https://doi.org/10.1007/978-94-6265-315-3_2

2.1 Introduction

When the Cold War ended, Dutch military education was in the last throes of a failed attempt to be recognized as academic, on par with civilian university education. The new strategic environment spelled the end for a draft law on academic officers' education first proposed in 1963. A 30-year process of education reform at the Royal Institute for the Navy (Dutch acronym KIM) and the Royal Military Academy (KMA) did not yield the desired result. The Ministry of Defence (MoD) faced major budget cuts, not only at the beginning of the post-Cold War period but throughout. Nevertheless, the Netherlands Defence Academy (NLDA) gained academic recognition in 2011. How did it manage to do this in such dire times?

This chapter looks at two explanations for the successful reform. One is that the change in the strategic situation led to the reform, that is to say, that policymakers decided to prepare the armed forces for their new tasks by changing the way officers were educated. As fitting as it would seem for top leadership at the MoD to consciously decide on long-term change in the quintessential instrument of state power, I will argue that this is not the way the reforms took place. Instead I will show that the reform was the outcome of processes at a lower level of decision-making, largely within the military education institutes themselves, and in response to changes in education policy as well as in the strategic situation.

Unless one takes an extreme view of the state as a rational unitary actor, it is no surprise that strategic decisions made at the top are to some extent affected by choices made during their implementation. There is likely a time lag, as educational reforms take time to crystallize and to be implemented. (For this reason it is not yet possible to assess the most recent changes in strategic outlook, after the Russian takeover of Crimea in 2014.) The institutions governing military education may be resistant to change or divided on the desirability of various options. The aims of the Ministry of Education don't necessarily align with those of the MoD. Because of these intervening variables, the outcome will never be exactly as imagined at the start of the process. A certain amount of path dependency is implied. It is not enough, therefore, to show that some deviation took place, to reject the first hypothesis we must show that the initiative lay at a lower level, or that policy frames other than political-military strategy had a bigger influence on the outcome, or both.

The research method most easily applied to the case is process tracing. Fortunately my colleague (and editor of this volume) Wim Klinkert has already written a history of the education reforms at the Netherlands Defence Academy and its forerunners.[1] Rather than redo the work Klinkert already did, I attempt here to draw out a few of the strands of that history and assess their explanatory value.

---

[1] Klinkert 2012.

The next section looks at educational content, whether change occurred and who had a say in it. The one after that discusses MoD policy. I argue there that military education was affected by various policies set by the ministry but that none of them articulated a specific policy on military education. In the penultimate section I show that there was much more dynamism at the level of the academy itself, prompted in large part by changes in education policy, thus shaped by the Ministry of Education rather than the Ministry of Defence. The NLDA achieved recognition by grabbing the opportunity held out by the Bologna declaration, a process which had nothing at all to do with military-strategic change.

2.2 Changes in Educational Content

Between the early 1990s and 2011 a large number of changes occurred, which I lack the space to discuss in detail. At the institutional level the most important change was the formation of a single Netherlands Defence Academy in place of two separate service academies and a separate school for advanced officers' education. While the forerunners of the NLDA used to offer education programs for officers in their branch of the armed services which were not accredited by the Ministry of Education, the NLDA now offers three university level bachelor degrees, four master degrees, one executive master at polytechnic level, a shorter officer training course aimed at students who already hold previous university or polytechnic diplomas, and a variety of very short programs to introduce trained specialists into the armed forces. This chapter focuses on the bachelor degree programs. However, from the early 2000s onwards the short officer-training program has been matched to the first months of the bachelor programs. This common core is followed by students from all three bachelor programs. It consists of overview courses in international security, strategy, military ethics, law, management and technology, and military operations. Because of the common core, the short program did not develop independently but has been driven along by the reform of the long program and thus has been affected by the accreditation process.

The forerunners of the bachelor programs were 4-year programs at the Royal Institute for the Navy and the Royal Military Academy. Both already had a common core followed by specialization. Aspiring officers in the technical branches (e.g. engineers) sometimes took courses at universities. The majority of aspiring officers took programs that mixed administration, economics, international politics and military operations, with further specialization in the 3rd and 4th year of the program. Three separate bachelor programs, one in Military Technical Studies, one in Military Management Studies, and one in War Studies replaced these programs. Military Technical Studies provides the armed forces with their complement of engineers as well as officers with an understanding of the technical aspects of their weapon systems. Military Management Studies provides controllers, personnel managers, logistics and medical officers and others whose main task is "behind the frontlines" (though that demarcation is not always clear anymore in today's battlespace). The utility of these programs is thus not in doubt. But to what extent have they changed the content of their courses in response to strategic developments? Technical studies adapted rather to changes in weapon systems than directly to strategic concerns. In fact, it was War Studies that began the cyber operations study program at the NLDA, focusing on legal and operational concepts. Military Management emphasized both the logistics of expeditionary operations and the ethics and psychological strain of messy new wars in its curriculum. War Studies divided its courses on military operations between regular warfare, counterinsurgency, peace support operations, and national operations, thus expanding course content on irregular operations. Of its two battlefield tours, one specifically integrates politics, law, and military operations in order to get a fuller view of contemporary conflicts and post-conflict situations; past tours have visited Bosnia, Kosovo, Turkey, Northern Ireland, Israel/Palestine and the Baltic states.[2]

From this I conclude that changes in educational content do follow changes in the strategic situation. But any match between the changed strategic situation and the new course content was not the result of any MoD directive. Instead Ministry of Education standards applied. These ensured academic freedom in regard not only to research but also to course content, which was set by program boards and by individual teachers. In the accreditation process, there is a small role for junior officers as recent graduates, and a similar role for the armed services as representatives of the work field, and the governing board of the academy (both before and after it became a foundation; see below) seats several officers and ex-officers. The program boards for the bachelors include cadets and military academic staff, i.e. officers who teach courses in their respective bachelor course and who, as academic staff, are expected to produce research as well. In this way there is some influence of the armed forces on the curriculum. But their civilian colleagues outnumber officer-teachers. Nor is this necessarily an impediment to strategic responsiveness. At company level, the lessons of the Afghanistan missions were easily forgotten because of frequent changes in personnel and a tendency to focus on the latest perceived threat, combined with a tendency to focus on the familiar, large-scale conventional conflict.[3] NLDA academics have, of their own accord, researched the new wars, and it appears they both delve deeper and have longer memories. Counterinsurgency, peacebuilding and related topics entered the classroom without prompting from the MoD. As the next section will show, the ministry's focus lay elsewhere.

---

[2] See Brinkel et al. Chap. 15 in this volume.
[3] De Winter 2015; Kitzen 2016.

2.3 Strategic Change, Defence Policy and Military Education

The first consequence of strategic change after 1989 was the peace dividend. The removal of the perceived direct threat to national security meant that national Defence could be scaled back. In other words: cuts to the military budget, which became worse at every subsequent financial crisis. Post-Cold War policy at the MoD and at branch headquarters (excepting the *Marechaussee* which expanded its border guard component) initially attempted to keep as much of the former capabilities intact as possible within a shrinking budget. At the start of the period, unused weapon systems were even put in storage rather than sold. The idea was that they would be ready to use again if the strategic situation changed for the worse, but as time went by, this was increasingly viewed as unlikely. A smaller budget for new weapon systems and for innovation generally was the costs of this preservation policy. That, too, became untenable over time. In these conditions, the replacement of the F16 fighter by the F35 Joint Strike Fighter became not only a hot button political issue but also a bone of contention between the branches, the army and navy fearing that their own budgets would be further squeezed in order to accommodate the air force's wishes.[4] Needless to say, such budgetary rivalry didn't mesh well with combined operations. Another way to retain operational capacity on a smaller budget was to use a volunteer reserve as a flexible workforce to be deployed when necessary. Some reservists have been deployed overseas multiple times, yet don't appear on the armed forces' regular peacetime payroll.[5] This approach fits with management ideas current in the civilian economy (which have also been taught at the Royal Military Academy since the 1980s). The MoD pushed for rationalization and efficiency in order to maximize capacity, much as the services did, while avoiding interservice rivalry as much as possible. Centralization of support services affected the military academies directly, as they were put in a separately run interservice branch staffed by personnel from each branch. Merging of branch units resulted, among others, in a single Defence Academy in place of the old service academies. The policy rationale for the change was to develop a common *esprit de corps* and improve interservice cooperation at lower levels; the recipients of the directive regarded it instead as an austerity measure. However, the decision to merge was taken in 2002 by parliament on the initiative of a MP, Mat Herben, rather than by the Defence ministry.

The government also decided it would no longer ask young men to sacrifice a year of their lives, ending the draft in 1996. The armed force went from professional core and cadre to full professional, with the happy (intended) consequence that it became much easier politically and legally to send soldiers on missions abroad. Career perspectives for officers changed as a consequence. The days when military

---

[4] Colijn et al. 2013.
[5] Rengers 2018.

professionals provided a cadre for units to be filled by conscript soldiers were over; lifetime employment was no longer guaranteed. The new personnel policy was "up or out", meaning that lower echelon officers who did not make the grade for the next higher rank were expected to leave the service (instead of staying on as officers for largely empty conscript units). Recruitment of quality personnel had been a problem before 1989, indeed was part of the rationale for the earlier push towards academic recognition. With these changes, the MoD expected its recruitment problems to increase. After some ten years deliberation, in 2005, it opted to sweeten the deal for military personnel by offering certified degrees so that those who would leave, would – they said hopefully – be regarded as capable workers in the civilian economy.[6]

After the Cold War, even as the budget shrank, the Dutch military shifted towards participating in multinational expeditionary operations. Dutch soldiers participated in 97 missions since 1989, ranging from observations missions on the Israel-Egypt border to mine clearing in Cambodia to peacekeeping in the Balkans to fighting jihadist groups in Afghanistan and Mali.[7] The fiasco at Srebrenica brought a sense of how hard the task was of maintaining peace in the middle of a civil war. Parliament and the cabinet responded with a check list of conditions to be taken into account before deciding on a mission. Cooperation with allies, preferably NATO allies, was crucial. Key terms were interoperability, joint and combined operations, and 3D or 3 block war.

As the section above makes clear, the new strategic situation did not mean fewer operations, quite the opposite. As professor in international relations Jaap de Wilde once remarked, the Dutch armed forces never saw so much action as after peace broke out.[8] What it did mean was different aims and constraints, and thus operations with a different character than foreseen during the Cold War. It also meant joint and combined operations, where Dutch soldiers had to cooperate with colleagues from a different branch of the armed forces as well as with allied units. Where the organizational structure had been focused on large-scale conventional warfare, the elements in that system were now often deployed separately, even at battalion level.

At the military academy the new missions were seen as an incentive to viewed as increasing demand for officers' education that included lessons on peacekeeping, on interorganizational cooperation, on strategic cultures, and on the society and culture of the various regions in which the armed forces went to work. However, the MoD had its hands full with the missions themselves and preparations in the short term and did not issue a policy on long-term preparation in the form of military education. In 2010 Army Command decided that exercises would henceforth be held in English, but again did not extend its policy to military education. Instead it was left to the academies to change their curricula as they saw fit.

---

[6] Van der Knaap 2005.

[7] Ministerie van Defensie 2018 [Dutch Ministry of Defence 2018].

[8] Personal communication. De Wilde said this during a panel discussion on the Eindrapport Defensie Verkenningen [White Paper focusing on the long term strategic perspective MoD].

While these strategic changes, and the various policies developed by the MoD to reorganize the military in response, shaped the expectations of military education, the ministry did not articulate a policy on military education. In fact, decisive steps in the process of reform came from the legislative rather than the executive branch. The aforementioned parliamentary motion by MP Mat Herben (a former MoD press officer) in 2002, overcame bureaucratic resistance against integrating the branch academies.[9] Another motion by Wasila Hachchi (ex-navy officer) in 2010 did the same for the organizational independence of the NLDA vis à vis the MoD, as a consequence of Ministry of Education demands.[10] As the motie-Hachchi shows, by 2010 the NLDA was already advanced on the path towards civilian accreditation. The next section explains how this came about.

2.4 Academic Initiative

At the start of the post-Cold War era, the Dutch military and naval academies had just seen their efforts to gain academic status rebuffed. Political resistance against the proposed law had rested on three pillars: general antimilitarism among some parties, distrust about academic freedom at a military-run institution, and doubts about the vocational orientation of the degree programs. The first of these the academies were powerless to challenge; only autonomous societal change could do that. The second and third they could perhaps overcome in a new attempt.

After 1993, the academies barely paused before launching cooperation agreements with civilian universities. These ensured their graduates access to university degrees requiring much less study than the normal university programs. As they were getting academic credit for military academy courses, the agreements implied a kind of recognition of quality. They also ensured their academic staff could hold positions at a civilian academy as well as at KIM and KMA and thereby gain recognition for their research programs. The first steps towards civilian recognition of military education therefore came from the academies themselves.

The decisive push for accreditation came from a working group led by Rob de Wijk, a former senior policy advisor at the MoD who had become professor of international relations at the Royal Military Academy. Its advise in 2001 led directly to educational reforms at the newly merged NLDA. As De Wijk and the working group drew support from both policy and military academic circles, for the purpose of answering the research question this appears to be a common effort.

Two outside factors favored a new attempt. The first was gradually increasing appreciation of the complexity of the military profession as a result of highly publicized overseas missions. The second was the EU education harmonization program, known as the Bologna Process, which standardized degree programs and

---

[9] Herben 2002.
[10] Hachchi 2010.

set the criteria for recognition. Meant to facilitate exchange between the member states, this also removed some obstacles for the NLDA.

The standard duration of an officer's education program was four years, the same length as a pre-Bologna academic degree program. Because practical military training and command skills had to be learned within this time, it had not been possible to squeeze in four years of academic education. But Bologna now set the length of a bachelor program at three years, at one stroke making it possible to combine the two without increasing the length of the program. This largely removed the objection that the academic program was too vocational. The academies proceeded to separate the two components into separate programs taught at separate times, reserving three full academic years for programs that as far as possible resembled university curricula in terms of content, prescribed literature, testing procedures, and so on.

Academics had already been incorporated in a faculty of military sciences separate from the teaching staff for the more vocational parts of the curriculum; at the merger of KIM and KMA into the NLDA, this faculty was made into a separate organizational unit directly under the director. The hiring process for academic staff was also improved so the number of qualified academics rose steadily; the administrative separation of academic staff from vocational teachers helped with appearances.

In 2004, in order to prevent universities in different member states refusing to recognize each other's diplomas, the EU set criteria for the various levels of education. (This follow-up from Bologna took place at Dublin, hence the terms are known as the Dublin criteria.) The NLDA took the opportunity to apply these to its own curricula, first by describing course content according to the Dublin guidelines and then raising standards where necessary. Two of the three bachelor programs (Military Management and Military Technical Studies) had equivalents at civilian academies which they took as examples. The third, War Studies, was not taught at any Dutch university but could point to several related fields as examples (international relations, conflict studies, strategic studies, history, law), as well as to civilian institutions abroad.

The remaining obstacle proved harder to deal with. Even after the three bachelor degrees were visited by the accreditation organization and found to have sufficient quality, the NLDA ran into a change of the law which now required degree-giving institution to be legally independent from their students' employers so they would not be pressured to lower standards. The Ministry of Education had balked at approving the military academies in the 1980s; now it again insisted on the NLDA living up to the letter of the law: the MoD would have to give up control over NLDA diplomas. During the discussions on previous, failed military education law, the ministry had insisted on retaining control. This time, the more gradual decision-making process had already committed the armed forces to many of the reforms in military education, so that giving up some formal authority appeared as a small step with a guaranteed return on investment. Nevertheless, a parliamentary motion was necessary to get the MoD to move; this was the motion by Wasila Hachchi mentioned in the previous section. It set up a Foundation with its own legal personality. The Foundation is responsible for giving degrees while loaning buildings and personnel from the MoD, which also retained a seat on the foundation's board for the NLDA commandant. As the other seats were filled with academics, this satisfied the Ministry of Education. Recognition by the MoE followed in 2011.

2.5 Conclusion

One could argue that adopting civilian education standards made good sense from a strategic perspective. The loss of prestige was the first reason, considering that the first attempt was made in the 19th century and another extended push at the height of the Cold War. This can be connected to the perception of a widening gulf between armed forces and society, which was expected to become worse after the draft was abolished. The second reason was recruiting and retaining the expertise of officers. The draft had insured a steady influx of university graduates, some of whom stuck around. As it was expected that many officers would leave the service before the retirement age, providing them with a civilian diploma was thought to show good employership (considered a moral imperative as well as a boon for recruitment). The third argument was that the armed forces now faced complex, multidimensional operations in wildly varying and often uncertain situations instead of a single enemy certain to come from one direction.

However, the initiative for reform came more often from the academy itself than from the Ministry of Defence. The process of education reform within the NLDA, and before that its constituent service academies, never stopped after the rejection of the earlier proposed law. The section above shows a dynamic process in which the academies themselves renewed their curricula and proposed institutional changes which the MoD subsequently accepted, sometimes after some prompting from parliament.

By contrast, the Ministry of Defence turned its attention elsewhere: to transformation towards an expeditionary force, ongoing operations, and budget cuts. All of these are weighty concerns but it is notable that the MoD did not develop a policy on military education to match the changes it worked on. Military education merited only a single line in the 2005 "vision letter" and in the 2010 report on future forces was not mentioned at all.[11] Even the first of these came three years after a parliamentary motion on the subject. Arguably this distraction benefited education reform as it meant the MoD did not articulate red lines, such as retaining control, which blocked the previous efforts. Instead, the question was put off until the very end, when it was the only remaining obstacle to reforms that were otherwise guaranteed to be successful.

Equally, if not more, crucial was the Bologna Process, which reshaped academic standards in such a way that it became much easier for the military academies to

---

[11] Van der Knaap 2005; Ministerie van Defensie 2010 [Dutch Ministry of Defence 2010].

conform. For the purposes of this chapter, the Bologna Process itself must be counted as an outside influence. But the decision to conform to Bologna standards and to ask for civilian recognition under its accreditation process was an inside job. It was again at the initiative of the academies, instigated by academic personnel, and overseen by the ministry of education.

Taken together, the evidence points clearly towards lower-level decision-making rather than a top-down policy-driven process.

References

Colijn K, Drent M E, Homan K, Rood J, Zandee D (2013) Clingendael's Visie op de Krijgsmacht van de Toekomst [Clingendael's vision on the armed forces of the future]. Clingendael, The Hague.
De Winter S (2015) The army after Afghanistan: A case study on military adaptation to counterinsurgency warfare within 12 Infantry Battalion Air Assault the Regiment Van Heutsz. MA thesis, NLDA, Breda.
Hachchi W (2010) Motie van het lid Hachchi c.s. [motion by MP Hachchi c.s.]. https://zoek.officielebekendmakingen.nl/kst-32500-X-19.html. Accessed 26 January 2019.
Herben M (2002) Motie van het lid Herben c.s. [motion by MP Herben c.s.]. https://zoek.officielebekendmakingen.nl/kst-28600-X-32.html. Accessed 26 January 2019.
Kitzen M (2016) The course of co-option: Co-option of local power-holders as a tool for obtaining control over the population in counterinsurgery campaigns in weblike societies - with case studies concerning Dutch experiences during the Aceh War (1873–c.1912) and the Uruzgan campaign (2006–2010). Dissertation, Amsterdam University, Amsterdam.
Klinkert W (2012) Mars naar de wetenschap: het streven naar de wetenschappelijk opgeleide officier, 1890–2011 [Striving for the academic status for officers' education, 1890–2011]. NLDA, Breda.
Ministerie van Defensie (2010) Eindrapport Defensie Verkenningen [Ministry of Defence (2010) Report Exploring Defence]. https://www.defensie.nl/downloads/rapporten/2010/03/29/eindrapport-verkenningen-2010. Accessed 25 May 2018.
Ministerie van Defensie (2018) Missie-overzicht [Ministry of Defence (2018) Overview Dutch missions]. https://www.defensie.nl/onderwerpen/historische-missies/missie-overzicht?trefwoord=&jaar-van=1989&jaar-tot=2018. Accessed 30 May 2018.
Rengers M (2018) "Zij zijn een maatje te klein voor hulp van defensie" [They are a little too small for help from Defence]. NRC Handelsblad, 25 May 2018.
Van der Knaap C (2005) Brief staatssecretaris over de invoering van een flexibel personeelssysteem bij Defensie [Letter from the underminister to the parliament on the introduction of a flexible personnel system]. https://www.parlementairemonitor.nl/9353000/1/j9vvij5epmj1ey0/vi3ao243elvs. Accessed 26 January 2019.

Dr. Maarten Rothman is associate professor of International Security Studies at the Faculty of Military Sciences of the Netherlands Defence Academy. His research focuses on the role of ideas in international politics, with a particular focus on democratic revolutions and the justification of violence. His dissertation (Purdue University, 2004) investigated the moral arguments arising from globalization. He has been teaching at the NLDA for 17 years and has previously published on the subject.

Chapter 3
Character Is (the) Key! The Application of Virtue Ethics to Improve Officers' Education

Joost Doense and Jaco de Bruijn

Contents

3.1	Introduction	28
3.2	Present Officers' Education	29
3.3	Factors of Influence	30
	3.3.1 Generation Y	31
	3.3.2 Adaptivity	32
	3.3.3 Ambidexterity	32
3.4	Framework of Military Virtues	33
3.5	Military Virtues and Officers' Education: Facing the Challenges	37
	3.5.1 Generation Y	38
	3.5.2 Adaptivity	38
	3.5.3 Ambidexterity	39
	3.5.4 Conclusion	40
3.6	Closure	40
References		41

Abstract Officers' education in The Netherlands is the responsibility of the Netherlands Defence Academy (NLDA). Within the NLDA the Royal Military Academy, the Royal Netherlands Navy College and the Faculty of Military Sciences each play an important part in teaching young cadets and midshipmen the necessary knowledge, skills and attitude to become a successful officer. Recent developments put the present model under pressure. Internationally, instability is

---

J. Doense (✉)
Royal Military Academy, Netherlands Defence Academy, PO Box 90002,
4800 PA Breda, The Netherlands
e-mail: j.doense@mindef.nl

J. de Bruijn
Royal Netherlands Naval College, Netherlands Defence Academy, PO Box 10000,
1780 CA Den Helder, The Netherlands
e-mail: jc.d.bruijn.01@mindef.nl

© T.M.C. ASSER PRESS and the authors 2019
W. Klinkert et al. (eds.), *NL ARMS Netherlands Annual Review of Military Studies 2019*, NL ARMS, https://doi.org/10.1007/978-94-6265-315-3_3

increasing leading to more emphasis on national security and rising Defence budgets. Technology is playing an increasingly dominant role with new warfare areas emerging like cyber and robotics enabled by artificial intelligence. The Netherlands Armed Forces anticipate on these developments by striving to become a more agile and adaptive organisation. Apart from possible changes in composition of the armed forces, future officers will increasingly have to deal with a complex, highly technological environment leading mixed and changing teams of specialists and still be able to achieve relevant results. To prepare them sufficiently, this chapter argues that all the institutions of the NLDA have to cooperate more closely than ever. In the opinion of the writers, character building has always been at the heart of officers' education and will continue to provide solutions for the future. For this they have introduced a framework consisting of military virtues serving as a backbone connecting the different elements of officers' education provided by the individual institutions.

Keywords Officers' education · character building · military formation · virtue ethics · adaptivity · leadership

3.1 Introduction

'Knowledge is power, but character is more'. This motto above the entrance to *het Zaaltje* – the living room of the midshipmen in Den Helder – underlines the core principle of the officers' education both at the Royal Military Academy (RMA) in Breda and the Royal Netherlands Naval College (RNNC) in Den Helder: an officer needs to acquire a vast amount of knowledge on varying subjects, but ultimately – in the fog of war, when push comes to shove – character will be decisive on winning or losing in battle. Historically, these two aspects – obtaining (academic) knowledge and building (military) character – not always went together easily. After all, the optimal climate for science differs from the optimal climate for obtaining military skills.

With the instigation of the Netherlands Defence Academy (NLDA) and concentration of academic education in the Faculty of Military Sciences (FMS), the above-mentioned aspects were in a way artificially separated. The FMS concentrates more on providing a knowledgebase for officer-cadets while the RMA and RNNC serve as a platform for leadership and character building. Although there will always be some healthy friction between military training and academic education, one could argue that the present construction results in a good balance, even synergy.

External developments are putting this model under pressure. Demographic changes require recalibration of the way we prepare our officers for their jobs. The knowledge needed to operate effectively in an increasingly complex environment puts extra pressure on already full curricula. To deal with this changing and unpredictable environment, the Netherlands Armed Forces (NAF) have to become more adaptable and flexible.[1] The likely effect will be that people join the NAF for shorter and sometimes interrupted periods and are nonetheless expected to deliver the same high standards as future officers. Education is pressed to be 'just in time, just enough' with emphasis on training 'on the job'.[2] This will create challenges for both previously mentioned aspects of officers' education. In this chapter we will investigate these challenges and provide possible solutions to ensure future officers are still able to think as well as fight and win.

Firstly, we will describe in broad terms the manner in which officer's education is organized at the moment. Thereafter we will analyse more in depth several challenges we identified with regards to providing the armed forces now and in the (near) future with good leadership. Then a framework based on virtue ethics will be introduced that could serve as a basis for officers' education. Finally, we will illustrate how this provides possible solutions for the challenges we identified, ending with conclusions and closing remarks.

3.2 Present Officers' Education

Today, civilians wanting to become an officer in the NAF can either apply for the Military Academic Course (MAC) or the Short Officer Course (SOC). The MAC is accessible for students straight out of secondary education (pre-university) and will last four to five years depending on the chosen study. The SOC is available for civilians in possession of (minimally) a bachelor degree who will train for approximately 1.5–2.5 years. Both MAC and SOC graduates will be able to apply for the same junior officer jobs and have identical career opportunities. The ratio between MAC and SOC entering the NLDA varies over the years and each service has a different policy.[3]

Officers' education both in Breda and Den Helder is built on the following pillars:

- *Academic (bachelor) education.* This part is the responsibility of the Faculty of Military Sciences (FMS) and enables officer-students to obtain an accredited Bachelor title. The FMS provides three programs: War Studies and Military Management Studies (both in Breda) and Military Systems & Technology (in Den Helder). Each program is available for both cadets and midshipmen

---

[1] Ministerie van Defensie 2017 [Dutch Ministry of Defence 2017].
[2] Ministerie van Defensie 2016 [Dutch Ministry of Defence 2016].
[3] For example, in 2019 the ratio MSC:SOC will be Army 45:192, Navy 68:75, Airforce 45:90 and Military Police 15:30. Source: Order NLDA 2019, November 2018, Annex F.

resulting in Army and Airforce cadets studying in Den Helder and Navy-midshipmen in Breda. The officer-students following the SOC will not participate in the academic program since they already have a Bachelor-degree (or higher).

- *Basic military training.* This is a broad area encompassing military skills and weapon drills, physical fitness and character building, socialization and leadership training. Every service has its own characteristics on how this part of the officers' education is executed based on future professional context and tradition, but there is a common denominator in the underlying objectives. Furthermore, the student societies *Cadettencorps* and *Korps Adelborsten* have an important role as their activities add significantly to the objectives of the military training. This is further amplified by the fact that they all join a boarding school system.
- *Specific military training.* Each cadet or midshipman within a service has chosen for a specific branch (e.g. IT, pilot, infantry, logistics) and needs specific training to be able to function at their first posting as a junior officer. This training is mostly carried out by the training organization of his/her future service or even branch (e.g. pilots or marines). However, some of the specific training is provided by the institution itself (e.g. Officer of the Watch at the RNNC). Although most of the specific military training will take place outside the NLDA, it is an integral part of the officers' education and remains the responsibility of the RMA and RNNC respectively.

In addition to these two main directions, there are several smaller courses which are taught mainly at the RMA. These comprise of the training of reserve officers and specialists (doctors, cyber-specialists, legal specialists, etc.).[4]

3.3 Factors of Influence

As stated in our introduction, there are many developments in the environment of the NLDA that have an influence on officers' education. Geopolitical developments, new technologies and changes in the labour market occur in an ever-increasing tempo. Our former Minister of Defence, Mrs. Hennis-Plasschaert concluded in her opening address to the Future Force Conference in 2017: "We have to be adaptive. In all perspectives. Uncertainty is the only constant."[5] In this section, we will take a closer look at the most dominant factors of influence we are facing with regard to officers' education.

---

[4] In 2019 the NLDA will train 90 specialists spread over the different services and 96 reserve officers (all Army). Source: Order NLDA 2019, November 2018, Annex F.

[5] Hennis-Plasschaert 2017.

3.3.1 Generation Y

The current generation of midshipman and cadets is the so-called millennials or "Generation Y". This generation, roughly born between 1980 and 2000, is characterized as flexible, free-thinking, curious and inquisitive, enterprising and with an inclination for technology. On the other hand, it is also characterized as easy-going, tough-to-manage, individualistic and raised with more freedom than senior generations.[6] The defence organization is by nature a hierarchical, traditional organization with many bureaucratic and technocratic characteristics.[7] Decades of budget cuts with corresponding reorganizations and centralizations have only reinforced the latter. Also, the NAF typically work in teams and not individually and lastly, the mission always comes first which puts organizational or general interest before individual interest, even when it comes to risk life or limb.

We should therefore be prepared when we introduce young people into an environment that is so completely at odds with the environment in which they grew up. In addition, we teach these young people to be critical and empowered as future leaders while at the same time we expect them to be disciplined, have a sound understanding of hierarchical relations and, not unimportantly, we teach them how to serve.

Candidates for the officers' training undergo a strict selection process and are therefore (in principle) qualified. Simultaneously, they are still young adults. The MAC-cadets come directly from secondary school and while their friends enjoy the liberties of student life, they are enrolled in a boarding school with a military regime. Although they entered voluntarily, they are confronted with strict boundaries compared to their civilian friends. The SOC-cadets have more life experience but they also have to relinquish previous autonomy due to the choice they made. One could argue they have to adapt even more than their younger colleagues.

The difficulty this provides is partly explained by the way the human brain develops in this stage of life. In particular, the development of more complex cognitive tasks such as self-control, planning and organizing and concentration takes place in the last years of brain development, while we expect these qualities to be present during officers' training.[8] On the other hand, since these qualities still need to be developed fully, this also provides the opportunity to shape them in accordance with the officers' (character) profile.

---

[6] Main 2017.
[7] Joosten 2017, p. 15.
[8] Mills et al. 2016.

3.3.2 Adaptivity

Traditionally, the NAF are perceived as a less interesting employer when the economy is flourishing as it is currently. Nevertheless, there is enough interest for a job as an officer. With 120 candidates for the RNNC and 360 for the RMA annually, both institutes are filled to capacity with candidates in the presently available courses with all services having the intention to even increase these numbers. The latter mainly to eliminate the current personnel shortages, but also because the organization is slowly growing again.[9] Anticipating further growth in the near future,[10] this additional requirement is expected to be lasting.

Besides quantity, the need for personnel in the NAF is more diverse than in the past due to a requirement for specialist knowledge like cyber or artificial intelligence. Furthermore, the NAF wants its organization to be flexible and adaptive to changing circumstances. To be able to cater for both these developments, the NAF will rely more on reservists.[11] This increasing adaptivity will likely change the composition of the NAF into a core of career military personnel and a flexible shell of reservists. Already there are several ongoing trials with specialists entering the organization with a short initial training to become an officer.[12] This raises the question to what extent they have internalized the norms and values of the military culture. In other words, do they possess enough 'character' besides their undisputed specialist knowledge?

3.3.3 Ambidexterity

Adaptivity does not only have consequences for the composition of the military, but also for the culture and the way we think. Adaptivity in this regard means "the ability to effectively anticipate (un)predictable changes, to process them and then respond in time to ensure optimal performance."[13] While it is often assumed that adaptivity is the ability to quickly switch between robustness and flexibility, TNO[14] argues differently. It states that an adaptive organization should have both properties at its disposal, albeit in proper balance: flexible enough to move swiftly but not so much robustness that it becomes rigid. This is called ambidexterity ("two-leggedness").

---

[9] For example due to the introduction of F35 and other new weapon systems. Although they will be partly replacing old systems thus creating a temporary requirement for personnel.

[10] Ministerie van Defensie 2018a, b, c [Dutch Ministry of Defence 2018].

[11] Ministerie van Defensie 2017 [Dutch Ministry of Defence 2017].

[12] For example, the training of 90 Airforce cadets in 2019 with an abbreviated SOC of 3 months. Source: Jaarplan NLDA 2019, Annex F.

[13] Herder et al. 2017, p. 6.

[14] TNO is a Dutch knowledge institute and the permanent partner of the MoD for a large number of innovative projects.

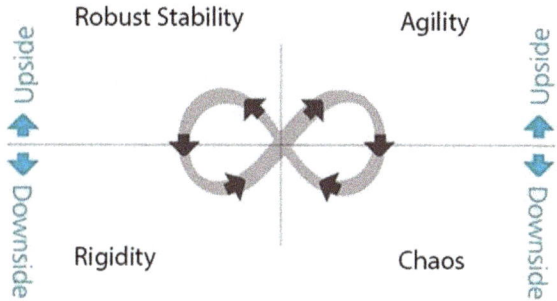

Fig. 3.1 Visualisation of the lemniscate of robustness and flexibility (ibid., p. 13). *Source* Herder et al. 2017

In an exploratory study TNO states that the degree of adaptivity of the Defence organization is mainly determined by the skill of its leader's ability to act in conflicting areas of tension.[15] In other words, the ability of leaders to assess and decide "and-and" instead of "or-or". Although the results of the TNO research is not yet included in official MoD-policy, it does provide an important perspective on leadership development for the near future and thus raises the question to what extent it should be included in officers' education (Fig. 3.1).

3.4 Framework of Military Virtues

Considering the challenges both RMA and RNCC are facing, we are convinced the only effective way to deal with them is through closer cooperation between RMA, RNCC *and* FMS. In our experience, due to the geographical distance (Breda – Den Helder) and cultural differences between the different services, the institutes within the NLDA have not always been capable of joining forces in the recent past. Although we fully recognize the importance of the unique identity of each institute, in our opinion it remains essential to find as much common ground as possible to be able to cooperate effectively. We therefore need to find a collective approach which, on the one hand, provides focus and, on the other hand, leaves enough room for the specific professional context, tradition and culture of each service.

As stated in our introduction, character building is at the core of officers' education. This core is usually formed by a certain set of values or virtues[16] laid down in a Code of Conduct or comparable document. Although military virtues based on virtue ethics have always been used for this purpose, albeit sometimes more explicitly than other, in the last decades the importance of virtue ethics has

---

[15] Herder et al. 2017, pp. 18–20.

[16] Although 'value' and 'virtue' are not the same, they are often interchanged. The term 'virtue' is closest to those characteristics of moral sound behaviour and good leadership in the military context and therefore used in this chapter. See: Oltshoorn 2011, p. 6; Dalenberg 2017, p. 51.

increased.[17] A likely explanation is the increasing complexity of modern warfare in relation to the emphasis (Western) society puts on moral just behavior by the military.[18] We have therefore further explored this domain for a collective NLDA-wide approach on officers' education.

An interesting perspective is offered by Brigade-General (ret.) Dr. P.H. de Vries in his extensive study of the theory developed by Alisdair MacIntyre on virtue ethics. In this study he applied the theory of MacIntyre to the military practice and developed a framework of military virtues. His goal was to develop "a suitable instrument to identify, instill and uphold the required moral standards in the military."[19]

The (simplified) theory of MacIntyre can be schematically described as follows:[20]

- People have certain desires (internal goods);
- They will try to participate in activities (praxis) where these desires can be fulfilled;
- Fulfilment will increase if one can excel in the execution of relevant activities;
- This will in its turn increase pleasure in the participation of the praxis;
- Striving for improvement will lead to certain generally accepted criteria within a praxis;
- These criteria will be internalized and will create an attitude (virtue) steering behavior.

In his study, de Vries argues that the military also constitute a practice. The application of Macintyre's theory on the military praxis has led to the following model of military virtues (Table 3.1). As explained by de Vries in the abstract of his thesis:[21]

> The military practice is characterized by the following constitutive elements: task, arms, cooperation, enemies, danger, an undetermined time and place, and rules that govern the practice. In relation to these constitutive elements, I identified the reasons why soldiers enjoy military activities. These are: satisfaction in accomplishing tasks, pride in wearing an uniform and bearing arms, a feeling of belonging as a result of close cooperation in a primary group, contentment in overcoming the enemy, excitement and thrill in facing danger, the challenge and adventure of strange places, and the structure and stability provided by clear rules. Based on the findings so far, I then proceeded to identify 7 virtues of military character and 1 virtue of military intellect. The virtues of military character are: sense of responsibility, military competence, comradeship, respect – for fellow soldiers, civilians and even the enemy – , courage, resilience, and discipline. These virtues of

---

[17] Oltshoorn 2011, p. 4.
[18] Oltshoorn 2011, p. 132; Vries 2013, p. 2.
[19] Vries 2013, p. vii.
[20] Vries 2014, p. 292.
[21] Vries 2013, pp. vii–viii.

Table 3.1 Model of military virtues (de Vries 2013, p. 83)

	Characteristics of military practice	Internal goods	Specific groupings	Virtues
Virtues of character				
1	**Task**	Fulfilment Achievement **Satisfaction**		**Responsibility**
2	**Arms**	Excitement Satisfaction **Pride**		**Competence**
3	**Cooperation**	Esteem Comfort **Belonging**	Members of the same primary group	**Comradeship**
			Other fellow soldiers	**Respect**
			Permissive, supportive civilians	
4	**Enemy**	Pride Satisfaction **Contentment**	Non-violent opposing civilians	
			Armed opposition, fighters	
5	**Danger**	Excitement Elation **Thrill**		**Courage**
6	**Undetermined time and place**	Challenge Tension **Adventure**		**Resilience**
7	**Rules**	Comfort Structure **Stability**		**Discipline**
Virtue of intellect				
	Action			**Practical wisdom**

Source de Vries 2013

military character are a prerequisite to establish what needs to be done, both practically and morally. How to achieve what needs to be done, is a matter of deliberation which requires the virtue of intellect: practical wisdom. This virtue-ethical framework is tangible; the virtues accommodate the pursuit of excellence and provide clear goals – and also yardsticks – for military education and training and personal development. The acquisition of these dispositions allows a soldier to be truly virtuous.

Although de Vries has developed his framework for the military practice in general, we think the theory of MacIntyre and the framework of de Vries is exceptionally suitable to be applied in the context of officers' education for a number of reasons:

(1) The main focus of his model is on the development of (the virtues of) character. This is in line with the historic motto of officers' education 'knowledge is power, but character is more'. The current importance of character was also

emphasized by the Netherlands Chief of Defence Admiral Bauer in his keynote speech at the opening of the Military Academic Year in 2018 as well as in his speech at the 2018 RMA graduation ceremony: "it is not only important to give young people the necessary academic education and military training, but the education [at RMA and RNNC] deals especially with personal development and character building. Now, maybe even more important than ever".[22]

(2) The community surrounding a genuine practice is a community of teachers and learners, with each individual community member filling each of these roles at different times.[23] "It belongs to the concept of a practice as I have outlined it … that its goods can only be achieved by subordinating ourselves within the practice in our relationship to other practitioners".[24] This applies to the environment of the RMA and RNNC as military educational institutions. However, it is not only visible in the relation between training staff and cadets, but also in the relation of cadets among themselves. In particular the *Cadettencorps* and *Korps Adelborsten* create an environment where first year cadets subordinate themselves to second and third year cadets even if they are older in age and already obtained a bachelor degree.

(3) History and tradition play an important part in a practice. The rules and standards of a practice have developed in the past and are binding on the present. Both the RMA and RNNC have rich histories and many traditions which relate back to the respective armed services and have been preserved until today. However, MacIntyre is not advocating blind loyalty to the past nor saying all change is bad. He is acknowledging that the present rests on the past and must take that past into account in its self-understanding and planning for the future. This is an important notion for a future officer and ties in to the 'historic method' as propagated by the FMS.[25] After all, future officers should realise: "History never repeats itself, man always does".[26]

(4) The framework can be connected to the current leadership model in use with the NAF. Leadership is one of the main subjects in the curriculum of officers' education. The motto of the current NAF leadership model is, 'being, doing, learning'.[27] 'Being' emphasizes the importance of character in a leader consisting of four characteristics: "courageous, responsible, servient and honest".

---

[22] Bauer 2018.
[23] Clayton 2005.
[24] MacIntyre 2013, p. 191.
[25] During his inaugural address at the NLDA historian Klinkert introduced his 'historic method' as part of officers' education. The 'historic method' comprises of analysis of military history in order to develop the reflective capabilities and critical thinking of aspirant officers. Klinkert 2018, p. 17.
[26] Voltaire 1759.
[27] Ministerie van Defensie 2013 [Dutch Ministry of Defence 2013].

These overlap largely with the virtues in the framework developed by de Vries. Furthermore, 'doing' and 'learning' is very much in line with the continuous *striving for excellence* objective of virtue ethics.[28] Thus, becoming more virtuous will likely make you a better leader.

(5) The model connects virtues of character with the virtue of intellect. To develop virtues of character requires deliberation or practical wisdom. This resembles the paradigm of the *thinking soldier* used by the FMS bachelor studies. The *thinking soldier* is based on the concept of the *reflective practitioner* developed by Donald Schön. In his studies he describes a progression from repeated following of rules to questioning, criticizing and reforming assumptions through a continuous process he calls "reflective conversation" with the situation.[29] Applied to the military context, this would largely coincide with the process of obtaining practical wisdom. In other words, a *virtuous soldier* will have to be a *thinking soldier*.

All in all, the model of military virtue offers the possibility to link all aspects of officers' education – basic and specific military training and academic education – for all services. Simultaneously, it does not require all courses to be identical since it caters for different narratives. In MacIntyre's theory, a narrative provides the necessary context in practices supports the development of the virtues and creates a unified identity.[30] The narrative for the Navy, the Army, the Airforce and the Military Police will all be different and consist of service-specific histories, stories and practices giving practical meaning to what it means to be in the military and in one of the services specifically. Still they will all lead to the same military virtues.

3.5 Military Virtues and Officers' Education: Facing the Challenges

In the previous section we showed that the introduction of a framework of military virtues well suits the overall objectives and structure of officers' education at both RMA and RNNC in combination with the academic education of the FMS. It could provide a collective approach enhancing cooperation between the different institutions of the NLDA while at the same time leaving enough room for an own identity. However, the main purpose of this chapter is to provide possible solutions for the challenges we identified for the (near) future. We will now analyse to what extent the framework can assist in facing these challenges.

---

[28] Vries 2013, p. 15.
[29] Schön 1983.
[30] Vries 2013, p. 101.

3.5.1 Generation Y

As shown in Sect. 3.2, there seems to be a large gap between the attitude of the *generation Y* candidate entering the course and the required attitude of a junior officer. It requires a lot of willpower to adapt and internalize the values of the military system. One of the most powerful aspects of virtue ethics is that it is based on individual desires (internal goods). According to a recent survey, the main reasons young people join the NAF are: variation, contribution to peace, working with different people, pride, the challenge, staying fit, comradery and obtaining discipline.[31] These are all internal goods that can easily be identified in the framework of military virtues. So, the use of this system will connect to their desires and motivate them to develop the required attitude.

Furthermore, in our experience the present generation is constantly searching for why things are the way they are, also pertaining to military training (Y also stands for 'why'). On many occasions, the reply by the staff will be: "That is the way we do things here.", which is, understandably, hardly satisfying. If used as a baseline for the curriculum, the framework could provide a clear direction on objectives thereby providing a coherent narrative that can easily explain the 'why' of training and enhance motivation.

Lastly, the framework of military virtues is a moral system created to develop the moral standards of a military professional. In the past there have been several studies on the risks of immoral behaviour at the NLDA.[32] Although a number of measures have been taken, recent incidents show that the institutions are still vulnerable to integrity issues.[33] This can probably never be completely excluded, but the features of generation Y as described in Sect. 3.2 will increase rather than decrease this vulnerability. In this view, choosing a moral system as backbone for officers' education makes a lot of sense and will definitely increase moral awareness both with students and staff.

3.5.2 Adaptivity

The development of the NAF to a more adaptable and flexible organisation has both a quantitative and a qualitative dimension. There is an increasing demand for more personnel with specific knowledge and skills. They will follow shorter or even no initial training at all and have a more flexible contract with MoD. While many of them might remain civilian, a substantial number will be military and become officers, albeit without the opportunity to undergo the full program of leadership development and character building supplied by the regular officers' courses. Still

---

[31] Moelker 2017, p. 48.
[32] Governance & Integrity/COID [Central Organization Integrity Defence] 2014.
[33] Ministerie van Defensie 2018a, b, c [Ministry of Defence 2018].

they will wear a uniform and are expected to possess the same professional attitude and moral competence.

This could be solved by extending the framework of military virtues to the environment outside the NLDA. As stated before, the intention of de Vries was to provide an instrument for the military practice in general and not specifically for officers' education at the RMA and RNNC. This means the framework could be applied integrally to the NAF as a whole making it possible for new (reserve) officers with little initial training to work on the development of military virtues in their working environment. After all, they should all speak the same language.

However, we realise that it would require a lot of effort and time to fully integrate the system in the entire organisation, let alone the (un)likeliness of an endorsed policy decision to do so. Nevertheless, the NLDA could still provide direction and guidance for both new officers and their environment based on the framework. After all, the system is designed on the military practice the new (reserve) officers will encounter every day in their working environment. So individual training in the form of a working manual (based on the regular curriculum) and supported by personal coaches from the Expertise Centre for Defence Leadership (ECLD) should enable them to develop the same professional attitude and moral competence as officers who completed the full course.

3.5.3 Ambidexterity

As we explained in Sect. 3.4, an adaptable organisation also requires a different way of thinking. The concept of ambidexterity means to be able to move mentally on a continuum between flexibility and robustness depending on the context, tying in with the underlying thought of the framework of military virtues. As explained by de Vries, conflict nowadays is unpredictable with little supervision and large responsibilities delegated to junior leaders.[34] This led him to study virtue ethics to support measured and context dependent decision making within a given mandate.

Looking at the framework we can identify virtues that will support robustness like *resilience* and *discipline* and on the other hand *courage* and *responsibility* that would enable flexible behaviour if required. Furthermore, the core principle of a virtue is the 'golden mean' between two extremes.[35] In this way one could argue that ambidexterity is the virtue that is created from the extremes of *rigidity* and *chaos*. Thus, for a person who has developed his skills in accordance with the framework of military virtues, the concept of ambidexterity will feel familiar and will be relatively easy to internalise.

---

[34] Vries 2013, p. 6.
[35] Van Iersel et al. 2002, p. 281.

Lastly, in a discussion paper on ambidexterity, the authors state the importance of a common intent connecting the system- and lifeworld in the Defence organisation.[36] It will function as a compass for the choice between a robust or flexible solution in a certain situation. Prerequisite is the ability of employees to relate to this common intent within their own working environment. In our opinion, the framework can be an important element of this common intent. It will provide direction and is firmly rooted in the everyday military practice.

3.5.4 Conclusion

As we have shown in this section of our chapter a framework of military virtues does provide answers to the challenges we see emerging for officer education in the NAF. It can give a better foothold to a new generation entering the RMA and RNNC, be useful for the young men and women becoming an officer via an alternative route and seems tailored for inclusion in the concept of ambidexterity. However, as our analysis does not really go into depth, additional research is required to verify if this concept based on virtue-ethics really does provide tangible and feasible solutions. Based on our initial investigation, we strongly believe this research will be worthwhile.

3.6 Closure

The Netherlands Armed Forces are on the brink of a very challenging period. The international environment is increasingly unstable, technology is changing at an ever-faster rate and personnel will become scarce. Furthermore, additional budget for MoD means another way of thinking after almost 30 years of budget cuts. How all this will develop exactly is unknown, but it is certain that there will be a greater appeal on the future leadership to steer these developments in the right direction.

The RMA and RNNC together with the FMS and other institutions of the NLDA have the responsibility to prepare the next generation officers for this uncertain future. Already this is done in a professional manor with a lot of hard work by many committed colleagues. However, we think an extra step is required (and possible) to enhance the current educational system. The framework of military virtues as developed by Brigade-general (ret.) de Vries provides several pointers that look promising in achieving valuable lasting improvements.

We are indebted to Brigade-general de Vries. He devoted 10 years of his retirement to study philosophy and produced a model of virtue ethics that is both complex and practicable. In this way he has proven himself a *thinking soldier* par

---

[36] Herder et al. 2017, p. 18.

excellence! For us he formed the inspiration to write this chapter. May he serve as a fine example of what is achievable when you combine knowledge with character in the best tradition of both the RMA and the RNNC.

References

Bauer R (2018) Kennis is macht, karakter is meer [Knowledge is power, but character is more]. Keynote speech at the opening of the academic year of the Netherlands Defence Academy https://www.defensie.nl/actueel/nieuws/2018/08/30/commandant-der-strijdkrachten-bauer-%E2%80%98kennis-is-macht.-karakter-is-meer%E2%80%99. Accessed 3 January 2019.

Clayton T (2005) Political Philosophy of Alasdair MacIntyre. The Internet Encyclopedia of Philosophy, ISSN 2161-0002 https://www.iep.utm.edu/p-macint/#H15. Accessed 28 December 2018.

Dalenberg S (2017) Officer, practice what you preach! Research on effects and interventions in military officer socialization at the Royal Military Academy (Doctoral dissertation). Radboud University, Nijmegen.

de Vries PH (2013) "The good, the bad and the virtuous": The virtue-ethical theory of Alisdair MacIntyre applied to military practice. (Doctoral dissertation) Radboud University, Nijmegen.

de Vries PH (2014) Morele vorming. Paard of wagen? [Article about moral education]. Militaire spectator 6:287–299.

Governance & Integrity/COID (2014) Integriteit bij de opleiding en vorming van adelborsten en cadetten aan de Nederlandse Defensie Academie; Duiding van risico's, perspectief op verbetering [Integrity in the training and education of the midshipmen and cadets at the Netherlands Defence Academy. Interpretation of risks, perspective on improvement]. https://gi-nederland.com/wp-content/uploads/Rapportage-Risicoanalyse-Integriteit-.pdf. Accessed 10 January 2019.

Hennis-Plasschaert J (2017) Turning the tide: the need to mobilise the force for good; Speech Minister of Defence on the occasion of the Future Force Conference 2017. https://www.government.nl/documents/speeches/2017/02/21/speech-minister-of-defence-on-the-occasion-of-the-future-force-conference-2017. Accessed 22 February 2019.

Herder A et al (2017) Theorie en praktijk van ambidexteriteit voor de Nederlandse Defensieorganisatie [Theory and practice of ambidexterity for the Dutch Defence organization]. TNO, The Hague.

Joosten E (2017) De toekomst van Defensie in een onzekere wereld; De deugden ethische oplossing voor het verbeteren van besluitvorming voor nieuw onderzoek (MSc-thesis) [The future of Defence in an uncertain world, MSc-thesis]. Erasmus University, Rotterdam.

Klinkert, W (2018) Vorming voor de toekomst: Mars en Clio; Militaire geschiedenis voor thinking soldiers, rede uitgesproken bij het aanvaarden van het ambt van hoogleraar Moderne Militaire Wetenschappen van de FMW van de NLDA [Education for the Future: Mars and Clio. Military History for Thinking Soldiers. Inaugural speech] Faculty Military Sciences, Breda.

MacIntyre A (2013) After Virtue. Bloomsbury, London.

Main D (2017) Who Are the Millennials? https://www.livescience.com/38061-millennials-generation-y.html. Accessed 20 January 2019.

Mills K et al (2016) Structural brain development between childhood and adulthood: Convergence across four longitudinal samples. https://www.sciencedirect.com/science/article/pii/S1053811916303512#!. Accessed 22 February 2019.

Ministerie van Defensie (2013) Visie Leiderschap Defensie [Ministry of Defence (2013) Vision on Leadership]. Expertise Center Leadership Defence, Netherlands Defence Academy, Breda.

Ministerie van Defensie (2016) Visie opleiden en individueel trainen; Leren en ontwikkelen bij defensie – 2030 [Vision on education and individual training. Learning and development in the military – 2030]. Ministry of Defence, The Hague.

Ministerie van Defensie (2017) Kamerbrief BS2016003367; Plan van aanpak uitvoering Total Force concept [Letter to the parliament about the implementation of Total Force concept]. Ministry of Defence, The Hague.

Ministerie van Defensie (2018a) Kamerbrief BS2018024659; Rapportage adaptieve krijgsmacht [Letter to the parliament; Report adaptive armed forces]. Ministry of Defence, The Hague.

Ministerie van Defensie (2018b) Kamerbrief BS2018031667; Nationaal plan defensie-uitgaven ten behoeve van de NAVO [Letter to the parliament about Defence spending on NATO]. Ministry of Defence, The Hague.

Ministerie van Defensie (2018c) Kamerbrief BS2018031444; Recente onderzoeken voorvallen [Letter to the parliament; recent investigations of incidents]. Ministry of Defence, The Hague.

Moelker R (2017) Research paper Recruteren uit een diepere vijver [Research paper about recruitment]. Faculty Military Sciences, Netherlands Defence Academy, Breda.

Oltshoorn P (2011) Military Ethics and Virtues; An interdisciplinary approach for the 21st century. Routledge, Abingdon.

Schön DA (1983) The Reflective Practitioner. How professionals think in action. Taylor & Francis, New York.

Van Iersel AHM, van Baarda ThA (red) (2002) Militaire ethiek; Morele dilemma's van militairen in theorie en praktijk [Military Ethics; moral dilemmas of soldiers in theory and practice]. DAMON, Eindhoven.

Voltaire (1759) Candide. http://www.gutenberg.org/files/19942/19942-h/19942-h.htm. Accessed 22 February 2019.

Colonel (Army) Joost Doense has since 2017 been commander of the Royal Netherlands Military Academy. He was commissioned in 1990. Initial postings included company and brigade level and two operational tours to Bosnia. After advanced staff college he was a planner at Army Staff and served in Afghanistan as chief operations. His subsequent battalion command included another tour in Afghanistan. Other postings included policy advisor at Defence Staff and deputy brigade commander, the latter while also being the military liaison to civil authorities.

Captain (Navy) Jaco de Bruijn is commander of the Royal Netherlands Naval College in Den Helder. After his initial training (1983–1988) at the Naval College, he joined the Naval Air Arm as navigator-communicator P3C Orion and subsequently tactical-coordinator for the Lynx-helicopter. He participated in several NATO-operations during the Yugoslavian conflict and Gulf War as TACCO and flight commander. Aside from a tour as squadron commander, he held several posts as a staff officer both with the Netherlands Royal Navy and the Ministry of Defence.

Chapter 4
A Performative Account of the Use of Oaths to Enhance Integrity Within the Military

Job Timmermans and Robert Bertrand

Contents

4.1	Introduction	44
4.2	Integrity	45
4.3	Oath-Taking	46
4.4	Performativity of Oath-Taking	48
	4.4.1 Characteristic 1: Infelicity	49
	4.4.2 Characteristic 2: Self-involvement	50
	4.4.3 Characteristic 3: Public Context	51
	4.4.4 Characteristic 4: Continuity/Structural Possibility of Infelicity	52
4.5	Discussion and Conclusion: Relevance to Educating and Training of Officers	54
References		55

Abstract Taking oaths has been part of military protocol dating back to the Bronze Age. For example, the pledging of allegiance to the flag, or the reciting of the soldier's creed, mark the connection and commitment of military personnel to the corps and its codes. Also, in the literature on business ethics, oaths have been recognized as a means of raising the level of integrity within organizations. The underlying idea is that the performing of such rituals makes a real difference to the individuals or organization keeping to their commitments. Therefore, a deeper understanding of the performative functioning of oaths as a means to entrench integrity within organizations and in its individual members could offer new insights into the steering of organizations towards integrity both theoretically and

---

J. Timmermans (✉)
Faculty of Military Sciences, Netherlands Defence Academy, PO Box 90002,
4800 PA Breda, The Netherlands
e-mail: jfc.timmermans@mindef.nl

R. Bertrand
Faculty of Military Sciences, Netherlands Defence Academy, Breda, The Netherlands
e-mail: rmm.bertrand@mindef.nl

practically. To this purpose, this chapter takes a closer look at how oaths function in the education and training of military officers: on the one hand, officers taking oaths as part of their own training and induction, and as part of their future role as an officer administering oaths on the other hand. Conceptually the assessment draws on the speech-act theories of Austin 1975 and Searle 1989.

Keywords Integrity · oaths · performativity · business ethics

4.1 Introduction

'That I do declare and solemnly swear.' These words were uttered by nearly thirty new staff members of the Netherlands Defence Academy (NLDA) at the Grand Hall of the Castle, as part of their induction ritual. As the commander of the NLDA just had made so eloquently clear in his public address during the ceremony, this oath was considered to be a cornerstone of the induction process, reminding the oath-takers of their duties and obligations in educating officers and creating the right ethical working and educational environment. This oath-taking ceremony is an example of the general rule that all new military and civil personnel take an oath or pledge when appointed within the Ministry of Defence, or directly after completing their initial military training (military personnel only).[1]

In the literature on business ethics, oaths have been recognized as a means to raise the level of integrity within organizations.[2] The underlying idea is that performing such rituals makes a real difference to the state of the individual or organization in keeping their commitments. A deeper understanding of the performative functioning of oaths as a means to entrench integrity within organizations and its individual members could offer new insight into the steering of organizations towards integrity both theoretically and practically. This certainly is the case for military organizations, especially for those institutes involved in the training and educating of military officers. Integrity not only lies at the heart of the military profession, having an ethical environment is also an essential prerequisite for the effective training of officers. Moreover, to ensure ethical behaviour, oaths and pledges have been part of military protocol dating back to the Bronze Age.

For these reasons, in this chapter the aim is to deepen our understanding of the relevancy and functioning of pledges as a means to enhance commitment and integrity in the training of officers. To this end, the chapter starts with a brief outline of the value and understanding of integrity (Sect. 4.2). This is followed by an introduction of the concept of oath-taking, including its historical background, purpose and meaning (Sect. 4.3). Next, a philosophical account of performativity is

---

[1] Civil Servant Statute of the Ministry of Defence (BARD) Article 70a, General Military Civil Servant Statute (AMAR), Article 126a.

[2] Anderson and Escher 2010; Wankel and Stachowicz-Stanusch 2011; Weaver et al. 2016.

brought forward, which then is applied to construct a performative account of oath-taking consisting of four characteristics: (1) Infelicity, (2) Self-involvement, (3) Public context, and (4) Continuity/Structural possibility of infelicity (Sect. 4.4). The chapter concludes by discussing the relevance of the performative conceptualisation of oaths to the education and training of officers.

4.2 Integrity

Nowadays, integrity is considered to be a core value of any professional organization, the (Dutch) defence forces being no exception. For instance, over the last few years, a Department has been initiated to enhance integrity within the Netherlands defence organization called the Central Organization Integrity Defence (COID), and a dedicated hotline has been set up where integrity violation can be reported.[3]

Notwithstanding having had attention from the literature for a long time, the concept of integrity still is contested.[4] Commonly, integrity is associated with having unity of character.[5] This implies consistency and lack of discrepancy in beliefs and actions. A person of integrity thus carries through her or his moral beliefs and values in her or his actions consistently and irrespective of external pressures or temptations.[6] In addition, integrity is associated with specific moral virtues or with moral virtue in general.[7] Integrity, for instance, has been associated with honesty, loyalty, fairness, truthfulness and faithfulness.[8]

This conceptualization of integrity corresponds to the definition currently used by the Dutch Ministry of Defence. This defines integrity as 'treating one another with respect and dignity, taking into account the legitimate interests and desires of all involved.' [our translation].[9] In line with the literature, this is a broad definition that underlines individual assessment and reflection.[10]

A consideration at the forefront of attention in both practical and academic contexts is how an organization can be steered towards integrity. Several strategies have been suggested such as building an organizational culture,[11] education and

---

[3] https://www.defensie.nl/onderwerpen/integriteit/defensie-en-integriteit, Accessed 7 January 2019.
[4] Rieke and Guastello 1995; Zarim et al. 2016.
[5] Audi and Murphy 2006.
[6] Windsor in Monga and Orlitzky 2017.
[7] Audi and Murphy 2006.
[8] Ibid.; Windsor in Monga and Orlitzky 2017.
[9] Dutch Ministry of Defence (2012) Aanwijzing SG A/984: Uitvoering van het integriteitsbeleid Defensie, p. 6.
[10] van der Steenhoven and Aalbersberg 2016.
[11] Kayes et al. 2007; Verhezen 2010.

training,[12] and the role of leadership.[13] One of the practical means of raising the level of integrity being suggested is the idea of oath-taking. Examples of the use of oaths within organizations can be found on company websites such as Unilever's[14] and Monsanto's,[15] and in the literature, especially, on business education.[16]

4.3 Oath-Taking

The use of a written or oral vow to underline a person's commitment to maintaining the highest standard of integrity can be traced back to the realm of professionalism in for instance the medical, legal and academic professions. Well-known, for instance, is the Hippocratic oath, which has been taken by physicians dating back to classical times. Also, in the military, taking oaths has a long history.

Although it is somewhat unclear what profession was first to introduce an oath or pledge, there is evidence of oaths and pledges in the military domain since ancient times. Written examples of a military oath have been found on cuneiform tablets with a Hittite origin. This oath had to be sworn by military servicemen before military commanders.[17] Further examples of military serviceman taking an oath can be found in ancient Egypt, Greece and the Roman Empire. For example, in ancient Athens a recruit ('*ephebos*') took an oath of allegiance – called ephebic – with as principal points the promise to defend the fatherland, to obey the laws and authorities, and to honour the State's cults – at least since the second half of the fourth century B.C.[18] Likewise, in the Late Roman times, legionnaires pledged their allegiance (the 'Sacramentum militare') to the Emperor and the State.[19]

Also in the Chinese and Japanese empire and in Middle and South America the Mayas, Aztecs and Incas, respectively, applied such rituals. In Western Europe, we see oaths applied in the military domain from Roman times till this day and age. In The Netherlands, the military oath became common practice when the young Republic developed a standing army under the command of Maurits Prince of Orange,[20] and from then on it remained the norm. Nowadays, oaths are applied in a

---

[12] Gonzalez-Padron et al. 2012.
[13] Manz et al. 2008.
[14] https://www.unilever.com/sustainable-living/our-strategy/business-integrity/.
[15] https://monsanto.com/company/commitments/our-pledge/.
[16] Anderson and Escher 2010; Wankel and Stachowicz-Stanusch 2011; Weaver et al. 2016.
[17] Oettinger 1976.
[18] Siewert 1977.
[19] Renatus 1996.
[20] Landolt 1861.

wide array of professions such as politicians, judges, lawyers, solicitors, notaries, doctors, Olympic athletes, (special) investigating officers. Due to recent debacles, broader attention in the realm of business ethics also stimulated the introduction of oaths for bankers, educators and in the future possibly for academic professors.

The appearance of modern-day oaths is still rooted firmly in the Christian tradition. The raising of the index finger, middle finger and thumb (often forgotten) when pledging an oath, symbolizes the Holy Trinity: the Father, the Son and the Holy Ghost. The closed ring finger and little finger, point to the Christian doctrine of the two natures – one human nature and one divine nature – of Jesus Christ. Together these are the core symbols of the Christian Faith.

However, over time we have also seen a gradual shift of the content of military oaths taken by military servicemen. Whereas ancient oaths tend to stress the all-time importance of loyalty of a serviceman to its commander, ruler or fatherland, modern-day oaths emphasise integrity and honesty more explicitly. This might be a result of a change in the task of the armed forces from supporting the goals of their commanders in ancient armies to having a broad spectrum of tasks both at home and abroad in modern-day armed forces. Not only their appearance but also the texts of modern-day oaths are still rooted firmly in the Christian tradition. Because of this, we often see a widely accepted alternative presented for non-religious persons, in the form of the more neutral affirmation.

The underlying idea is that performing such rituals makes a real difference to the state of the individual in keeping commitments. Oaths are considered to be the most important social-linguistic act of commitment because the taker of the oath offers a guarantee, which is accepted by the receiver of the oath in light of the rituals that are used.[21] Although oath-taking unmistakably has a religious background, in recent times, as the philosopher Jeremy Bentham[22] famously conveyed, it is related much more to moral engagement than to religion. By taking an oath, the utterance of the oath-taker takes a moral stance concerning a certain state of affairs and moves the oath-taker towards a commitment to the oath in future actions. For example, before testifying in court, by taking an oath, witnesses pledge to tell the truth.

By analysing the performativity of oath-taking, the argument is made that there is more to oath-taking than it being a one-off 'juridical' reminder raising the awareness about integrity. In turn, this analysis provides the ground to discuss the functioning of oath-taking as a means to enhance integrity as part of the training of officers.

---

[21] Loonen and Rutgers 2017.

[22] Bentham 1827.

4.4 Performativity of Oath-Taking

Before elaborating upon the performative account of oaths, first, the idea of performativity is briefly discussed. The idea to analyse communication in terms of its performativity first was introduced by J. L. Austin [23] and later further enhanced by J. Searle (1989)[24] and is known as the 'speech-act theory'. Performativity is understood as the capacity of speech and communication to act or to consummate an action.[25] Constative sentences – for example, 'snow is white' or 'Marry and John are married' – simply assert something to be descriptively true or false. In contrast, performative sentences – for example, 'I now pronounce you husband and wife' or 'I solemnly swear' – not only say something but actually do and create something new.[26] When uttering 'I now pronounce you husband and wife' the marriage officiant actually performs the marriage and creates a new entity, namely a married couple with particular rights and duties. Likewise, taking an integrity oath by an officer does not merely describe her/his commitment to act with integrity, but commissions the person to act accordingly.

Based on the speech act theory, the Dutch philosopher specializing in business ethics Vincent Blok[27] proposes a performative concept of ethical oaths that has four characteristics: (1) Infelicity, (2) Self-involvement, (3) Public context, and (4) Continuity/Structural possibility of infelicity. Together these characteristics provide a conceptual framework that allows analysing how the performativity of oath-taking functions as a means to embed a commitment to integrity within organizations. In the remainder of this section, each characteristic is discussed in detail, accompanied by practical illustrations. Primarily these illustrations are based on the oath-taking example of the induction ceremony of new NLDA personnel introduced at the beginning of this chapter. Although this is not a military oath in the sense that it involves civilians rather than military personnel, it does take place in a military context and concerns the training of military officers. Moreover, within the Dutch Ministry of Defence, oath-taking by civilians and military has a similar (formal) purpose and content.[28,29] In addition, further examples are included of oath-taking by military personnel within the Ministry of Defence in general.

---

[23] Austin 1975.
[24] Searle 1989.
[25] Hall 1999.
[26] Austin 1975.
[27] Blok 2013; Blok 2017.
[28] Dutch Ministry of Defence (2012) Aanwijzing SG A/984: Uitvoering van het integriteitsbeleid Defensie.
[29] Civil Servant Statute of the Ministry of Defence (BARD) Article 70a, General Military Civil Servant Statute (AMAR), Article 126a.

Table 4.1 Difference between constative and performative statements

Constative statement	Performative statement
Declaring that something is the case	A vehicle to do something and create something new
'John and Mary are married'	'I pronounce you man and wife'
True/false	The possibility of Infelicity: inappropriate, unsatisfactory, insincerity e.g. uttering 'I do' only is sensical in the act of marrying

Source Timmermans and Bertrand (2019)

4.4.1 Characteristic 1: Infelicity

As explained above, constative sentences are solely descriptive, i.e., they depict a certain state of affairs. Therefore, they are evaluated in terms of being true or false. For example, it is either true or false that 'coal is black'. Performative sentences function differently and, therefore, are evaluated differently. For example, it does not make sense to evaluate 'I name this ship the Queen Maxima' as true or false. Rather, a performative sentence is either appropriate or inappropriate, satisfactory or unsatisfactory given the context it is being uttered in. For instance, the sentence 'I do' is sensical when it is being uttered at a wedding ceremony, in the presence of a registrar and when the person uttering it is sincere about it, i.e., he or she has the right intentions and feelings (see Table 4.1).

All these possible ways of breaking rules when uttering a performative sentence are called 'infelicities' by Austin.[30] So, rather than truth-evaluable, performatives may be infelicitous. To evaluate performative sentences, Austin proposed six general rules:

1. **The existence of an accepted procedure.**
   For example, the oath-taking procedure of new staff members at the NLDA (or that of military personnel in general) involves vowing to the law or swearing to God, and the signing of a written statement by the oath-taker as well as the commander of the NLDA.
2. **The circumstances should be appropriate for the invocation of the procedures involved.**
   For instance, the induction ceremony took place in the Grand Hall of the Castle which is part of the housing of the NLDA, and all persons present wore appropriate clothing, for example, military ceremonial attire by military personnel. Also, after the oath-taking, the national anthem was played live, while the purpose and meaning of the oath-taking were elucidated by the commander's public address at the ceremony. Likewise, military oath-taking ceremonies are organized at dedicated places, with military ceremony and with appropriate

---

[30] Austin 1975.

military music and the presence of the banner or flag of the unit the military personnel is part of.
3. **The procedures must be executed correctly**.
   For example, the organizers took great care that the oath-taking ceremony was to be executed according to the protocol. First, by meticulously planning and allocating tasks via an official 'command' distributed a few weeks beforehand to the oath-takers and others involved. This command contained a sequence of events up to the minute of the preparations, the ceremony, and the aftermath describing what was to be executed and by whom. Second, before the ceremony, the oath-takers were instructed by a member of staff on the proceeding of the protocol. All this is considered standing practice at oath-taking ceremonies within the Ministry of Defence in general.
4. **The procedures must be executed completely**.
   For instance, at an oath-taking ceremony that takes place on a frigate, an air base or at the army barracks, the participants in the ceremony rehearse both ceremony and procedures and often the accompanying text of the oath is rehearsed publicly by the oath-takers. Also during the official ceremony, for each oath-taker, the complete wording of the oath itself is pronounced by the administering officer and then responded to by the oath-taker either by swearing or vowing.
5. **Congruency must exist between the intentions presupposed by the performative oath and the oath-takers actual intentions**.
   For instance, during the ceremony, the intention of new military personnel should be to act and behave with integrity during their work at for the Ministry of Defence when they utter the oath. This, however, is impossible to verify with certainty.
6. **Congruency between the intentions presupposed by the performative oath and the oath-takers actual behaviour**.
   For instance, in their dealings with students and co-workers, new NLDA staff members should uphold the values and norms of the NLDA and act with integrity. This can be verified by ex-post research.

General rules 5 and especially rule 6, clearly are related to integrity. In the discussion above (Sect. 4.2), integrity is understood as an alignment between intentions and actual behaviour. The possibility of incongruence between intentions and behaviour presupposed by the performative oath and the actual intentions and behaviour of the oath-taker, therefore, obviously may lead to a test of integrity. Consequently, integrity resides at the heart of oath-taking itself at two levels, namely the content of the oath and the living up to the oath.

4.4.2 Characteristic 2: Self-involvement

Next to the possibility of infelicity, the second characteristic of oath-taking is self-involvement. Performative statements always are in the first person singular, for example, in 'I pronounce you man and wife' or 'I solemnly swear'. This signals the involvement of the person uttering the oath in the performative sentence being uttered.

Two of the general rules of infelicity (5 and 6, see above) are concerned with the identity of the oath-taker. An oath is infelicitous when there is an inconsistency between the performative utterance and the actual intentions of the oath-taker, that is, the person that she or he wants to be, or between the person she or he wants to be and her or his actual behaviour.[31]

So, when the oath-takers at the NLDA ceremony proclaimed to behave with integrity, they not only *intended* to be acting with integrity but also state they intended *to be* the ones who are ethical or have integrity. By uttering the oath the self-performative articulates the professional identity of the staff member, which then affects his or her lifestyle, attitude and behaviour towards others.[32] Oath-taking thus concerns the identity as a professional and as a consequence her or his practical *commitment* to future action, as well as her or his attitudes and her or his feelings.[33] Furthermore, the involvement of the self in oath-taking is *transformative* of the identity of the oath-taker as it transforms her or his self or identity.

For example, before and during the oath-taking ceremony a certain nervousness or apprehension was palpable amongst the new staff members. Some tension-alleviating jokes were made and murmurs were heard of people rehearsing the words of their vow at the last minute. This can be interpreted to signal the intensity felt of living through that moment and, hence, the lasting impression it has was making on the partakers. Of course, the ceremony was carefully designed to make a lasting impression on the identity of the oath-takers, for example, by the historic setting, formal entourage and protocol, the speech by the commander underlying the purpose and significance of the ceremony. Moreover, by encouraging the oath-takers to invite close relatives and friends to be present at the ceremony helped to further enhance the personal involvement and commitment of the oath-taker to the ceremony. Again, these elements are common practice at oath-taking ceremonies within the Ministry of Defence.

4.4.3 Characteristic 3: Public Context

The involvement of family and friends as well as (close) colleagues is representative of the third characteristic of oath-taking: public context. Part of the performative of taking an oath involves the securing of uptake by the oath-taker. The person that the oath-taker wants to be by taking the oath is not just dependent on his or her subjective intentions, but is also determined by the public context and is articulated

---

[31] Blok 2013.
[32] Blok 2017.
[33] Evans 1963.

on the interaction with this public context.[34] The meaning of the oath is determined by the way it is understood by the public. For example, the oath at the NLDA ceremony gets its meaning because the public is present and understands what the oath is about and what the oath-takers intend by it. This understanding depends on the tradition of the oath, which shaped the way it was portrayed during the ceremony and was represented by the colleagues present, who themselves have taken a similar oath in the past. Also, the speech given by commander NLDA, which besides targeting the oath-takers themselves explicitly targeted the audience as well, affected the way the public understands the oath and its intentions.

Due to public involvement, the meaning and intention of the oath transcends the individual oath-takers and thereby provides binding power. By witnessing it, the uptake of the oath is warranted by the public at the ceremony. Moreover, by uttering the performative oath in front of the public, the oath-taker becomes the person who is responsive to the command of the public and the public becomes that to which the oath-taker is responsive in the oath-taking. So, at the NLDA ceremony and military oath-taking ceremonies in general, by taking the oath the oath-takers accept the demand by the public to act with integrity and become a person of integrity. While, at the same time, the public present takes on the role of witness and thereby becomes the authority under which the oath gets its meaning.

4.4.4 Characteristic 4: Continuity/Structural Possibility of Infelicity

Of course, meeting the felicity rules, being self-involved and having a public context while taking an oath does not guarantee (future) ethical behaviour. And, even if the three characteristics would be sufficient, the question must be raised how it can be established whether an oath actually works in the first place? I.e., whether an oath is able to determine and mark the identity and behaviour of an oath-taker according to its intentions? In the end, it is only by an actual act in light of an oath, that the oath becomes real, i.e. that the intentions and behaviour of the oath-taker are in alignment with each other and with the intentions of the oath. So, the ultimate test is the actual behaviour of the oath-taker, irrespective of the intentions to commit to some future action at the time of the ceremony.

However, living up to the oath by no means is trivial. The possibility of infelicity is looming at all times. Not only at the ceremony itself may incongruence between the intentions of the oath-taker and the intentions of the oath (rule 5) and/or the intentions of the oath-taker and her or his actual behaviour (rule 6) exist. These incongruences may occur at any stage after the ceremony too. Oftentimes, professionals have to operate in complex, dynamic contexts or have to act and decide under fundamental (epistemic) uncertainty. As a consequence, their acting involves

---

[34] Blok 2013.

taking risks and dealing with moral dilemmas. Moreover, according to the definition of integrity provided above, the possibility of incongruence between intentions and behaviour may involve a breach of integrity.

At the same time, the structural possibility of infelicity also provides proof that an oath is working. Firstly, when an oath-taker indeed is actually acting in light of the oath. But more importantly, secondly, through the ongoing struggle of the oath-taker against infelicity. While operating under uncertainty in complex, dynamic contexts, professionals encounter situations that challenge their integrity. Dealing with these situations calls for reflection on their intentions and behaviour in the light of the intentions of the oath, but also, on the intention of the oath itself. Therefore, living up to an oath involves an incessant appropriation and re-appropriation of the content of the oath by the oath-taker. As such, the performative understanding of oath-taking clarifies how the structural possibility of infelicity itself is the driver to live and act according to an oath.

Dealing with structural infelicity not only involves an effort by the individual oath-taker. Reflecting on what it means to live up the oath, i.e. be a person of integrity, also includes an ongoing conversation and negotiation with the public context. For example, NLDA staff-members may discuss difficult decisions they face with their spouses, friends or co-workers. Also, more formally, by debating within the NLDA organization about what it means to act with integrity in particular cases and in general, may result to a reconsideration of what living up to the oath entails. Eventually, such consideration may even end up affecting the oath-taking ceremony itself, such as, for example, the content of the speech given by the commander of the NLDA, or even the formulation of the oath itself.

In addition, the (re-)appropriation of the oath in the context of an organization can be supported by policies that enable reflection and dialogue on ethical issues, for example, a code of conduct, counsellors, education and training. Also, the institutional design concerning the governance structure, separation of functions, recruitment policies and reward systems can be geared towards accommodating ethical behaviour. The NLDA, for example, has a section dedicated to supporting integrity by providing advice and giving training, a professional code of conduct for students and staff members, and counselors and mediators across different levels of the organization. At the same time, however, it is less clear whether the institutional design of the NLDA is supportive of living up to the oath. For instance, the current governance structure, recruitment policy and reward systems foremost are dedicated to the supporting and preparing for military duties. The integrity violations that surfaced in a 2013 evaluation[35] and, more recently, the eight reports of unethical behaviour at the NLDA received by a hotline in 2018[36] raise the question whether such structural arrangements fully succeed in providing the context needed to support and maintain the integrity standard set forward by the new staff members' oath.

---

[35] Giebels et al. 2018, p. 15.
[36] COID [Central Organization Integrity Defence] 2014.

4.5 Discussion and Conclusion: Relevance to Educating and Training of Officers

Oaths have been part and parcel of the military tradition since classical times. From the advent of the Dutch Republic in the 17th century, they also became a cornerstone of the Dutch military. Taking a performative perspective on oath-taking allowed for a better understanding of oaths as a means to embed integrity within an organization. Four characteristics of oaths were discussed that analysed the functioning of oaths as a vehicle to embed integrity: first, the possibility of infelicity, second, self-involvement, third, public context, and fourth, continuity/structural possibility of infelicity. The characteristics not only provided insights with regard to the ceremony of oath-taking itself but also how the value of oaths can be sustained after the ceremony.

These insights are relevant to the training and educating of military officers from (at least) three perspectives:

(1) A direct consequence (first order effect) of a performative conceptualization of oaths is that it allows for a better embedding of integrity within the organization. On the one hand, raising the awareness of those involved in the ceremony about the functioning and importance of oath-taking as highlighted by the performative understanding can increase the effectiveness of the oath. As a consequence, the oath-takers, oath-givers and public will have the right attitude and feelings towards the oath, hence, enhancing the transformative aspects of the oath. On the other hand, also structural changes can be drawn from the analysis such as improving the ceremony and supporting the aftermath by adapting the institutional design and (integrity) policies of the host organization. For example, the military oath-taking ceremonies could be adapted as to pay more attention to (re-)appropriation to sustain the impact of the oath.

(2) More importantly, raising awareness and shaping the ceremony, policy, and institutions according to the performative understanding affects the acting in light of the oath by the oath-takers (second order effect). Behaving with integrity would be enhanced by creating awareness and understanding of the why and how of oath-taking and how it is related to integrity. Moreover, especially the awareness of and hence experiencing the structural struggle with infelicity would support the (re-)appropriation of the oath and thereby sustaining its impact. For example, awareness of this struggle would make it more transparent and thereby allows co-workers and students (the cadets and midshipmen in training to be officers) to be involved in the process of discussing and reflecting on (potential) infelicities and dilemmas encountered. Enhancing the integrity of the personnel this way supports constituting a safe working and learning environment at the NLDA that is attuned to its educational purposes. Furthermore, having insight about oaths enables the NLDA staff to transfer this knowledge to the students: implicitly, by setting an example through their

actions with integrity and struggling with infelicities; and explicitly, by including these insights into their training and teaching.

(3) And last but not less important, having these insights about oath-taking carriers over to the behaviour of the students (the cadets and midshipmen in training to be officers) themselves. Not only would this affect their behaving and acting with integrity during their training and education but also beyond it, in their professional lives as a military officer. For example, like the new staff-members at NLDA, starting a career as an officer involves taking an oath. Having an understanding of and conducting the ceremony according to the performative conceptualisation of oaths may increase and sustain the impact of their oath-taking. Moreover, in their role and responsibility as a leader, officers will be witnessing and administering oaths of others, for example, their subordinates. Again, having these insights and acting upon them enhances the positive impact of the oath-taking ceremony and the uptake beyond it. As such, oath-taking functions as a better tool to set the right ethical climate within the contexts the officer is involved in and co-responsible for.

To conclude, the analysis of a performative account of oaths provides insights that help to enhance the oath-taking ceremony and to sustain its impact beyond it. This way it supports the engraining of integrity in both staff members and students (officers in training) at the military academy. It must be noted though, that the current analysis rests on a philosophical argumentation, supported by the extant literature and historical evidence. Therefore, to further ground and expand the analysis it is recommended to test the performative conceptualisation and its insights in an empirical investigation.

Acknowledgement We would like to express our special gratitude to the commander NLDA General-Major Geerts and his staff for making available the official documents of the preparation and conducting of the NLDA oath-taking ceremony which was used as an example throughout this chapter.

References

Anderson M, Escher P (2010) The MBA oath: Setting a higher standard for business leaders. Penguin.
Audi R, Murphy PE (2006) The many faces of integrity. Bus Ethics Q 16:3–21.
Austin JL (1975) How to do things with words. Oxford University Press.
Bentham J (1827) Rationale of Judicial Evidence: Specially Applied to English Practice (in five volumes). Hunt and Clarke, London.
Blok V (2013) The Power of Speech Acts: Reflections on a Performative Concept of Ethical Oaths in Economics and Business. Rev Soc Econ 71:187–208.
Blok V (2017) Bridging the Gap between Individual and Corporate Responsible Behaviour: Toward a Performative Concept of Corporate Codes. Philos Manag 16:117–136.
COID (2014) Integriteit bij de opleiding en vorming van adelborsten en cadetten aan de Nederlandse Defensie Academie. Duiding van risico's, perspectief op verbetering [Integrity in the education and training of midshipmen and cadets at the Netherlands Defence Academy.

Interpretation of risks, perpective on improvement]. http://www.gi-nederland.com/wp-content/uploads/Rapportage-Risicoanalyse-Integriteit.pdf. Accessed 1 January 2019.
Evans DD (1963) The logic of self-involvement. SCM, London.
Giebels E, van Oostrum F, van den Bos K (2018) Onderzoek naar een sociaal veilige werkomgeving bij Defensie [Investigation into a socially safe work environment at Defence]. https://www.rijksoverheid.nl/documenten/rapporten/2018/10/15/onderzoek-naar-een-sociaal-veilige-werkomgeving-bij-defensie. Accessed 23 May 2019.
Gonzalez-Padron TL, Ferrell OC, Ferrell L, Smith IA (2012) A Critique of Giving Voice to Values Approach to Business Ethics Education. J Acad Ethics 10:251–269.
Hall K (1999) Performativity. J Linguist Anthropol 9:184–187.
Kayes DC, Stirling D, Nielsen TM (2007) Building organizational integrity. Bus Horiz 50:61–70.
Landolt HMF (1861) Militair woordenboek voor Nederlanders bewerkt [Military Dictionary edited for Dutchmen]. Sijthoff, Leiden.
Loonen T, Rutgers MR (2017) Swearing to be a good banker: Perceptions of the obligatory banker's oath in the Netherlands. J Bank Regul 18:28–47.
Manz CC, Anand V, Joshi M, Manz KP (2008) Emerging paradoxes in executive leadership: A theoretical interpretation of the tensions between corruption and virtuous values. Leadersh Q 19:385–392.
Monga M, Orlitzky M (eds) (2017) Integrity in Business and Management: Cases and Theory. Taylor & Francis, New York.
Oettinger N (1976) Die militärischen Eide der Hethiter. Harrassowitz, Mainz.
Renatus FV (1996) Vegetius: epitome of military science. Liverpool University Press.
Rieke ML, Guastello SJ (1995) Unresolved issues in honesty and integrity testing.
Searle JR (1989) How performatives work. Linguist Philos 12:535–558.
Siewert P (1977) The ephebic oath in fifth-century Athens. J Hell Stud 97:102–111.
Van der Steenhoven K, Aalbersberg M (2016) Moral fitness. Een onderzoek naar de integriteit van de defensieorganisatie ten aanzien van de omgang met commerciële partijen op het gebied van IT [Moral fitness. An investigation into the integrity of the defence organization with regard to dealing with commercial parties in the area of IT].
Verhezen P (2010) Giving Voice in a Culture of Silence. From a Culture of Compliance to a Culture of Integrity. J Bus Ethics 96:187–206.
Wankel C, Stachowicz-Stanusch A (2011) Management education for integrity: Ethically educating tomorrow's business leaders. Emerald Group Publishing.
Weaver M, Paxton S, Tan H, Crossan K (2016) Cultivating responsible business in Scotland through the lens of the Scottish business pledge. Scotland's Responsible Business Forum.
Zarim ZA, Zaki HO, Maridz NLM (2016) Motivation Factors: Impact on Sales Commission Plan Employees in a Telecommunication Company in Malaysia. Management 4:139–148.

Dr. Job Timmermans is an associate professor Business Ethics at the Faculty of Military Sciences of the Netherlands Defence Academy, The Netherlands. His interests cover the philosophical and sociological issues arising from the intersections of ethics, integrity and compliance within organizations. Previously, he has worked within several projects on Responsible Research Innovation (RRI) at Wageningen University (The Netherlands), De Montfort University (UK), and Delft University of Technology (The Netherlands).

Colonel Dr. Robert Bertrand RA RC RO is associate professor of Accounting, Control and Defence Economics at the Faculty of Military Sciences of the Netherlands Defence Academy. He joined the Royal Netherlands Air Force in 1995 and switched to the Royal Netherlands *Marechaussee* in 2009. He defended his Ph.D. on Contract Audits in 2016 at Maastricht University. His current research interests focus on Auditing, Compliance, Internal Control, Ethics and Leadership.

Part II
Educational Philosophy

Chapter 5
Officer *Bildung*: A Philosophical Investigation of Preconditions for Military Character Education

Marenne Jansen and Desiree Verweij

Contents

5.1 Introduction	60
5.2 Military Education Analysis	61
5.2.1 Why Character Education Matters	61
5.2.2 Practices of Military Education	63
5.3 Philosophical Underpinnings of Character Education	65
5.3.1 Aristotelian Virtue Ethics	65
5.3.2 *Bildung* as an Educational Concept	66
5.3.3 Contemporary Character Education	68
5.4 Preconditions and Implications	70
5.5 Conclusion	71
References	72

Abstract The importance of military leadership can hardly be underestimated. Military organizations worldwide continue to recognise the need for excellent leaders, if they are to deal with the complexities of warfare in the best possible way. Consequently, for the sake of the organization, as well as the individual, military academies seek to train their recruits to become outstanding leaders. To reach this objective, most, if not all, centre their educational programs around the ambition, not only to teach military and academic skills, but also to "develop leaders of character". Subsequently, countless learning programs and strategies aimed at character development exist. However, an initial analysis of contemporary military

---

M. M. Jansen (✉)
Radboud University, PO Box 9108, 6500 HK Nijmegen, The Netherlands
e-mail: marenne.jansen@minbuza.nl

D. E. M. Verweij
Faculty of Military Sciences, Netherlands Defence Academy, PO Box 90002,
4800 PA Breda, The Netherlands
e-mail: DEM.Verweij.01@mindef.nl

© T.M.C. ASSER PRESS and the authors 2019
W. Klinkert et al. (eds.), *NL ARMS Netherlands Annual Review of Military Studies 2019*, NL ARMS, https://doi.org/10.1007/978-94-6265-315-3_5

education shows that the practice of character education is far from straightforward. This chapter examines the philosophical underpinnings of character education and in doing so, aims to show the inherent difficulties faced by military academies in developing leaders of character. Finally, it argues that, in order to understand what it takes to implement military character education, one first needs to understand its preconditions. By formulating these preconditions and discussing their implications, this chapter aims to contribute to the re-evaluation of the dominant traditional paradigm in military education.

Keywords character education · military formation · *Bildung* · virtue ethics · educational philosophy · leadership

5.1 Introduction

The importance of military leadership can hardly be underestimated. Military organisations worldwide continue to recognise the importance of excellent leaders if they are to deal effectively with the complexities of modern warfare, including the ethical and operational complications emerging from the cultural, socio-political, and psychological characteristics of contemporary missions.[1] To manage these complexities, military organizations—from Hellenistic times through the formation of early European nation states to the present day—have underscored the importance of character education for military personnel.[2] Consequently, most Western military academies offer character education in order to support (aspirant) officers learning to navigate the complexities of modern warfare.[3] This training is designed with a specific focus on leadership qualities.[4] Therefore, most, if not all, Western military academies centre their educational programs around the ambition, not only to teach military and academic skills, but also to "develop leaders of character."[5]

In literature, this type of training is referred to as character building, character education, or moral education, and in various theoretical contexts, these terms are used interchangeably. There is no single shared definition of what "character," "good character," or "character education" actually refers to, and therefore the concept might appear rather ambiguous.[6] Nevertheless, there is a common understanding in mainstream academic discourse that "character education is any form of

---

[1] Beard 2014; Schut and Moelker 2015; Sherman 2010; Van Baarda and Verweij 2006.

[2] Caforio 2000, 2006; French 2003; Olsthoorn 2013; Richardson et al. 2004; Robinson 2007.

[3] Moelker 2000.

[4] Dalenberg 2017; De Vries 2013; Director General Leadership of the Royal Military Academy Sandhurst 2014; Matthews et al. 2006; Robinson 2007.

[5] Canadian Defence Academy 2005; Director General Leadership of the Royal Military Academy Sandhurst 2014; Netherlands Defence Academy 2016; United States Military Academy West Point 2015.

[6] Kristjánsson 2013; Van Baarda and Verweij 2006.

moral education that foregrounds the role of virtuous character in the good life."[7] Given its common understanding, this term and its associated definition will be used throughout this chapter.

Aside from its semantics, character education itself is a complex process. With this chapter, we aim to provide a philosophical background to the complex task of character education and in doing so, we aim to contribute to the discussion on the reassessment of the dominant paradigm in military education and its philosophical foundations.[8] We argue that, in order to understand what it takes to actually put military character education into practice, one needs to understand the preconditions for character education.

After a brief analysis of current practices of military character education, we re-asses the philosophical foundations of character education in Aristotelian virtue ethics and the tradition of *Bildung*—an educational tradition focusing on personal and intellectual maturation. In both traditions, there is substantial interest in the development of character. We discuss these perspectives because we believe they have the potential to deliver a substantial contribution to the development of theories on military education, and provide the basis of contemporary theories on character education.[9] Finally, we formulate preconditions for character education and discuss their implications for today's military character education.

5.2 Military Education Analysis

5.2.1 Why Character Education Matters

It is often argued that to adaptively handle the challenges of conflict, officers not only need to develop military and intellectual skills, but also moral competencies.[10] Literature supports this widely accepted assertion with two main arguments. The first is derived from the just war theory (*jus bellum justum*)—probably the best known ethical framework for military operations.[11] For a war to be legitimate, it not only needs to have a morally just cause and fulfil several other *jus ad bellum* ("right to war") criteria, but during the war, *jus in bello* ("right in war") criteria with regard

---

[7] Kristjánsson 2013, p. 272.
[8] Sookermany 2017.
[9] Biesta 2002, 2016; Dewey 2007; Good and Garrison 2010; Horlacher 2015; Løvlie and Standish 2002; Morgenbesser 1979; Nussbaum 2012; Sanderse 2012; Van Baarda and Verweij 2006.
[10] Beard 2014; Caforio 2000, 2006; Deakin 2008; Doty and Sowden 2009; Kennedy and Neilson 2002; Micewski and Annen 2005; Moelker 2000; Olsthoorn 2013; Richardson et al. 2004; Robinson et al. 2008; Visser 2002.
[11] Just war theory is probably best known from the work of Michael Walzer (2015), but dates back to Augustine and Thomas Aquinas, and is eloquently illustrated by Dyer's description of the true warrior: "[The warrior] does not want to kill people as such, but he will have no objections if it occurs in a moral framework that gives him justification—like war" (cited in Coker 2007, p. 6).

to the actual fighting need to be met as well. In order to evaluate whether a war, and the actions taken within a war, are justified, Michael Walzer states that training in morally responsible behaviour is a prerequisite for anyone working within an organization using (armed) power in conflict.

The second argument highlights the way in which developments in contemporary warfare have changed the nature of most military operations and consequently have affected the roles and tasks of military leaders. Aside from being a "warrior," a modern soldier needs to be able—depending on the particular assignment—to switch adaptively between multiple roles: "The modern soldier is no longer simply a warrior: he (or she) is at once a peacekeeper, diplomat, leader, sibling and friend."[12] In the face of such challenges, it has been often endeavoured to "incorporate a character-based training program, designed to develop virtues that will assist soldiers in fulfilling the multiple roles."[13] To do such demanding work and live with the often horrific experience of war, it is argued that military personnel have to be both morally and psychologically equipped. Shannon E. French explains that

> moral training in military education is needed because one would never want to see them sent off to face the chaotic hell of combat, without something to ground them and keep them from crossing over into an inescapable heart of darkness.[14]

French asserts that moral training helps to achieve this: "by setting standards of behaviour for themselves, accepting certain restraints, and even honouring their enemies, warriors can create a life-line that will allow them to pull themselves out of the hell of war and reintegrate themselves into their society."[15] Peter Olsthoorn adds that "incidents in Iraq and Afghanistan have shown that the required moderation does not always come naturally."[16] This is corroborated by research with regard to the behaviour of military personnel in Srebrenica,[17] Abu Ghraib,[18] the Central African Republic,[19] Somalia,[20] sexual abuse of women and girls by peacekeepers,[21] and serious misconduct by peacekeepers (both civilian and military) operating under a UN mandate.[22]

---

[12] Beard 2014, p. 274.
[13] Beard 2014, p. 274.
[14] French 2003, p. 11.
[15] French 2003, p. 7.
[16] Olsthoorn 2013, p. 365.
[17] Blocq 2006; Van Baarda and Verweij 2006.
[18] Giroux 2004.
[19] Carasik L (2015) Opinion: End Sexual Exploitation by Peacekeepers. america.aljazeera.com/opinions/2015/6/end-sexual-exploitation-by-un-peacekeepers.html (Accessed 16 October 2018).
[20] Maogoto 2000.
[21] Ndulo 2009.
[22] Grady 2016; Odello 2010.

Hence—be it because working in conflict zones requires a firm moral grounding because military misconduct should be prevented, or simply because officers need a moral compass—Western military academies emphasise character building "to assist members of the military in becoming men and women with a strong moral commitment."[23] However, although the objective of military academies is in most cases neatly defined, to actually "do" character education is neither a simple nor a straightforward process.[24]

5.2.2 Practices of Military Education

Traditionally, the right to become an officer was confined to the aristocracy. Hence, aspirant military officers were assumed to be well-behaved gentlemen, hardly in need of any subsequent character education. Teaching novices about the nobility of the officer corps was only considered relevant when the rank of officer became accessible to people from the lower social classes. It was said that they lacked the nobility of the "old" officers, and therefore needed a thorough education, including lessons in what was considered "officer behaviour."[25] Notably, this continues to the present day, and is being reinforced by military academies via the traditions of their cadet corps. For example, during hazing periods, cadets are drilled exhaustively until they know how to use the correct titles and exhibit the prescribed manners. However, it is debatable whether these "classes" actually constitute character education, or are more concerned with socialisation.[26] Character education is not solely a process of socialisation,[27] nor is it the result of the powerful influence of a "total" institution.[28] Rather, it depends on more than formal education alone, and is thus not solely a cognitive issue (see Sect. 5.3).

---

[23] Van Baarda and Verweij 2006, p. 9.

[24] The United States Military Academy West Point states as their aim to "[e]ducate, train, and inspire the Corps of Cadets so that each graduate is a commissioned leader of character committed to the values of Duty, Honor, Country and prepared for a career of professional excellence and service to the Nation as an officer in the United States Army" (United States Military Academy West Point 2015, p. VI). Saint-Cyr, the French military academy, is "dedicated to providing cadets not only with basic technical and tactical knowledge, but also with behavioral qualities and intellectual skills that will enable young officers to become decision-makers and face tomorrow's challenges" (Ecoles de Saint-Cyr Coëtquidan 2016, p. 3). Finally, in the United Kingdom, "the Royal Military Academy Sandhurst (RMAS) is where all officers in the British Army are trained to take on the responsibility of leading their fellow soldiers. During training, all officer cadets learn to live by the academy's motto: 'Serve to Lead'" (Royal Military Academy Sandhurst 2018, n.p.).

[25] Schoy 2011; Van Schilt 2011.

[26] Insightful studies on this topic have been conducted by Dalenberg (2017) and Van Schilt (2011).

[27] For example, see Ashforth et al. (2007), Guimond (1995), and Rones (2015).

[28] Anteby 2013; Goffman 1961; Moelker 2000.

Another common practice in military education is to anchor its moral component in codes of conduct.[29] This is done to mark the intention to shape, influence, and improve the characters of future officers.[30] However, the very assumption that codes of conduct are a useful vehicle for character education is problematic, as character education is "concerned with the development of inner discipline[;] it is not something that can be taught by cramming or drilling [and t]here are no checklists that can guarantee one becoming a good soldier."[31] Nevertheless, the teaching methods used are, more often than not, based on the traditional military educational paradigm, including hierarchical instruction methods and a plethora of rules used to regulate behaviour.[32] Whilst this approach is effective for teaching "a soldier how to load a weapon," Joe Doty and Walter Sowden argue that it is not the way to develop someone in "the moral or ethical arena. You cannot teach someone via PowerPoint to behave in the morally correct way."[33] Character education, thus, should be more than simply listing codes and teaching rules; it is about internalisation, rather than memorising.

A third problem with military character education programs is that the basic philosophical principles underlying them are "often very different from one nation to another and developed on an ad-hoc base rather than drawn from any systematically considered ethical theory or embedded within any pragmatic workable education program."[34] This statement is supported by an apparent academic disagreement on what military virtues actually are. Peter Olsthoorn lists honour, courage, loyalty, integrity, and respect as the five key military virtues, and argues that these virtues are rooted in (Aristotelian) virtue ethics.[35] Nancy E. Snow thinks that military virtues are based on utilitarianism, Kantianism, and Enlightenment ideals.[36] Meanwhile, Stephen Deakin[37] and Bradley C. S. Watson[38] consider them a combination of ethical theories, with influences from Christian ethics, relativism, and absolutism.

To summarise, the three basic problems with military character education programs are firstly, that ancient traditions are not sufficient, and secondly, that codes of conduct do not suit the ambition to equip military personnel with the desired

---

[29] Although there is no consensus on what the key virtues and values of a good officer are, military codes of most Western countries seem to be constructed using (more or less) the same virtues (Dalenberg 2017).

[30] Deakin 2008, p. 151; Franke 2000; Franke and Heinecken 2001.

[31] Wortel and Bosch 2011, pp. 21–22.

[32] Traditional military education is characterised by a "classic modernist view on education rooted in universalism, structure and objectivity" (Sookermany 2017, p. 310; see also Doty and Sowden 2009; Paile 2014).

[33] Doty and Sowden 2009, p. 70.

[34] Robinson et al. 2008, p. 1.

[35] Olsthoorn 2013.

[36] Snow 2009.

[37] Deakin 2008, p. 23.

[38] Watson 1999.

virtues and values. Finally, educational programs lack any grounding in ethical theory and a connection to educational design. Based on these conclusions, this chapter argues that, in order to understand how successful military character education can be implemented, one first needs to understand the preconditions for such character education. In the following section we therefore examine the philosophical foundations of character education, concentrating on those aspects especially relevant to the practice of military character education.

5.3 Philosophical Underpinnings of Character Education

5.3.1 Aristotelian Virtue Ethics

For many centuries, character education was based on the teachings of Aristotle. He laid the foundations for modern thinking on moral theory, virtue ethics, and the cultivation of (a moral) character.[39] For our purposes, three elements are noteworthy: (1) the goal of *eudaimonia* ("the good life") and how to achieve it; (2) the pupil; and (3) the relation between individual development and being part of the community.

Eudaimonia is a central concept in Aristotelian virtue ethics and is best translated as the fulfilment of human potential. Virtues are those qualities that will enable an individual to achieve *eudaimonia*, and virtue ethics aims to transform the young person into a flourishing human being.[40] To be virtuous is to find the right balance between two vices—for example, courage (a virtue) is balanced between rashness and cowardice (both vices). According to Aristotle, we can be gifted with natural traits and talents—in fact, we can even inherit a natural disposition to do, on occasion, the right thing—but this is not to be confused with the possession of virtue. Rather, via systemic training or habituation, the pupil will learn how not to fall prey to "their own emotions and desires," and will thus internalise virtuous behaviour.[41] A pupil of Aristotle is required to learn how to regulate one's own behaviour and, moreover, to internalise the rationality and behaviour appropriate for a virtuous life, which "is concerned with the development of inner discipline, with people beginning to look critically at themselves."[42] Self-regulation, personal development, and the internalisation of values are considered far more relevant than external rules, and it should therefore be unsurprising that, in the Aristotelian tradition, there is relatively little mention of rules and regulations. However, there

---

[39] MacIntyre 2013; Nussbaum 2013; Sanderse 2012.
[40] Kristjánsson 2013; MacIntyre 2013.
[41] MacIntyre 2013, p. 149.
[42] Wortel and Bosch 2011, p. 21.

are bound to be occasions in which no formula applies and, in these instances, the individual has to act for the right reasons, and out of trained habit.[43]

Yet, according to Aristotle, character education suits only a privileged group. Such a group consists of young men, endowed with intellectual, political, military, and creative talents and experience—those encouraged by their parents and previous teachers "to think of citizenship as their future sphere, [and] practical wisdom as their goal."[44] However, these criteria reveal a circular argument: in order to receive character education, one has to have a solid intellectual, cultural, and practical underpinning. Character education is thus not simply about the internalisation of new habits or behaviour, but rather builds upon existing internal dispositions.

Additionally, for Aristotle, the relationship between personal development and being a member of the community is important and unquestionable. He sees both personal development and being a member of the political community (*polis*) as essential for achieving *eudaimonia*. This idea reveals a more complex argument, explored by Alasdair MacIntyre, who explains that "the virtues are all in harmony with each other and the harmony of individual character is reproduced in the harmony of the state."[45] Thus, in Aristotle's conception of "the good life," the development of the individual and the community are intertwined.

5.3.2 Bildung *as an Educational Concept*

For Aristotle, character education is not an individual enterprise. Rather, being a flourishing individual is directly connected to being part of the community. Following a similar logic, *Bildung* idealists, such as Wilhelm von Humboldt, Werner Jaeger, and Johann Gottfried von Herder, emphasise the need for people to become educated members of the nation.[46] There are further similarities because, in the tradition of *Bildung*, ideals from ancient Greek culture were borrowed to establish a cultural and intellectual elite. The main features of *Bildung* are an idea of common kinship and the unity of mankind, and the adoption of classic insights as an educational and cultural ideal for the formation of both mind and character. This formation is a process of educating man towards his "true form"—the real and genuine human nature—and carries a normative notion of culture. The best way to educate, according to von Humboldt, is to let people develop themselves by means of a classic education.[47]

---

[43] MacIntyre 2013.
[44] Nussbaum 2013, pp. 55–56.
[45] MacIntyre 2013, pp. 156–157.
[46] Forster 2018.
[47] Humboldt 1963, p. 125.

Historically, *Bildung* has a wide variety of interpretations, ranging from the spiritual to the biological, and from the political to the educational. Whilst today we encounter *Bildung* mostly as a political and educational ideal, in its early usage, *Bildung* had a strong moral and spiritual meaning, instructing Christians to cultivate their talents and dispositions according to the image of God.[48] Yet, *Bildung* could also refer to a biological ideal. In the 16th century, the term *Bildung* was used, amongst others, by Gottfried Wilhelm Leibniz (1646–1786) to refer to "the development or unfolding of certain potentialities within an organism."[49] In the 18th century, *Bildung* evolved into a political term, mainly associated with a disciplining system for citizens. Herder's definition illustrates this transition: "*Bildung* refers to the products not of God's handwork, but of an impersonal genetic force that … drives human beings towards ever higher cultural achievements."[50] Noteworthy here is the idea of a higher culture that can only come into existence in a more developed and institutionalised society. Herder described this as a totality of experiences that imparts a coherent identity and sense of common destiny to a people. With this definition, he laid the basis for the modern political idea of the nation state. Around the same time, *Bildung* was introduced as an educational concept in the military. General von Scharnhorst, convinced that the improvement of the scientific and technical education of officers was necessary, found that "only well-educated people sought to alleviate the horrors of war, and that uneducated officers were just as bestial as the rank and file."[51]

Today, *Bildung* continues to carry this political and developmental connotation.[52] In its political meaning, *Bildung* is connected to an ideal society and a specific conceptualisation of the ideal citizen within such a society. This tradition takes a normative position, prescribing "the cultural content of education."[53] The supposition here is that character is to be imposed on the person—like an external (normative) state, or a formal competency, closely linked to the existence of a political community—to the point that, in its political meaning, the ideal of *Bildung* has become "entrapped in cultural arrogance and dull conformism."[54]

In the developmental tradition, *Bildung* refers to the humanist legacy, in which the focus lies on personal development and growth, and "the goal of education was to help students realise the ideal of modernity, which is for the individual to become a self-directed, self-formed person."[55] It emphasises "a specific kind of

---

[48] Biesta 2002; Horlacher 2004, 2015; Løvlie and Standish 2002; Reindal 2012.
[49] Schmidt 1996, p. 630.
[50] Herder 1784–91 cited in Boes 2008, p. 275.
[51] Von Scharnhorst 1793 cited in Schoy 2011, p. 9.
[52] Bauer 1997.
[53] Reindal 2012, p. 537.
[54] Løvlie and Standish 2002, p. 317.
[55] Good and Garrison 2010, pp. 52–53.

self-experience and self-development summarised in the phrase Sich-Bilden or 'self-education.'"[56] Central to the developmental tradition "is the question of what constitutes an educated or cultivated human being. The answer to this question is not given in terms of discipline, socialisation or moral training."[57] Instead, developmental *Bildung* idealises the kind of thinking that initiates a process "of how knowledge becomes internalised."[58] In this tradition, education is a long-term process that can be understood as a process of self-realisation or living up to one's full potential. The pupil receives the freedom to integrate knowledge and transform it internally and intrinsically.

The developmental interpretation of *Bildung*, referring to an educational ideal of strengthening students' innate powers and character developments, is currently extremely popular in research commissions on the future of education.[59] This popularity promotes the need for an education focused on self-experience, self-reflection, and self-development.[60] Here also, one can easily identify the expectation that *Bildung* supports both individual development and the formation of "good" (global) citizens. Proponents of this type of *Bildung* state that character education can only take place in open-ended learning situations—those guided by goals of individual development. Rather than pursuing measurable learning objectives, it focusses on forming a self-reflexive attitude.

5.3.3 Contemporary Character Education

Pursuing both political and developmental *Bildung* implies a certain tension between an external imposition and authentic development. This educational paradox is elaborated upon in contemporary theories on (character) education by authors such as David Graeber,[61] Martha Nussbaum,[62] Ewald Engelen, Fernandez

---

[56] Nordenbo 2002; Reindal 2012, p. 537.

[57] Biesta 2002, p. 378.

[58] Reindal 2012, p. 547.

[59] Løvlie and Standish 2002, p. 318.

[60] The former Dutch Minister of Education uses the term explicitly when discussing the future of education: "In the 21st century *Bildung* stands for a better understanding of the world, a strong moral compass and empathy, ground-breaking thinking and acting, and self-development driven by curiosity and critical thinking" (Ministerie van Onderwijs, Cultuur en Wetenschappen 2015, p. 6). This interest is not only prominent in The Netherlands. In Norway, a national research committee recommends understanding *Bildung* as a form of cultivation in the liberal arts tradition (Reindal 2012). A Yale report highlights various virtues as normative—for instance, critical deliberation, curiosity, autonomy, involvement, collaboration, and participation for the greater good. Thus, the report highlights the liberal arts tradition as a foundation for developing skills that can be utilised in whatever line of work a student eventually chooses (Committee on Yale College Education Working Groups 2003 cited in Reindal 2012, p. 536).

[61] Graeber 2015.

[62] Nussbaum 2012.

and Hendrikse,[63] Lars Løvlie and Paul Standish,[64] and Ger Biesta.[65] If we look at today's dominant educational paradigm, there is a preference for the use of externally imposed norms. Most educational programs have an extreme focus on efficiency, measurability, and quantifiable knowledge. However, as Nussbaum argues, to deal with the inherent complexities of real life, education should instead focus on more than calculable rational knowledge: we need liberal arts education to deal with the complexities of today's world, but also for the formation of democratic citizens of the world.[66] In a similar fashion, Biesta argues that

> the educational way, the slow, difficult, frustrating and weak way, may not be the most popular way in an impatient society. But in the long run it may well turn out to be the only sustainable way, since we all know that systems aimed at total control … eventually collapse under their own weight.[67]

The essence of this discussion was expressed by John Dewey, when he said that "to imposition from above is opposed expression and cultivation of individuality[;] to static aims and materials is opposed acquaintance with a changing world."[68] Similarly, Kristján Kristjánsson wonders:

> How can it be simultaneously true that the aim of moral education is to create individuals who, moved by their own conception of the good, cherish and assiduously apply their unencumbered autonomy and that this goal can best be achieved through means that necessarily involve an extrinsic motivation?[69]

Following the arguments of, among others, Nussbaum, Dewey and Biesta, it becomes clear that a lack of attention for the individual runs the risk of making character education an inward-looking practice, which henceforth, might eventually collapse under its own weight. In this argument we recognise the indissoluble, paradoxical connection between individual development and external norms. Neither Aristotle, nor Von Humboldt, nor the present-day authors mentioned above, intend(ed) to separate the two. Leading an active, community-oriented life in the *polis* is part of *eudaimonia*. Being a well-developed 18th-century German citizen implied being part of a modern nation state, whilst today, being equipped to deal with the complexities of the world requires a certain level of self-realisation and individual development in dialogue with the wider (globalised) world.

---

[63] Engelen et al. 2014.
[64] Løvlie and Standish 2002.
[65] Biesta 2016.
[66] Nussbaum 2012, pp. 95–120.
[67] Biesta 2016, p. 4.
[68] Dewey 2007, p. 19.
[69] Kristjánsson 2012, pp. 32–33.

5.4 Preconditions and Implications

The foregoing discussion makes clear the discrepancy between character education in its ideal form, and current practice at military academies. This section discusses four preconditions and their implications for military academies: (1) the insufficiency of rule-based education; (2) the development of rational habituation; (3) an understanding of *Bildung* as "building on"; and (4) an acknowledgement of the paradox within character education.

The first precondition—the insufficiency of rule-based education—states that rules alone do not constitute character education. Rules and regulations are explicitly not a part of Aristotelian character education; rather, they were considered merely an instrument for the *polis*. Virtue ethics and *Bildung* aim to help develop the individual into someone who can regulate his or her own behaviour, has a certain inner discipline and will, on that basis, not need external rules. This is in strong opposition to classic military education, which is best known for its hierarchy, rules, regulations, and disciplining learning environment.

Furthermore, virtue ethics are concerned with the internalisation of reasoning and appropriate behaviour—both for a virtuous life and in *Bildung*, reason is considered essential. Virtuous behaviour is the result of a trained rational approach—the ability to choose the mean between two vices, acquired through rational thinking and habituation. This leads to the second precondition, namely the development of rational habituation. Traditionally, military education is dominated by teaching drills and skills. Whilst this does imply habituation, it misses the point of a trained rational habit, since there is practically no reflection involved. Moreover, because moral training at military academies is often compressed into only a small number of lessons, the development of habituation in moral thinking is restricted.

The third precondition—understanding *Bildung* as "building on"—refers to the necessity to build on existing (practical) knowledge. Virtue ethics and *Bildung* both require a broad intellectual and practical background. Learning is considered a life-long process, starting with parental guidance and continuing through the practice of political membership. Thus, character education is, in essence, a slow, risky, and open-ended process. Ideally, a student is given time to transform internally and intrinsically. However, in a military context, a cadet is expected to learn morally responsible behaviour via a small number of lessons. Notably, from a philosophical perspective, character education differs from contemporary military education, not only in its extended time frame, but also in its emphasis on building on existing aspects of the individual's character. Most military education is based on the principle of "unlearning" existing behaviour and replacing it with new behaviours and skills specific to the military.[70] However, in character education, "the onus is not the usefulness of practical skills, but rather which potential is present in a student and how [that potential can] be developed to fruition in freedom."[71]

---

[70] Goffman 1961; Moelker 2000.
[71] Van Baarda and Verweij 2006, p. 12.

The final precondition is an acknowledgement of the paradox within character education. In virtue ethics, *Bildung*, and contemporary educational theory, the practice of self-development cannot be separated from the social and the political, and thus the normative environment in which self-development takes place. In fact, they are two sides of the same coin: individual self-development and the communal —social and political—contexts are intertwined. Any attempt to separate the two spheres runs the risk of creating a standardised, ineffective learning environment with only extrinsically motivated individuals, focussing strongly on the military context and losing sight of the social and political contexts. It is obvious that this will have detrimental effects on military operations—especially those that aim to "win the hearts and minds" of local populations.

5.5 Conclusion

It has become clear that, in order to deal with the complexities of 21st-century warfare, military organizations consider ethics and moral professionalism to be pivotal elements of adequate military leadership and education. Traditionally, this particular learning process has been the domain of character education. In this chapter it was argued that character education at Western military academies is more often guided by classic modernist traditions, hierarchy, and military socialisation than based on a coherent educational philosophy and strategy. With regard to the latter, we discussed how character education was understood in the context of Aristotelian virtue ethics, the tradition of *Bildung*, and contemporary educational philosophy. Based on this analysis, four preconditions for character education were formulated and the implications of these for contemporary military education were discussed. These preconditions and implications go against the dominant paradigm on (military) education, but have the potential to guide possible change, aiming to contribute to its wider reassessment.

It is important to realise that the preconditions for character education are established as a result of a constant deliberation of options: What should aspirant officers know? What do they want to know? What should they become, and what do they want to become? Exactly these deliberations lie at the heart of character education. By answering these questions for students and not letting them answer these questions themselves—by, for example, imposing more rules and regulations —an educational institute loses the opportunity for students to develop intrinsically motivated, ethical behaviour. Thus, students will most likely be better served with a less prescriptive form of education—one that exhibits a strong emphasis on self-development in a complex and multi-dimensional setting. As military academies aim to train leaders to function in future conflicts, it would be beneficial to teach them to think critically, instead of teaching them to thoughtlessly comply with the rules. The battlefields of the future are characterised by flexible complexity, and thus require reflective practitioners.

References

Anteby M (2013) Manufacturing morals: The values of silence in business school education. University of Chicago Press, Chicago.

Ashforth BE, Sluss DM, Saks AM (2007) Socialisation tactics, proactive behavior, and newcomer learning: Integrating socialisation models. Journal of Vocational Behavior 70(3):447–462.

Bauer W (1997) Education, Bildung and post-traditional modernity. Curriculum Studies 5 (2):163–175.

Beard M (2014) Virtuous soldiers: A role for the liberal arts? Journal of Military Ethics 13 (3):274–294.

Biesta G (2002) How general can Bildung be? Reflections on the future of a modern educational ideal. Journal of Philosophy of Education 36(3):377–390.

Biesta G (2016) The beautiful risk of education. Taylor & Francis, London.

Blocq DS (2006) The fog of UN peacekeeping: Ethical issues regarding the use of force to protect civilians in UN operations. Journal of Military Ethics 5(3):201–213.

Boes T (2008) Apprenticeship of the novel: The Bildungsroman and the invention of history, ca. 1770–1820. Comparative Literature Studies 45(3):269–288.

Caforio G (2000) The European officer: A comparative view on selection and education. Edizioni ETS, Pisa.

Caforio G (2006) Military officer education. In: Caforio G, Nuciari M (eds) Handbook of the sociology of the military. Springer, Cham, pp 255–278.

Canadian Defence Academy (2005) Leadership in the Canadian forces: Doctrine. publications.gc.ca/collections/collection_2013/dn-nd/D2-313-1-2005-eng.pdf. Accessed 19 October 2018.

Coker C (2007) The warrior ethos: Military culture and the war on terror. Routledge, London.

Dalenberg S (2017) Officer, practice what you preach! Research on effects and interventions in military officer socialization at the Royal Military Academy. Doctoral dissertation, Radboud University, Nijmegen.

Deakin S (2008) Education in an ethos at the Royal Military Academy Sandhurst. In: Robinson P et al (eds) Ethics education in the military. Ashgate Publishing, Aldershot, pp 15–29.

De Vries P (2013) "The good, the bad and the virtuous": The virtue-ethical theory of Alasdair MacIntyre applied to military practice. Doctoral dissertation, Radboud University, Nijmegen.

Dewey J [1938] (2007) Experience and education. Simon and Schuster, New York.

Director General Leadership of the Royal Military Academy Sandhurst (2014) Developing leaders: A British army guide. www.army.mod.uk/who-we-are/our-schools-and-colleges/rma-sandhurst/. Accessed 19 October 2018.

Doty J, Sowden W (2009) Competency vs. character? It must be both! www.dtic.mil/dtic/tr/fulltext/u2/a532524.pdf. Accessed 22 October 2018.

Ecoles de Saint-Cyr Coëtquidan (2016) Saint-Cyr Military Academy: Serving a common European ambition. docplayer.net/577756-Charuel-jb-tabone-escc-escc-dircom.html. Accessed 16 October 2018.

Engelen E, Fernandez R, Hendrikse R (2014) How finance penetrates its other: A cautionary tale on the financialization of a Dutch university. Antipode 46(4):1072–1091.

Forster M (2018) Johann Gottfried von Herder. In: Zalta EN (ed) The Stanford Encyclopedia of Philosophy (Spring Edition). https://plato.stanford.edu/archives/spr2018/entries/herder/. Accessed 17 December 2018.

Franke V (2000) Duty, honor, country: The social identity of West Point cadets. Armed Forces & Society 26(2):175–202.

Franke V, Heinecken L (2001) Adjusting to peace: Military values in a cross-national comparison. Armed Forces & Society 27(4):567–595.

French SE (2003) The code of the warrior: Exploring warrior values past and present. Rowman & Littlefield Publishers, Lanham, MD.

Giroux HA (2004) What might education mean after Abu Ghraib: Revisiting Adorno's politics of education. Comparative Studies of South Asia, Africa and the Middle East 24(1):5–27.
Goffman E (1961) Asylums: Essays on the social situation of mental patients and other inmates. Penguin Books, London.
Good JA, Garrison JW (2010) Traces of Hegelian Bildung in Dewey's philosophy. In: Fairfield P (ed) John Dewey and continental philosophy. Southern Illinois University Press, Carbondale, pp 44–68.
Grady K (2016) Sex, statistics, peacekeepers and power: UN data on sexual exploitation and abuse and the quest for legal reform. The Modern Law Review 79(6):931–960.
Graeber D (2015) The utopia of rules: On technology, stupidity and the secret joys of bureaucracy. Melville House, New York.
Guimond S (1995) Encounter and metamorphosis: The impact of military socialisation on professional values. Applied Psychology 44(3):251–275.
Horlacher R (2004) Bildung: A construction of a history of philosophy of education. Studies in Philosophy and Education 23(5–6):409–426.
Horlacher R (2015) The educated subject and the German concept of Bildung: A comparative cultural history. Routledge, Abingdon, Oxon.
Humboldt W (1963) Humanist without portfolio: An anthology of the writings of W. von Humboldt. Wayne State University Press, Detroit.
Kennedy G, Neilson K (2002) Military education: Past, present and future. Greenwood Publishing Group, Westport, CT.
Kristjánsson K (2012) Aristotle, emotions and education. Ashgate Publishing, Farnham.
Kristjánsson K (2013) Ten myths about character, virtue and virtue education: Plus three well-founded misgivings. British Journal of Educational Studies 61(3):269–287.
Løvlie L, Standish P (2002) Introduction: Bildung and the idea of a liberal education. Journal of Philosophy of Education 36(3):317–340.
MacIntyre A (2013) After virtue. Bloomsbury Academic, London.
Maogoto JN (2000) Watching the watchdogs: Holding the UN accountable for international humanitarian law violations of the "Blue Helmets". Deakin Law Review 5(1):47.
Matthews MD, Eid J, Kelly D, Bailey J, Peterson C (2006) Character strengths and virtues of developing military leaders: An international comparison. Military Psychology 18(sup1):S57–S68.
Micewski ER, Annen H (2005) Military ethics in professional military education: Revisited. Peter Lang, Bern.
Ministerie van Onderwijs, Cultuur en Wetenschappen (2015) De waarde(n) van weten. Strategische agenda Hoger Onderwijs en Onderzoek 2015–2025 [The value(s) of knowing: Strategic agenda higher education and research 2015–2025]. Ministry of Education, Culture and Research, The Hague.
Moelker R (2000) Hiding behind the pillars: Reflections on the education of officers at the Royal Netherlands Military Academy. In: Caforio G (ed) The European officer: A comparative view on selection and education. Edizioni ETS, Pisa, pp 123–139.
Morgenbesser S (1979) Introduction. In: Eames ER (ed) Dewey and his critics: Essays from the Journal of Philosophy. Modern Schoolman 56(4):377–378.
Ndulo M (2009) United Nations responses to the sexual abuse and exploitation of women and girls by peacekeepers during peacekeeping missions. The Berkeley Journal of International Law 27:127–161.
Nederlandse Defensie Academie (2016) Studiegids opleiding Militaire Bedrijfswetenschappen (MBW): Academisch jaar 2016–2017 [Study guide military business studies: Academy year 2016–2017]. Netherlands Defence Academy, Breda.
Nordenbo SE (2002) Bildung and the thinking of Bildung. Journal of Philosophy of Education 36(3):341–352.

Nussbaum MC (2012) Not for profit: Why democracy needs the humanities. Princeton University Press, Princeton, NY.
Nussbaum MC (2013) The therapy of desire: Theory and practice in Hellenistic ethics. Princeton University Press, Princeton, NY.
Odello M (2010) Tackling criminal acts in peacekeeping operations: The accountability of peacekeepers. Oxford University Press, Oxford.
Olsthoorn P (2013) Virtue ethics in the military. In: Van Hooft S, Saunders N (eds) The handbook of virtue ethics. Routledge, Abingdon, Oxon, pp 365–374.
Paile S (2014) European education and training for young officers: The European initiative for the exchange of young officers, inspired by Erasmus. Ministry of Defence and Sports of the Federal Republic of Austria, Vienna.
Reindal SM (2012) Bildung, the Bologna Process and Kierkegaard's concept of subjective thinking. Studies in Philosophy and Education 32(5):533–549.
Richardson R, Verweij D, Winslow D (2004) Moral fitness for peace operations. Journal of Political and Military Sociology 32(1):99–113.
Robinson P (2007) Ethics training and development in the military. Parameters: Journal of the US Army War College 37(1):23–36.
Robinson P, De Lee N, Carrick D (2008) Ethics education in the military. Ashgate Publishing, Aldershot.
Rones N (2015) The struggle over military identity: A multi-sited ethnography on gender, fitness and "the right attitudes" in the military profession/field. PhD thesis, Norwegian School of Sport Sciences, Oslo.
Royal Military Academy Sandhurst (2018) Preparing for excellence. www.army.mod.uk/who-we-are/our-schools-and-colleges/rma-sandhurst/. Accessed 16 October 2018.
Sanderse W (2012) Character education: A neo-Aristotelian approach to the philosophy, psychology and education of virtue. Eburon Uitgeverij, Delft.
Schmidt J (1996) The fool's truth: Diderot, Goethe, and Hegel. Journal of the History of Ideas 57(4):625–644.
Schoy M (2011) The Bundeswehr in the 21st century: Between Prussia's glory and design. http://www.dtic.mil/dtic/tr/fulltext/u2/a547910.pdf. Accessed 22 October 2018.
Schut M, Moelker R (2015) Respectful agents: Between the Scylla and Charybdis of cultural and moral incapacity. Journal of Military Ethics 14(3–4):232–246.
Sherman N (2010) The untold war: Inside the hearts, minds and souls of our soldiers. WW Norton & Company, New York.
Snow NE (2009) How ethical theory can improve practice: Lessons from Abu Ghraib. Ethical Theory and Moral Practice 12(5):555–568.
Sookermany AM (2017) Military education reconsidered: A postmodern update. Journal of Philosophy of Education 51(1):310–330.
United States Military Academy West Point (2015) The West Point Mission. www.usma.edu/about/sitepages/mission.aspx. Accessed 16 October 2018.
Van Baarda TA, Verweij DEM (2006) Military ethics: The Dutch approach: A practical guide. Brill, Leiden.
Van Schilt JT (2011) Herfsttij van het militaire elitegevoel: Het elitair zelfbeeld van aspirant-officieren op de Koninklijke Militaire Academie in de periode 1948 tot 2008. [The autumn of elitist sentiment in the military: The elitist self-image of aspirant officers at the Royal Military Academy in the period 1948 to 2008]. (Doctoral dissertation) Ridderprint, Ridderkerk.
Visser D (2002) Image and identity in military education: A perspective on the South African Military Academy. Society in Transition 33(1):173–186.
Walzer M (2015) Just and unjust wars: A moral argument with historical illustrations. Basic Books, New York.

Watson BC (1999) The Western ethical tradition and the morality of the warrior. Armed Forces & Society 26(1):55–72.
Wortel E, Bosch J (2011) Strengthening moral competence: A "train the trainer" course on military ethics. Journal of Military Ethics 10(1):17–35.

Marenne Jansen, MA works at the Advisory Council for International Affairs, while writing her Ph.D. at the Institute for Management Research of the Radboud University. Her research focuses on military leadership development, and the nexus between development and security. In addition, she is interested in educational philosophy, sustainable development and the role of international organizations. She has taught courses on these topics for bachelor and master students at various Dutch universities, international diplomats, and NGO employees.

Prof. Dr. Desiree Verweij is professor in philosophy and ethics at the Faculty of Military Sciences of the Netherlands Defence Academy. She also holds a chair at the Centre for International Conflict Analysis and Management (CICAM) of the Radboud University Nijmegen. Her research focuses on both fundamental and applied philosophy and ethics, including themes like Just War, moral responsibility and moral judgement.

Chapter 6
A Critical Appraisal of the *Bildung* Ideal in Military Ethics Education

Eva van Baarle and Desiree Verweij

Contents

6.1	Introduction..	78
6.2	Nietzsche's Concept of *Bildung*...	80
6.3	Foucauldian Art-of-Living..	83
6.4	Case Example: The Train-the-Trainer-Course in Military Ethics	86
	6.4.1 Background to the Case	86
	6.4.2 Applying the Ideal of *Bildung* and Art-of-Living in Ethics Education	87
6.5	Discussion...	90
	6.5.1 Being a Soldier..	90
6.6	Conclusion..	92
References..		93

Abstract This chapter explores the relevance of Michel Foucault's ideas on the 'art-of-living' concept for ethics education in military organizations. Given Foucault's intellectual indebtedness to Nietzsche we first present a theoretical analysis of the concept *Bildung* and subsequently focus on the 'art-of-living' concept in the work of Foucault. We then illustrate how the art-of-living concept has been used in a train-the-trainer course on military ethics and discuss the results thereof. We suggest that Foucauldian art-of-living may foster awareness of power dynamics with regard to military moral dilemmas and enable military personnel to consider alternative options to responsibly deal with moral dilemmas.

E. M. van Baarle (✉)
Faculty of Military Sciences, Netherlands Defence Academy, PO Box 90002
4800 PA Breda, The Netherlands
e-mail: em.v.baarle@mindef.nl

D. E. M. Verweij
Faculty of Military Sciences, Netherlands Defence Academy, Breda, The Netherlands
e-mail: DEM.Verweij.01@mindef.nl

© T.M.C. ASSER PRESS and the authors 2019
W. Klinkert et al. (eds.), *NL ARMS Netherlands Annual Review of Military Studies 2019*, NL ARMS, https://doi.org/10.1007/978-94-6265-315-3_6

Keywords Ethics education · Bildung · art-of-living · educational philosophy · military

6.1 Introduction

Ethics education is key to the armed forces;[1] its core function being 'to assist professionals to think through the moral challenges and dilemmas inherent in their professional activity and, by helping members of the profession better understand the ethical demands upon them, to enable and motivate them to act appropriately in the discharge of their professional obligations'.[2]

Military institutions act upon their responsibility to prepare military personnel for dealing with moral questions and dilemmas by providing various forms of ethics training courses, each with different explicit or implicit theoretical underpinnings.

Several authors claim that Foucault's theory on art-of-living provides a rich conceptual framework for ethics in organizations because it frames the employee as an 'active' ethical subject who is responsible for his or her own self-creation in contrast to a docile or 'normalized' subject whose self-creation is based on obedience to rules and values set out in a coherent doctrine. Foucault's art-of-living focusses on the importance of a critical attitude to processes of normalization (i.e. judgments about what is seen as corresponding to the standards that are considered appropriate in a given context) and so-called expert authority, while acknowledging the reality of processes of normalization in organizations.[3] However, Foucault's work still seems to have had little impact on the actual practice of applied ethics education in organizations.[4] Various authors have proposed to formulate organizational ethics in terms of a 'care of the self', that requires an active self-disciplined attention of the self to develop and transform oneself, to actively reflect, choose and act upon one's moral compass[5] and new ways of 'acting and being'.[6] The idea that the self can be transformed is one of the most popular themes taken up by management scholars.[7] Foucauldian art-of-living can be defined as a kind of critical self-direction and self-development within existing power relations and as the ability to learn to think critically. In contrast to ethical codes and pre-determined values, Foucauldian art-of-living requires an individual 'to attend effectively to the

---

[1] Van Baarda and Verweij 2006; Coleman 2013; Cook 2013; Robinson, de Lee and Carrick 2008; Olsthoorn 2008.

[2] Cook and Syse 2010.

[3] Barratt 2008; Iedema and Rhodes 2010; Munro 2014; Starkey and Hatchuel 2002; Van Baarle et al. 2018.

[4] Coleman 2013; Crane and Matten 2007.

[5] Munro 2014, p. 1127.

[6] Ibarra-Colado et al. 2006; Iedema and Rhodes 2010; Munro 2014, p. 1127; Randall and Munro 2010.

[7] Munro 2014; Kosmala and McKernan 2011; Loacker and Muhr 2009.

self, and to exercise and transform oneself'.[8] In educational theory as well, the Foucauldian art-of-living concept is regarded as relevant and fruitful.[9] These contributions are, however, mostly theoretical in nature. This chapter aims to explore the possibilities of applying a Foucauldian art-of-living approach in ethics education, reflecting on a Dutch train-the-trainer course on military ethics.

Specific aspects of military culture seem to influence how military personnel deal with moral issues and dilemmas. The following elements appear specifically relevant: being a soldier, group bonding, uniformity, hierarchy, lack of privacy, and masculinity.[10] For instance, the masculine ideal of a 'warrior hero'[11] who is in emotional control may not make it easy to engage in reflection allowing oneself to doubt, as this could be interpreted as being weak or vulnerable. The ability to recognize that there are ethical aspects worthy of consideration in the situation one is confronted with (referred to as 'ethical sensitivity') may seem obvious, but is not self-evident. Yet, this ability is crucial 'in a military environment where there is so much reliance on Standard Operating Procedures (SOPs), and such a strong pressure toward conformity and risk of group-think, this is an aspect of moral development we should perhaps reflect on more deeply'.[12] While reflection and developing self-awareness can be regarded as general aims of ethics education, strived for in many ethics programs, using insights from Foucault can be helpful to explicitly raise awareness of the tensions involved in situations of conformity, pressures and hierarchy.

This is in line with the work of Thornborrow and Brown who analysed paratroopers' discourse on work identities in a military organization, in an elite military unit and show how paratroopers are 'manufactured'.[13] Conceptions of being a paratrooper and the techniques of paratroopers' production form a tight web of discursive constraint. The idea that paratroopers are professional, elite and macho/combat-ready was, according to the soldiers, 'manufactured' in three principal ways:

> ... through 'rites of becoming' that restricted entry to the Regiment; storytelling (especially in using Regimental history); and through the maintenance of an informal culture of suspicion and surveillance.[14]

This raises important questions with regard to the possibility of ethics education within these institutional disciplinary forces. What are the organizational factors that might impact the ability of employees to critically think? Are they able to recognize the relevant power relations at stake in moral dilemmas and do they experience the possibility of choice?

---

[8] Foucault 1984b, p. 73.
[9] Biesta 1998, 2008; Gunzenhauser 2007; Infinito 2003; Nicoll et al. 2013; Pignatelli 2002.
[10] Van Baarle et al. 2015.
[11] Duncanson 2009; Morgan 1994.
[12] Cook 2013, p. 81.
[13] Thornborrow and Brown 2009, p. 355.
[14] Thornborrow and Brown 2009, p. 355.

Foucault is strongly inspired by Nietzsche in his critique on the philosophical canon regarding the 'rational subject', his concept of power and historical discontinuity.[15] For both philosophers, education and formation play a crucial role in these critiques and are embedded in the 'art of living' concept, which is, since classical times, a practical and didactical aspect of philosophy which the old Greeks and Romans called *'techne tou biou'* and *'ars vitae'* respectively. The concept was strongly marginalized in the course of the history of Western philosophy and only recently got the attention it deserves as a still crucial aspect of practical philosophy.[16] Given Foucault's intellectual indebtedness to Nietzsche, we first provide a theoretical analysis of Nietzsche's *Bildung* ideal, as an adequate background for understanding what Foucault was aiming at with his notion of art-of-living. We subsequently turn to the work of Foucault. In order to better understand Foucault's work, it is important to interpret Foucault's early and late works as a critical continuum,[17] which implies that art-of-living and 'the relation to oneself' should be understood in terms of power-relations. We then introduce the train-the-trainer course on military ethics to show how the Foucauldian ideas, discussed in the first part of this chapter, could be applied in practice. We conclude this chapter with a discussion of the question whether training soldiers to engage in autonomous and critical thinking is something we should be aiming at in a military context.

6.2 Nietzsche's Concept of *Bildung*

About 130 years ago Nietzsche proclaimed the 'death of God', a metaphor which implies the loss of absolute principles regarding truth and fundamental values. In his text he warns his readers against an all too flippant interpretation of his words. This warning makes sense against the backdrop of conflicting norms and values in present-day social, political and cultural settings. How do we form and educate young people (students) without the existence of a solid moral framework, a solid and generally acknowledged measure? Nietzsche's views on *Bildung* (education and formation) which were presented for the first time in a narrative that formed an integral part of six subsequent lectures presented at the 'Academic Society' in Basel in 1872, are relevant with regard to this question. We will take a closer look at the most relevant elements in this narrative with regard to both *Bildung* and the art-of-living.

The story Nietzsche tells his readers concerns a conversation between a philosopher and his companion that was overheard by Nietzsche and his friend when they were young students. At first the young students only listened, later on they participated in the conversation that took place on a hill in the woods, during

---

[15] See f.i. Rosenberg and Westfall 2018.
[16] Schmid 1998; Dohmen 2014; Teschers 2017.
[17] Deleuze 1994.

an afternoon and an evening. The setting is noteworthy, Nietzsche not only meticulously describes the "warmth of the sun endlessly mixed with blue autumn freshness",[18] he also makes clear that he, his friend and the philosopher and his companion all came to this place to discuss philosophical issues. In the case of the two young students this meant becoming philosophers themselves, discussing the existential issues related to their future lives, as Nietzsche points out.[19] The narrative, presented as a conversation, not only shows the importance of dialogue as a pedagogical instrument for Nietzsche, but also the need for space and time in order to learn to reflect and the inspiration coming from people who can actually teach a person something and can thus contribute to his or her *Bildung*.

The conversation starts with the philosopher's critical statements about the 'pedagogic poverty' of his time.[20] Education in grammar school used to be about *Bildung* and development, however this focus has been lost. The grammar school educated people for 'bookishness', and sometimes not even that. "Bookishness is for scholarly people, but a scholarly person is not the same as a developed and *bilded* person. There is a big difference between the two".[21] The philosopher points to the dry study of antiquity by the majority of the scholars and refers to 'bookishness' being a 'hypertrophic swelling up of an unhealthy body'[22] and grammar schools educating for 'bookish obesity'[23] and not for humanitarian *Bildung* as used to be the case.

The philosopher continues that everything is focused on becoming a money-making being and education being focused on realizing this goal as fast as possible. So what should be done? What is needed? One of the things mentioned is the importance of a naïve, trustful and personal relation to nature. A young person needs to be able to mirror himself in nature; to recognize himself in what he experiences in nature. In this way he will be able to learn to understand the connectedness of all things and reflect on who he is. This is also present in the description of the goal of *Bildung* as *HumanitätsBildung*[24] which refers to the connectedness to other people.

This idea of *Bildung* is quite contrary to what modern learning implies, according to the philosopher, namely learning how to manipulate nature. As such, *Bildung* is the opposite of the calculating, economized attitude towards one's surroundings. The nature metaphor with regard to *Bildung* is also present in Nietzsche's text *Schopenhauer als Erzieher* (Schopenhauer as educator).[25] Development and *Bildung* imply freeing a person, which means, as Nietzsche

---

[18] Nietzsche 1981b, p. 180.
[19] Nietzsche 1981b, p. 184.
[20] Nietzsche 1981b, p. 197.
[21] Nietzsche 1981b, p. 200.
[22] Nietzsche 1981b, p. 224.
[23] Nietzsche 1981b, p. 224.
[24] Nietzsche 1981b, p. 210.
[25] Nietzsche 1981a.

maintains, 'clearing away the ill weeds and garbage and the worms that corrode the soft core of the plant'.[26] This metaphor of *Bildung* as care for the young plant is an old Greek metaphor. Care and nourishment form the basis for flourishing; the more fertile the ground, the better the plant's roots can grow and branch off in all directions, laying a solid basis for flourishing. The concept 'rhizome' coined by the French (Nietzschean) philosopher Deleuze[27] is a comparable plant metaphor that can help to illustrate the strength of this classic image of the plant and its relevance in describing human flourishing and the art-of-living. 'Rhizome' means 'rootstock'; it refers to a root system with a multitude of branches. This concept plays an important role in Deleuze's philosophy, as it refers to connectedness and heterogeneity. Every point of the rhizome can be connected to any other point. Moreover, breakage and cracks form no problem; a broken rhizome can still grow in a different direction and enter into different connections. The concept thus refers to an abundance of connections and to openness and receptivity for change, a network of endless possibilities for growth.

The elements that form the metaphor of the plant are explicitly discussed in Nietzsche's text on *Bildung*. The importance of inspiration (nourishment) provided by good teachers (philosophers) is underlined, as is the importance of learning to listen and to speak (enter in a dialogue; present one's thoughts) and subsequently learning to reflect and think in a critical way, refraining from a too premature judgment. It is made clear that the goal of *Bildung* is not science, as such, it is the ability to answer the existential questions of one's own life and practice.

Bildung as education aims at freeing and helping people to flourish in and through connectedness with communities, and nature, of which they are an inalienable part. It implies openness and willingness to learn, acknowledging diversity and difference, which starts with acknowledging the diversity and differences within oneself.

This insight contributes to ethics education based on the art-of-living, for acknowledging diversity and difference in ourselves is a prerequisite for respecting the difference and diversity around us and thus the different values that people can adhere to. Dialogue can be viewed as an important pedagogical tool in achieving this.

Nietzsche's insights with regard to *Bildung* embedded in the 'art of living' concept, imply the need for space and time in order to learn to reflect critically, also and maybe especially, on the power relations that might hamper one's *Bildung*. It implies self-knowledge, the ability to enter in dialogue (being able to actually listen and express one's thoughts in an adequate way), and most of all it implies a close relation to practice. On the basis of these insights, we will now focus on the work of Foucault, who introduces several ideas for applying the art-of-living concept in ethics education that are inspired by Nietzsche.

---

[26] Nietzsche 1981a, p. 290.
[27] Deleuze and Guattari 1980.

6.3 Foucauldian Art-of-Living

In his earlier books, *Madness and Civilization*[28] *the Birth of the Clinic*[29] and *Discipline and Punish*[30] Foucault examines how power operates in our society. While one may be inclined to consider power as sovereign, in the hand of the government, and exerted by institutions such as local governments, the police and the Army, Foucault states that complex power relations are always present and are widely exercised and reproduced in institutions. Power relations are implicitly present in disciplining institutions, for instance in our educational systems, in hospitals and in psychiatry. These implicit power relations are often not made explicit in laws and the enforcement thereof, yet they construct the subject.

Foucault maintains that, due to these power relations, there is no external referent for certainty or truth. This also holds for 'truth' about the subject that is produced by science. Building on Nietzsche's 'death of God' metaphor, as discussed above, Foucault argues that both 'truth' and 'the subject' are constructed; 'human beings are made subjects'.[31] He examines how truth games (a set of rules and procedures by which truth is produced) were set up and how they were connected to power relations, in processes of objectification and categorization. In this context he introduces the term 'normalization', which refers to judgments about what is considered 'normal' and what is not in a given context. The term is closely related to another Foucauldian term: 'disciplinary technology' which aims at forging a 'docile body, that subsequently may be subjected, used, transformed and improved'.[32]

In *Discipline and Punishment,* Foucault introduces the terms normalization and disciplinary technology to show how subjects are 'produced'.[33] His architectural example of the Panopticon illustrates that when surveillance is permanent, 'the perfection of power should render its actual exercise unnecessary'.[34] Accordingly, if participants are disciplined in a similar way, they might be 'caught up in a power situation of which they are themselves the bearers'.[35]

One of the examples Foucault introduces to illustrate what he means by implicit power relations in disciplining institutions is the example of a soldier:

---

[28] Foucault 1965.
[29] Foucault 1973.
[30] Foucault 1977.
[31] Foucault 1982, p. 208.
[32] Foucault 1984a, p. 180.
[33] Foucault 1977.
[34] Foucault 1977, p. 200.
[35] Foucault 1977, p. 201.

> By the late eighteenth century, the soldier has become something that can be made; out of formless clay, an inapt body, the machine required can be constructed; posture is gradually corrected; a calculated constraint runs slowly through each part of the body, mastering it, making it pliable, ready at all times, turning silently into the automatism of habit[36]

Systematic surveillance, classification, hierarchy and military drill or the routinization of actions, are techniques aimed at the formation of a trained, docile body. As such, military personnel is 'produced', its 'normalization' takes place through the sharing and internalization of explicit and implicit norms during the military socialization process which aims for a perfect fit of military personnel in the military institutions and its culture.

While soldiers are presented as the prototypical example of the docile body constructed and produced by power relations, the later work of Foucault makes explicitly clear that due to these power relations there is always also space for freedom practices and therefore for the possibility of ethics:

> These power relations are ... mobile, reversible, and unstable. It should also be noted that power relations are possible only insofar as the subjects are free. If one of them were completely at the other's disposal and became his thing, and object on which he could wreak boundless and limitless violence, there wouldn't be any relation of power [but rather a state of domination]. Thus, in order for power relations to come into play, there must be at least a certain degree of freedom on both sides[37]

In the *History of Sexuality*[38] and in several interviews, Foucault stated that he tried to understand the way in which the human subject fits in these power relations, also referred to as 'critical activity'[39] and 'games of truth'.[40] Through the work of Pierre Hadot, Foucault discovered the importance of the 'techniques of the self' in the Greco-Roman world.[41]

The Greeks used a specific word to describe this: *'epimeleia heautou'*, which means working on or being concerned with something.[42] The care for the self is not purely an individual exercise; one always remains part of practices of power and truth games.[43] Nevertheless, one is able to decide how to shape the power relations one is part of. Power relations may appear to be forms of domination that seem immobile, yet, they can be modified, influenced or changed to a greater or lesser extend by individuals or social groups. This possibility to modify and change is omnipresent and as such not a privilege of the official authority, as one may be inclined to think. Foucault uses the notion of modifying power relations, rather than

---

[36] Foucault 1984a, p. 179.
[37] Foucault 1997, p. 292.
[38] Foucault 1984b.
[39] Foucault 1984b, p. 336.
[40] Foucault 1982, p. 281.
[41] Foucault 1984c, p. 342; Hadot 1995.
[42] Foucault 1984c, p. 359.
[43] Foucault 1997.

liberating oneself from power relations.[44] According to Foucault, we have to be careful not to fall back on the idea that there 'exists a human nature or base that ... has been concealed, alienated, or imprisoned in and by mechanisms of repression'.[45] In a military context, codes of conduct and underlying military values can be regarded as such power relations. A freedom practice does not exist apart from power relations, but 'it paves the way for new power relationships'.[46] Nevertheless, Foucault acknowledges that liberation is sometimes the political or historic precondition for freedom practices. One needs to be free from certain forms of repression in order to be able to use this freedom in a constructive way. Modifying these power relations, when necessary, Foucault states, is a practice of freedom.[47] These freedom practices include taking care of the self, an exercise of the self to develop and transform oneself, to actively reflect, choose and act upon one's moral compass, which starts with awareness of the values one holds. Foucault suggests that we can create our life by deciding how to give style to it and make a 'work of art' of our own life.[48] However, he does not provide a blueprint with respect to creating these practices nor does he mention explicit values or virtues one should strive for.

If we translate Foucauldian ideas into ethics education, it implies that fostering an ethics of art-of-living should first of all focus on awareness and advocate a way of life in which people become more self-aware.[49] This implies that one discovers oneself in one's concrete situation, in other words, people become aware of the power relations they are part of. Important questions are: What kind of power relations can be recognized, which institutions are involved, what effects do they have? Becoming aware of power relations might enable people to judge, and choose, how to shape these power relations. Instead of being a passive subject, an 'active subject constitutes itself in an active fashion through practices of the self'.[50] However, awareness of power relations, underlying values and possibly colliding values does not guarantee responsible moral decision-making. Nevertheless, it can be viewed as a pre-condition for morally responsible decision-making; without the awareness of choice, it seems impossible to carry out the techniques of the self, to defend and enlarge the space for freedom-practices within the disciplinary structures of organizations and of our society at large.

Foucault provides several techniques to put the art-of-living concept into practice, he introduces the importance of walking exercises determining one's motives, meditation, silence, listening to others and *hypomnemata*, keeping a diary or a

---

[44] Foucault 1997.
[45] Foucault 1997, p. 282.
[46] Foucault 1997, p. 284.
[47] Foucault 1984c.
[48] Foucault 1984c, p. 350.
[49] Vintges 2001.
[50] Foucault 1997, p. 291.

notebook.[51] Writing for oneself and others can function as a means to struggle with defects, such as anger, fear and envy. Following Foucault, ethics education can assist people to work on what Foucault refers to as 'the relationship with oneself'.[52]

6.4 Case Example: The Train-the-Trainer-Course in Military Ethics

6.4.1 Background to the Case

The second part of this chapter focusses on the way in which Foucault's ideas as discussed above have found their way into the train-the-trainer course on military ethics.

This course is organized four times per year by the Faculty of Military Sciences of the Netherlands Defence Academy. It was launched in 2006 by means of a five-day pilot. Since then, it has developed into a nine-day course consisting of three non-consecutive blocks of three days that provide participants the opportunity to put their newly acquired theory and tools into practice in between the blocks. This is subsequently reflected on during the course.

The course participants are mainly non-commissioned officers, who already teach military ethics to military personnel or plan to do so in the near future. In some courses officers participate as well. The participants work within the four Operational Commands (i.e. the Army; the Navy; the Air Force and the Military Police Corps).

The aim of the course is to train participants to become ethics trainers in their military work environment and at the same time foster their own moral competence. Fostering moral competence is not restricted to the knowledge domain; the willingness to act upon one's judgement is part of moral competence as well and indicates that it concerns a particular attitude. Notably, an important distinction can be made between 'schooling' and 'education'. 'Schooling (in German: *Ausbilden*; in Dutch: *opleiden*) refers to the teaching and learning of cognitive and practical knowledge, while the central focus of education (in German: *Bildung*; in Dutch: *vorming*) is the mastery and internalization of that knowledge'.[53]

For the majority of the participants, taking this course is a formal requirement for teaching military ethics at their respective military education establishments within the Dutch armed forces. More than half of the group is asked by their superiors to attend the course, the other participants apply for the course themselves.

---

[51] Foucault 1984c, p. 363.
[52] Foucault 1984c, p. 352.
[53] Van Baarda and Verweij 2006, p. 11; see also Wortel and Bosch 2011; Van Baarle et al. 2015.

6.4.2 Applying the Ideal of Bildung and Art-of-Living in Ethics Education

The theoretical ethical approach underlying this train-the-trainer course in military ethics has gradually moved from a focus on virtue ethics[54] to a focus on, what we would reconstruct as a Foucauldian art-of-living approach to ethics education.[55] There are parallels between a virtue ethics approach and the Foucauldian art-of-living approach to ethics education, as both approaches focus on character education. However, Foucault's approach differs from a virtue ethics approach in its emphasis on the role of power relations in practices, whereas, virtue ethics stresses the importance of developing excellence in a specific practice (for instance, being courageous in military combat). Foucault emphasizes the need for awareness of the power relations permeating one's practices and the need to incorporate this awareness in one's reflection on moral dilemmas. If the subject is indeed constructed and produced in the way Foucault has revealed, one has to (re)discover oneself in one's concrete environment and understand the ways in which one is formed in terms of power relations and related values in order to be able to think for oneself when confronted with moral dilemmas. As such, the Foucauldian art-of-living approach not only invites participants to reflect on themselves but also to take a critical look at their environment and on the norms and structures of the military institution they are part of. A sole focus on character can be regarded as a limitation of a virtue ethics approach since it overlooks the fact that unethical behaviour can also be 'the product of deficiencies in institutions or practices'.[56]

During the training, trainers assist participants to practice and discuss freedom practices by encouraging a reflective relation to the 'here and now'. Ethics courses as such also imply power relations, a pervasive operation of power associated with disciplinary processes and ultimately moral regulation. It is naive to propose that practices of reflection are separate and different from discursive practices.[57] With regard to power relations participants are explicitly invited to be co-responsible for the learning process during the training. While 'training' in a military context can sometimes be regarded as inducing certain behaviour, our concept of training implies an interactive way of education. During so-called 'co-directing sessions' participants can actively influence the program of the course by reflecting on the training and the group-process. This approach presupposes that trainers are willing to share power, to adapt the course to learning needs of participants, to be transparent in their choices and to be both willing and able to engage in self-reflection.

---

[54] Wortel and Bosch 2011.
[55] Van Baarle et al. 2018.
[56] Robinson 2007, p. 31; see also Cook 2015.
[57] Gilbert 2001.

The content of the training is based on theoretical notions on art-of-living by Foucault as inspired by Nietzsche (see Sect. 6.1). The training includes the following elements:[58]

First, participants of the course are made familiar with a dialogical way of interaction (prior to their participation in the Socratic dialogue as discussed in element three). They are provided with a list of dialogue-guidelines, including: taking time, listening carefully, suspending judgment, asking critical questions that stimulate the thinking process of all dialogue partners involved, thinking 'with' the dialogue partner, not 'against' him or her, analysing underlying values and not fixating on solutions, and finally reflecting critically on one's initial opinion, one's moral intuition, impression and emotions. During several exercises, participants learn to engage in a dialogue with each other by putting these guidelines into practice. This element is particularly inspired by Hadot's view that philosophizing is engaging in dialogue with oneself as well as with others.

Second, during the course, space is created for 'counter stories'[59] with regard to the military profession. These stories may include doubt, uncertainty and vulnerability and, as such, are not in line with stereotypes of 'military heroism'.[60] This element of storytelling recognizes value diversity in narratives, broadens the discourse and acknowledges diversity and difference with regard to what it means to be a soldier. This element can be seen as a translation of what Nietzsche aims at by *Bildung*, to foster openness and the willingness to learn, acknowledging diversity and difference, which starts with acknowledging the diversity and difference within oneself.

Thirdly, a key element of the course is a focus on Socratic thinking. The Socratic dialogue resembles what Nietzsche refers to as *Bildung* and Hadot as philosophy as a dialogue with oneself as well as with others. A Socratic dialogue provides insight into one's way of thinking, the values that one holds and the preconceived opinions one might have. We often believe things that, once we learn to critically think about them, turn out to be incorrect. A guideline for working on the art-of-living might focus on engaging in these dialogues in order to reflect on our own way of thinking, the way others think and to construct our own moral compass, learning to prioritize values, in order to become 'the helmsman of our own existence'.[61] One full day is devoted to engaging in a Socratic dialogue, by means of the 'hourglass model' method introduced by Kessels,[62] in which participants are first invited to formulate a fundamental ethical question based on their experiences in the military organization (for instance 'What is integrity?' or 'What is good leadership?'). This question is examined within the concrete context of a personal example of one of the participants. Thus, an example (i.e. a 'case') in which for instance 'integrity' or 'leadership' is at stake. Participants are invited to formulate a core statement with

---

[58] See Van Baarle 2017 for a more extensive discussion of these elements.
[59] Nelson 2001, p. 1.
[60] Thornborrow and Brown 2009, p. 368.
[61] Nietzsche 1981a.
[62] Kessels 2001.

regard to the case. For instance: 'doing x implied good leadership'. Subsequently, the participants identify values or principles on which the core statement is based. These values or principles that enable the group to answer the initial fundamental question not only apply to the specific case but are also valid in a broader sense. The trajectory within this moral inquiry, from the broad and abstract fundamental question to the concrete case and back to answers and general values or principles, resembles the figure of an hourglass. Biases, assumptions and values that direct the experience are reflected upon. This is also referred to as '*elenchus*', the process of 'approximation, refutation and reformulation'.[63] The answer to the question, although relevant, is not the most important part of the dialogue; most important is experiencing the process of engaging in a dialogue together and reflecting on the presented values and the ability to think together and develop openness to new ideas and suggestions.

Fourthly, recognizing and discussing power relations, as discussed by Foucault, is a crucial element of the course. This also implies focusing on tensions with regard to the power relations participants experience themselves in their daily practice. A short introduction on the work of Nietzsche and Foucault is followed by a session in which the participants are asked if they recognize power relations as introduced by Foucault in their own practice. Participants reflect on the possibility of (Foucauldian) freedom practices in the military organization and are asked to answer the following question: 'Am I 'imprisoned' or can I use my freedom within this organization?' This question refers to a previous session which includes both an introduction to Foucauldian art-of-living and the experience of watching the film *Das Experiment*[64] as a group. This movie shows that power relations, even inside a prison, are not fixed, but remain mobile and changeable. The question mentioned above aims to motivate all participants to reflect on power relations and freedom practices based on their own experiences, in order to allow for an in depth-discussion while at the same time providing focus.

During the train-the-trainer course participants recognize Foucault's concepts of normalization (e.g. judgements and prejudices about what is considered 'normal' and what is not) and disciplinary technology (e.g. the production of individual behaviour by techniques of control such as hierarchical observation, normative judgements, inspection and examination) within the military organization. One of the examples that can be mentioned in this context is a participant's reflection on the limits and difficulties of internalized disciplinary power in terms of military values, such as loyalty to the organization and a 'can do' mentality.[65]

---

[63] Miller 2007, p. 66.

[64] The German film 'Das Experiment' (2001: directed by Oliver Hirschbiegel) is inspired by the events of the Stanford Prison Experiment which was conducted in 1971 by a team of researchers led by Psychology Professor Philip Zimbardo at Stanford University.

[65] Van Baarle et al. 2018.

6.5 Discussion

The Foucauldian notion of art-of-living aims at fostering awareness of power relations, and at empowering people to use space for freedom practices, to actively choose and act upon certain values. It can be used in ethics education to foster participants' insight in themselves and in their concrete situation; it can help them to become aware of the power relations they are part of, and the way these power relations influence situations and prioritize certain values. Such reflections are helpful in stimulating moral awareness and making morally responsible decisions (i.e. decisions that take the different points of view of the stakeholders in question into account). According to Foucault, power relations imply the possibility of ethics, of choice and of modifying these power relations by means of freedom practices. Soldiers may be produced by power relations, but, as was discussed above, these power relations also imply that space can be created for freedom practices, since soldiers can be challenged to think for themselves, to become aware of tensions between values and to consider alternative options.

In this section, we discuss to what extend ethics education should be based on these philosophical ideals of *Bildung* and 'art-of-living', as discussed in the first part of this chapter. Soldiers need to be trained for specific situations, such as combat, in which they have to be able and willing to take on the tasks that are set to do without much hesitation. How can concepts such as *Bildung* and art-of-living assist soldiers in their daily practice? To what extend is training soldiers to engage in autonomous and critical thinking something we should be aiming at in a military context?

6.5.1 Being a Soldier

In Foucault's words, one slowly becomes 'a soldier', an identity which is transmitted by and reproduced through structures of the organization on a day to-day basis. Disciplinary mechanisms and institutional processes lead individuals to regulate their own conduct, turning them into self-disciplining subjects. As Foucault argues, under the panoptic gaze an individual 'becomes the principle of his own subjection'.[66]

Soldiers have taken an oath, or promise, which stresses loyalty to the head of state and military law. The military requires that soldiers carry out orders, especially in combat situations. However, at the same time, soldiers are required to think for themselves and refuse illegal or immoral orders, as is vehemently underlined in the codes of conduct of most armed forces.

Viewing oneself as a soldier who simply carries out orders may function as a self-protective decision, a psychological process by which the soldiers adaptively

---

[66] Foucault 1977, p. 202.

hide behind the military identity: 'an adaptive response to cope with one's [...] immoral treatment of others'.[67] Even if you are not the aggressor yourself, it is easier to justify that you cannot do anything about the immorality of a situation, since you are there to carry out a different task based on the idea that you are first and foremost a soldier.

The idea that one is first of all a soldier and secondly a human being may offer some kind of protection in executing tasks, but it may also encourage the blurring of moral standards. Since 'moral agency is manifested in both the power to refrain from behaving inhumanely and the proactive power to behave humanely'.[68] According to Bandura, moral disengagement not only arises as a result of sanitizing language and advantageous comparison, but also as a result of a 'disavowal of a sense of personal agency'.[69] Identifying oneself as a soldier with a duty to simply carry out orders, implicates a risk of displacement of responsibility[70] making soldiers not feel personally responsible for their actions.

One can ask the question whether soldiers would be better off without the ability to judge, if that ability renders them powerless. Verweij[71] argues that powerlessness can be the result of a self-dialogue leading to doubt: Is this something I should do? What are the consequences for me, and other people involved? The feeling of powerlessness can be inescapable; it can be generated by a tragic moral dilemma that leaves no other choice than a 'bad' one. However, this does not imply that not learning people to think (engage in self-dialogue) and judge solves the problem. Verweij asserts that it is precisely such self-dialogue that makes a person a human being. Without it, one may lose touch with oneself and one's humanity. In addition, soldiers may risk moral suffering if they fail to deal with moral dilemmas they encounter.[72] Being aware of one's personal moral values and the values of others, makes soldiers more sensitive to the moral dimension of situations. It may also strengthen their ability to communicate and justify to themselves and others why they choose to prioritize and act upon a specific value.[73]

Obviously, during combat, there are situations when executing orders under high pressure and within limited time makes engaging in reflection impossible. In such 'split second' situations it seems strange and even inappropriate to expect soldiers to engage in a dialogue and reflect on what action should be taken. In such situations, soldiers need to be able to put their training (including ethics education) into practice and take on their assigned tasks without much hesitation.

However, in most situations, during deployment as well as in peacetime, time and space are available to reflect on previous actions, to prepare for future actions

---

[67] Bastian et al. 2013, p. 157.
[68] Bandura 1999, p. 193.
[69] Bandura 1999, p. 193.
[70] Bandura 1999.
[71] Verweij 2010.
[72] Litz et al. 2009.
[73] Litz et al. 2009.

and to learn from experiences. In order to do this, soldiers should be trained in such a way that they are able to critically reflect, recognize different perspectives and values, and develop morally responsible judgement. As there will never be a rule or guideline that covers all future events, one will constantly need to reflect on and review existing guidelines and policies.[74] Reflection on rules creates room for the question whether certain rules are still adequate or should be changed.

This holds for all ranks. Yet, in most armed forces, the attitude with regard to ethics training strategies for officers and non-commissioned officers is different. While officers are often encouraged to develop virtues and to engage in autonomous, critical thinking, to recognize, and to actively reflect on practices and moral dilemmas, lower-ranking personnel are mainly trained to obey the institutional rules and legitimate orders of their superiors.[75] This bifurcation may be regarded as problematic. Military personnel of all ranks are morally and legally responsible for their actions in warfare and in the institutional setting. In combat situations it is often the 'strategic corporal' – a non-commissioned officer – who is faced with the most immediate and pressing ethical issues.[76] Non-commissioned officers have to find the courage to uphold the laws of war when external pressures of time and threat might tempt them to break these laws. As such, one may question the appliance of differing strategies regarding the ethics education for senior and less senior military personnel.[77]

6.6 Conclusion

In this chapter we explored the relevance of Foucault's 'art-of-living' concept against the backdrop of Nietzsche's ideas on *Bildung* for ethics education in military organizations. Ethics education focusing on the 'art of living' and *Bildung* ideal, of awareness of and reflection on power relations and active self-formation within existing power relations can offer an opportunity for organizations and their employees to understand how they have come to believe what they value. It can help them understand their own values as well as those of others. Finally, it assists employees in active reflection and decision making when faced with complex moral dilemmas in their daily practice.

Soldiers are not merely political assets (soldiers carrying out their duty) without agency. Within the discursive bounds imposed, they remain individuals who can construct their own identity. As such, they 'may shift the limits that define who they are, modifying and reconstituting themselves in other ways'.[78] However,

---

[74] Kramer 2007; Van Baarda and Verweij 2006; Robinson et al. 2008; Lucas 2015.
[75] Wolfendale 2008.
[76] Krulak 1999; Whetham 2010.
[77] Wolfendale 2008.
[78] Thornborrow and Brown 2009, p. 359

constituting oneself within a military context is not self-evident; it not only demands reflection, but also evaluation, training and education. Ethics education based on ideals of *Bildung* and art-of-living can play an important role in this ongoing learning process of both soldiers and their organizations. We suggest that Foucauldian art-of-living may foster awareness of power dynamics with regard to military moral dilemmas and enable military personnel to consider alternative options to responsibly deal with moral dilemmas.

References

Bandura A (1999) Moral disengagement in the perpetuation of inhumanities. Personality and Social Psychology Review, 3:193–209.
Barratt E (2008) The later Foucault in organization and management studies. Human Relations, 61:515–537.
Bastian B et al (2013) Losing our humanity: The self-dehumanizing consequences of social ostracism. Personality and Social Psychology Bulletin, 39:156–169.
Biesta G (1998) Pedagogy without humanism: Foucault and the subject of education. Interchange, 29:1–16.
Biesta G (2008) Encountering Foucault in lifelong learning. In: Nicoll K, Fejes A (eds) Foucault and Lifelong Learning: Governing the Subject. Routledge, London, pp 191–203.
Coleman S (2013) Military ethics: An introduction with case studies. Oxford University Press, Oxford.
Cook M (2013) Issues in military ethics, to support and defend the constitution. SUNY Press, Albany NY.
Cook M (2015) Military ethics and character development. In: Lucas G (ed) Routledge handbook of military ethics. Routledge, New York, pp 97–106.
Cook M, Syse H (2010) What should we mean by "military ethics". Journal of Military Ethics, 9:119–122.
Crane A, Matten D (2007) Business ethics: Managing corporate citizenship and sustainability in the age of globalization. Oxford University Press, Oxford.
Deleuze G, Guattari F (1980) Mille Plateaux. De Minuit, Paris.
Deleuze G (1994) Foldings, or the inside of thought. In: Kelly M (ed) Critique and power: Recasting the Foucault/Habermas debate. MIT Press, Cambridge MA, pp 315–374.
Dohmen J (2014) Over levenskunst; De grote filosofen over het goede leven [About the art of living; The great philosophers about the good life]. Ambo, Amsterdam.
Duncanson C (2009) Forces for good? Narratives of military masculinity in peacekeeping operations. https://doi.org/10.1080/14616740802567808.
Foucault M (1965) Madness and civilization: A history of insanity in the age of reason. Vintage Books, New York.
Foucault M (1973) The Birth of the Clinic An Archaeology of Medical Perception. Tavistock, London.
Foucault M (1977) Discipline and Punish. Vintage Books, New York.
Foucault M (1982) The Subject and Power. In: Dreyfus H, Rabinow P (eds) Michel Foucault: Beyond Structuralism and Hermeneutics. University of Chicago Press, Chicago, pp 208–229.
Foucault M (1984a) Docile Bodies. In: Rabinow P (ed) The Foucault reader. Pantheon Books, New York, pp 179–187.
Foucault M (1984b) Preface to the history of sexuality, Volume II. In: Rabinow P (ed) The Foucault reader. Pantheon Books, New York, pp 333–339.

Foucault M (1984c) On the genealogy of ethics: An overview of work in progress. In: Rabinow P (ed) The Foucault reader. Pantheon Books, New York, pp 340–372.
Foucault M (1997) The ethics of the concern for the self as a practice of freedom. In: Rabinow P (ed) Michel Foucault: Ethics, subjectivity and truth. Penguin, London, pp 281–303.
Gilbert T (2001) Reflective practice and clinical supervision: meticulous rituals of the confessional. Journal of Advanced Nursing, 36:199–205.
Gunzenhauser M (2007) Resistance as a component of educator professionalism. Philosophical Studies in Education, 38:23–36.
Hadot P (1995) Spiritual exercises. In: Davidson A (ed) Philosophy as a way of life. Blackwell, Oxford, pp 97–144.
Ibarra-Colado E et al (2006) The ethics of managerial subjectivity. Journal of Business Ethics, 64:45–55.
Iedema R, Rhodes C (2010) The undecided space of ethics in organizational surveillance. Organization Studies, 31:199–217.
Infinito J (2003) Jane Elliot meets Foucault: The formation of ethical identities in the classroom. Journal of Moral Education, 32:67–76.
Kessels J (2001) Socrates comes to market. Philosophy of Management, 1:49–71.
Kosmala K, McKernan J (2011) From care of the self to care for the others: Neglected aspects of Foucault's late work. Accounting, Auditing and Accountability Journal, 2:377–402.
Kramer E (2007) Organizing doubt. Self-organization and army units in crisis operations. Liber/ Copenhagen Business School Press, Copenhagen.
Krulak C (1999) The strategic corporal: Leadership in the three block war. Marines Gazette, 83:14–17.
Litz B et al (2009) Moral injury and moral repair in war veterans: A preliminary model and intervention strategy. Clinical Psychology Review, 29:695–706.
Loacker B, Muhr S (2009) How can I become a responsible subject? Towards a practice-based ethics of responsiveness. Journal of Business Ethics, 90:265–277.
Lucas G (2015) Routledge Handbook of Military Ethics. Routledge, New York.
Miller P (2007) The art of self-fashioning, or Foucault on Plato and Derrida. Foucault Studies, 2:54–74.
Morgan D (1994) Theater of war. Combat, the military, and masculinities. In: Brod H, Kaufman, M (eds) Theorizing masculinities. Sage Publications, London, pp 165–182.
Munro I (2014) Organizational ethics and Foucault's 'art of living': Lessons from social movement organizations. Organization Studies, 35:1127–1148.
Nelson H (2001) Damaged identities, narrative repair. Cornell University Press, Ithaca, NY.
Nicoll K et al (2013) Opening discourses of citizenship education: A theorization with Foucault. Journal of Education Policy, 28:828–846.
Nietzsche F (1981a) Friedrich Nietzsche werke 1, Schopenhauer als erzieher. K. Schlechta, Verlag Ullstein, Frankfurt am Main/Berlin.
Nietzsche F (1981b) Friedrich Nietzsche werke 3, Über die zukunft unsere bildungs-anstalten. K. Schlechta, Verlag Ullstein, Frankfurt am Main/Berlin.
Olsthoorn P (2008) The ethics curriculum at the Netherlands Defence Academy, and some problems with its theoretical underpinnings. In: Robinson P et al. (eds) Ethics education in the military. Ashgate, London, pp 119–132.
Pignatelli F (2002) Mapping the terrain of a Foucauldian ethics: A response to the surveillance of schooling. Studies in Philosophy and Education, 21:157–180.
Randall J, Munro I (2010) Foucault's care of the self: A case from mental health work. Organization Studies, 31:1485–1504.
Robinson P (2007) Ethics training and development in the military, Parameters: Journal of the US Army War College, 37:23–36.
Robinson P, De Lee N, Carrick D (2008) Ethics education in the military. Ashgate Publishing, Aldershot.
Rosenberg A, Westfall J (2018) Foucault and Nietzsche: A critical encounter. Bloomsbury Academic, London/Oxford/New York.

Schmid W (1998). Philosophie der Lebenskunst: Eine grundlegung. Suhrkamp, Frankfurt.
Starkey K, Hatchuel A (2002) The long detour: Foucault's history of desire and pleasure. Organization, 9:641–656.
Teschers C (2017) Education and Schmid's art of living: Philosophical, psychological and educational perspectives on living a good life. Routledge, New York.
Thornborrow T, Brown A (2009) Being regimented: Aspiration, discipline and identity work in the British parachute regiment. Organization studies, 30:355–376.
Van Baarda T, Verweij D (2006) Military ethics: The Dutch approach: A practical guide. Brill, Leiden.
Van Baarle E et al. (2015) Moral dilemmas in a military context: a case study of a train the trainer course on military ethics. Journal of Moral Education, 44:457–478.
Van Baarle E et al. (2017) What sticks? The evaluation of a train-the-trainer course in military ethics and its perceived outcomes, Journal of Military Ethics, 16:55–77.
Van Baarle E et al. (2018) The relevance of Foucauldian art-of-living for ethics education in a military context; theory and practice. Journal of Moral Education, 47:126–143.
Verweij D (2010) Geweten onder schot. Boom, Amsterdam.
Vintges K (2001) Must we burn Foucault? Ethics as art of living: Simone de Beauvoir and Michel Foucault. Continental philosophy review, 34:165–181.
Whetham D (2010) Ethics, law and military operations. Palgrave Macmillan, Basingstoke.
Wolfendale J (2008) What is the point of teaching ethics in the military? In: Robinson P et al (eds) Ethics education in the military. Ashgate, London, pp 161–175.
Wortel E, Bosch J (2011) Strengthening moral competence: A "train the trainer" course on military ethics, Journal of Military Ethics 10:17–35.

Prof. Eva van Baarle is an Assistant Professor of Military Ethics and Philosophy at the Netherlands Defence Academy. Her research focusses on fostering reflective practice and moral competence of military personnel by means of ethics education. She also works as a researcher at the Department of Medical Humanities at VU University Medical Centre in Amsterdam, The Netherlands.

Prof. Dr. Desiree Verweij is professor in philosophy and ethics at the Faculty of Military Sciences of the Netherlands Defence Academy. She also holds a chair at the Centre for International Conflict Analysis and Management (CICAM) of the Radboud University Nijmegen. Her research focuses on both fundamental and applied philosophy and ethics, including themes like Just War, moral responsibility and moral judgement.

Chapter 7
Reflective Practice in Synthetic Expeditionary Task Forces

Eric-Hans Kramer and Matthijs Moorkamp

Contents

7.1	Reflective Practice in Synthetic Expeditionary Task Forces	98
7.2	Reflective Practice as a Concept	99
7.3	Studying Reflective Practice in Military Task Forces	100
7.4	The Synthetic Organization as the Context for Reflective Practice	101
	7.4.1 The Conventional View on Task Force Design	102
	7.4.2 The Task Force as a Synthetic Organization	102
	7.4.3 Synthetic Task Forces and Reflective Practice	103
7.5	Reflective Practice in the Cases	104
	7.5.1 Understanding Environmental Dynamics	105
	7.5.2 Understanding Organizational Dynamics	106
	7.5.3 Designing Solutions for Organizational Challenges	107
7.6	Discussion	109
	7.6.1 Practitioners Shaping Organizational Context	109
	7.6.2 Reflective Practice and Purpose	110
7.7	Conclusion	111
References		112

Abstract According to Schön, a careful examination of artistry is important to understand the dynamics involved in the work of reflective practitioners. Such an examination is therefore crucial for ambitions to educate reflective practitioners. In this chapter we will argue that organizational characteristics of military task forces confront military professionals with specific challenges. These challenges highlight an

---

E.-H. Kramer (✉)
Faculty of Military Sciences, Netherlands Defence Academy, PO Box 90002
4800 PA Breda, The Netherlands
e-mail: FJ.Kramer@mindef.nl

M. Moorkamp
Institute for Management Research, Radboud University Nijmegen, Nijmegen,
The Netherlands
e-mail: m.moorkamp@fm.ru.nl

under-theorized aspect of reflective practice. Expeditionary military task forces are often characterized by underdeveloped design and coordination, which qualifies them as examples of what Thompson called "synthetic organizations". As a consequence, military professionals need to invest major effort into refining and reshaping their organizations while operating under dangerous and turbulent conditions. Reflective practice of military professionals is therefore simultaneously directed towards "self-designing" an organizational system and enacting the mission environment. Based on research projects carried out over the past 20 years we highlight our arguments by means of case study material. In this way we aim to contribute to developing the way the reflective practice concept can be incorporated into military education and research programs.

Keywords Reflective practice · synthetic expeditionary task forces · organizing

7.1 Reflective Practice in Synthetic Expeditionary Task Forces

By placing the concept of "the reflective practitioner" at the core of their educational philosophy, the Faculty of Military Sciences (FMS) in The Netherlands intends to prepare future officers for "reflective practice". Schön developed this concept to capture "how professionals think in action" and indicated they are more than instrumental problem solvers that select technical means suited to practical purposes.[1] Reflective practice refers to an iterative process of developing an understanding of ill-defined problems, developing interventions and evaluating subsequent effects. Embracing this concept in educational settings implies a particular understanding of the future work of professionals, in case of the FMS the future of military professionals. Therefore, it is important to develop an understanding of the kind of practices that constitute the core of the future working environment of these professionals. The starting point for this chapter is therefore Schön's suggestion to ask:[2] "what we can learn from a careful examination of artistry", that is, what we can learn from the experiences with practical problem solving by military professionals.

More specifically, this chapter focuses on reflective practitioners dealing with organizational challenges in expeditionary military task forces. The last two decades, the Netherlands Armed Forces has deployed several expeditionary task forces as a contribution to a broader international task force. Research indicates that a particular challenge of operating in such missions is that the deployed task force is constructed by "mixing and matching" existing organizational building blocks.[3] This particular way of deploying units was already used in for example the UNPROFOR, IFOR and SFOR missions in Bosnia in the 1990s, but also in the

---

[1] Schön 1987, p. 3.
[2] Schön 1987, p. 13.
[3] Kramer 2007; De Waard 2010; Moorkamp 2019.

SFIR mission in Iraq, the ISAF missions in Afghanistan and the present-day MINUSMA mission in Mali. Such missions constitute a particular context for reflective practice and confront practitioners with specific organizational challenges. The aim of this chapter is to develop an understanding of reflective practice in relation to organizational challenges in expeditionary task forces. In order to achieve this aim, this chapter reflects on the outcomes of different case studies.

7.2 Reflective Practice as a Concept

Schön's starting point for developing the concept of the "reflective practitioner" was a critique on views that perceive practitioners as instrumental problem solvers that select technical means to suit practical purposes.[4] His criticism is that a deductive process of technical rationality is only valid after the issue of problem setting has been dealt with and after a clearly delineated problem is formulated that fits a familiar category of problems that is covered by a theory. However, such requirements do not fit the uncertain, unique and value-laden character of the situations that confront practitioners. As a consequence of uncertainty, problem definitions are often not given, but need to be constructed by practitioners. Furthermore, the unique nature of many practical problems makes that they not always fit the categories and rules that constitute technical rationality. As for the value laden character of practical issues: to understand a given situation as a problem implies a normative orientation. For example, a diagnosis inevitably includes a normative judgment of what ought to be in the light of some standard.[5]

Important in Schön's characterization of reflective practice is the distinction between "reflection-in-action" and "reflection-on-action". Reflection-on-action refers to thinking back about the (un)expected outcomes of action.[6] Opposed to that reflection-in-action refers to thinking that[7] "(…) serves to reshape what we are doing while we are doing it". All in all, reflective practice involves developing a hypothetical definition of a problem situation, which practitioners refine by acting and reflecting on the outcomes of interventions. In his critique of technical rationality, Schön aims to avoid stepping into the opposite trap: he wants to avoid categories such as "intuition" and "talent" and aims to demystify the art of practical problem solving,[8] which is essential if "reflective practice" is to be any basis for

---

[4] Schön 1983, 1987.
[5] Van Strien 1997, pp. 686–687.
[6] Schön 1987, p. 26.
[7] Schön 1987, p. 26.
[8] Schön 1987, p. 13.
[9] Kinsella 2009.

education. "Reflective practice" has been particularly influential concept in academic debate in education.[9] Schön is credited for placing the relation between reflection and action on the agenda in organization studies[10] and his work has been influential in discussions on organizational learning[11] and education.[12]

While Schön[13] traces the origins of his concept back to the pragmatist educational philosopher John Dewey, Kinsella[14] relates it to the Aristotelian idea of *phronesis*. In organization science[15] as well as in management education[16] the relevance of *phronesis* has been recognized. *Phronesis* is usually characterized as "practical wisdom" that cannot be reduced to either *episteme* (intellectual grasp of a theory) or *techne* (mastery of arts and techniques).[17] Toulmin explains that:[18] "Far from being stated as abstract, universal and general propositions, practical wisdom is *shown* in concrete, particular, local actions to remedy a situation. Such knowledge (…) is never final, always *circumstantial*" (italics in original). In military studies *phronesis* has received considerable attention, but not predominantly in discussions about practical problem solving. Instead it has been brought up in the context of discussions about moral judgment and the importance of moral education in the military.[19] The discussions on the inherently value-laden concept of "reflective practice" indicate that moral judgment should not be understood as a "module" added to technical rationality. Instead, practical problem solving is inherently value laden, exactly because it cannot be reduced to technical rationality.

7.3 Studying Reflective Practice in Military Task Forces

It has been well-established in military studies that contemporary missions typically take place in dynamically complex, "reactive" environments[20] that not only confront practitioners with uncertainty, change, ambiguity and disruption, but also with intelligent opponents that act strategically in deceptive ways.[21] As such, these

---

[10] Yanow and Tsoukas 2009.
[11] For example Raelin 2007; Reynolds and Vince 2004.
[12] Raelin 2010.
[13] Schön 1992, p. 123.
[14] Kinsella 2012.
[15] Flyvbjerg 2002; Flyvbjerg et al. 2012.
[16] Maas 2006.
[17] Toulmin 1990, p. 190.
[18] Toulmin 1996, p. 210.
[19] Richardson et al. 2001; Toiskallio 2007.
[20] Kramer 2007; Bousquet 2008.
[21] Luttwak 2001.

missions appear to constitute a prototypical context in which reflective practice is of essential importance. At the Netherlands Defence Academy, expeditionary task forces have been studied for two decades.[22] Several case studies were developed to understand organizational challenges in these organizational contexts. The focus in these studies was on the operational units at the lowest hierarchical level and the everyday organizational challenges with which they struggled. Therefore, the "reflective practitioner" in this research was the operator that worked at that specific organizational level. The case studies were conducted using a qualitative research method based on interviews with military personnel of all ranks. The interviews focused on everyday practical problem solving in the specific organizational context in which they were involved. As such, the interviews focused on "reflection-on-action" as it is notoriously complicated – if not next to impossible – to study "reflection-in-action".[23] Based on a Grounded Theory perspective,[24] the aim was to develop theory about the challenges of organizing in such organizational settings.

Specifically at the operational level operators are directly confronted with dynamic complexity in their organizational environment. They are therefore potentially confronted with a gap between the assumptions on which the organizational framework was established and environmental challenges. In organizational literature, managing that gap is referred to as the essence of "normal work" of operators.[25] Our assumption is that by studying "normal work" it becomes possible to develop insight into reflective practices involved in developing processes, structures and systems in the context of "mixed and matched" temporary task forces. The empirical discussion below is not on focused on a particular case, but involves a meta-reflection on the research project.

7.4 The Synthetic Organization as the Context for Reflective Practice

The perceived role of reflective practice in temporary task forces depends on how the crucial dynamics in such organizational contexts are conceptualized. Here we want to contrast the conventional view on military task forces with a perspective that defines expeditionary task forces as "synthetic organizations". We argue that "reflective practice" has a central place when task forces are seen as "synthetic organizations" while in conventional views its opposite, i.e. "technical rationality" is assumed to play a crucial role.

---

[22] Vogelaar and Kramer 2004; Kramer 2007; Kramer et al. 2010, 2012; Van Bezooijen and Kramer 2014; Kramer and Moorkamp 2016; Moorkamp et al. 2016; Moorkamp 2017, 2019.
[23] Yanow and Tsoukas 2009.
[24] Glaser and Strauss 1967.
[25] Bourier 2002; Dekker 2005.

7.4.1 The Conventional View on Task Force Design

According to the conventional view, task forces:[26] "(…) are designed by taking basic unit building blocks and assembling them along hierarchical lines consistent with the demands of the mission and time-honored military traditions of command and control." Such a system is designed to structure the formal flow of communication and coordination.[27] This basic design is worked out further by more specific technical guidelines.[28] The conventional view of task force design fits with what Weick calls the architectural metaphor of organization design:[29] "Organizational design modeled along the lines of architectural design is viewed as a bounded activity that occurs at a fixed point in time. The activity is largely decision making, concentrated in a small group, which translates intention into plans." Coordination in such organizations is to take place along clearly pre-defined lines.[30]

The architectural metaphor relies on the assumption that behavior of operators in such systems is guided by technical rationality and essentially comes down to following rules. This is indicated by the way Snook describes behavior in military organizations:[31] "In generic terms, all actions within military organizations are guided by a broad set of doctrine, tactics, techniques and procedures". This view of organization design has frequently been criticized in organization science. According to Weick:[32] "(…) one-time design strategies make sense if the environment is basically placid, but continuous redesign is necessary when the environment becomes turbulent." Our conclusion is therefore that the conventional view on task force design overlooks fundamental characteristics of the dynamically complex conditions in which task forces are expected to operate.

7.4.2 The Task Force as a Synthetic Organization

A contrasting view on the nature of task forces can be sketched by means of James Thompson's "synthetic organization" concept. He characterizes a synthetic organization as a temporarily assembled "ad hoc" constellation that needs to deal with "great uncertainty". The synthetic organization derives its name from a necessary "process of synthesis", a process of connecting the previously unconnected. As Thompson emphasized:[33]

---

[26] Snook 2000, p. 33.
[27] Snook 2000, p. 38.
[28] Snook 2000, p. 37.
[29] Weick 2001, p. 57.
[30] Ockhuysen and Bechky 2009.
[31] Snook 2000, p. 34.
[32] Weick 2001, p. 60.
[33] Thompson 2008, p. 53.

(…) the synthetic organization must simultaneously establish its structure and carry on operations. Under conditions of great uncertainty, it must learn the nature and extent of the overall problem to be solved and the nature and location of relevant resources. At the same time it must assemble and interrelate the components, and it must do all this without the benefit of established rules or commonly known channels of communication. The synthetic organization cannot take inventory before swinging into action.

The example that Thompson uses is the prototypical disaster management organization that is composed of building blocks from different parent organizations.[34] Previous research has indicated that also expeditionary task forces are organizationally underdeveloped, need extensive shaping and reshaping of coordination and control while enacting a turbulent operating context. For this reason, the concept of the synthetic organization has been brought forward as a fruitful way of thinking about organizational challenges in such expeditionary task forces.[35] If an organization can be seen as a tool for accomplishing a complex task that requires collective effort, a synthetic organization is a tool built up of a (sparsely) interrelated assembly of organizational building blocks developed for a different kind of task, that needs to be shaped by its users in conditions of uncertainty, in order to deal with a task that is not yet fully understood.

The ideal-typical synthetic organization is characterized by inner contradictions and as a result the requirements for technical rationality are not in place. It is (perpetually) "unfinished": its design is not worked out, and cannot be worked out in advance as it lacks insight in "the nature and overall problem to be solved". It needs to develop functional integration along the way, while it operates in a challenging, and highly uncertain environment.[36] Interdependencies between the activities assembled parts are unclear, mechanisms to coordinate between parts are not (fully) in place and rules to guide behavior may be unclear as well. At the same time, the synthetic organization cannot work these out in advance, as it needs to act.

7.4.3 Synthetic Task Forces and Reflective Practice

Thompson does not work out the concept of the synthetic organization any further. We want to take a conceptual step by connecting it to the idea of reflective practice in the context of military task forces. We argue in this section that dealing with the inner contradictions of the synthetic organization requires reflective practice.

The struggles of Thompson's synthetic organization can be explained by relating them to Weick's philosophy of organizing. At the core of Weick's philosophy of organizing is the idea that organizations need to develop a pragmatic simplification

---

[34] See also Thompson and Hawkes 1962.
[35] Kramer and Moorkamp 2017; Moorkamp 2019.
[36] Thompson 2008, pp. 52–53.

of dynamically complex environments:[37] "The activities of organizing are directed toward the establishment of a workable level of certainty." In Weick's philosophy of organizing this simplification is inevitable but always provisional and might lead to overlooking relevant environmental dynamics: "organizations keep falling apart and they require "chronic rebuilding".[38] If an organization is confronted with dynamic complexity, it by definition cannot possess a finite system of rules and procedures to deal with those conditions. According to Weick, organizations therefore need to "enact" an environment on the basis of provisional knowledge. In doing so, they acquire the insights to make sense of the environment. That is, sense making is about "(…) the ongoing retrospective development of plausible images that rationalize what people are doing"[39] and implies the ability to make "better guesses in an unknowable world".[40] This combination of enactment and sense making seems to be core issues for the synthetic organization that operates in conditions of "great uncertainty" and that needs to "swing into action" with preliminary insights about the nature of the problem they need to deal with. The synthetic organization furthermore assembles and interrelates components and as such is essentially concerned with design and coordination. This issue can be related to Weick's claim that "to organize is to assemble ongoing interdependent action s into sensible sequences that generate sensible outcomes".[41]

Based on this perspective, we propose that in the specific context of the synthetic organization, the process of organizing requires "reflective practice" in the form of a complicated combination of enactment, sense making, coordination and design. In other words, if an organization is a tool to accomplish a complex collective task, enactment, sense making, coordination and design are the means by which reflective practitioners shape the tool required for the job at hand. The next section reflects on these patterns as they appeared in the cases.

7.5 Reflective Practice in the Cases

Given the specific focus of on organizational challenges in a dynamically complex environment, the cases discussed below distinguish between understanding environmental dynamics, understanding dynamics inside the organization and designing solutions for organizational challenges.

---

[37] Weick 1979.
[38] Weick 1979, p. 44.
[39] Weick et al. 2009, p. 129.
[40] Weick 2006, p. 1724.
[41] Weick 1979, p. 3.

7.5.1 Understanding Environmental Dynamics

One of the clearest patterns that can be observed in the cases is that operational units at the operational level were confronted with significant dynamic complexity in their operational environment.[42] Few people probably need convincing that military task forces experience dynamic complexity in their operational environments, as that is one of the very reasons military units are deployed. However, particularly in the UNPROFOR cases and in the TFU case, operational units encountered conditions that were particularly different from their expectations. For example, the TFU operation was expected to be a reconstruction mission, but developed into a combat mission.

Regarding the TFU mission, Kramer, De Waard and De Graaff observed that:[43] "(…) previous to the deployment of the Dutch troops the Afghan province Uruzgan was basically a white spot on the map. Furthermore, during deployment the local circumstances proved to be very changeable; the force of the Taliban opposition could vary significantly. Operational units were often the first to experience changes in the environment and acted therefore in a general sense as explorers." This is a clear example of the importance of enactment and sense making. Also in the 1990s during the UNPROFOR missions in Bosnia Herzegovina, Dutch logistic units were regularly confronted with shifting confrontation lines and were often the first witnesses of change,[44] while Dutchbat units that were shot at found it difficult to determine which of the local parties were firing at them and difficult to understand their intentions.[45] An issue related to this problem of uncertainty is that – strategically – it is difficult to determine what building blocks should be part of the synthetic task force. For example in the SFIR mission, the selection of these building blocks was adapted after experience in the mission area.[46] The operational environment was not merely "uncertain", but also "reactive" in the sense that local insurgents responded intelligently to the Dutch units. In each of the cases, it was reported that local insurgents studied operational tactics displayed by the Dutch task force. In the SFIR case, it was suggested that this enabled them to ambush a Dutch unit, as well as the subsequently deployed Quick Reaction Forces.[47] Making sense of such dynamics was a crucial issue in each of the cases that was studied.

---

[42] Kramer and Van Bezooijen 2018.
[43] Kramer et al. 2012, p. 242.
[44] Kramer 2007.
[45] Kramer 2007.
[46] Kramer 2009.
[47] Kramer et al. 2010.

7.5.2 Understanding Organizational Dynamics

In military studies the concepts of sense making and enactment are broadly used to refer to the process in military units of developing understanding of the operational environment. In our case studies, it was observable that operators frequently struggled to understand their own organization as well. In a sense, an internal sense making process was needed to develop such an understanding. For example, Moorkamp's analysis of TFU[48] indicated that operators working in different parts of the task force struggled to understand internal organizational dynamics, which became urgent after experiencing significant interferences such as near misses. Moorkamp discusses numerous examples of interferences, one particular example being interferences between Army and Airforce units. He for example quotes an Apache pilot:[49]

> We were constantly surprised over there by the Army … Everything that is not allowed on an airfield here [in the Netherlands] was happening over there … They suddenly decided to put up a large crane, or a balloon or a UAV … They were not thinking about the implications for us … So we had to train these Army guys in with whom they had to coordinate.

Such interferences can be explained by the fact that Army and Airforce units are not used to cooperate in the way they cooperated in TFU. This resulted in all kinds of (unexpected) interrelations between different activities while lacking appropriate coordination mechanisms.

This is one of the often-underestimated organizational consequences of operating in "mixed and matched" expeditionary task forces. If such task forces are large and composed of units from different backgrounds (TFU consisted of 49 different units including engineers, logistic units, Provincial Reconstruction Teams, infantry units, Airforce units, Military Police), it becomes increasingly problematic to understand how the behavior of different units interrelates. Also Snook[50] underlines this challenge in complex task forces: "(…) complex collective tasks, (…), require high degrees of both differentiation and integration. In addition to spawning differing cognitive and emotional orientations, taskforce mission requirements also created a myriad of complex interdependencies". This becomes particularly difficult if the different units involved enact a dynamically complex environment and consistently adapt their way of operating. This issue was not limited to TFU. In an analysis of an ambush,[51] which cost the life of one member of the Military Police, it appeared that there were numerous misunderstandings regarding procedures. Kramer[52] attributes this to the nature of the SFIR task force and notes that adding

---

[48] Moorkamp 2017, 2019.
[49] Moorkamp 2019, p. 109.
[50] Snook 2000, p. 178.
[51] Delahaij et al. 2009.
[52] Kramer 2009, p. 55.

specialized units to a battalion disrupts the normal way of working and requires a complex coordination process.

In discussing TFU, Moorkamp[53] indicates that as a result of the differences between organizational characteristics of a traditional army brigade and the expeditionary task force, existing rules for coordination had shortcomings:

> Forward Air Controllers subsequently experienced that, in shaping interactions with other units within TFU, existing rules and procedures had shortcomings and that application of these rules during operations resulted in safety issues. During training in brigade formation, FAC-ers[54] were used to deconflict fire support with 81-millimeter mortars only at the level of their company and inform battalion-staff afterwards. During brigade operations, this is possible because companies are assigned to separate geographical areas that do not overlap.

Working out – i.e. making sense of – the interdependencies between different specialized units is an essential and defining organizational challenge in synthetic organizations. The cases also show glimpses of a reflective practice process and emphasize that independencies sometimes were only insightful after incidents.

7.5.3 Designing Solutions for Organizational Challenges

Both issues discussed above required "reflective" problem solving activities by military professionals. One particular strategy oriented on reducing the complexity of a synthetic task force splitting up an Area of Responsibility (AOR) into smaller Areas of Responsibility for which a smaller group of units has integral responsibility. Such a design principle can potentially significantly reduce the complexity of the web of interrelating activities within the larger organizational system. This particular design strategy is typically used by Dutch contributions in Bosnia.[55] This is obviously a "conceptual" top-down design solution that is most often also developed and implemented in a hierarchical top-down fashion. However, TFU is an example in which the lowest hierarchical level also contributed to redrawing the lines of AORs.[56] Kramer relates this practice to the organization design principle of "building the whole in the parts", as put forward by Morgan.[57] Its success depends, however, on the very possibility to create loosely coupled organizational units that are guided by the design principle of "minimal critical specification". Also in TFU it was attempted to design AORs on basis of the principle of "the whole in the parts",[58] but Moorkamp's analysis of structural interferences between different parts

---

[53] Moorkamp 2019, p. 110.
[54] Acronym for "Forward Air Controllers".
[55] Kramer 2007.
[56] Kramer et al. 2012, p. 241.
[57] Morgan 1997.
[58] Kramer et al. 2012.

of the TFU task force indicated that this principle could not be systematically applied in this case,[59] possibly because centralized capacities interfered with local activities in the smaller Areas of Operations. In such instances "reflective practice" at the lowest hierarchical level is structurally impeded by complex interferences in the overall (international) task force.

A further consistent finding in the case studies was that operators "implicitly" created design solutions for the organizational challenges in the task force. That is, they developed solutions for different practical problems without a deliberate intention or even awareness to be involved in an issue of organization design. Their efforts were focused on repairing problems related to an underdeveloped organizational skeleton and to tailoring the task force to local conditions. In a sense, this is a defining characteristic of task forces: neither Dutchbat, Logtbat, IFOR, SFOR, SFIR nor TFU existed as an integral unit within the Armed forces. It is a characteristic that fits the definition of the synthetic organization, as this needs to assemble and interrelate components. The expeditionary task forces that we studied all needed to adapt their structure. Typically the operational levels contributed to refining and reshaping task force design. A particular example of a design solution that was developed in TFU was the so-called SUA or Smallest Unit of Action. Essence of the SUA concept was that different specialists required to perform a given patrol were grouped together. For this reason, Kramer, De Waard and De Graaff[60] underline that this practice of mixing specialists in a group contradicts the existing design philosophy of the Netherlands Armed Forces, as this emphasizes separating specialists in different groups. They furthermore underline that the SUA concept indicates the struggles of the Armed Forces to develop what De Waard and Kramer call "tailored taskforces".[61]

Military reflective practitioners also dealt with issues of group dynamics. In an analysis of the Logistic Support Battalion "Logtbat" that was active during UNPROFOR, Kramer[62] indicated that platoons experienced formerly unfamiliar group dynamics. As a result of a particular rotation policy one third of a platoon was rotated after two months of deployment while soldiers had a six-month tour of duty. Therefore, every two months platoons experienced an influx of new members. Not only demanded this that new members needed to learn the ropes of riding convoys in the uncertain and ever changing conditions in the civil war in Bosnia, also new members needed to integrate into the existing platoon. For leaders this situation was particularly demanding: at the start of their tour the unit they were supposed to lead was more far experienced in the local conditions.[63]

This discussion makes clear that reflective practice at the lowest hierarchical level played a significant role in developing organization design. Finding an

---

[59] Moorkamp 2017, 2019.
[60] Kramer et al. 2012.
[61] De Waard and Kramer 2008.
[62] Kramer 2007.
[63] Vogelaar and Kramer 2004.

appropriate organizational form is not – and indeed cannot be a – "one shot design" affair in synthetic organizations. At the same time, such reflective practice is limited by the fact that in complicated task forces not all interdependencies are clear at the bottom up level. The process of "self-design" can have effects beyond the horizon of units. As such, reflective practice is necessary but at the same time inherently imperfect in task forces that are unable to reduce structural complexity. This is the reason why Kramer and Moorkamp[64] underlined the inherent organizational vulnerabilities of expeditionary military task forces.

7.6 Discussion

By focusing on organizational challenges, this chapter discusses reflective practice in a slightly unusual way. Schön discusses examples such as architects designing houses and psychotherapists offering therapy. In such examples, attention is on reflective practice in relation to the very core of a profession and addresses questions like: what is an appropriate diagnosis for this particular patient? What is a good design for this particular building in this particular location? Some consider organizational issues as bureaucratic diversions that direct practitioners' attention away from the real issues.[65] However, the discussion in this chapter indicated that in the context of expeditionary military task forces "organizing" becomes part of the very core of the practice of military professionals, especially at the lowest hierarchical levels. In this section we want to discuss two further ways in which the military case studies offer a relevant perspective on reflective practice.

7.6.1 Practitioners Shaping Organizational Context

The practitioners that we studied struggled to understand organizational dynamics that greatly influenced their work. On occasion, this frustrated them immensely. A particularly significant conclusion is that the combined influence of organizational dynamics and the organizational context on the validity of established rules is not sufficiently understood in the Armed Forces. Here, the example is relevant of the FAC-er that found out that applying established procedures from the brigade context could lead to failure in the expeditionary context. This situation is reminiscent of what De Graaff and Kramer[66] call the "split brain problem" of the Armed Forces. They argue that practitioners in the expeditionary context may learn many

---

[64] Kramer and Moorkamp 2016.
[65] Verbrugge 2005.
[66] De Graaff and Kramer 2012.

things, but they have difficulties transferring lessons to the context of the parent organization. The example of the FAC-er makes clear that this split also complicates transfer in the opposite direction: it is not straightforward to transfer what is previously learned to the task force context. This seems to be a more significant threat to safety than what is obligatory referred to as "culture".

These arguments underline the importance of "self-design". Attention for self-design in military education could facilitate understanding of "issues of organizing" with which military professionals struggle. As expeditionary task forces are a significant part of the Dutch military "primary process" and as the FMS has placed the concept of the reflective practitioner at the core of their educational philosophy, it may be argued that military education should go beyond merely stressing the importance of "pragmatic problem solving" and "can-do mentality" for operating in expeditionary contexts and should prepare military professionals for the organizing issues that they encounter during expeditionary missions. As such, an emphasis on learning to apply organizational (design) knowledge to the specific context of expeditionary task forces seems to be a reasonable adoption of the reflective practice concept that is suitable for contemporary military challenges.

This particular view of reflective practice differs from how this is usually portrayed in organizational literature. For example, Yanow and Tsoukas emphasize that practitioners act in a world already interpreted and constituted:[67] "Practitioners, like others, act in a world already interpreted and already constituted; they achieve understanding through being and acting in it, not through isolated cognition of it. They are thrown into a world which is gradually disclosed to them through the actions they undertake". This is the very opposite of Weick's concept of enactment that emphasizes that as a result of dynamic complexity practitioners need to go beyond the world already constituted and interpreted. As "designers" reflective practitioners in military task forces contribute to working out the unfinished synthetic organization. As such they contribute to shaping the organizational and environmental context in which they work. This shows that in reflective practice, at least in military task forces, structure and agency mutually constitute each other.

7.6.2 Reflective Practice and Purpose

Another issue that emerges from our analysis is the meaningfulness of military missions. In Schön's examples it is uncontroversial that architects should design houses and psychotherapists should offer therapy. These are established practices in a sociological context that makes them meaningful. However, matters are more complicated during military missions in dangerous and turbulent environments.

---

[67] Yanow and Tsoukas 2009, p. 1349.

In such contexts it can become controversial if activities of practitioners can be a one-dimensional translation of previously formulated indisputable strategic intentions, as is also highlighted in the cases we discussed. Chia and Holt's idea of "strategy without design" might be informative here.[68] They argue that, in complex environments, strategy to a degree emerges out of the everyday problem solving activities of practitioners. Kramer, De Waard and De Graaff[69] argue that the strategic ambiguity at the onset of the TFU-mission (reconstruction versus combat) was pragmatically resolved by activities by the expeditionary task force. Particularly in complex military missions, reflective practitioners can experience that existing goals are unachievable, unjust or activities are counterproductive. In literature on trauma-related suffering in the military it has been well established that fundamental questions regarding the purposefulness of mission can have "injurious" effects[70] also in post-conflict rebuilding missions.[71] Similar effects are addressed in concepts such as "moral injury".[72] This underlines Schön's point that the work of practitioners is inherently value-laden. Although also psychotherapists and architects may come to question the very meaningfulness of their occupation, this seems particularly an issue in dynamic contexts in which the value-laden character of reflective practice is often directly related to purpose.

7.7 Conclusion

The aim of this chapter was to develop an understanding of reflective practice in the context of the organizational challenges of expeditionary task forces. It became clear that the characteristics of reflective practice can straightforwardly be observed in military case studies. At the same time, the experiences of military practitioners bring up organizational issues that are not frequently discussed in publications on reflective practice. This analysis makes clear that the concept of the reflective practitioner is both relevant and valuable for military education. Most importantly perhaps, this chapter indicates that the relevant organizational dynamics with which military practitioners are confronted are only partly understood but are central to experiences of military practitioners during missions. Developing further insight in these dynamics and possible organizational solutions might be an important step in developing a research and educational program that fits the aim to educate military professionals as reflective practitioners. At the same time, it may be of importance for further organizational development of the military organizational in general.

---

[68] Chia and Holt 2009, pp. 25–26.
[69] Kramer et al. 2012, p. 247.
[70] Lifton 2005; Shay 1994.
[71] Molendijk 2018; Molendijk et al. 2018.
[72] Litz et al. 2009.

References

Bourrier M (2002) Bridging Research and Practice: The Challenge of Normal Operations Studies. Journal of Contingencies and Crisis Management 10:173–180.

Bousquet A (2008) Chaoplexic warfare or the future of military organization. International Affairs 84(5):915–929.

Chia R, Holt R (2009) Strategy Without Design: The Silent Efficacy of Indirect Action. Cambridge University Press, Cambridge.

De Graaff MC, Kramer EH (2012) Leiderschap, uitzending en intelligent failure. De intelligente mislukking als hoeksteen van de lerende organisatie [Leadership, expeditionary missions and intelligent failure. The intelligent failure as the cornerstone of the Learning Organization]. Management and Organisatie 5:41–60.

Dekker S (2005) Ten Questions about Human Error: A New View of Human Factors and System Safety. Lawrence Erlbaum Associates Publishers, Mahwah NJ.

Delahaij R, Kamphuis W, Van Bezooijen B, Vogelaar ALW, Kramer EH, Van Fenema P (2009) Hinderlaag in Irak: een sociaal wetenschappelijke analyse [Ambush in Iraq: a social scientific analysis]. Netherlands Defence Academy, Breda.

De Waard EJ (2010) Engaging Environmental Turbulence. Organizational Determinants for Repetitive, Quick and Adequate Responses. ERIM, Rotterdam.

De Waard EJ, Kramer EH (2008) Tailored Task Forces: Temporary Organizations and Modularity. International Journal of Project Management.

Flyvbjerg B (2002) Making social science matter. Why social science fails and how it can succeed again. Cambridge University Press, Cambridge.

Flyvbjerg B, Landman T, Schramm S (eds) (2012) Real Social Science: Applied Phronesis. Cambridge University Press, Cambridge.

Glaser BG, Strauss AL (1967) The discovery of grounded theory: Strategies for qualitative research. Aldine, Chicago.

Kinsella EA (2009) Professional knowledge and the epistemology of reflective practice. Nursing Philosophy, (11), pp. 3–14.

Kinsella EA (2012) Practitioner Reflection and Judgement as Phronesis. In: Kinsella EA, Pitman A (eds) Phronesis as Professional Knowledge. Professional Practice and Education: A Diversity of Voices, vol. 1. SensePublishers, Rotterdam.

Kramer EH (2007) Organizing doubt. Grounded Theory, Army Units and Dealing with dynamic complexity. Copenhagen Business University Press, Copenhagen.

Kramer EH (2009) Het werken in samengestelde eenheden. In: Delahaij R et al. (eds) Hinderlaag in Irak: een sociaal wetenschappelijke analyse. Netherlands Defence Academy, Breda, pp 51–62.

Kramer EH, Moorkamp M (2016) Understanding Organizational Vulnerabilities in Military Taskforces. In: Beeres R et al. (eds) Netherlands Annual Review of Military Studies. Organizing for Safety and Security in Military Organizations. T.M.C. Asser Press, The Hague, pp 21–40.

Kramer EH, Moorkamp M (2017) The vulnerability of the synthetic organization. Acting purposely while being out of control. Paper presented at the annual Sociotechnical Roundtable, 12–15 September, New Brunswick, NJ.

Kramer EH, Van Bezooijen B, Delahaij R (2010) Sensemaking during operations and Incidents. In: Soeters J et al. (eds) Managing Military Organizations. Routledge, London.

Kramer EH, Van Bezooijen B (2018) Mission Command & the limits of self-organization. The challenges of organizing in expeditionary networks. In: Ydstebø P, Jeppson J (eds) Mission Command – Wishful Thinking? The Royal Swedish Academy of War Sciences, Stockholm.

Kramer EH, Waard de E, De Graaff M (2012) Task Force Uruzgan and experimentation with organization design. In: Van der Meulen J et al. (eds) Mission Uruzgan. Amsterdam University Press, Amsterdam.

Lifton RJ (2005) Home from the war. Learning from Vietnam Veterans, new edn. Other Press LLC, New York.

Litz B, Stein N, Delaney E, Lebowitz L, Nash W, Silva C, Maguen, S (2009) Moral injury and moral repair in war veterans: A preliminary model and intervention strategy. Clinical Psychology Review 29:695–706.

Luttwak E (2001) Strategy. The logic of war and peace, rev. edn. The Belknap Press of Harvard University Press, Cambridge, MA.

Maas JJA (2006) Organizational studies: (not-) smothering each other as a behavioural strategy. Critical Perspectives on International Business.

Molendijk T, Kramer EH, Verweij D (2018) Moral Aspects of 'Moral Injury': Analyzing Conceptualizations on the Role of Morality in Military Trauma. Journal of Military Ethics 17 (1):36–53.

Molendijk T (2018) Moral injury in relation to public debates: The role of societal misrecognition in moral conflict-colored trauma among soldiers. Social Science and Medicine 211 (C):314–320.

Moorkamp M, Wybo JL, Kramer EH (2016) Pioneering with UAVs at the battlefield: The influence of organizational design on the emergence of safety. Safety Science 88:251–260.

Moorkamp M (2017) Self-designing networks and structural influences on safety. Technical University, Delft.

Moorkamp M (2019) Operating under high risk conditions in temporary organization. A sociotechnical perspective. Routledge, London.

Morgan G (1997) Images of Organization, new edn. Sage, Thousand Oaks.

Okhuysen GA, Bechky BA (2009) Coordination in organizations: An integrative perspective. The Academy of Management Annals, 3(1):463–502.

Raelin J (2007) Toward an Epistemology of Practice. Academy of Management Learning and Education 6(4):495–519.

Raelin J (2010) Work-Based Learning: Valuing Practice as an Educational Event. New Directions For Teaching and Learning 124.

Reynolds M, Vince R (eds) (2004) Organizing Reflection. Ashgate, Aldershot.

Richardson R, Verweij D, Winslow D (2001) Moral Fitness for Peace Operations. Journal of Political and Military Sociology 32(1):99–113.

Schön D (1983) The reflective practitioner. Basic Books, New York.

Schön D (1987) Educating the reflective practitioner. Jossey-Bass Publishers, San Francisco.

Schön D (1992) The theory of inquiry: Dewey's legacy to education. Curriculum Inquiry 22 (2):119–139.

Shay J (1994) Achilles in Vietnam: Combat Trauma and the Undoing of Character. Scribner, New York.

Snook S (2000) Friendly Fire. The accidental shootdown of U.S. Black Hawks over Northern Iraq. Princeton University Press, Princeton.

Thompson JD (2008) Organizations in Action. Social Science Bases of Administrative Theory. Originally published in 1967. Transaction Publishers, New Brunswick.

Thompson JD, Hawkes RW (1962) Disaster, Community Organization and Administrative process. In: Baker GW, Chapman DW (eds) Man & Society in Disaster. Basic Books, New York, pp 248–300.

Toiskallio J (Ed) (2007) Ethical Education in the Military. What, How and Why in the 21st Century? National Defence University, Helsinki.

Toulmin S (1990) Cosmopolis: The Hidden Agenda of Modernity. University of Chicago Press, Chicago.

Toulmin S (1996) Concluding methodological reflections. Elitism and democracy among the sciences. In: Toulmin S, Gustavsen B (eds) Beyond theory. Changing Organizations through participation. John Benjamins Publishing Company, Amsterdam.

Van Bezooijen BJA, Kramer EH (2014) Mission command in the Information Age: A Normal Accidents Perspective to Networked Military Operations. Journal of Strategic Studies.

Van Strien PJ (1997) Towards a Methodology of Psychological Practice. Theory & Psychology 7 (5):683–700.

Verbrugge A (2005) Geschonden beroepseer [Violated professional pride]. In: Van den Brink G et al (eds) Beroepszeer, waarom Nederland niet werkt [Occupational pains. Why The Netherlands is not working well]. Boom Tijdschriften, Amsterdam, pp 108–123.

Vogelaar ALW, Kramer EH (2004) Mission Command in Dutch Peace Support Missions. Armed Forces and Society 30(2):409–431.

Weick KE (1979) The Social Psychology of Organizing. McGraw-Hill, New York.

Weick KE (2001) Making sense of the organization. Blackwell Business, Malden.

Weick KE (2006) Faith, Evidence and Action: Better Guesses in an Unknowable World. Organizing studies 27(11):1723–1736.

Weick KE, Sutcliffe K, Obstfeld D (2009) Organizing and the process of sensemaking. In: Weick KE (ed) Making sense of the organization. The impermanent organization. Wiley & Sons, Chichester, pp 129–151.

Yanow D, Tsoukas H (2009) What is Reflection-In-Action? A Phenomenological Account. Journal of Management Studies 46:8.

Prof. Dr. Eric-Hans Kramer is professor of Military Management and Organization at the Faculty of Military Sciences of the Netherlands Defence Academy. His research interests include integral organization theory, systems safety and the relation between organizational context and psychotrauma. His work has been published in various journals and books and he has also written a book entitled *Organizing Doubt*, which was published in 2007.

Dr. Matthijs Moorkamp is assistant professor of Organizational Design and Development at the Nijmegen School of Management of the Radboud University. His research interests include the relationship between organizational design, safety, security and crisis management, organizational networks and the development of organizational design theory. In his teaching, Matthijs is involved in several Bachelor and Master courses at the Nijmegen School of Management and the Radboud Management Academy.

Chapter 8
From Thinking Soldiers to Reflecting Officers—Facts and Reflections on Officers' Education

Tom Bijlsma

Contents

8.1 Introduction 116
8.2 What Is a Reflective Practitioner? 117
    8.2.1 Reflective Questions 117
    8.2.2 Myopic Learning 119
    8.2.3 The Role of Teachers 119
8.3 How to Educate Reflectivity/Reflectively? 120
    8.3.1 Two Concepts 120
    8.3.2 Experiential Learning Theory 120
    8.3.3 Problem-Based Learning 121
    8.3.4 Assessment of Reflectivity 122
8.4 What Are Military Applications of Reflectivity? 123
    8.4.1 Some Operational Perspectives 123
    8.4.2 Decision-Making 124
    8.4.3 Team Learning 124
    8.4.4 The Military Art 125
8.5 What Is the Actual Situation of Military Education? 126
8.6 Conclusion and Discussion 127
    8.6.1 Three Sub-conclusions 127
    8.6.2 Discussion 127
References 130

Abstract Reflectivity is an essential skill for every professional. According to Schön, reflectivity is the focal point for understanding and learning a craft. On top of this, for an operational serviceman/woman reflectivity is crucial to cope with the complex and ever-changing context he/she is working in. This prompts the question:

T. Bijlsma (✉)
Faculty of Military Sciences, Netherlands Defence Academy, PO Box 90002,
4800 PA Breda, The Netherlands
e-mail: T.Bijlsma.01@mindef.nl

© T.M.C. ASSER PRESS and the authors 2019
W. Klinkert et al. (eds.), *NL ARMS Netherlands Annual Review of Military Studies 2019*, NL ARMS, https://doi.org/10.1007/978-94-6265-315-3_8

what exactly is reflectivity? The importance from a military point of view is delineated at individual, team, and organizational level. Two concepts of reflective studying are introduced: the Experiential Learning Theory and Problem-Based Learning. With this frame, the actual situation on officers' education is explored. This leads to the conclusion that reflectivity should be given more attention in the curriculum and in the classroom. Concurrently, other competences for teachers are required and education, military training, and Corps processes need to be aligned, while the cadets need to adopt a more critical stance.

Keywords Reflective practitioner · officers · reflectivity · experiential learning · Problem-Based Learning · education

8.1 Introduction

Nowadays the playing field and context for a serviceman/woman is described by the acronym VUCA: Volatile, Uncertain, Complex, and Ambiguous. For more than fifteen years this perspective has been widely used in education at the U.S. Army War College.[1] The only way to cope with the operational threats and opportunities is, next to using his technical and soft skills, critical thinking, reflecting, and through this: learning.

Of course, these activities were already quite normal for each soldier during his postings and career. Operationally, for example, he is familiar with an After Action Review (AAR).[2] Hot and on the spot an action is evaluated and lessons are identified. In addition, for reflecting in military action a serviceman/woman applies Boyd's OODA-loop: Observe, Orientate, Decide, and Act.[3] The quality and frequency of constant repetition of this loop forms a crucial distinction between you and the enemy in a chaotic and dynamic (military) environment. The fastest soldier will outperform his opponent because he is in the lead and can proactively decide what the next step will be.

Still, in addition to this, over the past decades missions have become really VUCA: more (intensively) joint and combined, with NGO's and local parties, in diverse countries, cultures and religions, and with levelled Rules of Engagement. Therefore, because of all these developments critical thinking and reflecting have grown into essential, core competences. How far has educating these competences been walked in step with these developments?

As Schön states, "If professions are blamed for ineffectiveness and impropriety, their schools are blamed for failing to teach the rudiments of effective and ethical

---

[1] Stiehm 2010.
[2] Morrison and Meliza 1999.
[3] Osinga 2007.

practice."[4] He postulates that for studying and practicing a profession, from apprentice to master and beyond, the ability to reflect is essential. In addition, it is in their vocational and scientific education that students will professionally become acquainted with reflection. So, when referring to officers, the quality of the military academy and schools is a distinctive element for these practitioners, not only from Schön's perspective (reflectivity as the focal point for understanding and learning a craft) but also from the operational military context (reflectivity and learning as an essential element prerequisite for coping with VUCA).

The structure of this chapter is shaped around the following questions. First of all: What is a reflective practitioner? This question relates to reflective questions and the role of teachers. Secondly: How to educate reflectivity/reflectively? The answer will introduce two concepts of reflective studying, followed by possibilities for assessing them. Thirdly: What are military applications of reflectivity? The answer to this question is split into three levels: the individual, the unit, and the military organization. The next and final question, referring to reflectivity, is: What is the actual situation of military education? At the end three conclusions are drawn, followed by some discussion points.

The title of this chapter suggests a path from novice to master, from cadet or midshipman to experienced officer. That is indeed my intention. However, in essence, looking at the content and the corresponding processes, critical thinking and reflecting are two sides of the same coin.

8.2 What Is a Reflective Practitioner?

8.2.1 Reflective Questions

A reflective practitioner is a craftsman thinking about his job by asking questions. The reflective question itself is the core of reflectivity. The answers are secondary; even (the knowledge of) not finding an answer is helpful. But, where to start with questioning? In other words, is there a structure to follow while reflecting on your action or an event?

First of all, reflective questions can be arranged according to the time line.[5] These are consecutively: Reflection for action, – in action, and – on action.

Reflection for action helps one to participate in, plan, and be mentally prepared for possible oncoming actions, forethought. It can be a help to gain the initiative after an event or to speed up to the front side of the problem.

---

[4] Schön 1987, p. 8.
[5] Plack and Greenberg 2005.

Reflection in action is reflecting in the moment, on the spot. Reflection in action requires functioning on two levels at the same time. First of all, there is the ongoing task and occupational activities themselves, staying situationally aware, while at the same time questioning, observing, assessing, and, dependent on this process, adjusting. From a psychological point of view, it looks like one has a dissociative identity disorder, or split personality. From organizational perspective, it is called ambidexterity.

Reflection on action is about reflecting after each activity or event, sharpening and deepening the competencies by exploring the lessons learned.

Secondly, another aspect is content dependency. These questions start with What, How, and Why respectively. The content reflection is aimed at a better understanding. These are mostly What-questions. The process reflection aims at evaluating the chosen strategy and exploring other strategies. These are mostly How-questions. The most intense way of reflection focusses on assessing own assumptions, values, beliefs, heuristics, and biases. The corresponding questions are the most difficult to ask and answer. These are mostly Why-questions and are about double- and triple loop learning.[6]

In all the above-mentioned situations, the questioning can be done alone. The risk of blind spots and not probing deeply and widely enough is always present. The section below on myopic learning will address a big pitfall ensuing from this. Reflection with colleagues (from informal during a coffee break to a formal method like intervision), with a coach, a senior/mentor, or with friends or spouse, are just a few examples of the many possibilities. These forms can be mixed as written or verbal reflections. The verbal reflection with others will take the shape of a dialogue, not a debate. In this dialogue, the Socratic method is a form that is quite appropriate. A prerequisite for such reflective cooperation is a safe and open learning environment.

Apart from the variety in interlocutors, reflective moments may take place anytime and anywhere. In real operations, people will reflect in action on the spot in the heat of the moment, and on action at official evaluations or at informal discussions at the coffee corner or water cooler. This may depend on the structure and processes, and on the need and openness in the team. A limited British research project (based on grounded theory) on reflecting leaders proved most leaders reflect (on action) away from work and the office.[7] In an educational context, however, place and time for reflection are more scheduled or regulated. During a practicum for instance, a master or teacher will tell about his thoughts and choices while working, as an example of reflection in action. This brings us back to the start of educating the reflective practitioner and the purpose of this chapter. First, let us look into a cited danger.

---

[6] Argyris 2000; Tosey et al. 2012.

[7] Patterson 2015.

8.2.2 Myopic Learning

There is a possible obstacle in the long term. As mentioned, knowing what kind of questions to ask when reflecting is important. Questions about the basic perspective of problem solving will lead to single-loop learning.[8] Questioning the issue from a higher level will display a new array of solutions, and this double-loop learning, according to Argyris, is the most difficult form for professionals to apply. "Highly skilled professionals are frequently very good at single-loop learning. After all, they have spent much of their lives acquiring academic credentials, mastering one or a number of intellectual disciplines, and applying those disciplines to solve real-world problems. But ironically, this very fact helps explain why professionals are often so bad at double-loop learning. Put simply, because many professionals are usually successful at what they do, they rarely experience failure. Moreover, because they have rarely failed, they have never learned how to learn from failure. So whenever their single-loop learning strategies go wrong, they become defensive, screen out criticism, and put the "blame" on anyone and everyone but themselves. In short, their ability to learn shuts down precisely at the moment they need it the most."[9] This is a real danger for officers as each mission and rotation has its own context and VUCA is the norm.

8.2.3 The Role of Teachers

How do vocational students acquire this specific professional artistry, this occupational mastery? A safe learning environment for this is a practicum, a place to practice and learn a job. In line with this, most schools have to rigorously rethink their pedagogical assumptions and have to accommodate the reflective practicum as a key element of professional education.[10] The teachers will become coaches.

Apart from being coaches, teachers are walking examples of reflectivity as well. Professional artistry, like teaching, is a set of competences displayed in practice. It is often difficult to describe those competences, even by the professionals themselves. It is based on a lot of tacit knowledge. By observing and questioning the 'knowing in action', the implicit and tacit knowledge and experience can be made explicit. On the other hand, a practitioner can reflect on experience himself. He reflects on a particular situation after the event in order to learn from it and to inform future practice. So, start watching and questioning the masters, and through this learn to watch and question yourself when in action. As a baby, everybody has learned implicitly, or first of all, instinctively, by reflection to survive and become

---

[8] Argyris 2000.
[9] Ibid., p. 279.
[10] Schön 1987, p. 18.

an adapted member of the family and society. The essence of a reflective student is learning to use his reflectivity again, but now in a professional setting.

After this, the graduated and experienced professional/ex-student can make his organization a learning environment by coaching his team, i.e., helping others to learn. This forms a crucial element for team learning and a learning organization.

The competences of the teachers are crucial, but of course, this is related to a certain educational concept. Two concepts are elaborated on in the following section.

8.3 How to Educate Reflectivity/Reflectively?

8.3.1 Two Concepts

The basis of Schön's educational philosophy is reflection. Some universities and academies have already experience with this kind of education. However, even the 'conservative' ones have elements in their curriculum. This section will introduce two concepts of reflective studying: the Experiential Learning Theory and Problem-Based Learning. Seen from a distance they share a lot, but basically, they have a different vision regarding learning. The core distinction is the intrinsic motivation of the student; the results of the process are learner driven. The following subsections will illuminate both the roles of students and teachers (!) when educating reflectivity, and to educate reflectively. The last section is about possibilities to assess reflectivity.

8.3.2 Experiential Learning Theory

At the end of the last century, experiential learning was developed as an alternative for traditional education.[11] Scholars like Dewey, Lewin, and Kolb were in the forefront of this stream with their holistic ideas about human learning and developing.[12] This Experiential Learning Theory (ELT) can be described by some generally shared propositions. First of all, it is the learning process that is the core, not the outcomes. Therefore, the primary focus of the educational process, and of the institute employing ELT, must be engaging students in a process that best enhances their learning. In the words of Dewey more than a century ago, "Education must be conceived as a continuing reconstruction of experience: … the process and goal of education are one and the same thing."[13]

---

[11] Kolb and Kolb 2005.
[12] E.g. Kolb 1984.
[13] Dewey 1897, p. 79.

Another basic element of experiential learning is recurrent relearning; challenging the knowledge and beliefs of the student so they can be examined and tested in a new context, and integrated in a richer mind. This short description of the learning process leads us to the third element: arranging dispute, opposition, and dialectical modes of adaptation, in e.g. reflection and feeling. From this follows a fourth cornerstone: learning is a holistic process of adaptation to the world. It is not just the brains; it engages the total person, in all the layers of Bateson.[14]

Therefore, it is not the teacher-centered transmission of models and theories that is important in the learning process, but it is the learner-centered reflection whereby (social) knowledge is created. The teacher facilitates and coaches the student to complete the Kolb-circle: experiencing, reflecting, thinking, and acting, wherever he is starting, and at the diverse dimensions of ratio and emotion. Through this, reason and emotion are strongly paired in their influence on learning and memory. It is up to the institute and teachers to create an open and safe culture, free of fear and anxiety and full of positivity and attractions. Over an extended period of time, there is a combination of formative and summative assessments to check and enhance the learning process.

Of course, a dogmatic way of implementing ELT is not the solution; there are drawbacks or gaps.[15] However, it is the philosophy about learning and (personal) growth that makes the difference.

8.3.3 Problem-Based Learning

The second concept of learning reflectivity, or learning reflectively is called Problem-Based Learning (PBL). For a few decades now, Maastricht University has used PBL as its key method of instruction. In small groups students work together on real life problems or cases. This concept is more structured than ELT. Each student has to study and prepare group selected specific aspects and after some time, there are presentations and discussions about the findings. A tutor is present at the mandatory meetings to monitor the process and the content and ensures students alternate the roles. So, there is active student participation on diverse aspects, starting from analysing the case or problem. A critical stance to literature and a critical appraisal of each other is fostered. From the start skills like knowledge acquisition, collaboration, communication, and leadership are triggered and developed.

A Chinese meta-analysis about undergraduate medical courses concludes that PBL can increase course examination excellence rates.[16] PBL is more effective when applied to laboratory courses than to theory-based courses. Another study is

---

[14] Bateson 1979.
[15] E.g. Miettinen 2000.
[16] Zhang et al. 2015.

in line with these results.[17] PBL demonstrates a superior efficacy for longer-term knowledge retention and in the application of knowledge. This first effect is also borne out in another meta-analysis.[18] Students in PBL remembered more of the acquired knowledge, while, on the other hand, they gained slightly less knowledge. There is a robust positive effect of PBL on the skills of students.

Working with PBL (in an international context) is culturally dependant. It is good to keep in mind there are no uniform processes and outcomes when an institution wants to implement this method.[19]

Reviewing international studies for effects and differences between PBL and Lecture Based Learning (LBL), it is striking how many medical courses make use of PBL. Is that because a medical professional has to reflect more frequently, has to learn continuously, and has to see his patient more holistically than other professionals in their fields? In their research on the reflective practitioner in the medical field Plack & Greenberg take this line, "Reflection is particularly important in medicine, in which evidence-based practice and client-centred care require the physician to analyse best evidence while considering his or her values and assumptions vis-à-vis the values, beliefs, and goals of each patient. It enables trainees to recognize their own assumptions and how those assumptions might impact the therapeutic relationship and their clinical decisions. Reflection also helps practitioners develop a questioning attitude and the skills needed to continually update their knowledge and skills, which is essential in today's rapidly changing global health care environment."[20]

8.3.4 Assessment of Reflectivity

If a learning outcome of a course is to develop the capacity for reflective practice, assessment is necessary to assure the well-formulated level or norm. An (accredited) educational institute has to assess reflective learning like other outcomes of courses. However, because of the nature of reflecting there are two impediments to be overcome. First of all, a great deal of the outcome is subjective knowledge, which can only be recognized and assessed by the student himself. Neither a tutor nor a teacher can observe or hear all individual activities during PBL or Experiential Learning. Secondly, it is about reflections on experiences. Not all those experiences, and their successive reflections and learning, can be planned, they are emergent; and because of this, so are the learning outcomes.

---

[17] Yew and Goh 2016.
[18] Dochy et al. 2003.
[19] Frambach et al. 2012.
[20] Plack and Greenberg 2005, p. 1546.

Bourner tackled both challenges by comparing critical thinking with reflective thinking.[21] By asking the reflective questions, a student can show his ability to reflect. The Korthagen model is a structured example of this and is used in many countries.[22] This model is also known as the ALACT model, an acronym for the five phases: Action, Looking back on the action, Awareness of essential aspects, Creating alternative methods of action, and Trial.

Basically, an assessment of the reflective process and outcome can draw on two sources. First, a self-report, that is, the learner's own account, in the form of a reflective document. Secondly, an other-report, accounts by others of the learner's reflective activity, in the form of written excerpts of dialogue-with-others.

An example of the former (and mutatis mutandis of the second) is a 'Personal learning portfolio'. A student's instruction on the structure could be, "A personal learning portfolio is a public document (intended for assessment). This is a compilation of learning intentions, accounts of learning activities, learning outcomes, records of reflective dialogues. It includes evidence from a variety of sources including your private learning journal/diary/log, and, most important of all, a reflective document detailing your learning process. The personal learning portfolio, while confidential to you, is intended for assessment, and therefore you will need to consider what to include/exclude and adopt a style which is appropriate for others to read who may not have witnessed the event or process."[23] In line with the educational context of reflective learning a teacher can use a lot of formative tests and tools, leading to a summative test or portfolio.

8.4 What Are Military Applications of Reflectivity?

8.4.1 Some Operational Perspectives

After this general introduction on reflectivity, we arrive at the question: how and when is this reflectivity concept applicable to the military? Alternatively, more exactly and true, to what extent is this concept already (implicitly) applied? The introduction already mentioned AAR and the OODA-loop. For now, a snap shot will be taken at three operational levels: the officer (individual), the unit or team (learning), and military operations (an organizational concept).

---

[21] Bourner 2003.
[22] Korthagen and Vasalos 2005.
[23] Brockbank and McGill 2007, p. 103.

8.4.2 Decision-Making

Military decision-making is an essential part of the job because in a dynamic and chaotic environment it is sometimes about life and death. An operational decision making model for reflection in action is the Recognition Primed Decision (RPD) model.[24] The process of creating and keeping up situational awareness, which is to some extent incorporated in this RPD model, precedes taking a decision.[25]

During operations commanders use the military decision making process (MDMP) as the fundamental basis. The MDMP is a 'rational' and linear tool for solving problems and making decisions. Knowing people are not rational, apart from the blurred input of the process and the chaotic context the military commander faces, a lot of heuristics and biases are used to fill the process to come to the best solution. In that case, the process and outcome are rather more intuitive than analytic. In essence, there is nothing wrong with intuitive decision-making. Reflection in action can help the commander (and his staff) to be aware of the (implicit) assumptions, frames, mental models, heuristics, and biases used. Otherwise, reflection on action will hopefully do, but then the option for correcting that specific action has passed.

In this respect, Schön notes about reflection in action, "… a critical function, questioning the assumptional structure of knowing-in-action. We think critically about the thinking that got us into this fix or this opportunity; and we may, in the process, restructure strategies of action, understandings of phenomena, or ways of framing problems."[26] These reflections add real and lasting value to the primary task of a professional officer: taking tough decisions.[27]

8.4.3 Team Learning

When we look closer at the operational aspects of the military, it turns out that reflection, and with this, learning, is crucial. Engaged in military operations, an officer, in some cases, only has himself to fall back on. In those cases, he has no peers, or supporting units, to help him with 'reflecting/learning in action'. He has to know his strong and weak points related to reflecting and learning and as a professional practitioner, he has to work on them. And in severe cases stress, sleep deprivation, and fatigue will deplete reflection. Sometimes an officer is all on his own, but he may still be responsible for life and death in some far away corner of the world. Because of the dynamics and uncertainties the military has to cope with,

---

[24] Klein 1998.
[25] Endsley 1995.
[26] Schön 1987, p. 28.
[27] Williams 2010.

learning in the hot seat is important. In addition, there is no learning without reflection.

Yet, when working with his team on the planning process in training or during actual operations, an officer must understand the strengths and weaknesses of his vocational and decisional reflection knowledge and experience. Through this he can ask (himself) the right questions (e.g. double loop learning), and organize discussion (e.g. when falling short). By using his tools and techniques, and team members, he is prevented from conducting the latest mission or war by blindly obeying the standing rules and doctrines or relying too much on his experience. The process of reflection in- and – on action with (help of) his team is called team learning.[28] With teams being the building blocks of a (military) organisation, this team reflection and team learning is the next stage after Schön's reflective practitioner, the reflective team.

8.4.4 The Military Art

Schön studied and explored his concept especially within artistic professions, such as architecture, music, and psychoanalysis. These professions are difficult to grasp for they lack a textbook and roadmap when climbing to mastery. Every challenge or order is unique with its own constraints for, e.g., time, money, and expectations of the diverse stakeholders about outcome. Precisely in those situations of learning by doing, reflection is a useful tool for growing and professionalizing.

Planning and leading military operations have corresponding substantive and contextual similarities with those artistic professions, even verbally. The concept of operational art was added to U.S. Army doctrine in the mid-1980s. Operational Art is called "The employment of military forces to attain strategic and/or operational objectives through the design, organization, integration, and conduct of strategies, campaigns, major operations, and battles. Operational art translates the joint force commander's strategy into operational design, and, ultimately, tactical action, by integrating the key activities at all levels of war."[29] This concept was soon adopted by NATO and marked the recognition of creativity as an important competence for operational commanders.[30]

Military operational art incorporates a kind of artistic expression akin to the performing and design arts studied by Schön, so the recommendations for the system and conduct to educate and train these military practitioners might be alike.

The conclusion is that already long before the start of the VUCA-era officers had to be critical thinkers and reflective practitioners. Nowadays these competences are even more important for a military professional. Let us return to the focus of this

---

[28] Bijlsma 2009.
[29] Joint Chiefs of Staff 2001, p. 318.
[30] Naveh 1997.

chapter: how to educate reflectivity/reflectively? As was stated in the introduction, Schön argued that someone's own educational system determines to a large extent whether these professionals will be reflective.[31]

8.5 What Is the Actual Situation of Military Education?

As a matter of fact, also at the U.S. Army Command and General Staff College a reflectivity debate took place.[32] Additionally, other authors consider the reflective U.S. military practitioner as the core of the ever-developing professional body of knowledge.[33]

In our Dutch schools and institutions, the military now work with Competency Based Education and Training. Some benefits of this concept are that it is individualized, emphasizes outcomes (what to know and do), and allows a flexible route how to achieve the norms. Fundamentally, this is not contradictory to reflection in-action or on-action, it is one of the routes. However, especially at master-level, when reflective practice in practica is the main method of transferring tacit knowledge to explicit knowledge, the common competence-based concept falls short. Alternatively, transformational competencies can close this gap, as already at a more basic level the competence 'critical thinking' forms a small bridge to reflection itself.

All in all, for parts of the Netherlands Defence Academy, specifically for the military training at the Military Academy and the Naval Institute, and for the scientific curriculum the Faculty Military Sciences, Experiential Learning should be more than flipping the classroom or blended learning. Some other didactical activities are needed. But above this, a mind shift is required. First of all, from the student's side, so it is clear he is responsible for his own learning process and personal growth. The teachers equally have to adapt their relationship with the students and have to embrace or expand roles such as coach, tutor, instructor, and even philosopher. The end terms and learning goals do not have to change all at once, maybe later when opportunities emerge to align output and outcome (!) to the process.

When exploring Problem-Based Learning, it turned out this concept was favoured by medical education because "Reflection also helps practitioners develop a questioning attitude and the skills needed to continually update their knowledge and skills, which is essential in today's rapidly changing global health care

---

[31] Schön 1987, p. 8.
[32] Klingaman 2004; Paparone 2014.
[33] Paparone and Reed 2011.

environment."[34] It seems there are a lot of similarities between the medical and military worlds and their practitioners. Maybe it is worthwhile to explore the possibilities of PBL in military education.

8.6 Conclusion and Discussion

8.6.1 Three Sub-conclusions

Based on the previous sections we can draw some sub conclusions. First of all, Schön makes his point about the reflective practitioner, a professional who can learn and grow further by frequently reflecting in – and – on action. To facilitate this artistic process schools have to implement these learning mechanisms and adapt their curricula to the practice.

Secondly, it makes clear a reflective soldier is of added value; with all future developments it can even be said that reflectivity is a 'condition sine qua non'. A soldier, especially an officer, has to be critical of his own behavior and performance and embrace the attitude of a learning professional. By his reflection in- and – on action he can coach, teach, and inspire others as well, leading to team learning.

Thirdly, there is a lot of successful experience with reflectively learning and teaching reflectivity, and corresponding assessments as well. Maybe the concept of Experiential Learning Theory or Problem-Based Learning does not fit 100% in a military educational setting. Still, many elements can, maybe (partially), be transferred to and translated into military schools and academies (on selected courses).

8.6.2 Discussion

Bearing in mind these three 'theoretical' sub conclusions, we turn to the Dutch institute and daily practice of military officers' education. In this Discussion I will only point out some essential elements and conditions to successfully implement a form of reflection in officers' education. For a well-embedded, integral, and realistic plan of action, too many changes have to occur at the Netherlands Defence Academy. These I will address as well, but from a change management perspective we know a transformational change will take considerable time. In an aphoristic way, I will address the elements to professionalize reflectivity.

Practise what you preach

Apart from the educational process, cadets are subjected to a shaping process as well. This process is about influencing belief, persuasion, opinion, and even traits

---

[34] Plack and Greenberg 2005, p. 1546.

and qualities and developing them in a particular way. Ultimately, a military officer is different from a generic civilian manager. Especially in an operational setting, it is presumed the officer will show distinctive behaviour. A precondition for a congruent shaping process for a cadet is exemplary behaviour from all staff members, military and civilian, from the faculty and from the military academy or institute, from the first day on. So, when reflectivity is taken as a key element for an officer, from the first day the cadet and midshipman lives and works in his academy or institute, he can see, hear, smell, and sense reflectivity. And this goes far beyond the educational setting with a practicum à la Schön or some form of PBL!

Leading by example

An important aspect of establishing a reflective climate is organizational conditions. Ultimately, reflectivity leads to insight and learning and at macro-level the goals and targets of the organizational subunits will be attuned, synchronized. Will it then be possible to settle the everlasting fight for academic (faculty) and military (operational green and blue) time and events? This is not a wicked problem, but still very topical and (negatively) powerful because this challenge lies with the highest organisational level of the Netherlands Defence Academy and is visible almost daily for students and staff. Does the cadet or midshipman become a different person when he changes his beret (the classroom) for a helmet (on exercise) and vice versa? Not rationally, but in reality there are two separate worlds. Not a bright example and starting point for our people, officers and managers, to spread the word about the essence of a Thinking Soldier or endorse the growth towards a Reflective Officer.

Practise what you teach

Apart from the highest level, the decision to embrace reflectivity as one of the leading principles in education and shaping has consequences for everyone. The teacher, coach, instructor, and commander: all have to show exemplary behaviour. Related to their job, the teacher at the faculty as well as the instructor at the military academy or institute has to adopt and implement reflective learning methods.

There is an essential condition to implement this aphorism successfully at the faculty. The root cause of a crisis in professionalism is the prevailing epistemology of practice, according to Schön.[35] Educational institutes unroll their professional knowledge through efficient curricula and arrangements for research. The more academic research as output, the more scientific status; and the more professional knowledge is gathered, the better it is to be taught in classes to prepare the students for their oncoming tasks and challenges in society. The starting point for change is not exploiting more research-based knowledge (still important!) but exploring more artistry from the craftsman.

---

[35] Schön 1987.

Semper fidelis or Semper ludens?

The third pillar of officers' education has not been mentioned yet, but can play a role as well: the Corps of cadets and the Corps of midshipmen. In line with their mission they are oriented towards reflectivity. There is a playground or sandbox (in time, place, money, and other facilities) and every Corps association has its own advisor. Corps activities can enhance academic and military skills, such as project management, logistics, and leadership. A kind of PBL can accompany the planning, realisation and evaluation of these recurrent activities.

The motto of the Corps of cadets is Semper fidelis. Loyal to the rules and orders? This loyalty can be applied to the reflective shaping process and turn Fidelis into Ludens. This is related to the playground: playing to explore their competences; one big practicum with advisors as masters; learning by doing.

Think big, start small

If PBL is (still) a step too far, there are possibilities to introduce elements of learning, and teaching, reflectively. A student may be instructed to write a critical reflection on a studied book, a paper to read, or on certain didactical activities. A typical lead question to elaborate on with this method is: what aspects do I think are valuable for me as an officer (cadet), and why; and what elements are less usable, and why? When repeating this every class a growing document or portfolio will emerge.

Another possibility is stop teaching a fixed, teacher-led course. Give the students more tasks, preparation opportunities, and use class for plenary feedback and (reflective) discussion. Even with Leids level 200, it is manageable and study-able with coaching and a healthy learning climate.

Manage your own mirror

Speaking of coaching, there are many educated colleague-coaches in the Dutch military, who may be approached voluntarily. Maybe it is a bridge too far to assign a coach to each cadet, as he has already a diversity of people (his commander, other officers and NCO's from his company, instructors, faculty teachers, study mentor, advisor from the Corps) who will claim a coaching role when necessary. However, at some moments a coach could be useful for (young) officers, the reflective practitioners. At the U.S. Navy Submarine Command Course, for example, they use Executive Coaching by dedicated military psychologists.[36] This intensive reflective trajectory is not about vocational skills, but about leadership in all its aspects. A commander of a nuclear submarine is a valuable asset. There are many other cheaper and easily accessible opportunities for our military. Mindfulness, for example, is a form of reflectivity that can be applied everywhere and anytime. For some researchers a next and last phase of a reflective practitioner at master level is

---

[36] Nieuman 2017.

being mindful.[37] In this phase, the reflective practitioner is fully aware of his patterns of actions, thinking, feeling, and intentions, without distortion. He is focused, receiving all relevant input and is living/working in the moment.

References

Argyris C (2000) Teaching smart people how to learn. In: Israelit SB (ed) Strategic Learning in a Knowledge Economy. Routledge, pp 279–295.
Bateson G (1979) Mind and Nature: A necessary Unity. Dutton, New York.
Bijlsma T (2009) Teamleren bij de Nederlandse Krijgsmacht [Team learning in the Dutch Armed Forces]. Koninklijke De Swart, The Hague.
Bourner T (2003) Assessing reflective learning. Education + training 45(5):267–272.
Brockbank A, McGill I (2007) Facilitating reflective learning in higher education. McGraw-Hill Education.
Dewey J (1897) My pedagogic creed. The School Journal. LIV(3):77–80.
Dochy F, Segers M, Van den Bossche P, Gijbels D (2003) Effects of problem-based learning: A meta-analysis. Learning and Instruction 13(5):533–568.
Endsley M (1995) Toward a Theory of Situation Awareness in Dynamic Systems. The Journal of the Human Factors and Ergonomics Society 37(1):32–64.
Frambach JM, Driessen EW, Chan LC, van der Vleuten CP (2012) Rethinking the globalisation of problem-based learning: How culture challenges self-directed learning. Med Educ 46:738–747.
Johns C (ed) (2017) Becoming a reflective practitioner. John Wiley & Sons.
Joint Chiefs of Staff (2001) Joint Publication 1-02. Department of Defense Dictionary of Military and Associated Terms, Washington, DC.
Klein GA (1998) Sources of power: How people make decisions. MIT Press, Cambridge, MA.
Klingaman JJ (2004) Teaching the operational art using reflective practice. SAMS, U.S. Army Command and General Staff College, Fort Leavenworth, KS.
Kolb AY, Kolb DA (2005) Learning Styles and Learning Spaces: Enhancing Experiential Learning in Higher Education. Academy of Management Learning & Education 4(2):193–212.
Kolb DA (1984) Experiential learning: Experience as the source of learning and development. Prentice-Hall, NJ.
Korthagen F, Vasalos A (2005) Levels in reflection: Core reflection as a means to enhance professional growth. Teachers and Teaching 11(1):47–71.
Miettinen R (2000) The concept of experiential learning and John Dewey's theory of reflective thought and action. International Journal of Lifelong Education 19(1):54–72.
Morrison JE, Meliza LL (1999) Foundations of the after action review process (No. IDA/HQ-D2332). Institute for Defense Analyses, Alexandria, VA.
Naveh S (1997) In Pursuit of Military Excellence. Frank Cass, London.
Nieuman AH (2017) Memo; Reisverslag [travel report] USN Submarine Command Course 54. Ministry of Defence, Royal Netherlands Navy, Den Helder.
Osinga FP (2007) Science, Strategy and War; the strategic theory of John Boyd. Routledge.
Paparone CR (2014) Two Faces of Critical Thinking for the Reflective Military Practitioner. Military Review 94(6):104–110.
Paparone CR, Reed GE (2011) The Reflective Military Practitioner: How Military Professionals Think in Action. Military Review 67:66–76.

---

[37] Johns 2017.

Patterson E (2015) 'What are leaders' experiences of reflection?' What leaders and leadership developers need to know from the findings of an exploratory research study. Reflective Practice 16(5):636–651.
Plack MM, Greenberg L (2005) The reflective practitioner: Reaching for excellence in practice. Pediatrics 116(6):1546–1552.
Schön DA (1987) Educating the reflective practitioner. Jossey-Bass, San Francisco.
Stiehm JH (2010) U.S. Army War College: Military education in a democracy. Temple University Press.
Tosey P, Visser M, Saunders MN (2012) The origins and conceptualizations of 'triple-loop' learning: A critical review. Management Learning 43(3):291–307.
Williams BS (2010) Heuristics and biases in military decision making. U.S. Army Combined Arms Center Fort Leavenworth, KS.
Yew EHJ, Goh K (2016) Problem-Based Learning: An Overview of its Process and Impact on Learning. Health Professions Education 2(2):75–79.
Zhang Y, Zhou L, Liu X, Liu L, Wu Y, Zhao Z, Yi D, Yi D (2015) The Effectiveness of the Problem-Based Learning Teaching Model for Use in Introductory Chinese Undergraduate Medical Courses: A Systematic Review and Meta-Analysis. https://doi.org/10.1371/journal.pone.0120884.

LtCol (res) Dr. Tom Bijlsma is an assistant professor of Military Management Studies at the Faculty of Military Sciences of the Netherlands Defence Academy. After his four-year study at the Royal Military Academy he served as an army officer for ten years. Subsequently, after working for five years as a management trainer/management consultant in the commercial sector, he moved to teaching. His research focuses on learning processes and change management and his preference lies in studying and teaching this focus area from the human-factor perspective.

Chapter 9
Five Critical Success Factors for Coaching: A Perspective on Educating Reflective Practitioners

Ger van Doorn

Contents

9.1 Introduction	134
9.2 Five CSFs for Coaching in Relation to Adaptive and Reflective Capacities Within Organizations	135
9.2.1 CSF-1—Context: Environmental Awareness When Working and Learning	138
9.2.2 CSF-2—Yardstick: Goal-oriented Working and Learning	139
9.2.3 CSF-3—Ownership: Self-management in Working and Learning	139
9.2.4 CSF-4—Iceberg: Congruence Within One's Competence Household	140
9.2.5 CSF-5—Here & Now: Experiential Learning	142
9.3 Guiding Employees from the CSF Perspective	143
9.3.1 Context-oriented Guidance (CSF-1)	143
9.3.2 Goal-oriented Guidance (CSF-2)	144
9.3.3 Self-management-oriented Guidance (CSF-3)	144
9.3.4 Competence-oriented Guidance (CSF-4)	144
9.3.5 Experience-oriented Guidance (CSF-5)	145
9.4 Discussion	145
9.4.1 Implications	146
9.4.2 Brief Reflection Upon FMS-NLDA's Current Educational Practice	147
9.4.3 Limitations and Opportunities	148
References	149

The author wishes to express his gratitude to Professor Myriame Bollen, Professor Eric-Hans Kramer and Mrs. Tine Molendijk MSc for their comments on earlier versions of this chapter, GJD.

G. J. van Doorn (✉)
Faculty of Military Sciences, Netherlands Defence Academy, PO Box 90002, 4800 PA Breda, The Netherlands
e-mail: GJM.v.Doorn@mindef.nl

Abstract Due to ever faster and drastically changing operational contexts, organizations today have to be increasingly flexible. This requires staff to become adaptive, based on a mode of instantaneous 'learning while working', often referred to as *reflective practice*. Consequently, coaching – i.e. facilitating learning – is about to appear as 'the new leadership'. Van Doorn and Lingsma (2017) defined five so-called *critical success factors* (CSFs) *for coaching*, and used them for the *ex-ante* and *ex-post* evaluation of both the *process* (enabling learning) and its *product* (learning outcomes). This chapter examines how the theoretical CSF-perspective may offer a practical framework for organizational learning and—more detailed—for the education of reflective practitioners. This question will be addressed by answering two sub questions: (1) How do CSFs relate to reflective and adaptive capacities within organizations? (2) How can managers apply the CSFs to the benefit of their employees' learning? It is argued that, generally speaking, the five CSFs—the 'spectacles with five glasses'—offer a suitable perspective on learning and development within organizations, aiming for their adaptability, based on a well-founded reflective practice. Specific attention is paid to its fitness for the education of future military leaders.

Keywords Coaching · Critical Success Factor · Leadership · Educational Philosophy · Organizational Learning · Adaptability · Reflective Practitioner · Informal Learning · Workplace Learning

9.1 Introduction

As the (global) social environment of organizations is changing rapidly and radically,[1,2] their operational context is becoming less predictable. Today, managers and employees alike have to relate to their respective circumstances in the nimblest possible manner. This requires *adaptive ability*,[3] for which, in turn, they need a substantial capacity for 'learning while working', based on *reflective practice*,[4] preferably integrated within organizational learning.[5]

Until recently, leadership focused mainly, if not exclusively, on employee *performance*. Since roughly a decade however, a shift in emphasis can be seen to *learning capacities*, at *all* levels within organizations. As a result, coaching is gaining recognition as 'the new leadership',[6,7,8] defined by Van Doorn and

---

[1] Montuori 2000.
[2] Stacey 2007.
[3] Cundill et al. 2012.
[4] Schön 1983, 1987.
[5] Reynolds 2017.
[6] Bass and Avolio 1990.
[7] Harper 2012.
[8] Yukl 2013.

Lingsma (2017) as: 'the guidance of learning by individuals, groups and organizations, so as to increase their on the job effectiveness'.[9] To this end, the authors distinguish five *critical success factors* (CSFs), that serve to test both the process (facilitating learning) as well as its results (learning outcomes).[10] The authors view CSFs as crucial to organizational success.[11]

This chapter investigates how CSFs can provide a practical framework for organizational learning; more specifically, for finding out whether organizations, by means of integrated *reflective practices*, can learn to act adequately on change (*adaptivity*). The main question to be addressed is: How do the five CSFs – as identified by Van Doorn and Lingsma – offer a perspective on the education of reflective practitioners? Based on a literature search, this question will be elaborated on in two ways. First, how do CSFs relate to reflective and adaptive capacities within organizations? Second, how can managers apply the CSFs while guiding their people?

The discussion section revolves around the consequences of the CSF perspective for the design, structure and evaluation of educational programs for future (military) leaders.

9.2 Five CSFs for Coaching in Relation to Adaptive and Reflective Capacities Within Organizations

This section discusses the first question, i.e. how coaching – i.c. coaching leadership – relates to reflective and adaptive abilities within *learning organizations* (LO). Following Argyris and Schön (1978), the LO-concept attempts to clarify how reflective practice is part of it, adaptivity being the intended effect. According to Senge and Sterman (1992), and corroborated, amongst others, by O'Keeffe (2002), organizations have to develop continually to cope with environmental change. Senge furthermore suggests that organizations transform into communities to which their workers feel connected,[12] as this will increase motivation and improve performance. An LO is seen as an organization transforming itself, by facilitating ongoing learning. Senge distinguishes five strengths or 'disciplines', characterising LO-members: (1) personal mastery, (2) awareness of mental models, (3) a collective vision on the organization, (4) team learning, and (5) the 'umbrella discipline' connecting the other four: systems thinking.

Typically, LOs are aware of their own strengths and weaknesses, enabling them to remove obstacles blocking successful performance. Such obstacles are seen to

---

[9] Van Doorn and Lingsma 2017, p. 33.

[10] (1) – Environmental awareness, (2) – Goal orientation, (3) – Self management, (4) – Competence (5) – Experiential learning. Labels or metaphors used: *Context, Yardstick, Ownership, Iceberg* and *Here & Now*.

[11] Rockart 1979.

[12] Senge et al. 2008.

thwart preconditions for organizational learning. For instance, personal mastery does not result solely from formal education and training, but substantially leans on informal learning in the workplace.[13] Based on pro-activity, critical reflection and creativity,[14] informal learning relates to *experiential learning, self-directed learning, action learning* and *transformative learning*,[15] all especially useful strategies for educating adults.[16]

To foster informal learning in the workplace, a healthy learning culture, characterised by e.g., coaching and coaching leadership, is necessary. Adhering to traditional hierarchy and 'old values' in leadership styles can be obstacles to implement a culture in which learning abilities may flourish.[17]

The ability to act adequately upon external influences[18] renders LOs adaptive. Due to their personal mastery, employees learn faster and improve incessantly. Consequently, the pace in organizational change becomes more up-tempo, enabling LOs to keep up with abrupt environmental developments. However, to regard an LO as the sum total of all individual learning fails to take into account the need to *transfer* and *integrate* what has been learned into the organization as a whole,[19] necessitating *interaction* amongst individual learners.[20] Today, organizational capacities for learning are defined by the extent of vertical cooperation between individuals, teams and management, and their contributions must complement each other to be effective.[21] Järvinen and Poikela (2001) stress the meaning of simultaneous learning at all three levels, whilst Høyrup (2004), highlighting the importance of both individuals and group interaction, advocates integration of reflective practices within LOs.

Notably, the LO-concept appears to focus explicitly on strengthening the adaptive capacities of both organizations and their employees. Promoting the self-evident reflection on learning processes, it emphasises one's own responsibility for the relationship with the working environment, the purposefulness and congruency of one's actions, within the well-understood setting of currently relevant learning experiences. As such, the LO concept seems to be fully in line with Van Doorn and Lingsma's 2017 five CSFs, as explained below.

According to the authors, the five factors underpinning successful coaching comprise *environmental awareness, goal orientation, self-management, competence* and *experiential learning* (see Fig. 9.1). In times of rapid change, they consider it even more important when organizational members take their own

---

[13] Eraut 2004.
[14] Watkins and Marsick 1992.
[15] Conlon 2004.
[16] Merriam et al. 2007.
[17] Easterby-Smith et al. 2000.
[18] Pedler et al. 1997.
[19] McDougall and Beattie 1998.
[20] Fenwick 2008.
[21] Mooijman and Olthof 1999.

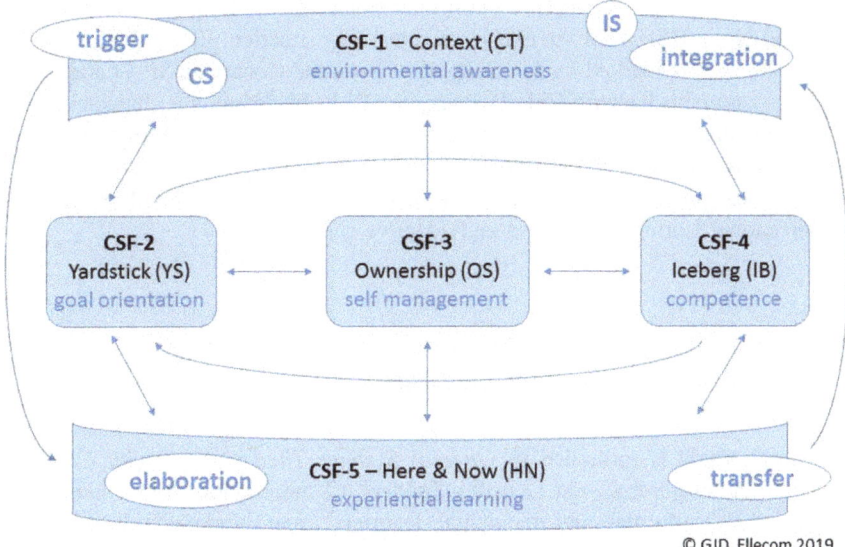

Fig. 9.1 The five Critical Success Factors of Coaching (CSFs) interconnected. *Source* Van Doorn (2019)

responsibility (CSF-3) to learn purposefully (CSF-2) about the actual situation they find themselves in (CSF-5), develop the skills required, based on a critical reflection upon their considerations and motives (CSF-4), and apply their newly acquired competences in novel situations, in a context-adaptive process (CSF-1).[22]

As Fig. 9.1 shows, the **Context** (KSF-1) serves both as coaching's point of departure as well as its focal point. It is triggered by a learning need within the current situation (CS), and the integration of the learning results eventually has to take place there as well, in the intended situation (IS). With the **Yardstick** (CSF-2) as a metaphor,[23] the learner indicates both his actual and desired position. The journey to bridge the gap between these two (CS ≠ IS) requires him to take full **Ownership** (CSF-3) of the process, deliberately centralised in this diagram. The **Iceberg** metaphor (CSF-4) depicts the multi-layered structure of his so-called 'competence household' of doing, thinking and feeling (see Sect. 9.3.4). He works on this within the **Here & Now** (CSF-5) of the learning environment, in order to then apply the learnings within the **Context** (CSF-1) of his work environment. Circle completed …

Now, generally speaking, what makes these factors 'critical' to coaching and leadership alike? A lack of goal orientation (Yardstick, CSF-2) and self-management

---

[22] Van Doorn and Lingsma 2017.

[23] Please note that (2) *Yardstick* and (4) *Iceberg* are **not** the CSFs themselves, only just the metaphors depicting their essence, GJD.

(Ownership, CSF-3) is likely to result in unnecessary loss of energy in the Here-and-Now (CSF-5) of the experiential learning situation. If, in addition, a coachee's situation is marked by *non-alignment* (*with* the Context, CSF-1) and *incongruence* (*within* his Iceberg, CSF-4), then, inevitably, his learning is characterised by a 'limited intelligent use of human and material resources'. Continuation of the process should then be seriously reconsidered.

In the next part of this section, the five CSFs will be elaborated with reference to organizational learning, reflective and adaptive capabilities.

9.2.1 CSF-1—Context: Environmental Awareness When Working and Learning

CSF-1 (Context) is grounded in *General Systems Theory*,[24,25] *Social Cognitive Theory*[26] and *Organizational Learning Theory*,[27,28] more specifically, *communities of practice*,[29] informal and incidental learning[30] and workplace learning.[31,32] Learning and development are characteristic to *adaptive systems*, i.e., organizations that respond adequately to both internal and external signs.[33,34] So-called *complex adaptive systems* constitute a specific variant, deriving their complexity from various interconnected elements, their adaptivity stemming from the ability to learn and change accordingly.[35] This is exactly why coaching—guiding the learning—must be system-oriented.[36]

Coaching effectiveness should not only be assessed by looking (linearly) at the process and its outcomes, since a coachee's working environment is likely to (circularly) impact his actual performance far more.[37] Relevant aspects include e.g., how coachees coordinate within their team or department or how they cooperate with customers, cooperating organizations, competitors etc. Organizational adaptivity requires *all* members to involve in focused self-reflection, as, often, in

---

[24] Von Bertalanffy 1950, 1972.
[25] Checkland 1985.
[26] Bandura 1986, 1988.
[27] Argyris 1999.
[28] Senge and Sterman 1992.
[29] Wenger 2000.
[30] Marsick and Watkins 2001.
[31] Billett 2004.
[32] Van Woerkom and Poell 2010.
[33] Baumann 2015.
[34] Espejo et al. 1996.
[35] Lansing 2003.
[36] Van Doorn and Lingsma 2017.
[37] MacKie 2007.

longer-term relationships, important others, such as one's team-leader, turn out to be part of the problem instead of the solution.[38]

9.2.2 CSF-2—Yardstick: Goal-oriented Working and Learning

In complex adaptive systems, learning capabilities relate directly to intentional, goal oriented behaviour. Whether organizations act effectively largely depends on *goal alignment* at various organizational levels.[39] Members are connected to the organization by means of their own yardstick, indicating where they currently stand and which direction they tend to take, preferably aligned with the organizational course, involving value driven activities.[40,41]

Furthermore, *setting goals* appears contextually sensitive.[42] Facilitating their achievement means taking into account reciprocal relationships between, on the one hand, someone's thoughts, feelings and behaviours (internally), and his environment[43] (externally) on the other. Mutual adjustment between these connections requires ongoing reflection on this.

A clear yardstick to measure effective behaviour is conditional to any chance of success in a coaching process. However, if the coachee is not bothered by the gap between CS and IS, his intrinsic motivation to remedy the situation will be low. Many of us may know what we want to get rid of (the CS regretted), but not yet where to go (an unclear IS). The responsibility to act on the ensuing delta is at the core of CSF-3, self-management.

9.2.3 CSF-3—Ownership: Self-management in Working and Learning

Self-management, an acknowledged pinnacle to organizational learning,[44] demands a supportive environment.[45] Bandura (2001) argues a self-evident relation between workplace environment (CSF-1), goal orientation (CSF-2) and ownership (CSF-3).

---

[38] Tobias 1996.
[39] Boyatzis 2006.
[40] Biesta 2010.
[41] Eccles and Wigfield 2002.
[42] Pintrich 2000.
[43] Grant et al. 2009.
[44] Margaryan et al. 2009.
[45] Butler 2002.

Three processes, impacting each other as well as the environment, are relevant:[46] (1) *monitoring* own behaviour and effects; (2) *assessing* own behaviour; and, (3) affective *self-regulation*. The reciprocal influence between one's own thinking and doing and a network of social influences[47] is referred to as the *interactionist perspective* of Bandura's Social Cognitive Theory.

Someone's ownership of his learning-while-working-process becomes manifest in his tendency to reflect on himself and his experiences, so as to better deal with the initial situation that urged him to seek guidance. Thus, the connection between ownership and context is made explicit, and *adaptivity* would require him to be attentive to his relationships with others within their shared workplace setting, using all available horizontal, vertical and diagonal interaction lines. However, if he only takes responsibility for his specialist field or domain, he may very well be a senior craftsman, but as a team member there is still a junior.

In complex LOs (CSF-1), clearly designated ownership is important for both individual and teamwork.[48] Self-regulated learning by individuals, on its own, however, does not suffice.[49] In addition, collective learning processes should be *integrated*[50] by informal learning in the workplace.[51,52] Ellinger (2004) refers to *self-directed learning* as an approach in which learners manage the planning, execution and evaluation of their own learning experiences.[53] They refrain from external attribution,[54,55] claiming accountability for their own actions, thoughts and motives, as represented by the next CSF.

9.2.4 CSF-4—Iceberg: Congruence Within One's Competence Household

Individual competences are closely related to the organization's *core competences*,[56] the former being grounded in personal characteristics, such as knowledge and motivation; the latter regarding the qualities organizations need to convince their customers and to distinguish themselves from other suppliers. Competence

---

[46] Schunk 2001.
[47] Bandura 1991.
[48] Siemieniuch and Sinclair 2002.
[49] Confessore and Kops 1998.
[50] Littlejohn et al. 2012.
[51] Boekaerts and Minnaert 1999.
[52] Marsick and Watkins 2015.
[53] Caffarella 2000.
[54] Lefcourt 2014.
[55] Weiner 1985.
[56] Rakickaite et al. 2011.

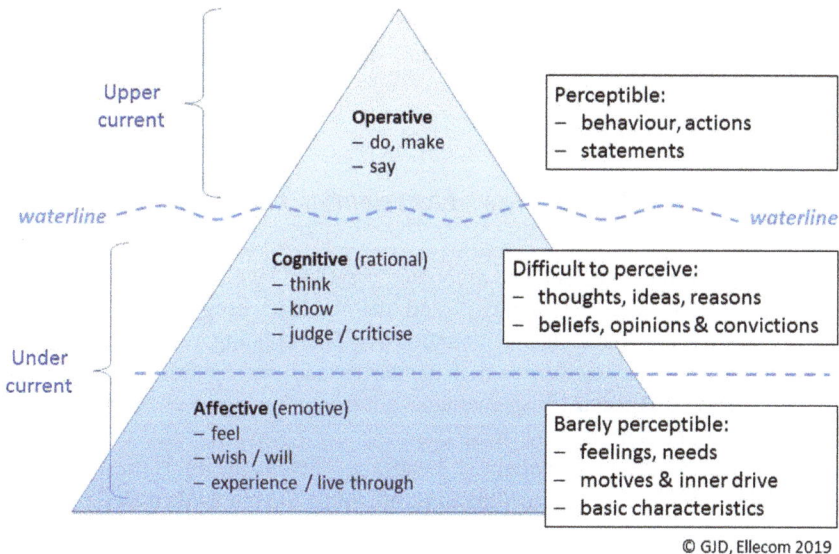

Fig. 9.2 The three-layered Iceberg: operative (upper current), cognitive and affective (under current). *Source* Van Doorn (2019)

development, therefore, is a prerequisite for competitive advantage.[57] Since the competence-based approach to organizational learning has become increasingly context-dependent and context-oriented, CSF-4 and CSF-1 nowadays are inextricably intertwined.[58,59] In other words, the fulfilment of the organizational mission, vision and strategy[60] requires a parallel development of individual and core competences.[61] McClelland (1973, 1998) used the Iceberg metaphor to explain the layered structure of competences[62] (see Fig. 9.2).

Continuous vertical alignment between the iceberg's layers is needed for individuals to act congruently, i.e. in line with their thoughts and feelings.[63] However visible their behaviour may be though, by no means so are their underlying thoughts and feelings, since they are to be found below the waterline. Experiential learning-by-doing (operatively) results from an interplay between the cognitive and

---

[57] Prahalad and Hamel 2006.
[58] Suikki et al. 2006.
[59] Boyatzis 2008.
[60] Wickramasinghe and de Zoyza 2009.
[61] Van Doorn 2017.
[62] Spencer and Spencer 1993.
[63] Sheldon and Kasser 1995.

the affective,[64] and coaching largely consists of the reflection on these two layers of a coachee's internal system, within the Here & Now of his momentary experience (CSF-5).

9.2.5 CSF-5—Here & Now: Experiential Learning

Experiential learning is considered embodied practice:[65] we relate to our social and natural habitat as physical beings,[66] and the need to keep or restore balance (*homeostasis*) forces us to learn continuously. The ongoing recalibration of this relation requires us to *transform* both ourselves and our environment during an infinitely adaptive process; a perpetuous confrontation between CSFs-1 and 4 within the current Here & Now (CSF-5).

Kolb's (1984, 2009) Experiential Learning Theory (ELT) is meaningful to LOs.[67] However, defining EL as 'learning by doing' seems inadequate.[68] It would be better to use 'learning by *reflection* on one's doing', for only the reflection confers meaning to the 'doing'.[69] Schön (1983, 1987) distinguishes between 'reflection *on* action' and 'reflection *in* action', by either looking back on one's actions afterwards, or observing them critically at the very same moment.

Reflection is often defined as a merely cognitive process. Instead, Van Woerkom and Poell (2010) explicitly advocate involving one's unconscious motives and emotions in the practice of critical reflection. Awareness of one's subjective experiences matters for learning fundamentally, by simultaneously paying attention to doing, thinking *and* feeling in the here and now.[70] This comprehensive view regarding the concept of competences—operative, cognitive *and* affective[71]—is in line with the internal and external systems approach to (organizational) learning.

Feedback is most convincing if directly and recognisably connected to the same experience, shared by coach and coachee. This enables the former to instantaneously link his interventions to the latter's concrete and observable behaviour,[72] by first trying to understand it within the momentous here and now.[73] Linking this actual learning situation to the 'there and then' work situation (CSF-1) bestows coaching its immediate relevance and accuracy.

---

[64] Pos et al. 2008.
[65] Kupers 2008.
[66] Merleau-Ponty 1962.
[67] Vince 1998.
[68] Farrell 2012.
[69] Van Doorn and Lingsma 2017.
[70] Jordan et al. 2009.
[71] Van Doorn and Lingsma 2017.
[72] Leising and Bleidorn 2011.
[73] Lievens et al. 2018.

This section has addressed the first question, as to how CSFs relate to reflective and adaptive capabilities within organizations. They appear fit-for-use, as CSF-1 (Context) offers a framework for goal-oriented, self-managed competence development (CSFs 2, 3 and 4), whereas reflection-upon-experience within the Here & Now (CSF-5) underpins actions with insights, thereby giving organizational adaptivity a firmer basis.

Next, in Sect. 9.3 an answer is sought to the second question, about how leaders can apply CSFs while guiding their employees during their reflective learning processes.

9.3 Guiding Employees from the CSF Perspective

Managers can use the five CSFs to facilitate their employees' reflection, both *on* and *in* action, thus increasing organizational effectiveness.[74] Altogether the CSFs offer the 'spectacles with five glasses', thus enabling learners and their facilitators to focus precisely on learning processes—including their content—so as to explore and fully comprehend them. For each CSF, this section will elaborate on its anticipated contribution to this endeavour.

9.3.1 Context-oriented Guidance (CSF-1)

CSF-1 refers to the employee's awareness of the environment, which exerts a big influence on his workplace behaviour.[75] Obviously, his manager must be attentive to this too, if only just to facilitate the former's coping. Moreover, to fulfil this complex task coherently, he has to coach *all* his team members.[76] He deliberately brings to the foreground the unpredictability of the context, to subsequently invite them to make it manageable, always in close cooperation with one another.

Contextually geared interventions start by the manager exploring the environment, preferably together with his employees,[77] comprising task and role diversity, organizational positions held by key players etc.[78] To make people navigate more skilfully the complexity of social network relations, information flows may be visibly mapped out using sociograms[79] or interactiograms.[80]

---

[74] From now on in this chapter we will no longer speak about 'coach and coachee', as in the previous sections, but about 'manager and employee', GJD.
[75] Peltier 2011.
[76] Feldman and Lankau 2005.
[77] Hawe et al. 2009.
[78] Foster-Fishman et al. 2007.
[79] Huang et al. 2007.
[80] Fürstenberg 2013.

9.3.2 Goal-oriented Guidance (CSF-2)

CSF-2 refers to the employee's level of goal orientation. Goals can been seen as cognitive representations of desired outcomes.[81] Performance improves when managers set them clearly and concretely, as is generally recognised.[82] Bandura (1986) argues that *goal setting* (CSF-2) and *self-regulation* (CSF-3) are inextricably linked. Other authors also find relations between self-regulation and learning (Green et al. 2006) whereas Gregory et al. (2011) find that effectiveness increases by active *goal setting* and *seeking feedback*, thus relating to CSFs 1, 2 and 3.

9.3.3 Self-management-oriented Guidance (CSF-3)

CSF-3, ownership, refers to the employee's basic attitude. Does he regard himself as the designer of his own learning, or as a victim of the situation? Characteristically, *learner autonomy* entails the shift of emphasis within the didactic process 'from teaching to learning' and, consequently, modern educational systems focus on *student-centred learning* rather than on teaching staff.

Employees can be guided in two ways, either by control or by supporting their autonomy.[83] The latter way would fit in with workers taking responsibility for planning, executing and evaluating their own learning activities.[84] Often, ownership begins by reflection on the extent to which somebody already engages in self-management.

9.3.4 Competence-oriented Guidance (CSF-4)

CSF-4 concerns the employee's competence at the levels of doing, thinking and feeling, plus the degree of congruence between these three. Again, the approach is learner-centred,[85] based on self-management (CSF-3) with the manager as *facilitator*, well aware of the taxonomy of didactic goals.[86]

Romiszowski's (1981, 2016) taxonomy, at a behavioural level, distinguishes *reproductive and productive skills*. The former are based on procedures, protocols and instructions, and can be learned by repetition. These skills are suited to deal with standardised situations, relying on routine actions, not requiring any creativity.

---

[81] Dickinson and Balleine 2012.
[82] Boekaerts et al. 2012.
[83] Reeve 2009.
[84] Sierens et al. 2009.
[85] Frank et al. 2010.
[86] Van Doorn and Lingsma 2017.

The latter, on the other hand, cannot be learned by practicing routines, because these simply never came about. They *per se* have to be dealt with by tackling unforeseen problems in not-standardised situations. Learners will have to approach a reality unknown to them creatively, choosing from equally unknown alternate actions, while often being pressed for time. Only agility of mind and swiftness of action—improvising ability—may lead to the desired adaptivity.

9.3.5 Experience-oriented Guidance (CSF-5)

CSF-5 is geared towards experiential learning, and not necessarily defined by the manager being around.[87] This approach is also learner-centred, allowing the employee to make his own discoveries from direct experience.[88] In doing so, ownership is challenged (CSF-3). Managers, facilitating their employee's process of reflection, can give support by granting space to develop adequate self-management skills,[89] e.g., by offering coaching.[90] Questioning is an important technique,[91] especially, when followed up by putting the answers to the test. By remaining non-judgemental, managers can help their employees to develop into self-regulating problem solvers.[92]

It appears, managers have ample opportunities to apply the CSFs while guiding their people during the reflection upon their own performance, looking through 'the spectacles with five glasses'. Learning effects are dependent on techniques used to enable reflection, such as *problem-based learning*,[93] *problem solving*, *critical questioning*, as well as to have learners themselves voice and synthesise their own learning outcomes. To support reflection, Gray (2007) suggests *storytelling*, conversation and dialogue, *critical incident analysis* and the use of reflective metaphors.

9.4 Discussion

The five CSFs for coaching can serve as tools to operationalise reflective practice within organizations in order to increase their adaptivity. Moreover, as coaching offers a basic didactic philosophy for training professionals as reflective practitioners, the five CSFs are of value for educational purposes. This section generally

---

[87] Rogers et al. 2013.
[88] Moon 2004.
[89] Heron 1999.
[90] Brockbank 2006.
[91] Wood Daudelin 1997.
[92] Barnett 1995.
[93] Löbler 2006.

outlines some possible consequences for the training of future managers, soon to be the new guides of their employees' learning. More specifically, brief attention is paid to the design, structure and evaluation of the educational program at the Faculty of Military Sciences (FMS-NLDA). A closer look is given to the way in which the reflective practitioner may already have taken shape as an educational objective. In addition, a quick scan is also carried out to see whether the (theoretical) CSF perspective has already found its way to the (practical) implementation of education, possibly even as part of the didactic concept.

9.4.1 Implications

As discussed in Sect. 9.3, managers may apply CSFs to guide their employees' learning, experientially and informally. To do so, they themselves need to be educated as *reflective practitioners* to remain adaptive, both individually and as part of a learning collective.[94] One wonders how this would translate to job- and competence profiles, and what requirements as to knowledge, skills and professional attitudes should be added to educational profiles to enable *continuous improvement*[95] for all organizational members.

In general terms, professional education should aim at: (1) promoting *mastery* at all organizational levels, during informal learning processes in the workplace; (2) promoting *learning conditions* for informal learning to take place. e.g., coaching (others) and peer group learning;[96] (3) promoting *collective learning processes*,[97] focusing on *interaction* among individual learners and vertical cooperation between individuals, teams and management; (4) focusing on *levels of reflection*, within both the internal and external system; (5) focusing on *each CSF's essence*, remaining aware of their critical aspects.

Specifically, professional education can prepare future managers for CSF-related tasks:

– CSF-1—facilitate employees to deal more effectively with their *environment*, clarifying its complexities, and invite them to make these manageable, together with others;
– CSF-2—help employees to learn *purposefully* while working, giving them concrete directions;
– CSF-3—encourage employees' *ownership* in an autonomy-supporting way, starting with the reflection on their current degree of self-management;

---

[94] Ruijters 2016.
[95] Cohen-Vogel et al. 2015.
[96] Van Doorn and Lingsma 2013.
[97] Lee and Roth 2007.

- CSF-4—guide employees in *congruent-competent behaviour*, focusing on both reproductive (routinely) and productive (creative-improvising) skills;
- CSF-5—let people make their own discoveries based on *direct learning experiences*, facilitating reflection and self-direction.

To promote employees' goal and competence orientation, examine their basic attitude and stimulate their self-management, the leader-coach has various working models available.[98] Beattie (2006) puts forward a hierarchy of nine facilitating behaviours, of which the basic forms 'performing skillfully' and 'providing information' occur most often, closely resembling traditional leadership behaviour. More subtle and sophisticated ones though, such as 'challenging' and 'reinforcing desirable behaviour', require additional development, since they are not part of many manager's natural repertoire.[99]

Vocational education programs aiming to train future managers as supervisors of reflective practitioners, should show a certain degree of reflection themselves, regarding at least five aspects of their tasks and responsibilities: (1) actively invite to a self-evident, natural reflective practice in a psychologically safe learning environment; (2) promote the five CSFs and act accordingly and recognisably; (3) be permissive instead of directive; (4) be inviting instead of indoctrinating; (5) nurture autonomy rather than dominate.

9.4.2 Brief Reflection Upon FMS-NLDA's Current Educational Practice

When we now briefly examine how the FMS-NLDA is currently operating from the CSF perspective described above, the following can be noted. The vision and policy, mentioned in the Education Quality Manual (EQM[100]), aims to develop students into *thinking soldiers*, who are expected to operate effectively within unpredictable environments. They should be able to apply theoretical insights creatively to cope with problems in the field. Their attitude has to be critical, and they need to grasp the assignment's broader context.

The EQM's *Curriculum Structure* (Section 2) shows that FMS deliberately pursues the reflective practitioner concept. Additionally, it can be deduced from the *Educational Organization* (Section 3) that CSFs 1, 3 and 5 (*environmental awareness, self-management, experiential learning*) have been incorporated within the planned approach. To this end, teaching staff are expected to apply didactic principles of 'active learning' and associated methods, such as small group-working, dialogue, collaboration and peer feedback.

---

[98] See for instance: Van Doorn and Lingsma 2017, pp. 505–614.
[99] Beattie 2006.
[100] Faculty of Military Sciences (FMS) 2016.

Less favourably though, the EQM's *Evaluation* Section (5) appears to focus more on the *quantity* of FMS's output, thus seemingly refraining from its initially formulated goal 'to educate reflective practitioners', which is more of a *qualitative* nature. The same goes for the *Guidance and Mentoring* Section (6), solely aiming at 'getting students to study within the official timeframe.' So, due to the moulding of the *qualitative* objective (reflective practitioners) into numbers, plotted in time, the final test of the result mainly takes place in *quantitative* terms. Furthermore, it is not entirely clear how FMS brings about the self-reflective attitude and approach of teachers themselves, whereas precisely *that* should induce the desired reflective practice among students.

By and large, the specific objective of reflective practitioning—preferably students' new, lifelong habit—could benefit from a more consistent implementation; not only within the design phase of training programs (*ex-ante*), but—plausibly even more important—of the evaluation phase (*ex-post*) as well. A CSF-tailored articulation, *in qualitative terms* of *process and content*, may give further substance to the educational objective initially stated.

9.4.3 Limitations and Opportunities

Discussing organizational adaptivity, the reader might find this chapter only to contain 'yesterday's news'. After all, according to Hargrove (1995) and Wierdsma and Swieringa (2002), the above considerations do not go beyond Argyris' (1999) *single loop learning*, i.e. behaviour *improvement*. Its *innovation* requires *double loop* learning though, its ongoing *development* even *triple loop*.[101] Far from being a superficial affair, real—transformative—learning, takes place within the middle and bottom layers of McClelland's (1993) Iceberg (CSF-4).

Furthermore, mere adaptivity may be deemed conflicting with CSF-3: ownership. By simply adjusting to their environment, organizations can be estimated as reactive followers, rather than proactive designers of their own process.[102] This raises the question whether we would not better invest in developing anticipatory and innovative rather than adaptive capabilities. In Romiszowski's (1981) words: should not we transform from reproductive performers to productive creators of a new reality? Especially when research shows that learning and personal mastery thrive better in innovative organizations than in adaptive ones.[103]

Third, although adaptivity is connected to incidental learning in the workplace[104] and the leader-coach is supposed to give impetus to informal learning

---

[101] Wierdsma and Swieringa 2002.
[102] Covey 1989.
[103] Llorens-Montes et al. 2004.
[104] Eraut 2004.

particularly,[105] this does not mean that formal learning should be looked down on. According to Tynjälä (2008) informal and formal learning should amalgamate to develop new expertise for dealing with change, as almost all workplace situations entail elements of both variants.[106] Ellström (2011) adds that heed should be paid to the integration of individual and organizational competences. Nisbet, Lincoln and Dunn (2013) nonetheless note that informal and inter-professional learning still rarely takes place.

More recently even, Ruijters (2018) remarks that 'new leadership typologies, necessary in learning organizations, still remain limited.' According to this author, the direction to take would involve creating space for the whole of human beings, both leaders and employees. It is about 'knowing what is going on, working from values, establishing connections between people, across functions, within their own system and beyond.'[107]

A world to win, it seems …

References

Argyris C (1999) On organizational learning, 2nd edn. Blackwell, New York.
Argyris C, Schön DA (1978) Organizational learning: A theory of action approach. Addison-Wesley, Reading, MA.
Bandura A (1986) Social foundations of thought and action: a social cognitive theory. Prentice Hall, Englewood Cliffs, NJ.
Bandura A (1988) Organizational application of Social Cognitive Theory. Australian Journal of Management 13:275–302.
Bandura A (1991) Social cognitive theory of self-regulation. Organizational Behaviour and Human Decision Processes 50:248–287.
Bandura A (2001) Social cognitive theory: An agentic perspective. Annual Review of Psychology 52:1–26.
Barnett BG (1995) Developing reflection and expertise: Can mentors make the difference? Journal of Educational Administration 33:45–59.
Bass BM, Avolio BJ (1990) The implications of transactional and transformational leadership for individual, team, and organizational development. Research in Organizational Change and Development 4:231–272.
Baumann O (2015) Models of complex adaptive systems in strategy and organization research. Mind and Society 1–15. http://link.springer.com/article/10.1007/s11299-015-0168-x. Accessed 14 May 2015.
Beattie RS (2006) Line managers and workplace learning: Learning from the voluntary sector. Human Resource Development International 9:99–119.
Biesta GJ (2010) Why 'what works' still won't work: From evidence-based education to value-based education. Studies in Philosophy and Education 29:491–503.
Billett S (2004) Workplace participatory practices: Conceptualising workplaces as learning environments. Journal of Workplace Learning 16:312–324.

---

[105] Conlon 2004.
[106] Marsick 2009.
[107] Ruijters 2018, p. 162.

Boekaerts M, Minnaert A (1999) Self-regulation with respect to informal learning. International Journal of Educational Research 31:533–544.

Boekaerts M, Smit K, Busing F (2012) Salient goals direct and energise students' actions in the classroom. Applied Psychology 61:520–539.

Boyatzis RE (2006) An overview of intentional change from a complexity perspective. Journal of Management Development 25:607–623.

Boyatzis RE (2008) Competencies in the 21st Century. Journal of Management Development 27:5–12.

Brockbank A (2006) Facilitating reflective learning through mentoring and coaching. Kogan Page, London.

Butler D (2002) Qualitative approaches to investigating self-regulated learning: Contributions and challenges. Educational Psychologist 37:59–63.

Caffarella RS (2000) Goals of self-learning. In: Straka GA (ed) Conceptions of self-directed learning: Theoretical and conceptual considerations. Waxmann, Münster, pp 37–48.

Checkland P (1985) From optimizing to learning: A development of systems thinking for the 1990s. Journal of the Operational Research Society 36:757–767.

Cohen-Vogel L, Tichnor-Wagner A, Allen D, Harrison C, Kainz K, Socol AR, Wang Q (2015) Implementing educational innovations at scale: Transforming researchers into continuous improvement scientists. Educational Policy 29:257–277.

Confessore SJ, Kops WJ (1998) Self-directed learning and the learning organization: Examining the connection between the individual and the learning environment. Human Resource Development Quarterly 9:365–375.

Conlon TJ (2004) A review of informal learning literature, theory and implications for practice in developing global professional competence. Journal of European Industrial Training 28:283–295.

Covey SR (1989) The seven habits of highly successful people. Simon & Schuster, New York.

Cundill G, Cumming GS, Biggs D, Fabricius C (2012) Soft systems thinking and social learning for adaptive management. Conservation Biology 26:13–20.

Dickinson A, Balleine BW (2012) Causal cognition and goal-directed action. In: Heyes C, Humber L (eds) The evolution of cognition. MIT Press, Cambridge MA, pp 185–204.

Easterby-Smith M, Crossan M, Nicolini D (2000) Organizational learning: debates past, present and future. Journal of Management Studies 37:783–796.

Eccles JS, Wigfield A (2002) Motivational beliefs, values, and goals. In: Fiske ST, Schacter DL, Sahn-Waxler C (eds) Annual Review of Psychology. Annual Reviews, Palo Alto CA, pp 109–132.

Ellinger AD (2004) The concept of self-directed learning and its implications for human resource development. Advances in Developing Human Resources 6:158–177.

Ellström PE (2011) Informal learning at work: Conditions, processes and logics. In: Malloch M, Cairns L, Evans K, O'Connor BN (eds) The SAGE handbook of workplace learning. Sage, London, pp 105–119.

Eraut M (2004) Informal learning in the workplace. Studies in Continuing Education 26:247–273.

Espejo R, Schuhmann W, Schwaninger M, Bilello U (1996) Organizational transformation and learning: A cybernetic approach to management. Wiley & Sons, Chichester.

Faculty of Military Sciences (2016) Education Quality Manual. Netherlands Defence Academy (NLDA), Breda.

Farrell TS (2012) Reflecting on reflective practice: (re)visiting Dewey and Schön. TESOL Journal 3:7–16.

Feldman DC, Lankau MJ (2005) Executive coaching: A review and agenda for future research. Journal of Management 31:829–848.

Fenwick T (2008) Understanding relations of individual-collective learning in work: A review of research. Management Learning 39:227–243.

Foster-Fishman PG, Nowell B, Yang H (2007) Putting the system back into systems change: A framework for understanding and changing organizational and community systems. American Journal of Community Psychology 39:197–215.

Frank JR, Snell LS, Cate OT, Holmboe ES, Carraccio C, Swing SR, Harris KA (2010) Competency-based medical education: Theory to practice. Medical Teacher 32:638–645.

Fürstenberg F (2013) Grundfragen der Betriebssoziologie [Basic questions of business sociology]. Springer, Berlin/Heidelberg.

Grant AM, Curtayne L, Burton G (2009) Executive coaching enhances goal attainment, resilience and workplace well-being: A randomised controlled study. The Journal of Positive Psychology 4:396–407.

Gray DE (2007) Facilitating management learning: Developing critical reflection through reflective tools. Management Learning 38:495–517.

Green LS, Oades LG, Grant AM (2006) Cognitive-behavioral, solution-focused life coaching: Enhancing goal-striving, well-being, and hope. The Journal of Positive Psychology 1:142–149.

Gregory JB, Beck JW, Carr AE (2011) Goals, feedback, and self-regulation: Control theory as a natural framework for executive coaching. Consulting Psychology Journal: Practice and Research 63:26–38.

Hargrove R (1995) Masterful coaching: Inspire an 'impossible future' while producing extraordinary leaders and extraordinary results, 3rd edn. Wiley & Sons, San Francisco.

Harper S (2012) The leader coach: A model of multi-style leadership. Journal of Practical Consulting 4:22–31.

Hawe P, Shiell A, Riley T (2009) Theorising interventions as events in systems. American Journal of Community Psychology 43:267–276.

Heron J (1999) The complete facilitator's handbook. Kogan Page, London.

Høyrup S (2004) Reflection as a core process in organisational learning. Journal of Workplace Learning 16:442–454.

Huang W, Hong SH, Eades P (2007) Effects of sociogram drawing conventions and edge crossings in social network visualization. Journal of Graph Algorithms and Applications 11:397–429.

Järvinen A, Poikela E (2001) Modelling reflective and contextual learning at work. Journal of Workplace Learning 13:282–290.

Jordan S, Messner M, Becker A (2009) Reflection and mindfulness in organizations: Rationales and possibilities for integration. Management Learning 40:465–473.

Kupers W (2008) Embodied inter-learning: An integral phenomenology of learning in and by organizations. The Learning Organization 15:388–408.

Lansing JS (2003) Complex adaptive systems. Annual Review of Anthropology 32:183–204.

Lee YJ, Roth WM (2007) The individual-collective dialectic in the learning organization. The Learning Organization 14:92–107.

Lefcourt HM (2014) Locus of control: Current trends in theory and research, 2nd edn. Taylor & Francis, East Sussex.

Leising D, Bleidorn W (2011) Which are the basic meaning dimensions of observable interpersonal behaviour? Personality and Individual Differences 51:986–990.

Lievens F, Lang JWB, d Fruyt F, Corstjens J, van de Vijver M, Bledow R (2018) The predictive power of people's intra-individual variability across situations: Implementing whole trait theory in assessment. Journal of Applied Psychology 103:753–771.

Littlejohn A, Milligan C, Margaryan A (2012) Charting collective knowledge: Supporting self-regulated learning in the workplace. Journal of Workplace Learning 24:226–238.

Llorens-Montes FJ, Garcia-Morales VJ, Verdu-Jover AJ (2004) The influence on personal mastery, organisational learning and performance of the level of innovation: adaptive organisation versus innovator organisation. International Journal of Innovation and Learning 1:101–114.

Löbler H (2006) Learning entrepreneurship from a constructivist perspective. Technology Analysis & Strategic Management 18:19–38.

MacKie D (2007) Evaluating the effectiveness of executive coaching: Where are we now and where do we need to be? Australian Psychologist 42:310–318.

Margaryan A, Milligan C, Littlejohn A, Hendrix D, Graeb-Koenneker S (2009) Self-regulated learning in the workplace: Enhancing knowledge flow between novices and experts. Paper presented at the 4th International Conference on Organizational Learning, Knowledge and Capabilities (OLKC), Amsterdam.

Marsick VJ (2009) Toward a unifying framework to support informal learning theory, research and practice. Journal of Workplace Learning, 21(4), 265–275.

Marsick VJ, Watkins KE (2001) Informal and incidental learning. In: Merriam SB (ed) The new update on adult learning theory: New Directions for Adult and Continuing Education. Jossey-Bass, San Francisco, pp 25–34.

Marsick VJ, Watkins KE (2015) Informal and incidental learning in the workplace. Routledge, London.

McClelland D (1973) Testing for competence rather than for 'intelligence'. American Psychologist 28:1–14.

McClelland D (1998) Identifying competencies with behavioural-event interviews. Psychological Science 9:331–339.

McDougall M, Beattie RS (1998) The missing link? Understanding the relationship between individual and organisational learning. International Journal of Training and Development 2:288–299.

Merleau-Ponty M (1962) Phenomenology of perception. Routledge, London.

Merriam SB, Caffarella R, Baumgartner L (2007) Learning in adulthood: A comprehensive guide, 3rd edn. Wiley, New York.

Montuori LA (2000) Organizational longevity: Integrating systems thinking, learning and conceptual complexity. Journal of Organizational Change Management 13:61–73.

Mooijman E, Olthof S (1999) Van leren naar lerend vermogen [From learning to learning ability]. Opleiding en Ontwikkeling 12:37–41.

Moon J (2004) A handbook of reflective and experiential learning: Theory and practice. Routledge, London.

Nisbet G, Lincoln M, Dunn S (2013) Informal interprofessional learning: An untapped opportunity for learning and change within the workplace. Journal of Interprofessional Care 27:469–475.

O'Keeffe T (2002) Organizational Learning: a new perspective. Journal of European Industrial Training 26:130–141.

Pedler M, Burgogyne J, Boydell T (1997) The Learning Company: A strategy for sustainable development, 2nd edn. McGraw-Hill, London.

Peltier B (2011) The psychology of executive coaching: Theory and application, 2nd edn. Routledge, Hove, East Sussex.

Pintrich PR (2000) An achievement goal theory perspective on issues in motivation terminology, theory, and research. Contemporary Educational Psychology 25:92–104.

Pos AE, Greenberg L, Elliott R (2008) Experiential therapy. In: Lebow J (ed) Twenty-first century psychotherapies. Wiley, Hoboken, NJ, pp 80–122.

Prahalad CK, Hamel G (2006) The core competence of the corporation. Springer, Berlin/Heidelberg.

Rakickaite J, Juceviciene P, Vaitkiene R (2011) Structure of professional service firm's organizational competence. Social Sciences 73:51–61.

Reeve J (2009) Why teachers adopt a controlling motivating style toward students and how they can become more autonomy supportive. Educational Psychologist 44:159–175.

Reynolds M (2017) Organising reflection. Routledge, London.

Rockart JF (1979) Chief executives define their own data needs. Harvard Business Review 57:81–93.

Rogers CR, Lyon HC, Tausch R (2013) On becoming an effective teacher: Person-centred teaching, psychology, philosophy, and dialogues with Carl R Rogers and Harold Lyon. Routledge, London.

Romiszowski AJ (1981) A new look at instructional design. Part I. Learning: Restructuring one's concepts. British Journal of Educational Technology 12:19–48.

Romiszowski AJ (2016) Designing instructional systems: Decision making in course planning and curriculum design. Routledge, London.

Ruijters MCP (2016) Het is de toon die de muziek maakt: componeren van ontwikkelstrategieën [It's the tone making the music: composing development strategies]. Tijdschrift voor Management en Organisatie 70:79–93.

Ruijters MCP (2018) Leidinggeven aan leren en ontwikkelen. In: Ruijters MCP, Queeste naar goed werk; over krachtige professionals in een lerende organisatie [Quest for good work; about powerful professionals in a learning organization]. Vakmedianet, Deventer, pp 159–169.

Schön DA (1983) The Reflective Practitioner: How professionals think in action. Basic Books, New York.

Schön DA (1987) Educating the reflective practitioner. Jossey-Bass, San Francisco.

Schunk DH (2001) Social cognitive theory and self-regulated learning. In: Schunk DH, Zimmerman BJ (eds) Self-regulated learning and academic achievement: Theoretical perspectives, 2nd edn. Erlbaum Mahwah NJ, pp 125–151.

Senge PM, Smith B, Kruschwitz N, Laur J, Schley S (2008) The necessary revolution: How individuals and organizations are working together to create a sustainable world. Currency Doubleday, New York.

Senge PM, Sterman JD (1992) Systems thinking and organizational learning: Acting locally and thinking globally in the organization of the future. European Journal of Operational Research 59:137–150.

Sheldon KM, Kasser T (1995) Coherence and congruence: Two aspects of personality integration. Journal of Personality and Social Psychology 68:531–543.

Siemieniuch CE, Sinclair M (2002) On complexity, process ownership and organisational learning in manufacturing organisations, from an ergonomics perspective. Applied Ergonomics 33:449–462.

Sierens E, Vansteenkiste M, Goossens L, Soenens B, Dochy F (2009) The synergistic relationship of perceived autonomy support and structure in the prediction of self-regulated learning. British Journal of Educational Psychology 79:57–68.

Spencer LM, Spencer SM (eds) (1993) Competence at work: models for superior performance. Wiley & Sons, New York.

Stacey RD (2007) Strategic management and organisational dynamics: The challenge of complexity to ways of thinking about organisations, 5th edn. Pearson Education, Harlow.

Suikki R, Tromstedt R, Haapasalo, H (2006) Project management competence development framework in turbulent business environment. Technovation 26:723–738.

Tobias LL (1996) Coaching executives. Consulting Psychology Journal: Practice and Research 48:87–95.

Tynjälä P (2008) Perspectives into learning at the workplace. Educational Research Review 3:130–154.

Van Doorn GJ (2017) Organisatie coaching op basis van de vijf kritieke succesfactoren [Organizational coaching based on five critical success factors]. Tijdschrift voor Coaching [Magazine for Coaching] 13:81–91.

Van Doorn GJ, Lingsma MM (2013) Intervisiecoaching; kortdurende begeleiding van lerende groepen [Coaching peer consultation; short-term guidance of learning groups], 2nd edn. Boom, Amsterdam.

Van Doorn GJ, Lingsma MM (2017) De vijf kritieke succesfactoren voor coaching; kennis en kunde voor de competente coach [Five critical success factors of coaching; knowledge and skills for competent coaches]. Boom, Amsterdam.

Van Woerkom M, Poell RF (eds) (2010) Workplace learning: Concepts, measurement and application. Routledge, London.

Vince R (1998) Behind and beyond Kolb's learning cycle. Journal of Management Education 22:304–319.

Von Bertalanffy L (1950) An outline of general system theory. The British Journal for the Philosophy of Science 1:134–165.

Von Bertalanffy L (1972) The history and status of general systems theory. Academy of Management Journal 15:407–426.

Watkins KE, Marsick VJ (1992) Towards a theory of informal and incidental learning in organizations. International Journal of Lifelong Education 11:287–300.

Weiner B (1985) An attributional theory of achievement motivation and emotion. Psychological Review 92:548–573.

Wenger E (2000) Communities of practice and social learning systems. Organization 7:225–246.

Wickramasinghe V, de Zoyza N (2009) A comparative analysis of managerial competency needs across areas of functional specialization. Journal of Management Development 28:344–360.

Wierdsma AFM, Swieringa J (2002). Lerend organiseren; als meer van hetzelfde niet helpt [Learning while organising; when more of the same offers no relief], 2nd rev. edn. Noordhoff, Groningen.

Wood Daudelin M (1997) Learning from experience through reflection. Organizational Dynamics 24:36–48.

Yukl GA (2013) Leadership in organizations (8th edn). Prentice-Hall, Upper Saddle River, NY.

Lieutenant Colonel Ger van Doorn, MSc is an academic lecturer on Leadership, Ethics and HRM and a researcher at the Faculty of Military Sciences of the Netherlands Defence Academy, as well as a personal, executive and team coach on call for the Expertise Centre for Defence Management (ECLD). Together with Marijke Lingsma – a widely acknowledged pioneer of coaching in The Netherlands – he wrote *Intervisiecoaching; kortdurende begeleiding van lerende groepen* [Coaching peer consultation; short-term guidance of learning groups] (2013) and *De vijf kritieke succesfactoren voor coaching; kennis en kunde voor de competente coach* [Five critical success factors of coaching; knowledge and skills for competent coaches] (2017). His research focuses on coaching's ontological and epistemological foundations and the implications for its practitioners.

Chapter 10
Mindfulness in the Dutch Military – Train Your Brain

Anouk van Tilborg, Tom Bijlsma and Susanne Muis

Contents

10.1	Introduction	156
10.2	Theory	158
10.3	Hypotheses	159
	10.3.1 One, Mindfulness	159
	10.3.2 Two, Stress	160
	10.3.3 Three, Working Memory	161
	10.3.4 Four, A and B, Situational Awareness	162
	10.3.5 Five, Wellbeing	163
10.4	Methods	163
	10.4.1 Design	163
	10.4.2 Procedure	164
	10.4.3 Participants	164
	10.4.4 Mindfitness Training	165
	10.4.5 Measurements and Materials	165
	10.4.6 Analysis	168
10.5	Results	168
10.6	Discussion	173
	10.6.1 Practical Implications	175
References		176

A. van Tilborg (✉)
GenDx, Utrecht, The Netherlands
e-mail: anoukvantilborg@gmail.com

T. Bijlsma
Faculty of Military Sciences, Netherlands Defence Academy, PO Box 90002, 4800 PA Breda, The Netherlands
e-mail: T.Bijlsma.01@mindef.nl

S. Muis
University Utrecht, Utrecht, The Netherlands
e-mail: susannemuis@hotmail.com

© T.M.C. ASSER PRESS and the authors 2019
W. Klinkert et al. (eds.), *NL ARMS Netherlands Annual Review of Military Studies 2019*, NL ARMS, https://doi.org/10.1007/978-94-6265-315-3_10

Abstract Mindfulness training (MT) programs are, apart from curative MT programs (e.g., PTSD treatment), not yet widely offered in the military. However, military (wo)men, who are often exposed to extremely stressful situations, might benefit from the "preventive" effects of MT (e.g., stress-reduction, enhanced wellbeing, increased military resilience), and with this facilitating and deepening their reflectivity. In order to meet busy military schedules, the current research investigates the potential effects of an individual, low-dose, self-training mindfulness intervention (i.e., 10-day Mindfitness training) in a Dutch military sample (N = 173) that was subdivided into an intervention- and a waitlist-control group. By using a pre-/post-test design, the effects of our MT on mindfulness, stress, wellbeing, working memory capacity, and situational awareness were explored. Concluding from a multivariate analysis of covariance, the intervention had a negative effect on stress, and a positive effect on mindfulness, wellbeing and (self-rated) situational awareness. These results indicate the need to further explore the potential benefits of implementing individual (both extensive and low-dose) MT programs in the (Dutch) military domain.

Keywords Mindfulness · mindfitness · self-training · stress · wellbeing · working memory capacity · situational awareness

10.1 Introduction

Like in most crisis management organizations, in the military, being physically fit used to be intertwined with being a professional. However, nowadays, mental fitness is also acknowledged to be very important for a professional soldier's wellbeing and performance. For example, during the high-stress situations during deployment, military (wo)men must be high in military resilience (i.e., coping with and recovering from stress). This does not imply that they are insensitive to stress, but rather that they are more resistant to stress by "bouncing back".[1] Furthermore, not only the soldier's body, but also his/her mind must "stand at attention". In such a state of high environmental awareness, one can think more clearly, make more optimal decisions, and thereby one's actions are optimized.[2] One of the most important constructs in the military domain that is linked to decision- and performance optimization, is situational awareness (SA).[3] SA starts with one's perception of the (usually dynamic) direct environment. Thus, if military can be trained in achieving higher levels of attention and better (e.g., more open and a less biased) perception of the environment, this will likely increase their situational awareness, decision-making and consequently their military performance.

---

[1] Schok et al. 2010.
[2] Stanley and Jha 2009.
[3] E.g. Endsley 1988.

In other (large) organizations, there is already growing interest in implementing mindfulness training (MT). Not only is mindfulness implemented in well-known organizations such as Google, but also the U.S. Army is using MT in order to enhance workplace functioning.[4] Also, research on the outcomes of MT within the American police force and firefighters indicates that individuals in high-risk occupations benefit from MT.[5]

Still, even though MT enhances attention and reduces mind wandering, there is generally a substantial scepticism within the military domain regarding the topic of "mindfulness". This is unfortunate, given that research in the domains of psychology, neuroscience, and medicine indicates that MT results in positive outcomes concerning constructs such as attention, cognition, emotions, wellbeing, behaviour and physiology. Yet, when it comes to military-relevant outcomes, MT does not only have the potential to alter subsystems of attention,[6] but it can also bolster military resilience[7] in the sense that individuals get better at coping with stressful situations (i.e., enhanced military/stress resilience). Also, MT bolsters cognitive functioning (e.g., working memory capacity) and protects against its predeployment-related degradation,[8] which often occurs during a predeployment period. Moreover, given that there is a high risk of Post-Traumatic Stress Disorder (PTSD) in the military domain, it is also important to mention that mindfulness can successfully treat (and even reduce chances of developing) PTSD.[9] To conclude, engaging in MT exercises corresponds to lower general stress levels and higher levels of wellbeing and positive affect.[10] Thus, MT may yield promising results in terms of military wellbeing and performance before, during and after deployment. Therefore, it is important that the military is informed about the potential benefits of MT so that individuals or even complete units within the military domain might reconsider their opinion regarding mindfulness.

However, regardless of the evidence on the benefits of MT, not much is done when it comes to researching on MT in the Dutch military. Even though MT programs for Dutch military (wo)men are offered by *Vormingscentrum* Beukbergen and yoga teachers are educated within the Dutch military since the beginning of 2017, there are still some constraining factors that keep MT from being implemented within the Dutch military domain. The organization might be too masculine and task-focused to accept MT; many military might think that mindfulness is too "woolly". Besides this, a pilot study (Bijlsma et al. 2016, n.p.) on the effects of a MT with half the crew of a Dutch submarine was unsuccessful and this was mainly due to practical reasons. More specifically, the researchers learned that a 2-week

---

[4] Good et al. 2016, p. 115.
[5] Kaplan et al. 2017.
[6] Jha et al. 2007.
[7] E.g. Johnson et al. 2014.
[8] Jha et al. 2010.
[9] Stanley et al. 2011.
[10] E.g. Good et al. 2016.

MT, which required participants to engage in four plenary sessions is absolutely unpractical for an operational military unit.

Yet, research in a civilian population indicates that even brief, self-training in mindfulness is effective.[11] Hence, the current research replicated the self-training program with some changes for the military domain. As a result, our study contributes to the literature on mindfulness in that we explore a different occupational domain (i.e., the Dutch military) and focus on military related important outcomes. More specifically, we aim to investigate whether our 10-day, economic, mindfulness-based self-training program ('Mindfitness in the Military; Train your Brain') enhances mindfulness, wellbeing, working memory capacity and situational awareness, while decreasing stress in Dutch military (wo)men. Participants were administered to either the MT group or the waiting list-control group and completed a pre- and post-test survey. Only the MT group engaged in the training in-between both tests. The waiting list-control group was provided with the training after completing the post-test questionnaire.

10.2 Theory

Mindfulness originates from the Buddhist philosophy, wherein "clear-minded attention to and awareness of what is perceived in the present" is highlighted.[12] Nowadays, one of the most cited definitions of mindfulness is that of Kabat-Zinn, who defines mindfulness as "paying attention in a particular way, on purpose, in the present moment, and nonjudgmentally".[13] Still, an operational definition was lacking, therefore Bishop et al. made the effort to establish one.[14] They propose that mindfulness is the self-regulation of attention. Mindfulness is the act of bringing awareness to current experience (i.e., observing of and attending to the dynamic field of thoughts, feelings, and sensations) by regulating the focus of attention. Regulating attention requires attentional stability (i.e., sustaining attention on a current target with less mind wandering), attentional control (i.e., selecting appropriate targets from among a field of potential targets) along with task switching (i.e., flexibility of attention so that attentional focus can be brought back), and attentional efficiency (i.e., economical use and allocation of attentional resources).[15]

According to a four-stage model by Lutz et al., the practice of focused attention involves the development of at least four different faculties, including; (1) sustained attention to a target object, (2) a monitoring faculty (which is able to detect mind

---

[11] Hülsheger et al. 2013, 2015.
[12] Good et al. 2016, p. 116.
[13] Kabat-Zinn 1994, p. 4.
[14] Bishop et al. 2004.
[15] Good et al. 2016, p. 119.

wandering), (3) the ability to disengage from a distracting object (i.e., attention switching), and the (4) ability to redirect focus promptly to the chosen object (i.e., selective attention).[16] As focused attention training advances, one does not rely on the first faculty anymore due to the development of a well-trained monitoring faculty. Simply put, one does not need an explicit target object (e.g., breathing) anymore in order to cognize mind wandering. This implies that MT would increase focused attention and on-task (rather than off-task) thinking.

Furthermore, mindfulness is the opposite of "mindlessness", which is a state of behaving and thinking on "autopilot" without having meta-awareness (i.e., being aware of one's awareness) of one's attention. Thus, mindful individuals typically engage in experiential processing, whereas being mindless is associated with mere conceptual processing. In other words, mindful individuals have the capacity to witness events, thoughts and emotions as they are rather than interpreting them in ways that are biased by personal memories, learned associations, or future projections.[17] They are able to observe things as if for the first time (i.e., the "beginner's mind"), by taking a de-centred perspective.[18] From this perspective, mind wandering is detected more easily. Consequently, when mind wandering occurs, they can gently direct their attention back to the present moment.

In sum, mindfulness is not an act of suppressing (off-task) thoughts,[19] but can be seen as a metacognitive (i.e., cognition about one's cognition) skill that involves attentional awareness and allocation of attentional resources.

10.3 Hypotheses

10.3.1 One, Mindfulness

Since mindfulness is a skill that can be trained,[20] several MT programs exist. One of the most well-known MT programs is Jon Kabat-Zinn's Mindfulness-Based Stress Reduction (MBSR) program, which aims at treating a variety of psychological (and physiological) disorders and enhancing patients' quality of life.[21] However, nowadays a wide range of MT programs for the non-clinical domain are available as well.[22]

Research indicates that primarily via its effect on attention, MT positively affects human functioning. By improving attentional stability, attentional control, and

---

[16] Lutz et al. 2008.
[17] Good et al. 2016, p. 117.
[18] Safran and Segal 1990.
[19] Bishop et al. 2004.
[20] Bishop et al. 2004.
[21] Jha et al. 2007.
[22] E.g., Good et al. 2016.

attentional efficiency, consequently other domains of human functioning (e.g., cognitive, emotional, behavioural, physiological) are altered.[23] Both immediate (i.e., state mindfulness) and long-term (i.e., trait mindfulness) effects of MT on human functioning have been established. Even though long-term, consistent and extensive MT promotes lasting changes in cognition and wellbeing,[24] minimum doses of MT appear effective too. For example, it was found that only 15 min of training resulted in better decision-making.[25] Also, neuroelectric and neuroimaging studies have shown that both trait- and state-like changes in the brain occur as a consequence of meditation.[26] For instance, more neural efficiency is already achieved at 3 h of MT[27] and structural changes occur at 11 h of training.[28]

Given that we developed our own MT program (Mindfitness training), which we based on Hülsheger et al. 2013 low dose, 10-day self-training mindfulness intervention and the Mindfulness-based Mindfitness Training (MMFT or M-Fit),[29] it is important to implement a manipulation check. Therefore, our first hypothesis is that there will be a significant increase in self-reported mindfulness after engaging in the low-dose Mindfitness self-training.

H1: The 10-day Mindfitness training will have a positive effect on mindfulness.

10.3.2 Two, Stress

Secondly, we aimed to replicate the well-established and well-documented finding that MT reduces stress. According to Stanley and Jha, stress is "produced by real or imagined events that are perceived to threaten an individual's physical and mental wellbeing".[30] Furthermore, they conceptualize stress as a perceived internal response rather than something that is external to the individual. Stress is not necessarily bad. In fact, the right amount of stress can optimize one's decisions and performance. However, excessive and/or chronic stress have negative consequences on both the physiological and the psychological level. More specifically, being exposed to too much stress leads to poorer decisions, and difficulties with learning and processing new information. Given the need to protect military (wo)men from these negative consequences of (excessive/chronic) stress-exposure and the finding

---

[23] Good et al. 2016.
[24] Zeidan et al. 2010.
[25] Hafenbrack et al. 2013.
[26] E.g., Cahn and Polich 2006.
[27] Moore et al. 2012.
[28] Tang et al. 2010.
[29] Stanley and Jha 2009.
[30] Stanley and Jha 2009, p. 145.

that MT can be a means to reduce stress,[31] it is important to investigate the potentially beneficial effects of MT.

Prior research indicates that MT is negatively related to perceived stress levels, results in faster recovery to baseline levels,[32] alters the stress response (e.g., reduction in cortisol-levels) and the brain's structural properties (i.e., neuroplasticity). However, due to the setup of the current research, we rely on subjective measures of stress. Therefore, it is hypothesized that our MT will decrease perceived stress-levels.

H2: *The 10-day Mindfitness training will reduce perceived stress-levels.*

10.3.3 Three, Working Memory

Furthermore, stress relates to unfavourable outcomes such as the degradation of cognitive resources. One of the negatively affected cognitive resources is working memory capacity (WMC),[33] which is a component of the human memory that "acts as a short-term buffer for holding and processing information that links attention to higher-order cognition".[34] There is functional overlap between working memory and attention and attention is considered as the "gatekeeper" for working memory. Therefore, attention is not only important for encoding new information, but also for the maintenance of information by activating certain parts of memory (i.e., working memory), so that they become the focus of attention.[35] Those individuals that are high in WMC, have better attentional skills, higher fluid intelligence (i.e., the ability to use information instead of merely knowing facts), and perform better at abstract problem-solving tasks. On the contrary, low-WMC individuals have poorer academic achievement, experience more episodes of mind wandering, and are more likely to suffer from PTSD, anxiety disorders and substance abuse.[36] In sum, deterioration of cognitive resources increases the risk of cognitive failures and emotional disturbances, thereby decreasing military (operational) effectiveness and individual wellbeing. Thus, since excessive and/or chronic stress-exposure is inevitable for military, especially during deployment, it is important to protect their WMC from deterioration.

Several intervention studies suggest that MT increases both working memory capacity[37] and flexibility, which is partly mediated by the effect of MT on

---

[31] E.g., Grossman et al. 2004.

[32] Brown et al. 2012.

[33] E.g., Taverniers et al. 2011; Jha et al. 2010; Stanley and Jha 2009.

[34] Good et al. 2016, p. 199.

[35] Awh et al. 2006.

[36] Stanley and Jha 2009, p. 148.

[37] E.g., Roeser et al. 2013; Jha et al. 2010; Stanley and Jha 2009; Mrazek et al. 2013.

attention.[38] Thus, in order to provide greater cognitive resources to military personnel, thereby equipping them better for responding to the cognitive and emotional challenges during deployment, it is suggested that MT is implemented in military training.[39] In order to establish support for the latter statement, we aim to proof that MT increases soldiers' WMC.

H3: The 10-day Mindfitness training will improve working memory capacity.

10.3.4 Four, A and B, Situational Awareness

In turn, WMC is linked to several mental faculties that are essential for military effectiveness.[40] One of these faculties is situational awareness (SA), which is a construct that is defined in multiple ways. The best-established definition is explained through Endsley's three-level model. According to this model, SA exists out of (1) "the perceptions of the elements in the environment within a volume of time and space" (e.g., self, others, the wider environment), (2) "the comprehension of their meaning" (in the current situation), and (3) "the projection of their status in the near future".[41] Consequently, SA feeds forward into decision-making, then altering the state of the environment, which then feeds back to SA again. It is theorized that high SA in military (wo)men allows them to make more optimal (military) decisions, which leads to optimization of their actions in critical, complex, dynamic situations.[42]

Based on the assumption that state mindfulness widens the scope of attention, thereby allowing one to see more peripheral stimuli, it seems valid to hypothesize that MT will increase SA.

H4A: The 10-day Mindfitness training will increase situational awareness.

In fact, Jha et al. 2017 already found that "MT may promote greater SA in the range of complex, ambiguous, uncertain, and stressful environments in which service members find themselves – from battlefield combat, to peacekeeping operations, to humanitarian missions and disaster relief", but the authors did not zoom in on the role of working memory in increasing SA by means of MT.[43] Since WMC is important for SA[44] and WMC can be enhanced by means of MT, we hypothesize that the effect of MT on SA is partly mediated by WMC.

H4B: The 10-day Mindfitness training will increase situational awareness and this effect is partially mediated by working memory capacity.

---

[38] E.g., Good et al. 2016, p. 120; Jha et al. 2014, 2017.
[39] Jha et al. 2010.
[40] Stanley and Jha 2009.
[41] Endsley 1988, p. 792.
[42] Darwin and Melling 2011.
[43] Jha et al. 2017, p. 11.
[44] E.g., Gutzwiller and Clegg 2013.

10.3.5 Five, Wellbeing

To conclude, we aim at replicating the well-established finding that engaging in MT positively affects wellbeing. Prior research on the MT-wellbeing relationship incorporates outcomes such as enhanced vitality, positive affect, satisfaction with life,[45] adaptive coping in stressful situations,[46] and decreased depression.[47] More specifically, MT alters emotional valence/tone (i.e., the overall positivity or negativity of emotions)[48] in that it relates to experiencing less negative emotional valance/tone. In addition, MT shortens the emotional lifecycle,[49] which relates to quicker recovery from negative emotions.[50] An important issue for the military.

Furthermore, MT generally exist out of multiple components (e.g., didactic instruction, social support, mindfulness exercises) and it is not clear which of these components contributes most to enhancing individual wellbeing.[51] Yet, research suggests that mindfulness itself results in positive outcomes regarding wellbeing.[52] Given that our MT is a self-training and does not involve components such as group sessions that might confound the effect of MT on wellbeing via social support, the fifth hypothesis of the current research is that the Mindfitness training, which merely involves engaging in mindfulness exercises, contributes directly to increased subjective wellbeing.

H5: The 10-day Mindfitness training will increase subjective wellbeing.

10.4 Methods

10.4.1 Design

The current study can be considered as a mixed pre-test/post-test design given that all dependent variables (i.e., wellbeing, stress, working memory capacity, situational awareness, mindfulness) were measured at both t0 and t1, except for the Situational Judgement Test (SJT), which is one of the two measures for assessing SA, for it was only administered at t1. Therefore, scores on the SJT are treated as a between-group measure, whereas the other scores are both within-group/within-individual and between-group/between-individual measures.

---

[45] E.g., Brown and Ryan 2003.
[46] E.g., Weinstein et al. 2009.
[47] E.g., Christopher and Gilbert 2010; Brown and Ryan 2003.
[48] Eberth and Sedlmeier 2012.
[49] Davidson et al. 2000.
[50] Good et al. 2016.
[51] Bishop 2002.
[52] Weinstein et al. 2009.

10.4.2 Procedure

The study was approved by the University's Ethical Review Committee Psychology and Neuroscience (ERCPN) and informed consent was derived from each participant before taking part in the study. We were able to promote our research by paying visits and sending e-mails to military troops during two months. We randomly assigned participants to either the Mindfitness training- or waitlist-control group based on the order at which they signed up (via e-mail). Since several military units signed up as a group, we decided to take a stratified randomization approach in order to balance the distribution of the MT intervention- and the waitlist-control groups within these units. Also, this would allow for sub analysis (per military group). All participants were told that they could start (with the pre-test) whenever it suited them best during an (for most of them) oncoming six-week period. The major difference between the two conditions was that participants in the experimental group engaged in the mindfulness training directly after completing the pre-test (t0), whereas the waitlist-control group was provided with the mindfulness exercises after the post-test (t1). In doing so, we only assessed the effect of the MT on the dependent variables in the experimental condition and could compare this to the non-MT group (i.e., the waitlist-control group). More specifically, participants in the experimental condition were asked to complete an online survey at day 0 (t0) and at day 11 (t1). At day 0, they received the MT package so that they could engage in the training from day 1–11. On the other hand, participants in the waitlist-control condition were asked to complete the online survey at day 0 (t0) and at day 11 (t1). After having received the t1-survey these participants were able to download the MT package.

10.4.3 Participants

Initially, 649 individuals signed up for taking part in our study. However, we had to exclude civilians. Eventually, 374 individuals completed the first (t0) online questionnaire and 220 individuals also completed the second (t1) online questionnaire. Then, we had to exclude those individuals that completed the second (t1) questionnaire more than 14 days after the first (t0) questionnaire (N = 36) and those that (accidentally) indicated that their age was lower than their tenure (N = 5). Finally, we had to exclude 6 individuals from the experimental group, given that their self-reported MT practice time was equal to 0 days and 0 min. Consequently, the final sample comprised 173 participants (mean age 38.87, SD = 10.59).

The waitlist-control group contained 110 individuals (mean age 38.27, SD = 10.93). There were 91 men and 19 women in this group and their mean tenure was 17.62 years (SD = 11.32). Out of the 110, 46 participants were from the land forces, 17 from the air forces, 36 from the navy, and 11 from the military police. In terms of hierarchy, 22 participants were soldiers or corporals, 37 were non-commissioned officer/NCO, and there were 51 officers.

The experimental, or MT intervention group comprised 63 participants (mean age 39.92, SD 9.98) among which 52 men and 11 women. The mean tenure in the experimental group was 19.01 years (SD 10.15). Furthermore, 25 participants were from the land forces, 7 from the air forces, 25 from the navy, and 6 from the military police. In terms of hierarchy, there were 6 soldiers or corporals, 20 non-commissioned officers/NCOs, and 37 officers in the MT intervention group.

10.4.4 Mindfitness Training

We aimed at providing the military (wo)men a convenient MT program that both fits their busy military schedules and their mindset. Therefore, the MT program was mainly based on Hülsheger et al.'s 2013 10-day mindfulness intervention that, unlike MT programs such as Kabat-Zin's[53] well-established MBSR protocol, does neither require long, nor plenary sessions. We excluded one in this culture potential "soft" exercise (i.e., the "Love and Kindness Exercise") and imported two exercises from Jha et al.'s[54] Mindfulness-based Mind Fitness Training (MMFT). The Mindfitness Training eventually comprised a three-minute breathing space exercise, mindful activity exercise, mindful listening exercise, body scan, walking meditation exercise, and an object-focus exercise.

After having uploaded the pre- (the experimental group) or post-test (the waitlist-control group) questionnaires on the online platform Qualtrics, one could download the Mindfitness Training with some music files. The six exercises were executed 10-days in a row. Following the guidelines and the training schedule, participants would engage in MT exercises for approximately 5–15 min per day distributed over a morning- and an afternoon practice.

10.4.5 Measurements and Materials

The pre- (t0) and post-test (t1) questionnaires were created on the online research platform Qualtrics. The t0 online survey for both the experimental group and the waitlist-control group consisted out of demographic questions, the Mindful Attentional Awareness Scale (MAAS), Perceived Stress Scale (PSS), Personal Wellbeing Index for Adults (PWI-A), the Situational Awareness Rating Technique (SART), and a shortened OSPAN test. The t1 questionnaire for both the experimental group and the waitlist-control group consisted out of the MAAS, PSS,

---

[53] Kabat-Zinn 1990.
[54] Jha et al. 2010.

PWI-A, SART, a shortened OSPAN test, and a Situational Judgement Test (SJT). Yet, for the experimental group, there was also a question regarding their practice-time included in the t1 questionnaire.

Demographics. In order to explore potential between-group differences, we enquired about the participants' gender, age, military service, function, rank, tenure, and whether one was deployed or not. Also, we established participants' experience with mindfulness training, meditation, yoga, tai chi or other types of attention-/relaxation training in that it might influence their baseline level of mindfulness.

Mindfulness. The Mindful Attention Awareness Scale (MAAS) was used in order to establish the participant's trait mindfulness by measuring the absence of mindfulness (i.e., mindlessness). The MAAS exists out of 15 items (e.g., "I find myself doing things without paying attention"), each scored based on a 6-point Likert scale varying from "almost always" to "almost never". Higher scores indicate higher self-rated mindfulness. The original, English version of the MAAS[55] was translated into Dutch and validated by Schroevers et al.[56] It was concluded that the Dutch version of the MAAS is valid, reliable, and generic (i.e., it can be applied in a variety of domains). Therefore, we felt confident to use this translation of the scale for the current research. In our sample, Cronbach's alpha was 0.89 (N = 173) and the test-retest reliability was established at 0.79 (N = 172) over the 10–14 day period.

Stress. In order to establish general stress levels, the Perceived Stress Scale (PSS) was used.[57] This self-report measure of stress is used to determine the extent to which one has experienced his/her life as stressful during the past month (e.g., "In the last month, how often have you felt difficulties were piling up so high that you could not overcome them?"). The original PSS exists out of 14 items. Yet, the authors suggest to use the short version, existing out of 10 items, since it procures a good reliability as well.[58] Therefore, we decided to use the PSS-10 and found validated (e.g., Cronbach's alpha = 0.87; Albers 2011) Dutch versions (e.g., Vrije Universiteit Brussel, n.d.) of the scale. In addition, we planned to use a Dutch translation of the PSS-10. In the current sample, we found that Cronbach's alpha equals 0.89 and the test-retest reliability at 0.70 over the 10- to 14-day period (N = 173).

Situational Awareness. Two measurement methods were used to assess SA. At both t0 and t1, we included the Situational Awareness Rating Technique (SART)[59] and at t1 we added a self-made SJT. The SART is a widely used, post-trial, subjective rating technique that aims at establishing a quantitative assessment of SA and exists out of 10 items, which correspond to 10 dimensions (e.g. Instability of the situation, Complexity of the situation, and Information quantity). An

---

[55] Brown and Ryan 2003.
[56] Schroevers et al. 2008.
[57] Cohen and Williamson 1988.
[58] E.g., Cohen et al. 1994.
[59] Taylor 1990.

example-item is: "How many variables are changing within the situation? Are there many varying factors (high) or are there very few variables changing (low)?" The questions are scored on a 7-point Likert scale, ranging from "Low" to "High". Since we did not find a Dutch translation of the scale, we translated the questions ourselves and found that Cronbach's alpha in the current sample was 0.59 and the test-retest reliability comprised 0.39 over a 10–14 day period (N = 173).

In addition to the SART, a self-made Situational Judgement Test was administered (at t1) in order to establish a more objective measure than the SART. The purpose of the SJT was to establish the extent of awareness in a decision-making task. More specifically, we instructed the participants that they carefully had to look at a situation in the form of a newspaper article, which we based on an existing one,[60] for they would be asked to make decisions about the situation afterwards. We informed them that they had 4 min to study the article and that they could continue with answering the questions after 3 min if they wanted to. However, we were not interested in their answers on this first set of questions. Rather, we scored their answers on the second set of questions, which existed out of 12 questions and regarded (seemingly redundant) details from the text and pictures (e.g., "In which hand was the basketball player holding the ball?") instead of aspects that would be directly relevant in order to make a decision.

Working Memory Capacity. In order to establish each participant's WMC, we conducted an online WMC test. In line with Mrazek et al.,[61] we measured WMC by means of an Operation Span (OSPAN) task. The OSPAN is a complex span task, which implies that a simple span task (e.g., to remember and recall letters) is combined with an interleaved processing task (e.g., solving math problems).[62] We used a shortened version of the OSPAN test.[63]

Wellbeing. The Personal Wellbeing Index for Adults (PWI-A[64]) was used in order to measure perceived wellbeing. By means of this 8-item scale, satisfaction with 8 life domains (e.g. standard of living, personal health, and achieving in life) is established. The eighth item, which regards satisfaction with religion, can also be answered by choosing the "not applicable" option. In addition, it was asked how satisfied the participants were with life as a whole (i.e., "Thinking about your own life and personal circumstances, how satisfied are you with your life as a whole?"). Officially, this item is not part of the PWI-A, but is often added to measure overall life-satisfaction and to test for the construct validity of the scale.[65] In the current sample, Cronbach's alpha for the PWI-A-9 and the PWI-A-8 (the latter does not enquire about satisfaction with religion) were 0.84 and 0.89 respectively.

---

[60] AD 2016.
[61] Mrazek et al. 2013.
[62] Redick et al. 2012, p. 164.
[63] Conway et al. 2005.
[64] International Wellbeing Group 2013.
[65] E.g., Van Beuningen 2012; International Wellbeing Group 2013.

Furthermore, we found a test-retest reliability of 0.78 over the 10–14 day period (N = 173).

10.4.6 Analysis

We conducted a power analysis in G*Power (version 3.1) based on Virgili's[66] meta-analysis on the effectiveness of mindfulness interventions. Hence, the input for the analysis was a mean effect size of 0.68, 95% confidence interval (CI) [0.58, 0.78], resulting in a required sample size of at least 96 participants, with 48 participants in each of the two conditions.

The data were analysed with IBM SPSS Statistics version 24. To check whether the 10-day MT intervention was effective in increasing mindfulness (i.e., manipulation check) we conducted a MANOVA with Time (t0 and t1) and Condition (waitlist-control group and MT intervention group) as the independent variables, and MAAS-scores as the dependent variable. Also, we used a MANOVA to check for equivalence between groups based on the t0 demographic data. If we would find significant differences between the two groups, we would need to control for these variables (i.e., include them as covariates) in the MANCOVA on the t1 scores (i.e., MAAS, PWI-A, PSS, SART, SJT, and OSPAN scores) with t0 scores (i.e., MAAS, PWI-A, PSS, SART, and OSPAN scores) as covariates. The mediation hypothesis (H4B) was tested by conducting a regression analysis.

An alpha of 0.10 was used for all analyses, for we expected a specific direction of the effects (e.g., positive for mindfulness and negative for stress). To conclude, Cronbach's alphas as well as test-retest reliability measures were determined for the MAAS, PSS, PWI-A, and the SART in order to establish the psychometric properties (i.e., reliability) of these scales (see Sect. 10.4 above).

10.5 Results

After establishing the raw scores for all outcome variables (see Table 10.1), and Pearson Correlation scores (see Table 10.2) were calculated, we started with a manipulation check (H1) and found a statistically significant difference in scores on the MAAS as a function of Time and Condition (F1, 170 = 7.702, p < 0.006; Wilk's Lambda = 0.957). Therefore, the 10-day MT intervention is effective in increasing self-rated mindfulness (see Fig. 10.1).

In order to test Hypotheses 1, 2, 3, 4A, and 5, a multivariate analysis of covariance (MANCOVA; N = 171) was conducted, using pre-test measures as covariates. Concluding from a MANOVA, we did not need to include other

---

[66] Virgili 2015.

Table 10.1 Means and standard deviations of the main outcome variables for both groups at t0 and t1

	Waitlist-control group (N = 110)		Experimental group (N = 63)	
	M	SD	M	SD
MAAS scores (t0)	3.81	0.68	3.65	0.77
MAAS scores (t1)	3.81	0.72	3.84	0.69
PSS scores (t0)	2.21	0.66	2.21	0.63
PSS scores (t1)	2.16	0.67	2.03	0.56
PWI-A scores (t0)	7.25	1.22	7.44	0.75
PWI-A scores (t1)	8.2	1.72	7.66	0.91
OSPAN scores (t0)	14.22	6.93	14.53	6.51
OSPAN scores (t1)	16.35	6.74	15.91	6.4
SART scores (t0)	19.25	6.88	18.11	6.17
SART scores (t1)	19.88	6.16	21.16	5.37
SJT scores (t1)	8.33	1.75	8.16	1.41
Days between t0 and t1	11.81	1.41	11.83	1.36
Training time (in days) (t1)	x	x	6.87	2.42
Training time (in minutes) (t1)	x	x	103.57	67.26

Source van Tilborg et al. 2019

covariates (e.g., tenure, rank, age) in the MANCOVA, since the MT intervention group and the waitlist-control group did not significantly differ on the demographic variables that were established at t0. Results of the MANCOVA were (marginally) significant (Wilk's Lambda = 0.931, = F6, 159 = 1.970, p = 0.073). With pre-test differences controlled, univariate tests support a group effect for the effect of the 10-day Mindfitness training on mindfulness (F1, 0.945 = 0.945, p = 0.022) well-being (F1, 1.951 = 1.951, p = 0.057) and stress (F1, 0.059 = 0.059, p = 0.084). Thereby, hypotheses 1, 2 and 5 are supported (see Table 10.3 for the adjusted means). We found partial support for the effect of the intervention on situational awareness, for there was a significant group difference regarding SART scores (F1, 101.861 = 101.861, p = 0.052), but not for the SJT scores (F1, 1.519 = 1.519, p = 0.448). Therefore, hypotheses 4A is not fully supported. To conclude, the data failed to support hypothesis 3, meaning that there was no group difference regarding working memory capacity (F1, 12.781 = 12.781, p = 0.512).

To conclude, we tested whether the effect of 10-day Mindfitness training on SA is partially mediated by WMC (H4B). We did so by using the stepwise approach for the regression analysis. It was first tested for path C', then for path A, and then for path B (see Fig. 10.2). Only if all paths are statistically significant, there is a significant indirect effect of the 10-day MT on SA through WMC.[67] Since we found

---

[67] Kenny 2016.

Table 10.2 Intercorrelations between study variables

	1	2	3	4	5	6	7	8	9	10	11	12
1. Gender												
2. Age	−0.130											
3. Experience with meditation	0.119	0.073										
4. Experience with mindfulness	0.140	0.159^b	0.610^a									
5. Experience with yoga	0.237^a	0.111	0.403^a	0.299^a								
6. Experience with Tai Chi	0.053	0.066	0.310^a	0.332^a	0.325^a							
7. Experience (other)	−0.151	−0.097	0.289	0.403	0.497^b	0.402						
8. Tenure	−0.150^b	0.914^a	−0.025	0.110	0.073	0.013	−0.138					
9. Military department	−0.002	−0.282^a	−0.038	−0.090	−0.076	−0.024	0.000	−0.193^b				
10. Rank (low/medium/high)	0.095	0.437^a	0.108	0.162^b	0.114	0.125	−0.075	0.412^a	−0.163^b			
11. t1_t0 (in days)	0.050	−0.154^b	0.053	0.042	0.043	0.024	0.304	−0.151^b	−0.026	−0.106		
12. SART (t0)	−0.067	−0.034	0.045	−0.017	−0.053	0.021	0.219	−0.007	0.109	−0.087	−0.094	
13. SART (t1)	0.015	0.121	−0.037	−0.082	0.051	−0.085	−0.099	0.124	0.153^b	0.062	0.050	0.388^a
14. OSPAN score (t0)	0.079	−0.061	−0.028	−0.061	−0.039	0.002	−0.515^b	−0.069	0.074	0.053	0.068	0.198^a
15. OSPAN score (t1)	−0.048	−0.087	−0.026	−0.105	−0.015	−0.038	−0.313	−0.105	−0.004	0.111	−0.008	0.139
16. PWI-A (t0)	−0.055	−0.134	−0.078	−0.037	0.037	0.025	−0.101	−0.153^b	0.095	0.147	−0.098	0.302^a
17. PWI-A (t1)	−0.052	−0.074	0.034	−0.068	0.001	−0.027	−0.161	−0.099	0.031	0.176^b	−0.023	0.214^a
18. PASS (t0)	0.140	0.065	0.031	0.000	0.065	0.001	0.176	0.079	−0.054	−0.084	0.016	−0.368^a
19. PASS (t1)	0.113	−0.159^b	−0.004	0.016	0.058	−0.013	0.170	−0.108	0.071	−0.207^a	0.073	−0.289^a
20. MAAS (t0)	−0.044	0.134	0.002	0.035	−0.088	−0.020	−0.132	0.135	−0.030	0.096	−0.074	0.255^a
21. MAAS (t1)	−0.047	0.187^b	0.001	−0.007	0.006	0.022	−0.121	0.189^b	−0.082	0.155^b	−0.068	0.279^a
22. SJT score (t1)	−0.113	0.182^b	0.012	−0.013	−0.037	0.035	0.115	0.188^b	0.019	0.211^a	−0.006	−0.009
23. MT (days) (t1)	0.042	0.432^a	0.084	−0.025	0.192	0.133	0.122	0.353^a	−0.015	−0.001	−0.202	−0.277^b
24. MT (minutes) (t1)	0.144	0.346^a	0.205	0.129	0.279^b	0.152	−0.193	0.302^b	−0.093	0.184	−0.103	−0.246

(continued)

Table 10.2 (continued)

	13	14	15	16	17	18	19	20	21	22	23
1. Gender											
2. Age											
3. Experience with meditation											
4. Experience with mindfulness											
5. Experience with yoga											
6. Experience with Tai Chi											
7. Experience (other)											
8. Tenure											
9. Military department											
10. Rank (low/medium/high)											
11. t1_t0 (in days)											
12. SART (t0)											
13. SART (t1)	0.247[a]										
14. OSPAN score (t0)	0.121	0.573[a]									
15. OSPAN score (t1)	0.344[a]	0.158[b]	0.125								
16. PWI-A (t0)	0.329[a]	0.194[b]	0.218[a]								
17. PWI-A (t1)	−0.366[a]	−0.226[a]	−0.240[a]	0.780[a]							
18. PASS (t0)	−0.426[a]	−0.289[a]	−0.223[a]	−0.671[a]	−0.511[a]						
19. PASS (t1)	0.278[a]	0.120	0.092	−0.586[a]	−0.615[a]	0.703[a]					
20. MAAS (t0)	0.366[a]	0.148	0.122	0.314[a]	0.247[a]	−0.583[a]	−0.440[a]				
21. MAAS (t1)	0.122	0.062	0.061	0.355[a]	0.362[a]	−0.524[a]	−0.540[a]	0.792[a]			
22. SJT score (t1)	−0.021	−0.195	0.010	0.147	0.115	−0.083	−0.134	0.148	0.157[b]		
23. MT (days) (t1)	0.017	−0.193	0.106	−0.008	0.018	0.131	−0.062	−0.080	−0.025	0.068	
24. MT (minutes) (t1)				−0.097	−0.022	0.227	0.009	0.000	0.002	0.149	0.679[a]

Note The SJT score was only obtained at t1 for both the waitlist-control and the experimental condition. MT (days) and MT (minutes) refers to the self-reported pracitce-time of individuals in the experimental group at t1. [a]Correlation is significant at the 0.01 level (2-tailed), [b]Correlation is significant at the 0.05 level (2-tailed)
Source van Tilborg et al.

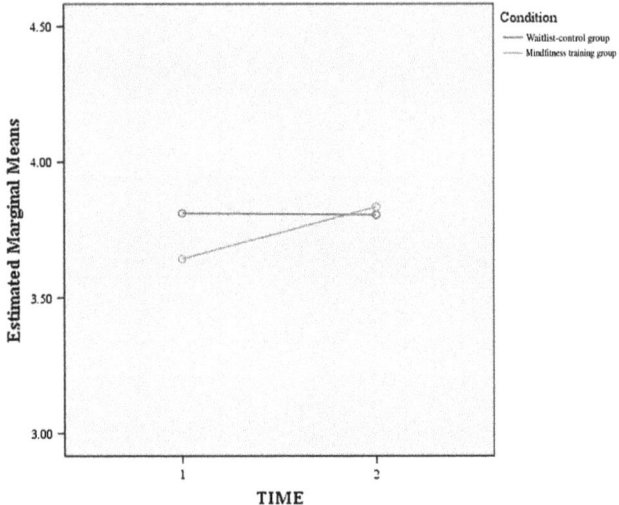

Fig. 10.1 Changes in MAAS scores over time as a function of condition. *Source* van Tilborg et al. 2019

Table 10.3 Adjusted means for mindfulness, stress, wellbeing, situational awareness, and working memory capacity for both the waitlist-control group and the MT intervention group

Dependent variable	Condition	Mean	Std. error
Stress (PSS score at t1)	0	2.157	0.042
	1	2.033	0.057
Wellbeing (PWI-A score at t1)	0	7.332	0.070
	1	7.559	0.094
Mindfulness (MAAS scores at t1)	0	3.763	0.041
	1	3.921	0.055
Working memory capacity (OSPAN scores at t1)	0	16.406	0.522
	1	15.825	0.705
Self-rated situational awareness (SART scores at t1)	0	19.783	0.495
	1	21.424	0.669
Objective situational awareness (SJT scores at t1)	0	8.335	0.156
	1	8.134	0.210

Note 0 = waitlist-control group and 1 = MT intervention group
Source van Tilborg et al. 2019

a significant relationship between scores on the MAAS, which is our indicator of mindfulness, and Situational Awareness scores (path C′ in Fig. 10.2; b = 0.336, p = 0.000), but not between scores on the MAAS and scores on the OSPAN test (path

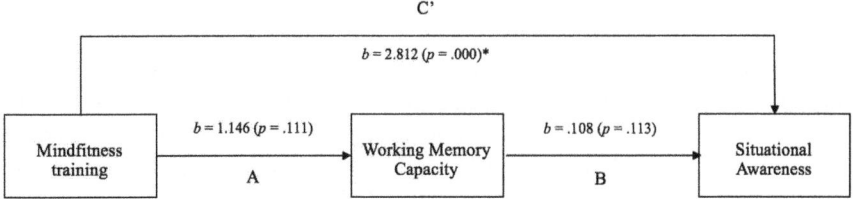

Fig. 10.2 Stepwise approach in the regression analysis (*Significant at the 0.01 level). *Source* van Tilborg et al. 2019

A; b = 0.122, p = 0.111), nor between WMC and SA (path B; b = 0.108, p = 0.111). As a result, we conclude that no mediation occurred and thus the data fail to support Hypothesis 4B.

10.6 Discussion

In the current study, we investigated the effect of a low-dose, 10-day, self-training mindfulness program on mindfulness, stress, wellbeing, working memory capacity, and (both objective and subjective) situational awareness, which we presented to our participants as a 10-day Mindfitness self-training. The data support the MT's effectiveness in terms of increasing mindfulness and wellbeing, while reducing stress. This means that we succeeded in replicating Hülsheger et al.'s[68] findings that even a low-dose, economic, self-training mindfulness intervention effectively enhances mindfulness, but this time in a different population. However, contrary to our expectations, the data failed to support the MT's effectiveness on working memory capacity and only partially support the training's effectiveness on situational awareness.

Potentially, the content and duration of the MT was not sufficient to enhance WMC and SA. Yet, Mrazek et al. found that even a 2-week MT program can be effective in improving WMC.[69] However, their MT program involved not only "homework" (self-training) exercises, but also didactic and group MT sessions. Perhaps, the information and the feedback that was provided in those sessions is more effective than mere self-training. This might hold true for SA as well. More specifically, the MMFT, which successfully enhanced SA in U.S. marines, also involves didactic components, group MT sessions, and daily half an hour exercises for homework. Thus, even though the content of our training was quite similar to the above-mentioned MT programs, the difference in duration (e.g., longer sessions)

---

[68] Hülsheger et al. 2015.
[69] Mrazek et al. 2013.

and other relevant components (e.g., didactic and/or group sessions, and longer daily exercises) might explain the difference in results.

In addition, we cannot be sure about the actual MT practice time of the participants that engaged in the current research. As can be seen in Table 10.1, the average, self-reported time that the participants spent on the Mindfitness exercises was 6.87 (SD = 2.42) days, or 103.57 (SD = 67.26) minutes. Given that we expected participants to devote approximately 5–15 min per day to the mindfulness exercises during the 10-day training, the reported training time (in minutes) meets with this expectation. However, the total number of days that the participants averagely spent on the training might be insufficient in order to benefit from the training.

In terms of the quality of the measurements that were used in the current research, we must mention that contrary to the validated, Dutch versions of the MAAS, PSS, PWI-A-8, and PWI-A-9 (α = 0.895, 0.896, 0.843, and 0.889 respectively), we did not find validated, Dutch versions for self-rate SA measures. Therefore, we translated the SART ourselves (from English to Dutch). Unfortunately, even though we found a significant test-retest reliability for the SART, Cronbach's alpha for our translation of this scale is 0.594, which indicates a poor internal consistency of this scale in the current sample. This might be due to that the situation that the participants took in mind related to a difficult decision when completing the SART questionnaire differed too much and could therefore not be compared (both between- and within individuals). Apart from the SART, we also must be critical regarding the SJT. Even though both the SART and the SJT were supposed to measure SA, we did not find a significant intercorrelation between scores on the SJT at t1 and scores on the SART at both t0 ($r = -0.009$, $p = 0.903$) and t1 ($r = 0.122$, $p = 0.112$) meaning that there is no significant convergent validity between the SART and SJT. Therefore, it is questionable whether the construct (SA) was measured.

Finally, even though the OSPAN test was constructed by following an existing, validated script[70] and we felt confident with taking Conway et al.'s[71] advice to use a shortened version, one could argue that a variety of measures should be used in order to measure WMC, since this reduces the chance of specific method-variance.[72]

Another challenge that we faced, is that the waitlist-control group was almost twice the size (N = 110) of the MT group (N = 63) due to exclusion and experimental mortality. Even though we conclude from the Power analysis that our sample size is sufficient, this does not necessarily compensate for the chance that group differences are due to participant attrition instead of the Mindfitness training, thereby threatening the internal (and consequently external) validity of the current

---

[70] Millisecond Software LLC 2016.
[71] Conway et al. 2005.
[72] Lewandowsky et al. 2010.

research.[73] Potentially, the amount of participant dropout in the experimental group was higher than in the waitlist-control group because participants in the latter group were not required to engage in the Mindfitness training between the t0 and t1 measure and therefore perceived their participation in the study as less demanding than the participants in the experimental condition. Most participants that were no longer able to or did not want to participate in the study anymore informed us via e-mail. They indicated that they found it hard to combine the training with their daily activities (especially those that were deployed), that they unexpectedly had to take part in a (large-scale) military exercise, or that they considered the exercises of the Mindfitness training as "too woolly".

Furthermore, we could have enquired about general (dis)interest in mindfulness in addition to enquiring about base-line experience with mindfulness, meditation, yoga, Tai Chi, or other forms of relaxation-/focus exercises. In doing so, we might have been able to explain the dropout. Also, such data would be helpful in controlling whether only individuals that are intrinsic interested in mindfulness signed up for the study or not.

Although we must acknowledge the above-mentioned limitations of our study, it seems nevertheless that even a short, economic, self-training mindfulness intervention is an effective tool for enhancing mindfulness, increasing wellbeing, and reducing stress in Dutch military (wo)men. We had the unique opportunity to conduct our research in the military domain and to spread awareness about the potential benefits of MT among military (wo)men, who are known to be rather sceptical when it comes to the topic of mindfulness. In terms of the design, we were able to implement a pre-/post-test design, which has various advantages over a cross-sectional design.[74] To conclude, we established a participant pool that existed out of participants from all four armed services (i.e., air force, land forces, military police, and the navy) instead of focusing on only one of these, which was the case in prior research (e.g., U.S. Marine Corps[75]). In doing so, we increase the generalizability, or external validity, of our findings.[76]

10.6.1 Practical Implications

Given that our 10-day MT is effective with respect to mindfulness, wellbeing and stress-reduction, the Dutch military might benefit from offering (and encouraging military (wo)men to take part in) similar short, self-training MT programs. Especially since this form of MT does not require costly, time-consuming, and hard to coordinate plenary sessions, it is both economically more attractive for the

---

[73] Barry 2005.
[74] E.g., Hart 2007.
[75] Stanley et al. 2011.
[76] E.g., Barry 2005.

organization to offer the MT program and more convenient for military (wo)men to engage in the MT. Thus, in addition to MT programs (e.g., by *Vormingscentrum* [training center] Beukbergen) and yoga classes that are already offered in the Dutch military, we suggest that (either brief or more intensive) MT programs should be offered to (Dutch) military (wo)men. In doing so, MT can serve as a preventive instead of a curative (e.g., PTSD treatment[77]) approach in terms of stress-reduction,[78] increased positive affect,[79] enhanced wellbeing[80] and higher military resilience.[81] As a matter of fact, prevention is better than cure.

And with this, all these beneficial effects will facilitate reflectivity.

References

AD (2016) Partygirls beroven juwelen NBA vedette ter waarde van 700.000 [Partygirls robbing jewellery NBA-vedette to the value of 700.000]. http://www.ad.nl/andere-sporten/partygirls-beroven-juwelen-nba-vedette-ter-waarde-van-700-000~a8d05991/. Accessed 10 April 2017.

Albers T (2011) Eindelijk, mijn scriptie over uitstellen [Finally, my thesis on putting things off]. Thesis University of Twente.

Awh E, Vogel EK, Oh SH (2006) Interactions between attention and working memory. Neuroscience 139(1): 201–208.

Barry AE (2005) How attrition impacts the internal and external validity of longitudinal research. The Journal of School Health 75(7):267.

Bishop SR (2002) What do we really know about mindfulness-based stress reduction? Psychosomatic Medicine 64(1):71–83.

Bishop SR, Lau M, Shapiro S, Carlson L, Anderson ND, Carmody J, Segal ZV, Abbey S, Speca M, Velting D, Devins G (2004) Mindfulness: A proposed operational definition. Clinical Psychology: Science and Practice 11(3):230–241.

Brown KW, Weinstein N, Creswell JD (2012) Trait mindfulness modulates neuroendocrine and affective responses to social evaluative threat. Psychoneuroendocrinology 37(12):2037–2041.

Brown KW, Ryan RM (2003) The benefits of being present: mindfulness and its role in psychological well-being. Journal of Personality and Social Psychology 84(4):822.

Cahn BR, Polich J (2006) Meditation states and traits: EEG, ERP, and neuroimaging studies. Psychological Bulletin 132(2):180.

Christopher MS, Gilbert BD (2010) Incremental validity of components of mindfulness in the prediction of satisfaction with life and depression. Current Psychology 29(1):10–23.

Cohen S, Williamson GM (1988) Perceived stress in a probability sample of the United States. In: Spacapan S, Oskam S (eds) The social psychology of health. Sage, Newbury Park CA.

Cohen S, Kamarck T, Mermelstein R (1994) Perceived stress scale. Measuring stress: A guide for health and social scientists.

Conway ARA, Kane MJ, Bunting MF, Hambrick DZ, Wilhelm O, Engle RW (2005) Working memory span tasks: A methodological review and user's guide. Psychonomic Bulletin & Review 12(5):769–786.

---

[77] Stanley et al. 2011.

[78] E.g., Grossman et al. 2004; Brown et al. 2012.

[79] E.g., Good et al. 2016.

[80] E.g., Weinstein et al. 2009.

[81] E.g., Johnson et al. 2014.

Darwin J, Melling A (2011) Mindfulness and Situation Awareness. Paper number 040, 16th ICCRT Symposium.

Davidson RJ, Jackson DC, Kalin NH (2000) Emotion, plasticity, context, and regulation: Perspectives from affective neuroscience. Psychological Bulletin 126:890–909.

Eberth J, Sedlmeier P (2012) The effects of mindfulness meditation: A meta-analysis. Mindfulness 3:174–189.

Endsley MR (1988) Situation awareness global assessment technique (SAGAT). Proceedings of the IEEE 1988 National Aerospace and Electronics Conference, NAECON 1988, 789–795.

Good DJ, Lyddy CJ, Glomb TM, Bono JE, Brown KW, Duffy MK, Baer RA, Brewer JA, Lazar SW (2016) Contemplating mindfulness at work: An integrative review. Journal of Management 42(1):114–142.

Grossman P, Niemann L, Schmidt S, Walach H (2004) Mindfulness-based stress reduction and health benefits: A meta-analysis. Journal of Psychosomatic Research 57(1):35–43.

Gutzwiller RS, Clegg BA (2013) The role of working memory in levels of situation awareness. Journal of Cognitive Engineering and Decision Making 7(2):141–154.

Hafenbrack AC, Kinias Z, Barsade SG (2013) Debiasing the mind through meditation: Mindfulness and the sunk-cost bias. Psychological Science 25:369–376.

Hart M (2007) Design, International Journal of Childbirth. Education 22(1):22.

Hülsheger UR, Alberts HJ, Feinholdt A, Lang JW (2013) Benefits of mindfulness at work: The role of mindfulness in emotion regulation, emotional exhaustion, and job satisfaction. Journal of Applied Psychology 98(2): 310.

Hülsheger UR, Feinholdt A, Nübold A (2015) A low-dose mindfulness intervention and recovery from work: Effects on psychological detachment, sleep quality, and sleep duration. Journal of Occupational and Organizational Psychology 88:464–489.

International Wellbeing Group (2013) Personal Wellbeing Index, 5th edn. Australian Centre on Quality of Life, Deakin University, Melbourne.

Jha AP, Morrison AB, Parker SC, Stanley EA (2017) Practice is protective: Mindfulness training promotes cognitive resilience in high-stress cohorts. Mindfulness:1–13.

Jha AP, Rogers SL, Morrison AB (2014) Mindfulness training in high stress professions: Strengthening attention and resilience. Mindfulness-based treatment approaches: A clinician's guide:347–366.

Jha AP, Stanley EA, Kiyonaga A, Wong L, Gelfand L (2010) Examining the protective effects of mindfulness training on working memory capacity and affective experience. Emotion 10(1):54.

Jha AP, Krompinger J, Baime MJ (2007) Mindfulness training modifies subsystems of attention. Cognitive, Affective, & Behavioral Neuroscience 7(2):109–119.

Johnson DC, Thom NJ, Stanley EA, Haase L, Simmons AN, Shih PAB, Thompson WK, Potterat EG, Minor TR, Paulus MP (2014) Modifying resilience mechanisms in at-risk individuals: a controlled study of mindfulness training in Marines preparing for deployment. American Journal of Psychiatry 171(8):844–853.

Kabat-Zinn J (1990) Full Catastrophe Living. Using the Wisdom of Your Body and Mind to Face Stress, Pain, and Illness. Delta, New York.

Kabat-Zinn J (1994) Mindfulness meditation for everyday life. Hyperion, New York.

Kaplan JB, Bergman AL, Christopher M, Bowen S, Hunsinger M (2017) Role of Resilience in Mindfulness Training for First Responders. Mindfulness:1–8.

Kenny DA (2016) Mediation. Accessed June 21, 2017 from http://davidakenny.net/cm/mediate.htm.

Lewandowsky S, Oberauer K, Yang LX, Ecker UK (2010) A working memory test battery for MATLAB. Behavior Research Methods 42(2):571–585.

Lutz A, Slagter HA, Dunne JD, Davidson RJ (2008) Attention regulation and monitoring in meditation. Trends in Cognitive Sciences 12(4):163–169.

Millisecond Software LLC (2016) User Manual for Inquisit's Automated Operation Span. http://www.millisecond.com/download/library/v5/ospan/automatedospan.manual. Accessed 4 April 2017.

Moore A, Gruber T, Derose J, Malinowski P (2012) Regular, brief mindfulness meditation practice improves electrophysiological markers of attentional control. Frontiers in Human Neuroscience 6:18.

Mrazek MD, Franklin MS, Phillips DT, Baird B, Schooler JW (2013) Mindfulness training improves working memory capacity and GRE performance while reducing mind wandering. Psychological Science 24(5):776–781.

Redick TS, Broadway JM, Meier ME, Kuriakose PS, Unsworth N, Kane MJ, Engle RW (2012) Measuring working memory capacity with automated complex span tasks. European Journal of Psychological Assessment 28(3):164–171.

Roeser RW, Schonert-Reichl KA, Jha AP, Cullen M, Wallace L, Wilensky R, Oberle E, Thomson K, Taylor C, Harrison J (2013) Mindfulness training and reductions in teacher stress and burnout: Results from two randomized, waitlist-control field trials. Journal of Educational Psychology 105:787–804.

Safran JD, Segal ZV (1990) Interpersonal process in cognitive therapy. Basic Books, New York.

Schok ML, Kleber RJ, Lensvelt-Mulders GJ (2010) A model of resilience and meaning after military deployment: Personal resources in making sense of war and peacekeeping experiences, Aging & Mental Health 14(3):328–338.

Schroevers M, Nykliček I, Topman R (2008) Validatie van de Nederlandstalige versie van de Mindful Attention Awareness Scale (MAAS), Gedragstherapie [Validation of the Dutch version of the Mindful Attention Awareness Scale (MAAS) Behavioural therapy].

Stanley EA, Jha AP (2009) Mind fitness. Improving operational effectiveness and building warrior resilience. Joint Force Q 55:144–151.

Stanley EA, Schaldach JM, Kiyonaga A, Jha AP (2011) Mindfulness-based mind fitness training: A case study of a high-stress pre-deployment military cohort. Cognitive and Behavioral Practice 18(4):566–576.

Tang Y-Y, Lu Q, Geng X, Stein EA, Yang Y, Posner MI (2010) Short-term meditation induces white matter changes in the anterior cingulate. Proceedings of the National Academy of Sciences 107:15649–15652.

Taverniers J, Smeets T, Van Ruysseveldt J, Syroit J, von Grumbkow J (2011) The risk of being shot at: Stress, cortisol secretion, and their impact on memory and perceived learning during reality-based practice for armed officers. International Journal of Stress Management 18 (2):113.

Taylor RM (1990) Situational Awareness Rating Technique (SART): The development of a tool for aircrew systems design. AGARD, Situational Awareness in Aerospace Operations 17:23–53.

Van Beuningen J (2012) The Satisfaction with Life Scale examining construct validity. Statistics Netherlands, The Hague.

Virgili M (2015) Mindfulness-Based Interventions reduce psychological distress in working adults: A meta-analysis of intervention studies. Mindfulness 6(2):326–337.

Weinstein N, Brown KW, Ryan RM (2009) A multi-method examination of the effects of mindfulness on stress attribution, coping, and emotional well-being. Journal of Research in Personality 43(3):374–385.

Zeidan F, Johnson SK, Diamond BJ, David Z, Goolkasian P (2010) Mindfulness meditation improves cognition: Evidence of brief mental training. Consciousness and Cognition 19 (2):597–605.

Anouk van Tilborg, MSc studied Psychology at Maastricht University, The Netherlands. She specialized in Work & Organizational Psychology as well as Health & Social Psychology, spent a semester abroad at Stellenbosch University, South Africa, and wrote her Bachelor's Thesis on "Selfies". During her Master's research internship, she collaborated with the Netherlands Defence Academy in Breda to write her Thesis on "Mindfulness in the Military". In the second half of 2017 she studied for a second master and is now, in 2019, working as HR Associate at GenDx.

LtCol (res) Dr. Tom Bijlsma is an assistant professor of Military Management Studies at the Faculty of Military Sciences of the Netherlands Defence Academy. After his four-year study at the Royal Military Academy he served as an army officer for ten years. Subsequently, after working for five years as a management trainer/management consultant in the commercial sector, he moved to teaching. His research focuses on learning processes and change management and his preference lies in studying and teaching this focus area from the human-factor perspective.

Susanne Muis, MSc started her psychology studies in Tilburg and subsequently decided to follow the master program Work and Organizational Psychology in Maastricht. She found that improving the well-being of employees was one of the most interesting aspects of the study, so she was glad to be able to study the effects of mindfulness on different aspects within the Dutch Military. After completing her study in Maastricht in 2017 she started the study Veterinary Medicine in Utrecht.

Chapter 11
The Impact of Educational Characteristics on the Development of Cadets from Novices to Experts

Charlotte Annink and Nicole van Mook

Contents

11.1	Introduction	182
11.2	Novice to Expert	183
11.3	Military and Academic Education	184
11.4	Individual and Collective Learning	185
11.5	Role of Teachers	186
11.6	Professional Identity	188
11.7	Learning Strategies	189
11.8	Conclusion	191
References		192

Abstract The purpose of this chapter is to illustrate how teachers affect the development of cadets from novices to experts. In pursuit of this purpose, this chapter addresses the following question: *How can teachers contribute to the development of cadets from novices to experts, within five predetermined characteristics?* The five characteristics that have been distinguished are as follows: (1) individual and collective learning, (2) military and academic education, (3) the role of teachers, (4) professional identity and (5) learning strategies. Findings show that these characteristics are all related to the development of cadets from novices to experts and contain several activities teachers need to implement in the educational program, so they can stimulate the development from novices to experts of cadets. The most important activities teachers need to implement, according to these five predetermined characteristics, are stimulating the reflective ability of cadets, pro-

---

C. J. M. Annink (✉) · N. N. M. van Mook
Netherlands Defence Academy, PO Box 90002, 4800 PA Breda, The Netherlands
e-mail: CJM.Annink@mindef.nl

N. N. M. van Mook
e-mail: NNM.v.Mook@mindef.nl

viding enough time to practice knowledge and skills and differentiating between individual and collective learning needs.

Keywords academic education · collective learning · expert · individual learning · learning activities · learning environment · learning process · learning strategies · military education · novice · organizing learning · professional identity · role of teachers

11.1 Introduction

To perform her constitutional tasks, The Netherlands has to be able to depend on her armed forces under any circumstances in an immediate and unconditional capacity. As a result, the armed forces must be constantly prepared and available for (operational) deployment anywhere in the world for as long as necessary. In order to meet these expectations, the armed forces and therefore its officers, should be able to anticipate on and cope with rapidly changing circumstances. This requires a high degree of flexibility and a strong innovative capacity. This, together with an increasing expectation that officers should be experts in their profession, will have consequences for the academic and military education of the subaltern officers. The Netherlands Defence Academy accommodates this education for the Dutch armed forces. Her teachers, instructors and educational specialists are responsible for designing, developing and teaching the educational program. To be able to do so they need to have a clear understanding of what the concept 'expertise' is and how to achieve this. For them it is of great importance not only to understand the concept, but to be able to contribute to the development of novice to expert during the initial education of officers. The purpose of this chapter is to illustrate this contribution. To make this contribution tangible five characteristics have been defined using the essential qualifications of the initial officers' education. The five characteristics that have been distinguished are: (1) military and academic education, (2) individual and collective learning, (3) the role of teachers, (4) professional identity and (5) learning strategies. In pursuit of the abovementioned purpose, this chapter addresses the following question: *How can teachers contribute to the development of cadets[1] from novices to experts, within five predetermined characteristics?*

To answer this question, this chapter will first provide a theoretical framework about the development from novice to expert. Thereafter, the five characteristics will be defined, placed into context and it will be determined which activities teachers can implement to affect the development from novice to expert. This chapter ends with a conclusion.

---

[1] This means: cadets of the army, the air force, the navy and the military police.

11.2 Novice to Expert

In the late 20th century Dreyfus and Dreyfus[2] came up with a model for defining different levels of skilfulness. At first, this model was primarily used within the field of nursing. In the early 21st century this model was employed in other fields as well, for example within the field of computer information science education and even within the military.[3] The model Dreyfus and Dreyfus came up with is called the Dreyfus five-stage model of expertise. The first stage of this model is called novice. A novice is someone that is completely new or has limited experience within an area or a field and who does not possess a significant amount of pre-existing knowledge or skills.[4] Generally, a novice is taught to follow guidelines and procedures. When a novice has acquired more than just a few rules, exercising the skills require so much concentration that the capacity to talk or to listen to advice is severely limited.[5] After a period of exposure to a field or domain, a novice progresses to become an advanced beginner, the second stage. Through (practical) experience in coping with real situations, the advanced beginner starts to recognize meaningful elements of the field or domain (due to a perceived similarity with prior examples). The third stage is called competent practitioner. A competent practitioner organizes experiences into formal decision-making processes. Competent practitioners construct conceptual models that aid them in their decision-making process. Because of these conceptual models, general performance is more fluid. Moreover, such practitioners have an increased ability to handle complex situations. After the stage of competence the next stage follows, this is the stage of proficiency. A proficient practitioner reads a situation quicker and smoother than a competent practitioner. Proficiency develops over time, but only if experience is assimilated. The practitioner sees patterns clearly, but has to think about the best course of action. Finally, in the last stage, the practitioner becomes an expert. They not only see patterns clearly, they also immediately see how to achieve their goal (because of their optimised processes). In other words, experts are able to act on their intuition.[6]

In the beginning of the initial officers' education at the Netherlands Defence Academy, cadets are considered to be novices. Depending on the start qualifications cadets are novices regarding their military and/or academic knowledge and skills. During their initial education, which can take one to four years, they go through the different stages of the Dreyfus five-stage model of expertise, so as eventually to become an expert.

---

[2] Dreyfus and Dreyfus 1986, pp. 16–52; Dreyfus and Dreyfus 1996, pp. 29–32.
[3] Dunphy and Williamson 2004, p. 107; Hinton 2013, pp. 1–16; Sookermany 2012, p. 590.
[4] Dunphy and Williamson 2004, pp. 108–112; Shuell 1990, p. 537.
[5] Dreyfus and Dreyfus 1986, pp. 16–52.
[6] Chmiel and Loui 2004, p. 19; Dreyfus and Dreyfus 1986, pp. 16–52; Dreyfus 2004, p. 177; Dunphy and Williamson 2004, p. 110.

11.3 Military and Academic Education

The Netherlands Defence Academy provides initial officers' education. The educational program consists of a military learning-teaching trajectory and an academic learning-teaching trajectory. The military learning-teaching trajectory consists, among other things, of basic military skills, such as learning to shoot, to apply first aid in (combat) situations, to apply command and control processes in (combat) situations and to lead teams. The primary learning objective of this trajectory is to teach cadets how to apply military and leadership skills within (inter)national situations and contexts. The academic learning-teaching trajectory is a bachelor's program for cadets in which three directions can be distinguished: (1) War Studies, (2) Military Management Studies and (3) Military Systems & Technology. The primary learning objective of this trajectory is to develop cadets into reflective professionals, who are capable of applying critical thinking skills, based on profound knowledge of theoretical concepts and frameworks, in any given situation, in order to make a well-informed, deliberate decision.

Initial officers' education is offered to three different target groups: (1) cadets who have graduated from preparatory scientific education, (2) cadets who have graduated from higher vocational education and academic education and (3) experienced non-commissioned officers. These target groups are novices in different areas of the initial officers' education. For example, cadets of the first two target groups are novices regarding the military education and the military organization, while target groups one and three are novices regarding academic education. During the initial officers' education cadets develop from novices to experts within the different areas of education, so that every graduated cadet has the same level of expertise a sub-lieutenant needs for the entry-level job. Therefore, the target group affects the duration of the educational program. For example, cadets who are novices regarding both forms of education (military and academic) require four years to eventually become an expert.

The initial officers' education at the Netherlands Defence Academy is provided by different kinds of teachers; some teachers contribute to the primary learning objective of the military learning-teaching trajectory, while others contribute to the primary learning objective of the academic learning-teaching trajectory. However, this distinction is not cast in stone. For instance, (civilian) academic teachers contribute to the military learning-teaching trajectory by applying a military conduct such as presenting and dismissing class at the beginning and end of the lesson. The same applies the other way around: military teachers contribute to the academic learning-teaching trajectory by asking critical questions about the why and the how of procedures while cadets follow these same procedures. As a result, critical thinking and reflection are stimulated.

In order to be the most effective in stimulating the development from novice to expert in the different areas of education, the collaboration between military and academic teachers is essential. This collaboration at least consists of meetings about the educational program (containing both trajectories) and the role of teachers within this educational program. Those meetings enhance awareness of the position of the course within the educational program, the prior knowledge and skills cadets have acquired, how teachers can complement this and at the same time prepare cadets for future courses. After reaching this awareness teachers will be able to stimulate the development from novice to expert, in the area of education the individual cadet needs it the most, so that every cadet can achieve the two main learning objectives of the military and academic education.

11.4 Individual and Collective Learning

Our perspective is that the purpose of education is to facilitate and further improve learning. This learning process can take place in many different ways, on many different levels: from individual learning to collective learning. During individual learning the cadet is consuming and storing new concepts, constructing knowledge and developing skills and behaviours.[7] A cadet is part of a team, therefore the individual learning process can also affect the learning process of the group. During collective learning the team is constructing collective knowledge and meanings by exploring complex situations from different perspectives, which will lead the team to insights they can only reach as a collective.[8] This process is characterised by social influences from the attitudes and behaviour of the team members on the cognition and behaviour of the individual cadet.[9] Therefore, it is important to respect (the contribution of) each individual.[10]

In order to facilitate collective learning there are many different conditions to consider. For example, the ability to reflect: collective learning breaks down when a team fails to reflect on their own actions or when they fail to make changes following discussion and reflection.[11] As well as sufficient time to first specialize knowledge and skills as an individual: an individuals' contribution is more effective when an individual first specialises their knowledge and skills.[12] And a safe learning environment; where sharing knowledge and showing specific behaviour is valued and supported.[13]

Collective learning is more important for the armed forces than for civil organisations because military teams differ in crucial ways from civil teams as a consequence of the nature of military (team)work; they need to execute their tasks

---

[7] Fenwick 2008, pp. 4–6.
[8] Kimmerle et al. 2015, p. 121.
[9] Hedlund et al. 2015, p. 3.
[10] Fenwick 2008, p. 6.
[11] Hedlund et al. 2015, p. 3.
[12] Currie and Kerrin 2004, pp. 11–16.
[13] Edmondson 2002, pp. 257–263; Fenwick 2008, p. 6; Hedlund et al. 2015, p. 14.

in highly complex environments that are full of stressors, pressures and threats which may have implications on life-or-death situations.[14] Collective learning is thus of great importance for accomplishing military tasks. At the Netherlands Defence Academy, collective learning is forced upon cadets due to the boarding school system, but there are many other elements that stimulate collective learning as well.

One of those elements is the teacher. They contribute to the individual and collective learning of cadets by taking into account the three conditions as mentioned above. First of all, teachers can stimulate and facilitate reflection, for example by asking critical questions and providing direct and postponed feedback on skill acquisition and behaviour of cadets. Secondly, teachers could focus on individual learning first and then slowly progress to collective learning. In order to do so, teachers need to formulate learning objectives, differentiate between individual learning needs and design suitable learning-teaching trajectories. Teachers also have to monitor the acquisition of knowledge and skills and the ability to reflect and cope with feedback on an individual level and with feedback to the group as a whole. When cadets' abilities to reflect and deal with feedback are sufficient, teachers should use appropriate learning activities to facilitate collective learning. Thirdly, teachers can put effort into creating a safe learning environment. To realise such an environment they need to make sure that cadets have enough opportunities to practice skills in an authentic environment, have the opportunity to ask for help and can receive guidance from them. Therefore, teachers need to value and support the sharing of knowledge, incite specific behaviour and create a judgement-free environment. Finally, teachers can consider designing learning-teaching trajectories with increasing complexity and self-regulation. Altogether, teachers at the Netherlands Defence Academy need to be prepared to take responsibility in facilitating individual and collective learning according to the abovementioned conditions. If a teacher is not prepared or does not have the tools to facilitate this, it will hamper the development of cadets from novices to experts.

11.5 Role of Teachers

As mentioned above teachers have a meaningful role regarding the learning process and development of cadets. This section focuses on the influence teachers have on regulating students' learning processes and development. The most abstract way of doing so is by implementing three different functions of education: (1) cognitive function, (2) affective function and (3) regulative function. The cognitive function of education is used to clarify and present learning content for cadets, for instance by defining learning objectives, structuring the lessons and giving opportunities to

---

[14] Essens et al. 2009, pp. 295–305; Veestraeten et al. 2014, p. 77.

practice skills. The affective function of education is used to construct and maintain a positive learning environment. This can be obtained by motivating, activating and challenging cadets. The regulative function of education is used to guide the learning process of cadets. This starts with managing expectations, but also includes monitoring study progress, providing feedback and stimulating reflection.[15]

Teachers fulfil different roles within these functions of education. In general there are six different roles teachers can have during a lesson or a course: (1) a diagnostician, (2) a challenger, (3) a model learner, (4) an activator, (5) a monitor and (6) an evaluator.[16] Firstly, the teacher needs to be able to adequately diagnose (previously) acquired knowledge, skills, attitudes and the learning and thinking strategies cadets did or did not master or master unsatisfactorily. This diagnosis helps the teacher determine how to introduce new content and skills in a way that integrates with cadets' learning needs. This also helps them to prevent cadets from learning ineffective learning and thinking strategies. Secondly, the teacher needs to be able to challenge cadets to learn and apply new knowledge, to learn and try out new skills and learning and thinking strategies in several different situations.[17] In order to do so, a safe and positive learning environment is conditional.[18] This challenge does not only come from the teacher, but is incorporated in the educational program; the continuous shift between military and academic education. Thirdly, the teacher needs to be able to be a role model.[19] For example, the teacher thinks out loud while conducting a procedure. This way the teacher makes knowledge and skill acquisition explicit and overt.[20] Fourthly, the teacher needs to be able to activate the use of knowledge, skills, attitudes and the learning and thinking strategies by means of different learning activities such as questions, tasks and exercises, etcetera.[21] Fifthly, the teacher needs to be able to take a step back and monitor the study progress of cadets. At the same time the teacher helps cadets who are in need, so that they are also able to accomplish the learning objectives. This way, the teacher is a monitor who provides cadets with feedback and feedforward.[22] Lastly, the teacher needs to be able to evaluate the quality of the learning process of cadets to determine to what extend cadets have accomplished the learning objectives.[23] When teachers are capable of fulfilling the six roles in relation to the functions of education, they will aid in the development from novice to expert of cadets.

---

[15] Kallenberg et al. 2014, pp. 46–55.
[16] Vrieling et al. 2018, pp. 685–686; Vermunt and Verloop 1999, pp. 274–275.
[17] Muhonen et al. 2018, p. 16; Vrieling et al. 2018, p. 692.
[18] Hattie 2012, p. 2.
[19] Vrieling et al. 2018, pp. 691–692.
[20] Vermunt and Verloop 1999, pp. 274–275.
[21] Kallenberg et al. 2014, pp. 139–176; Vrieling et al. 2018, pp. 690–694.
[22] Hattie 2012, p. 2; Vrieling et al. 2018, p. 692.
[23] Kallenberg et al. 2014, pp. 21–44; Vermunt and Verloop 1999, pp. 274–275.

11.6 Professional Identity

Personal identity is one of the subjects during the recruitment of candidate officers. This form of identity is considered to be an accumulation of values, standards, self-conception and self-definition. The foundation of this identity is realised during childhood and adolescence.[24] At the start of the initial officers' education their personal identity will be complemented with a professional identity. In other words: the professional identity is an expansion of the personal identity. Developing a professional identity is a condition for working effectively within the military organisation because the various tasks officers perform are based on a fundament of shared values.[25] One of the tasks is leading a team, for example, a team consists of subordinates who have already developed a professional identity. Therefore, it is important that officers have a professional identity which enables them to lead the team containing all those (different) professional identities.

As well as the personal identity, the professional identity takes time to develop. This development starts at the beginning of the education at the Netherlands Defence Academy, when cadets are novices regarding the professional identity, with exception of experienced non-commissioned officers. At this developmental stage the professional identity is characterised by an inner insecurity regarding their own leadership. During this stage significant role models, peers and superiors, are very important for cadets because they are considered to have authority, to be secure about themselves and to be able to adapt their behaviour depending on the situation.[26] During the educational program the professional identity grows through seeing role models show exemplary behaviour, then imitating that same behaviour and getting feedback on the execution of that behaviour. Due to this the self-esteem of cadets will grow.[27] Additionally, promotion in rank and being appreciated by the team are experiences that contribute to the development of self-esteem and therefore the development of a professional identity. The development of professional identity will only be realised to a certain extent because the educational program takes place in a simulated representation of reality. In order to take the development to a higher level it is necessary that officers experience the core tasks of their profession: an operational deployment. The professional identity will only be established after experiencing an operational deployment.[28]

Throughout the different stages of professional identity development, the teacher fulfils an important role. Teachers can foster some personal characteristics, such as willingness to try new things, being goal oriented and having an open attitude. The teacher also needs to stimulate reflection and provide realistic and challenging

---

[24] Marcia 1966, p. 552.
[25] Bachrach 2015, pp. 10–11.
[26] Hoi Kok Siew and Hwee Ling Koh 2015, p. 4; Larsson et al. 2006, p. 74.
[27] Larsson et al. 2006, p. 75; Marcia 1966, p. 552.
[28] Larsson et al. 2006, p. 75.

exercises and tasks within the military context.[29] Besides these curricular activities, the teacher is also a role model. In order to illustrate what is meant by teachers as role models, two examples will be described. Firstly, teachers need to address inadmissible behaviour of cadets. Another example is the so-called "crown system" at the Royal Netherlands Military Academy, an institution within the Netherlands Defence Academy. The "crown system" is a parallel organisation of the staff. This means cadets can apply for a position as a "crown" of key staff members in order to get acquainted with the corresponding tasks of that position. This system serves the purpose of role models, who are important for the development of the professional identity, in two ways: (1) the "crown" has a role model, namely the staff member, (2) the "crown" functions as a role model for the other cadets.

11.7 Learning Strategies

To anticipate and cope with rapidly changing circumstances, lifelong learning is essential for an officer.[30] In order to develop academically and learn effectively, officers need to be able to regulate their learning process on their own. An exemplary characteristic of self-regulated learners is that they have mastered a number of learning strategies to facilitate learning and enhance performance. While applying learning strategies cadets need to be able to take into consideration the different contexts and characteristics of learning situations.[31]

Four categories have been defined with regard to learning strategies. Firstly, cognitive strategies, which an officer can use to develop new knowledge, understanding and skills regarding a specific domain or task. Secondly, metacognitive strategies; these strategies can be used to regulate cognitive and affective learning processes. Thirdly, management strategies, an officer can use these strategies to create an ideal learning environment. Finally, motivational strategies, which an officer can use to cope with emotions that arise during the learning process.[32] Each of these four categories of learning strategies consist of several sub-strategies, see Table 11.1.

It is important that cadets master the different learning strategies as soon as possible because these strategies can help them cope with all the different learning situations they will encounter. Depending on their prior education, some cadets may need to put more effort into mastering these strategies than others have to. For example, cadets who have graduated from higher vocational education or academic education are likely to have mastered learning strategies already. These cadets are considered to have already taken the first steps to becoming an expert than cadets

---

[29] Bartone et al. 2007, p. 501; Larsson et al. 2006, p. 77.
[30] Van Keulen 2016, pp. 44–47.
[31] De Boer et al. 2013, p. 9; De Smul et al. 2018, p. 215.
[32] De Boer et al. 2013, p. 10; Vermunt and Verloop 1999, pp. 260–263.

Table 11.1 Explanation of sub-strategies belonging to the four categories of learning strategies (De Boer et al. 2013, pp. 26–27)

Learning strategies	Sub-strategies	Explanation
Cognitive strategies	Rehearsal	A cadet repeats and re-reads in order to learn and eventually apply the content
	Elaboration	A cadet relates new knowledge and skills to already existing knowledge and skills
	Organisation	A cadet distinguishes prominent and detailed information
Metacognitive strategies	Planning and prediction	A cadet writes a plan, that contains information about how the task is performed and which preconditions are applicable
	Monitoring and control	A cadet monitors the progress of the learning process and adjusts accordingly
	Evaluation and reflection	A cadet evaluates and reflects on the accomplished process and product
Management strategies	Management of the self	A cadet is committed to completing the task, regardless of circumstances
	Management of the environment	A cadet creates the best circumstances for learning
	Management of others	A cadet asks advice and collaborates with peers
Motivational strategies	Self-efficacy	A cadet believes in the ability to complete the task
	Task value	A cadet believes the task is relevant and/or important
	Goal orientation	A cadet is able to name the personal goal of the task

Source De Boer et al. 2013

who have graduated from preparatory scientific education (they are likely to be considered novices regarding learning strategies).

To facilitate cadets in mastering learning strategies there are various interventions and activities teachers and more experienced peers can apply. Scaffolding can be considered as an intervention teachers or peers can administer to support the learning process of a cadet. This intervention consists of three main characteristics: (1) Contingency, which means the teacher or peer provides tailored support, (2) Fading, which means that over time the support gradually withdrawals and (3) Transfer of responsibility, which means the cadet gradually gets more responsibility to perform the task over time.[33] Furthermore, a teacher or peers can apply several activities, such as asking detailed questions, asking for prominent and detailed information, creating a safe environment, having cadets experience success, giving compliments, activating prior knowledge, giving feedback and stimulating reflection in order to stimulate the development of learning strategies.[34]

---

[33] Muhonen et al. 2018, p. 68.
[34] Kallenberg et al. 2014, pp. 45–52; Vermunt and Verloop 1999, p. 268.

11.8 Conclusion

Recapitulating, this chapter set out to provide an answer on the following question: *How can teachers contribute to the development of cadets from novices to experts, within five predetermined characteristics?* The answer to this question may help teachers to improve the educational program, so cadets will be able to go through all stages of the Dreyfus five-stage model of expertise. This may eventually contribute to officers having a higher degree of flexibility and a stronger innovative capacity. On the long term, this may influence the functioning of officers during operational deployment anywhere in the world for as long as necessary.

The illustrated characteristics are related to the development of cadets from novices to experts. Each of the five characteristics contain several activities teachers need to implement in the educational program, so they can stimulate the development from novice to expert. The analysis of the above mentioned five predetermined characteristics shows that the question could be answered best by means of the following four domains of education, which are tangible for the teacher: (1) learning activities, (2) learning environment, (3) learning process and (4) organising learning. Findings on these four domains will be discussed below.

Firstly, teachers can implement at least three learning activities according to Sect. 11.4, the role of teachers, professional identity and learning strategies. The first learning activity is practising knowledge and skills in an authentic environment during tasks and exercises. Teachers need to establish an environment that meets the professional context as close as possible, in which cadets are offered enough time to practice. Differentiating between individual and collective learning needs is the second learning activity teachers should implement. To do so teachers need to diagnose (previously) acquired knowledge, skills, attitudes and the learning and thinking strategies cadets did or did not master or master unsatisfactorily. After which teachers need to make sure their educational program fits the individual and collective learnings needs. The third learning activity teachers should be aiming for is challenging their cadets by increasing the complexity of tasks and exercises. Teachers can achieve this by implementing scaffolding in the educational program.

Secondly, teachers need to be able to accomplish a safe learning environment according to the following sections: individual and collective learning, the role of teachers, professional identity and learning strategies. This safe environment could be realised by making sure the group respects individual contributions and values and supports sharing knowledge and showing specific behaviour. Therefore, it is of great importance that teachers supervise the interactions within the group.

Thirdly, teachers should enforce several activities to stimulate the learning process of cadets according to the sections individual and collective learning, military and academic education, the role of teachers, professional identity and learning strategies. The learning process of cadets is stimulated by their ability to reflect on their own behaviour, to deal with received feedback and to learn and apply learning strategies. Therefore, teachers should be capable to mentor their cadets, to motivate them, to stimulate individual and collective reflection, to provide direct and postponed feedback on skill acquisition and behaviour, to be their role model and to monitor the learning process and adjust accordingly.

Finally, teachers need to be able to organise learning according to the sections individual and collective learning, military and academic education and the role of teachers. Designing learning-teaching trajectories is essential for teachers to organise learning. Formulating learning objectives and structuring educational content are two elementary components of learning-teaching trajectories. Another essential component is the collaboration between military and academic teachers. As a result of this collaboration teachers are able to act on the awareness of their position within the educational program. Another result of this collaboration could be the contribution of (civilian) academic teachers to the military learning-teaching trajectory and the other way around: military teachers contribute to the academic learning-teaching trajectory. Nevertheless, this collaboration should not be limited to teachers, but it should also include developers, instructors, educational specialists and everyone else who influences the development of cadets.

References

Bachrach D (2015) Profielschets van de officier van de Nederlandse Krijgsmacht [Profile of the officer of the Dutch armed forces]. Ministry of Defence, The Hague.
Bartone PT, Snook SA, Forsythe GB, Lewis P, Bullis RC (2007) Psychological development and leader performance of military officer cadets. The Leadership Quarterly 18:490–504.
Chmiel R, Loui MC (2004) Debugging: from Novice to Expert. ACM SIGCSE Bulletin 36:17–21.
Currie G, Kerrin M (2004) The Limits of a Technological Fix to Knowledge Management: Epistemological, Political and Cultural Issues in the Case of Intranet Implementation. Management Learning 35:9–29.
De Boer H, Donker-Bergstra AS, Kostons DDNM, Korpershoek H, Van der Werf MP (2013) Effective Strategies for Self-regulated Learning: A Meta-analysis. University of Groningen, Groningen.
De Smul M, Heirweg S, Van Keer H, Devos G, Vandevelde S (2018) How competent do teachers feel instructing self-regulated learning strategies? Development and validation of the teacher self-efficacy scale to implement self-regulated learning. Teaching and Teacher Education 71:214–225.
Dreyfus SE (2004) The Five-Stage Model of Adult Skill Acquisition. Bulletin of Science Technology & Society 4:177–181.
Dreyfus HL, Dreyfus SE (1986) Mind over Machine: The Power of Human Intuition and Expertise in the Era of the Computer. MacMillan, New York.
Dreyfus HL, Dreyfus SE (1996) The relationship of theory and practice in the acquisition of skill. In: Benner P, Tanner CA, Chesla A (eds) Expertise in Nursing Practice: Caring, Clinical Judgement and Ethics. Springer Publishing Company, New York, pp 29–47.
Dunphy BC, Williamson SL (2004) In Pursuit of Expertise: Toward an Educational Model for Expertise Development. Advances in Health Sciences Education 9:107–127.
Edmondson AC (2002) The Local and Variegated Nature of Learning in Organizations: A Group-Level Perspective. Organization Science 13:128–146.
Essens P, Vogelaar A, Mylle J, Blendell C, Paris C, Halpin S, Baranski J (2009) Team Effectiveness in Complex Settings: A Framework. In: Salas E, Goodwin G, Burke S (eds) Team Effectiveness in Complex Organizations. Psychology Press 293–320.

Fenwick T (2008) Understanding Relations of Individual-Collective Learning in Work: A Review of Research. Management Learning 39:227–243.

Hattie J (2012) Visible Learning for Teachers: Maximizing Impact on Learning. Routledge, Abingdon-on-Thames.

Hedlund E, Börjesson M, Österberg J (2015) Team Learning in a Multinational Military Staff Exercise. Small Group Research 46:179–203.

Hinton C (2013) The military taught me something about writing: How student veterans complicate the novice-to-expert continuum in the first-year composition. Composition Forum 28:1–16.

Hoi Kok Siew D, Hwee Ling Koh (2015) Understanding the process of military leaders' development as professionals. National Institute of Education, Singapore 1–18.

Kallenberg T, Van der Grijspaarde L, Ter Braak A, Baars G (2014) Leren (en) Doceren in het Hoger Onderwijs [Education (and) Teaching in Higher Education]. Boom Lemma Uitgevers, The Hague.

Kimmerle J, Moskaliuk J, Oeberst A, Cress Ulrike (2015) Learning and Collective Knowledge Construction with Social Media: A Process-Oriented Perspective. Educational Psychologist, 50–2:120–137.

Larsson G, Bartone PT, Bos-Bakx M, Danielsson E, Jelusic L, Johansson E, Moelker R (2006) Leader Development in Natural Context: A Grounded Theory Approach to Discovering How Military Leaders Grow. Military Psychology 18:69–81.

Marcia JE (1966) Development and Validation of Ego Identity Status. Journal of Personality and Social Psychology 3:551–558.

Muhonen H, Pakarinen E, Poikkeus AM, Lerkkanen MK, Rasku-Puttonen H (2018) Quality of educational dialogue and association with students' academic performance. Learning and Instruction 55:67–79.

Shuell TJ (1990) Phases of Meaningful Learning. Review of Educational Research 60:531–547.

Sookermany A (2012) What is a skillful soldier? An epistemological foundation for understanding military skill acquisition in (post) modernized armed forces. Armed Forces & Society 8:582–603.

Van Keulen GW (2016) Beleidskaders Opleiden en Individueel Trainen heroverwogen en afgestemd [Policy framework education and individual training: reconsidered and aligned]. Ministry of Defence, The Hague.

Veestraeten M, Kyndt E, Dochy F (2014) Investigating Team Learning in a Military Context. Vocations and Learning 7:75–100.

Vermunt JD, Verloop N (1999) Congruence and friction between learning and teaching. Learning and Instruction 9:257–280.

Vrieling E, Stijnen E, Bastiaens T (2018) Successful learning: balancing self-regulation with instructional planning. Teaching in Higher Education 23:685–700.

Charlotte Annink, MSc is an educational specialist working for the staff of the Netherlands Defence Academy, where she is assigned to the Language Centre of Defence. In her work she focuses on educational quality management, assessment, writing and implementing educational policies, designing and developing language courses and learning-teaching trajectories.

Nicole van Mook, MSc is an educational specialist working for the staff of the Netherlands Defence Academy and is assigned to the Royal Netherlands Military Academy of the Netherlands. In her work she focuses on educational quality management, the Netherlands Qualification Framework (NLQF), assessment, designing and developing curriculums, and writing and implementing educational policies.

Chapter 12
Determinants of Academic Performance in Bachelor Theses: Evidence from the Faculty of Military Sciences at the Netherlands Defence Academy

Robert Beeres and Myriame Bollen

Contents

12.1	Introduction	196
12.2	NLDA-FMS Bachelor's Degree Program Military Management Studies (MMS)	198
12.3	Hypotheses	200
	12.3.1 Gender and Academic Performance	200
	12.3.2 Age and Academic Performance	201
	12.3.3 Services and Academic Performance	202
12.4	Methodology	203
12.5	Results	203
12.6	Conclusion and Discussion	205
References		206

Abstract Using the grades obtained for Bachelor's theses as a yardstick, this chapter examines factors influencing the academic performance of undergraduate students in military management studies at the Faculty of Military Sciences at the Netherlands Defence Academy. To this end, over the last six years surveys have been conducted amongst 184 cadets and midshipmen, representing all services (i.e., Navy, Army, Air Force and Military Police) in the Netherlands Armed Forces. Academic performance is measured by comparing the grades obtained for Bachelor's theses from 2013 until 2018. We apply various statistical tests to

---

R. Beeres (✉) · M. Bollen
Faculty of Military Sciences, Netherlands Defence Academy, PO Box 90002,
4800 PA Breda, The Netherlands
e-mail: RJM.Beeres@mindef.nl

M. Bollen
e-mail: MTIB.Bollen.01@mindef.nl

© T.M.C. ASSER PRESS and the authors 2019
W. Klinkert et al. (eds.), *NL ARMS Netherlands Annual Review of Military Studies 2019*, NL ARMS, https://doi.org/10.1007/978-94-6265-315-3_12

investigate the effects of different factors on the students' achievements. Amongst others, statistical results show that neither service, nor gender, nor age can be associated with academic performance.

Keywords Academic performance · Netherlands Defence Academy · Age · Gender · Services · Undergraduate Students

12.1 Introduction

In the wake of the Bologna Declaration, the so-called "two-cycle degree system, encompassing both undergraduate Bachelor's degree programs and graduate Master's degree programs" has spread across Europe. Writing a thesis concludes the majority of such programs.[1] At the Faculty of Military Sciences, Netherlands Defence Academy (FMS-NLDA), from 2011, the two-cycle degree system has been formally embedded and institutionalized within all military scientific degree programs and all FMS degree programs are concluded by a thesis.

The main difference between theses written at either a Bachelor's or Master's level refers to the extent and quality of the student's independent study behavior as opposed to the amount and intensity of teaching staff's supervision needed to perform at least sufficiently. This chapter, by using the grades obtained for Bachelor's theses as a yardstick, accounts for the findings on the academic performance of undergraduate students (cadets and midshipmen), at the verge of obtaining their Bachelor's degree in military management studies (BSc MMS).[2]

There exists an extensive body of literature on determinants and predictors for academic performance. Historically, those who pursued an academic education or a career in academia and scholarship appeared mainly driven by "academic curiosity" and "scientific exploration". Foremost, however, for any aspiring academic to even consider taking up such a career, access to ample financial means was required. To date, on the other hand, academic scholarship appears to be looked at as a means "to better job placement, financial stability, effective family planning and better quality of life, rather than exploring human phenomena".[3] In other words, instead of fulfilling a quest for knowledge, *Bildung* and reflection, from this perspective, academic education would mainly serve as a way to gain wealth and prosperity.

To define academic performance or academic achievement two layers can be distinguished. First, the object academic performance is operationalized, e.g., as "a measure that is tied to educational endeavors", or, "some method of expressing a student's scholastic standing", or, "the knowledge attained or skills developed in

---

[1] Meeus et al. 2004, p. 300.
[2] The academic performance of three civilian MMS students is not part of this study.
[3] Gomez 2016, p. 3.

the school subjects", or, "the level of proficiency attained in academic work".[4] Next, and varying in concreteness, ways to measure the operationalized concept are put forward, such as, "that requires a demonstration of skills to verify that learning as occurred", or else, "by test scores or marks assigned by the teacher", or, "by percentage of marks obtained by students in examination".[5] When measuring academic performance both researchers and teachers use Grade Point Average scores (GPAs), standard assessment scores, or grades obtained on courses or on Bachelor's or Master's theses.

As it turns out, across the globe, researchers profess their interest and beliefs in a vast number of factors that, potentially, are thought to be able to influence academic performance. Within the scope of this chapter, we have chosen to limit ourselves by providing an overarching categorization of factors in the overview below.

From international academic performance literature, we have derived five categories (distinct types) of determinants or predictors for academic performance.[6] The first category concerns demographic determinants (e.g., age, ethnicity; gender, geography, marital status).[7] In this category, research findings vary considerably. It appears relatively popular to attempt to find relations between gender and academic performance. In this regard, the hypothesis that women score higher on academic performance as compared to men is tested often.[8] Pivotal to the second category, encompassing psychological predictors, is the idea that superior intelligence positively relates to superior academic performance. In this line of research, personality traits (mainly measured by the so-called Big Five Factors; agreeableness, conscientiousness, extraversion, neuroticism and openness) are directly related to academic performance.[9] Significant relations are reported between conscientiousness and academic performance.[10] The third category distinguishes behavioral factors that impact academic performance. The corresponding literature connects "health behaviors" and academic performance.[11] For instance, So and Park investigated relations between "tobacco use, substance use, sexual behavior, violence, physical activity (exercise versus sedentary activity) and nutrition" and academic performance.[12] Amongst other findings, the authors conclude that "for Korean adolescents, not eating three meals a day regularly, the odds of a lower academic performance increased".[13] Next, within the fourth

---

[4] Gomez 2016, p. 4; Lavin 1965, p. 18; Sukhsarwala et al. 2015, p. 286.

[5] Gomez 2016, p. 4; Lavin 1965, p. 18; Sukhsarwala et al. 2015, p. 286.

[6] Various authors use various categorization and ordering systems to distinguish between determinants for academic performance. The categorization overview presented in this section is constructed by us and is based on multiple systems.

[7] Faisal et al. 2017; Farooq et al. 2011; Khan et al. 2012; Naderi et al. 2009.

[8] Sheard 2009, p. 192.

[9] Kassarnig et al. 2018; Mansoor and Mansoor 2018; Poropat 2009.

[10] Sheard 2009, p. 189.

[11] Bradley and Greene 2013; Busch et al. 2014; So and Park 2016.

[12] So and Park 2016, p. 123.

[13] So and Park 2016, p. 125.

category pertaining to socio-economic factors (e.g., parental education and occupation, access to loans, residence status),[14] Engel et al. find that military deployments "have modest adverse effects in most academic subjects, with lengthy deployments and deployments during the month of testing associated with the largest detrimental effects".[15] Finally, the influence of environmental factors as determinants for academic performance has been researched extensively.[16] For example, Wu et al. studied the impact of the learning environment (e.g., number of teachers per program, number of students per class) as well as "greenness of school surroundings" on academic performance. The findings support "a relationship between the "greenness" of the school area and school-wide academic performance".[17] Although the findings of Wu et al. relate to academic performance at elementary schools, in higher education, also, e.g., teacher-student ratio, libraries, the availability of an electronic learning environment etc. are taken into account in assessing the feasibility of degree programs. We think therefore that Wu's findings may be extrapolated to academic performance of undergraduate and graduate students.

We aim to contribute to this body of knowledge by exploring demographic effects of age, gender and service (Navy, Army, Air Force, and Military Police) on the academic performance in military management of specific undergraduate cadets and midshipmen.

To this end, in the next, second, section, we discuss the foundations of the bachelor's degree program MMS to clarify our decision to use the bachelor's thesis – the program's closure, so to speak – as the yardstick for academic performance. Our hypotheses are introduced in the third section and in the fourth section we will explain the methodology. In the fifth section, we will present the findings and, last, we will offer a conclusion and discussion.

12.2 NLDA-FMS Bachelor's Degree Program Military Management Studies (MMS)

Totaling 180 ECTS,[18] MMS consists of four phases, (1) Joint Officers Course; (2) Fundamentals in military management; (3) Field Specific Tracks and (4) Capstones and thesis research. The first phase, the Joint Officers Course, is part of all three NLDA-FMS Bachelor's degree programs, and, next to academic skills,

---

[14] Azhar et al. 2014; Engel et al. 2010.
[15] Engel et al. 2010, p. 73.
[16] Shabani 2013.
[17] Wu et al. 2014, p. 1.
[18] European Credit Transfer system. In The Netherlands' higher education realm, 1 ECTS equals 28 study hours. Scientific Bachelor's degree programs consist of 180 ECTS, whereas, vocational Bachelor's degree programs equal 240 ECTS. The study load across Dutch Master's degree programs varies from 60 ECTS to 180.

offers introduction courses relevant to all services and all three degree programs. As such, some extent of common ground and coherence across degree programs is created.

During the second phase, Fundamentals, three thematic learning pathways are discerned connecting domains or specializations within domains that, together, are viewed as the building blocks that construct the interdisciplinary program. The learning pathway Psychological and Social Dynamics in Expeditionary Deployments (PSDED) encompasses the building blocks derived from social – and behavioral sciences as well as institutional, governance and legal aspects. The learning pathway Organizing for Military Deployments (OMD) is construed from business – and management studies as well as from governance studies and law. The learning pathway Deployability, Sustainability and Performance (DSP) is made up of (defence) economics, technology and logistics. In addition, the Fundamentals phase includes part of the program's courses on research methods.

Next, two Field Specific Tracks offer in-depth knowledge, considered relevant to operate in a specific military working field and, as such, are thought to connect scientific- and practice based knowledge. The track Leadership in Crisis Situations is related to PSDED, whereas the track Operational Logistics and Defence Economics is related to DSP.

The Capstones and thesis phase consists of four integrative capstone courses and thesis research. Three out of four courses are related to the three thematic learning pathways: Systems, Networks and Safety (PSDED), Project management (OMD) and Strategic Defence Sourcing (DSP). The fourth course, Military Innovation and Technology, reflects on the organizational implications of technology in the military. Characteristically, these capstone courses aim to integrate and deepen insights, obtained from the Basics phase, by putting forward military relevant themes, challenges and controversies. As such, Synthesis capstone courses offer cadets and midshipmen the possibility to actively discover connections between scientific- and practice based knowledge that is needed for critical thinking and creative problem solving. These academic skills are needed to engage in the ensuing thesis research.

Thesis research constitutes the final part of MMS in which students prove they are able to investigate a clearly defined area of interest, thereby acting independently, to a large extent. Typically, thesis research starts by writing an Individual Research Plan. Students select a specific academic problem of their own choice and proceed with a problem definition and research questions. They show their grasp of a relevant body of literature as well as their ability to underpin their intended empirical research with a suitable research design and methods for data collection, – processing and – analysis of their findings. Last, in writing their thesis report, students show they are able to communicate their findings properly, well-structured and understandable. According to us, and corroborated by independent accreditation panels of academic peers, by taking this approach to thesis research, the Bachelor's degree program MMS enables its students to academically distinguish themselves. FMS-wide, the importance attached to this final undergraduate academic feat shows from the installment of a special annual award for the best Bachelor's thesis across all three programs. This is seen to enhance performance.

12.3 Hypotheses

This section elaborates on the hypotheses to be tested in this chapter.

12.3.1 Gender and Academic Performance

Statistics are being used increasingly to discover differences between males and females. For instance, Barua et al. find females to be "more cautious", "less aggressive", "less risk-seeking", "more risk averse" and "more compliant with regulations".[19] Based on their findings, the authors state that financial statements produced by female chief financial officers are of higher quality than financial statements produced by their male counterparts.[20]

Relations between gender and academic performance have been tested likewise. However, relatively often, these statistical tests appear to lack hypotheses formulated ex-ante and, moreover, little explanation is provided to account for the differences. Examples of such statistical testing can be found in the work of Faisal et al. These authors do not find differences in academic performance of male and female medical students in Pakistan.[21] In their study among students in business administration in Pakistan, Mansoor and Mansoor, on the other hand, discover male students to obtain higher academic results than female students.[22] Conducting research at the Pakistani University of Agriculture at undergraduate level, Khan et al. find the "performance of female students is obviously better than that of males".[23]

Other studies do formulate an expectation prior to statistical testing. Shabani, for instance, expects that due to "socio-cultural considerations prevailing in Tanzania and most African countries, male students will perform better than female students".[24] From her findings, however, no statistically significant differences between males and females can be noted.[25] Based on the grounds that "much of the existing literature appears to be in agreement that the learner identity of female

---

[19] Barua et al. 2010, pp. 26–27.
[20] Barua et al. 2010, p. 37.
[21] Faisal et al. 2017, p. 206.
[22] Mansoor and Mansoor 2018, p. 965.
[23] Khan et al. 2012, p. 799.
[24] Shabani 2013, p. 7.
[25] Shabani 2013, p. 38.

students leads them to work harder and more consistently"; Sheard expects females will outperform males.[26] Testing this expectation at undergraduate level at a university in the Northeast of the UK, the author finds this expectation corroborated.[27] We conclude the relation between the variables gender and academic performance is still open to debate. Against this background, we formulate our first null-hypothesis as follows.

H_{10}: There is no difference between male and female students regarding their academic performance.

12.3.2 Age and Academic Performance

Based on our literature study, and compared to the academic interest in relations between gender and academic performance, the relation between age and academic performance seems less extensively investigated. In general, investigations resemble research on the previous hypothesis. As to undergraduate students in Tanzania, Shabani expects "that age wise performance will decrease with age"[28] and this expectation is corroborated by her finding that "students in younger ages performed academically better than their counterparts". According to the author, a "plausible explanation for this observation is that at young ages students are more likely to have sharper minds and are more preoccupied with academic matter than at advanced ages".[29]

Amongst a group of Iranian undergraduate students,[30] Naderi et al., however, find age and academic performance to be positively related. However, the authors do not venture any explanations. Sheard argues that "mature-age graduates, in contrast to younger students, appear to try to work out the meaning of information for themselves, do not accept ideas without critical examination of them, relate ideas from their studies to a wider context, and look for reasons, justification, and logic behind ideas". Based on these arguments, the author expects "mature-age students would outperform young students in measured academic performance criteria".[31] As a matter of fact, when measuring academic performance by means of GPA, the author finds a positive significant relation. However, when measuring academic performance by the yardstick "dissertation (or thesis) grade" no significant relations between age and academic performance are noticeable.[32] In reference

---

[26] Sheard 2009, p. 192.
[27] Sheard 2009, p. 198.
[28] Shabani 2013, p. 7.
[29] Shabani 2013, p. 39.
[30] Naderi et al. 2009, p. 109.
[31] Sheard 2009, p. 192.
[32] Sheard 2009, p. 196.

to Sheard's previous arguments, this seems a remarkable finding. Against this background, we formulate our second null-hypothesis as follows.

H_{20}: Age and students' academic performance are not associated.

12.3.3 Services and Academic Performance

In our literature review we have not come across any references regarding previous research into the relation between the services and academic performance. Spanning the period from 1828 until 1989, Groen analyses obtained study results among cadets of the Royal Netherlands Military Academy (RNLMA).[33] Groen finds that, from 1948 until 1989, Air Force cadets score significantly worse than Army cadets.[34] However, in that time and age, at military academies, academic success was measured by using the yardstick "officer's diploma". As a result, part of the so-called academic performance consisted of practice based military skills, drills and competencies that, nowadays, would not be considered academic qualifications per se. Moreover, as Groen's extensive overview ends 30 years ago, and, apart from its historical interest, cannot be used to obtain explanations or insights into relations between services and academic performance to date.

In order to formulate a hypothesis regarding relations between services and academic performance, we could attempt to connect to Builder's characteristics of the cultures in services.[35] The author finds the ways in which the services measure themselves (as to their performance) to be a principal cultural characteristic. According to Builder, for the Navy, mainly, size matters, "which it measures, first, pertaining to the number of its capital ships", i.e., frigates, to be followed by the extent of balance within the fleet, in other words, "the numbers of other ships, by category, and, more recently, in the aggregate".[36] "For the Air Force", Builder continues, "the aerodynamic performance and technological quality of its aircraft have always been a higher priority than the numbers". When measuring itself, the Air Force is first and foremost concerned about "the kind of quality of its aircraft (speed, altitude, maneuverability, range, armament) to be followed by "the numbers".[37] Last, Builder considers the Army as the "most phlegmatic of the three services about measuring itself". "The Army may refer to the number of active divisions, to its state of modernization of readiness, as percentages of the whole, but the basic measure remains the number of people. And the Army is accustomed to that number varying, depending upon the commitment of society and the

---

[33] Groen 2003, pp. 534–538.

[34] Groen 2003, p. 534.

[35] Builder 1989, pp. 17–29 also see De Ruiter 2018, p. 106.

[36] Builder 1989, p. 21.

[37] Builder 1989, p. 21.

Table 12.1 Overview variables

Variable	Abbreviation	Measurement
Academic performance	PERF	Students' academic performance is measured as the grade obtained for the bachelor's thesis
Gender	GEN	Female = 1; Male = 2
Age	AGE	Age expressed in years
Service	SERV	Army = 1; Air Force = 2; Navy = 3 and Military Police = 4

Source R. Beeres and M. Bollen, 2019

government to defined causes".[38] Against this background, one would expect the Air Force to be the most academically oriented service (geared towards performance measurement), second, the Navy (geared towards quantitative measurement and fleet balance) and, last, the Army (geared towards measuring numbers of military). Builder does not discuss the Military Police as a separate service but, instead, views this command to originate from the Army and, hence, to be subject to the same cultural characteristics, including its approach to itself. Against this background, we formulate our third null-hypothesis as follows.

H_{30}: There exists no relationship between the service, the student is destined for and the students' academic performance.

12.4 Methodology

The data to test our hypotheses has been collected by the Faculty of Military Sciences educational offices. From 2013–2018, these data has been presented annually to account for the results on MMS bachelor theses. For this chapter, the data has been processed and analyzed by means of SPSS. Table 12.1 encompasses the variables used to test our hypotheses (column 1), abbreviation (column 2) and the way in which each variable has been measured (column 3).

12.5 Results

This section reports on our findings as a result from testing the hypotheses formulated ex ante. From Table 12.2, it becomes clear, the typical "mean" MMS Bachelor's graduate is male, almost 24 years of age, scoring 7.35 out of 10 for his Bachelor's thesis. Although the spreading of MMS students across the services is not reported on in Table 12.2, it is an important factor in interpreting the findings,

---

[38] Builder 1989, p. 22.

Table 12.2 Descriptive statistics of variables used

	Variables	N	Mean	Median	S.D.	Max.	Min.
Dependent variable	PERF	184	7.35	7.30	0.77	10	5.5
Independent variables	GEN	184	1.68	2.00	0.47	2	1
	AGE	184	23.60	23.00	1.77	31	21
	SERV	184	1.87	2.00	0.94	4	1

Note All variables are defined in Table 12.1
Source R. Beeres and M. Bollen, 2019

Table 12.3 Correlation analysis

	PERF	GEN	AGE	SERV
PERF	1	−0.069	0.091	0.120
GEN	−0.050	1	0.020	−0.044
AGE	0.033	0.029	1	0.061
SERV	0.111	−0.027	0.084	1

Note All variables are defined in Table 12.1
Source R. Beeres and M. Bollen, 2019

so we will offer these data as follows: Army (85 cadets); Air Force (48 cadets); Navy (41 midshipmen); Military Police (10 cadets).

Table 12.3 presents correlations between the variables. Numbers above the diagonal refer to Pearson correlation coefficients, whereas numbers below the diagonal are Spearman correlations. From Table 12.3, furthermore, it follows that when comparing Spearman and Pearson correlations, no deviances regarding the direction of the relations between variables can be observed.[39] Last, in Table 12.3 none of the variables are significantly related to each other.

From Table 12.4, it turns out none of the null-hypotheses can be rejected. In other words, in this research we have found that the variables gender, age and service are not significantly associated with academic performance.

Finally, Table 12.5 presents the results of a one-way ANOVA analysis. Table 12.5 shows the variable academic performance does not significantly differ between services. Despite this finding, however, when using the mean as yardstick, Navy students are acknowledged to obtain the highest grades for the MMS Bachelor's thesis, to be followed by the Military Police, the Army, and, ranking on the fourth position, the Air Force.

---

[39] Hartmann 1997, p. 160.

Table 12.4 OLS regressions

	(1)	(2)	(3)	(4)	(5)
GEN	−0.069 (−0.930)	–	–	−0.117 (−0.956)	−0.109 (−0.889)
AGE	–	0.091 (1.231)	–	0.040 (1.249)	0.037 (1.158)
SERV	–	–	0.120 (1.626)	–	0.091 (1.512)
Constant	7.540 (35.207)	6.421 (8.404)	7.165 (56.846)	6.549 (8.383)	6.480 (8.229)
Adjusted R2	0.001	0.003	0.009	0.002	0.009
Observations	184	184	184	184	184
F-value	0.865	1.515	2.644	1.214	1.577

Note All variables are defined in Table 12.1
Source R. Beeres and M. Bollen, 2019

Table 12.5 Academic performance related to service

	SERV	N	Mean	SD	F	Df	Sig.
PERF	Army	85	7.31	0.79	2.11	3	0.10
	Air Force	48	7.19	0.60			
	Navy	41	7.58	0.91			
	Military Police	10	7.49	0.58			

Note All variables are defined in Table 12.1
Source R. Beeres and M. Bollen, 2019

12.6 Conclusion and Discussion

Using the grades obtained for Bachelor's theses as a yardstick, in this chapter we ask whether the factors gender, age and/or service can be associated with the academic performance of undergraduate students in military management studies at the Faculty of Military Sciences of the Netherlands Defence Academy. We have found no significant associations, neither between the factors, nor between the factors and academic performance.

Are these findings remarkable? We do not think so. For, although regularly acclaimed otherwise, from our cross-national literature study it already appeared that age/academic performance and gender/academic performance could not be systematically related. Moreover, the relation service/academic performance has not been studied previously. Groen concludes that the cadets' geographical, social and religious backgrounds impacted their study results at the military academy only very slightly.[40] Based on our current findings, the same would apply regarding age, gender and service. We share Groen's point of view when she argues that instead of the cadet's background roots, the extent to which the individual cadet's personality, social, intellectual and physical capacities merge into the personal, social, intellectual and physical educational program offered at RNLMA, will impact study results.[41]

Our findings may also be interpreted in another way. As, from the normal distribution of the dependent variable 'grade obtained for Bachelor's thesis' and the non-significant relations between (in)dependent variables, it can be concluded that teaching staff assessing these theses do not discriminate regarding gender, age nor service. In other words, regardless of their age, gender and/or service cadets and midshipmen are all treated the same.

We conclude this chapter by offering two recommendations for further research. First, we could validate our findings nationally, by repeating this research amongst the other two bachelor's programs at FMS-NLA. Second, the use of our research design presents a relatively efficient way to conduct international comparative research into the determinants for academic performance across military academies.

References

Azhar M, Nadeem S, Naz F, Perveen F, Sameen A (2014) Impact of parental education and socio-economic status on academic achievements of university students. European Journal of Psychological Research 1:1–9.
Barua A, Davidson LF, Rama DV, Thiruvadi S (2010) CFO gender and accruals quality. Accounting Horizons 2:25–39.
Bradley BJ, Greene AC (2013) Do health and education agencies in the United States share responsibility for academic achievement and health? A review of 25 years of evidence about the relationship of adolescents' academic achievement and health behaviors. Journal of Adolescent Health 52:523–532.
Builder C (1989) The masks of war: American military styles in strategy and analysis. John Hopkins University Press, Baltimore.
Busch V, Loyen A, Lodder M, Schrijvers AJ, van Yperen TA, de Leeuw JR (2014) The effects of adolescent health-related behavior on academic performance: a systematic review of the longitudinal evidence. Review of Educational Research 84:245–274.
De Ruiter RM (2018) Breuklijn 1989. Continuïteit en verandering in het Nederlandse defensiebeleid 1989–1993 [Faultline 1989. Continuity and change in Dutch defence policy 1989–1993]. University of Amsterdam, Amsterdam.
Engel RC, Gallagher LB, Lyle DS (2010) Military deployments and children's academic achievement: Evidence from Department of Defense Education Activity Schools. Economics of Education Review 29:73–82.
Faisal R, Shinwari L, Hussain SS (2017) Academic performance of male in comparison with female undergraduate medical students in Pharmacology examinations. Journal of Pakistan Medical Association (JPMA) 67:204–208.

---

[40] Groen 2003, p. 538.
[41] Groen 2003, p. 538.

Farooq MS, Chaudhry AH, Shafiq M, Berhanu G (2011) Factors affecting students' quality of academic performance: a case of secondary school level. Journal of Quality and Technology Management 7:1–14.

Gomez Jr FE (2016) Predicting Academic Performance: A Commitment Perspective. https://scholarworks.sfasu.edu/cgi/viewcontent.cgi?referer=https://scholar.google.nl/&httpsredir=1&article=1076&context=etds.

Groen P (2003) De bloem der natie. Achtergronden van de KMA-cadetten 1828–2003. In: Groen P, Klinkert W (eds) Studeren in uniform [Studying in uniform. 175 years Royal Netherlands Military Academy 1828–2003], Sdu Uitgevers, The Hague, pp 491–548.

Hartmann FGH (1997) Accounting for performance evaluation. Effect of uncertainty on the appropriateness of accounting performance measures. Maastricht University, Maastricht.

Kassarnig V, Mones E, Bjerre-Nielsen A, Sapiezynski P, Dreyer Lassen D, Lehmann S (2018) Academic performance and behavioral patterns. EPJ Data Science 7:1–16.

Khan BB, Nawaz R, Chaudhry KM, Hyder AU, Butt TM (2012) Evaluation of comparative academic performance of undergraduate students at university level. The Journal of Animal & Plant Sciences 22:798–801.

Lavin DE (1965) The prediction of academic performance. A theoretical analysis and review of research. Russell Sage Foundation, New York.

Mansoor S, Mansoor T (2018) Correlation of personality and learning styles of students with their academic performance. Pakistan Armed Forces Medical Journal 68:963–968.

Meeus W, Van Looy L, Libotton A (2004) The bachelor's thesis in teacher education. European Journal of Teacher Education 27:299–321.

Naderi H, Abdullah R, Aizan HT, Sharir J, Kumar V (2009) Creativity, age and gender as predictors of academic achievement among undergraduate students. Journal of American Science 5:101–112.

Poropat AE (2009) A meta-analysis of the five-factor model of personality and academic performance. Psychological Bulletin 135:322–338.

Shabani Z (2013) Determinants of undergraduate students' academic performance in examination at Ardhi University. Doctoral dissertation, Mzumbe University. http://scholar.mzumbe.ac.tz/bitstream/handle/11192/652/MSc_MPA_Zaituni%20Shabani_2013.pdf?sequence=1.

Sheard M (2009) Hardiness commitment, gender, and age differentiate university academic performance. British Journal of Educational Psychology 79:189–204.

So ES, Park BM (2016) Health behaviors and academic performance among Korean adolescents. Asian Nursing Research 10:123–127.

Sukhsarwala B, Kacker P, Mukundan CR (2015) Academic motivation, dispositional mindfulness, emotional maturity and academic achievement of college students. International Journal of Management & Behavioural Sciences 6/7:282–296.

Wu CD, McNeely E, Cedeño-Laurent JG, Pan WC, Adamkiewicz G, Dominici F, Lung SCC, Su HJ, Spengler JD (2014) Linking student performance in Massachusetts elementary schools with the "greenness" of school surroundings using remote sensing. PloS One 9:e108548.

Prof. Dr. Robert Beeres is professor of Defence Economics at the Faculty of Military Sciences of the Netherlands Defence Academy in The Netherlands.

Prof. Dr. Myriame Bollen is professor of Civil-Military Interaction at the Faculty of Military Sciences of the Netherlands Defence Academy, where she chairs the department of Military Management Studies and she is a visiting professor at the Baltic Defence College in Estonia.

Part III
Didactical Solutions

Chapter 13
Iconic Images and Military Education: A Delicate Relationship

Henk de Jong and Floribert Baudet

Contents

13.1 Introduction – The Relevance of Studying Iconic Images 212
13.2 How to Go About It? Taking up Iconic Images 214
13.3 What to Study? War Imagery and (Military) History: Options and Challenges 215
13.4 The Educational Approach: Contextualised Image Analysis 217
13.5 (Visual) Education of Thinking Soldiers: Solutions at the Faculty of Military
 Sciences 219
13.6 Conclusion 223
References and Recommended Literature 225

Abstract As military professionals operate in a complex environment full of confusing and contradictory visual (dis)information, academically trained officers, at least, should possess an awareness of the consequences of 'manoeuvring' in this equally allusive and persuasive domain of visual rhetoric. In this domain, so-called 'iconic images' can transfer important (political) messages and therefore may be used to influence all those involved in conflicts. In this chapter we argue that studying relationships between form, content and function in iconic images of war positively enhances our cadets' and midshipmen's understanding of the complex nature of conflict, war and warfare and the responsibilities of the officer therein. A true 'thinking soldier' also needs critical tools from the toolbox of the (art) historian.

Keywords Military education · thinking soldier · visual culture · iconic images · war photography · war movies · visual metaphors and rhetoric

---

H. de Jong (✉) · F. Baudet
Faculty of Military Sciences, Netherlands Defence Academy, PO Box 90002, 4800 PA
Breda, The Netherlands
e-mail: h.d.jong@mindef.nl

F. Baudet
e-mail: FH.Baudet@mindef.nl

© T.M.C. ASSER PRESS and the authors 2019
W. Klinkert et al. (eds.), *NL ARMS Netherlands Annual Review of Military Studies 2019*, NL ARMS, https://doi.org/10.1007/978-94-6265-315-3_13

13.1 Introduction – The Relevance of Studying Iconic Images

The camera is an instrument that teaches people how to see without a camera.[1]

Joe Rosenthal's photograph of the raising of the American flag on Iwo Jima on 23 February 1945 is indisputably one of the iconic images of the Second World War.[2] It came to represent heroism, endurance, mourning and loss and inspired for example the well-known monument to the US Marines at Arlington Cemetery. *Raising the Flag on Iwo Jima* was copied many times since. Dutch troops reproduced it once again in 2015 (Fig. 13.1). Their photo shows an almost identical composition, a similar leaning flag post and the same desperate stretching experience. It suggests that Dutch servicemen in a Mali backwater identified with American Marines in a hard-fought amphibious landing in the Pacific seventy years earlier and through them attributed meaning to their own experience.

It has been argued that such iconic images are much more than impressive or historically important documentary photographs, or merely aesthetically appealing.[3] Authors like Hariman, Lucaites, Bredekamp, Kjeldsen, and Perlmutter have for this reason stressed the importance of studying the 'visual eloquence', 'visual rhetoric' and 'visual language' therein.[4] Melching has pointed out their meaning for our understanding of conflict, war, warfare and remembrance more in general.[5] They all suggest that iconic images through their 'power of epic concentration' detach themselves from their original context and develop in their 'afterlife' into independent symbols that represent something far more general and universal.[6] Images like these therefore are instrumental in legitimising beliefs, values and ideals; they embody, evoke and imply the stories that are fundamental to a community and take central stage in the realm where collective identities and memory are formed, political ideologies crystallise, *grand narratives* are constructed, collective remembrance is celebrated and public debate takes place on crucial values. In short, they mobilise people.[7]

This is especially so when technological advances have made it possible to manipulate (and disseminate) images at an unprecedented scale. This may have far-reaching consequences in the real world especially when they result in engineered iconic images that actually wield the power attributed to them. In a world

---

[1] Dorothea Lange in Meltzer 2000/1978, p. vii.
[2] Black 2012; Carruthers 2011; Aasman et al. 2010; Van Creveld 2008; Berger and Mohr 1995.
[3] Melching 2018, pp. 81–99. See also: Aasman et al. 2010.
[4] Hariman and Lucaites 2007; Bredekamp 2010; Kjeldsen 2017; Perlmutter 1998, 1999.
[5] Melching 2018, pp. 81–82.
[6] Melching 2018; Hunt and Schwartz 2010, pp. 259–271; Hariman and Lucaites 2007; Perlmutter 1999.
[7] Also in Kjeldsen 2017; Hunt and Schwartz 2010; Jansen 2010; Bredekamp 2010; Hariman and Lucaites 2007; Von der Dunk 2007; Fogu 2003; Perlmutter 1998, 1999; Mitchell 1994.

Fig. 13.1 Dutch soldiers of the United Nations Multidimensional Integrated Stabilization Mission in Mali. *Source* © Alex 'Lonny' *Volkskrant*, 22-04-2015

where most people's views on 'what is going on' in politics, and life in general, are influenced by images and clips on social media, it is difficult to underestimate their mobilizing and destabilizing impact. Even if its precise nature is not clear yet, no political or military organization can afford to ignore this latest development within the *Visual Turn*.[8] The mind itself has become a kind of battlefield.[9]

It is obviously not only the adversary that engages in using imagery, our own side does so as well, both intentionally and inadvertently. It is therefore vital for military leaders to be able to understand and counter the visual codes, visual rhetoric and the related ways of influencing that are facing, or, in fact, *surrounding* all of us. Such ability will improve 'situational awareness' substantially, as it stimulates better understanding of the visual signs and its (implied) messages from friend and foe. 'Pics' are not enjoyable and fairly inconsequential illustrations, but in fact important sources of information and producers and conveyers of meaning in their own right, with their own specific visual logic, persuasiveness, dangers and possibilities.[10] Training young officers' receptiveness in this respect is essential and our academic military curriculum provides for this.

In the following pages we will illustrate how we have translated this realisation into our academic curriculum. We will outline the search for original effective

---

[8] Patrikarakos 2017; Bouwmeester 2017; Gorman 2009; Perlmutter 2008; Rutherford 2004; Knieper and Müller 2005; Visser 2002; Journal of Visual Culture.

[9] Compare Bouwmeester 2017; Carruthers 2011; Osgood and Frank 2010; Rutherford 2004; Knightley 2004; Bennet and Palatz 1994.

[10] Ibidem, and: Aasman et al. 2010, pp. 121–141; Knieper and Müller 2005; Perlmutter 1999; Berger and Mohr 1995; Mitchell 1994.

didactical forms that supply our students with the relevant analytical tools and insights required. Secondly, we will discuss learning goals, teaching methods and effects of the relevant courses on our students.

13.2 How to Go About It? Taking up Iconic Images

Iconic images thus hold centre stage in public debates and ultimately in the political and military arena as well. In fact, they provide the framework with which societies and individuals absorb the shock of actual war, and with which they try and make sense of it.[11] However, translating an understanding of the importance of iconic images into a military academic curriculum has not proved to be an easy task.

Studying images was long considered to be 'off topic'. The still dominant idea that the media and certain iconic images such as Eddy Adams' photo of the execution of Viet Cong prisoner Nguyen Van Lem by Brigadier General Nguyen Ngoc Loan, the footage from My Lai, and the photograph of nine-year-old 'napalm-girl' Phan Thi Kim Phuc in particular, had caused the American defeat in Vietnam could and should have stimulated military interest in the power of imagery *as such*.[12] It did not.

At the same time, in academia the idea that iconic images almost by definition have critical potential held sway.[13] From the Vietnam case many scholars extrapolated that emotions evoked by iconic images could invariably be linked to protests, criticism, disapproval and 'calls to action', whereas of course iconic images are equally capable of endorsing world-views and ideologies and fairly uncritically validating group identities.[14]

Ironically, such ideas only served to bolster the conviction in military establishments that the press fatally undermined the war effort. After 1975, the US Ministry of Defence curtailed the freedom of movement of the press during military operations and efforts were made to turn the power of the media to their advantage.[15] Embedding journalists, conducting media-ops and info-ops, and framing of messages for specific internal and external target groups became common practice.[16] This only intensified in the post-Cold War era when strategic communication became the buzzword. As the various post-1989 types of operations found their way into our academic curriculum, so did the notion of 'hybrid warfare' and with it

---

[11] Melching 2018; Cadava 1997.

[12] On Vietnam, imagery and the role of the press: Taylor 2003; Devine 1999; Bates et al. 1998; Hammond 1998; Wyatt 1995; Walsh and Aulich 1989; Hallin 1989; Kamber 2013; Tucker et al. 2012; Carruthers 2011; Fabian and Adam 1992.

[13] For example: Melching 2018, pp. 82–84.

[14] Melching 2018, pp. 82–84; Kamber 2013; Bredekamp 2010. But see Gorman 2009; Van Creveld 2008; Hariman and Lucaites 2007; Von der Dunk 2007; Lowenthal 1998; Haskell 1993.

[15] Carruthers 2011; Knightley 2004.

[16] Ibidem, and Paul and Kim 2004.

came an increased interest in the power of imagery that, at times, seemed to take on mythological proportions.[17]

However, as historians we strongly felt that the challenges we face with regard to imagery as conveyors of messages and propaganda, if you will, are not fundamentally new. The past offers a staggering array of illuminating case studies on (iconic) imagery and its (mis)use. We also believed that our historical method, which analyses phenomena both *in* time and *through* time, would also work with imagery.[18] Applied for example to the history of war imagery, propaganda, manipulation and influencing, a focus on context, changes and continuity undoubtedly raises sensitivity toward surprising and unexpected (alternative) visual languages. At the same time this approach demonstrates that many aspects from the past regarding the relation of *imago* and *narratio* still echo today and therefore have relevance for today.[19] Such a discovery profoundly deepens young officers understanding of the power of iconic images and the delicate relationship between media, societies and public opinion.

We complement this with another method: critical image-analysis, which is of an almost *art*-historical nature.[20] We follow the approach also advocated by Hariman, Lucaites, Bredekamp, Kjeldsen and Perlmutter, who, as said in the introduction, stress the importance of studying the 'visual eloquence', 'visual rhetoric' and 'visual language'.[21] We combine these approaches, in order to enable our students to better read 'visual narratives', identify implicit subplots and understand the use of visual symbolism in general.

13.3 What to Study? War Imagery and (Military) History: Options and Challenges

The 'why?' and 'how?' thus answered, the question of 'what?' came next. Well aware that our students will be military leaders, their future roles offered some guidelines as to subject matter. Even so, when we started selecting material, we immediately faced the ubiquitous nature of (war) images. With it came the understanding that *all* individual and collective memory is visual in nature to a large extent. It is evidently filled to the brim with iconic images that clearly often emanate

---

[17] Bouwmeester 2017; Gorman 2009.

[18] On the characteristics, methods and (ab)use of (military) history: Baudet 2011; Van Creveld 2008; Tosh and Lang 2006; Hughes and Philpott 2006; Morillo 2006; Murray and Sinnreich 2006; Black 2004; Lynn 1997; Charters et al. 1992; Mearsheimer 1988.

[19] Berger and Mohr 1995; Haskell 1993; Mitchell 1994.

[20] D'Alleva 2012; Adams 1996; Nelson and Shiff 1996; Mitchell 1994; Johnson 1988.

[21] Kjeldsen 2017; Bredekamp 2010; Hariman and Lucaites 2007; Perlmutter 1998, 1999.

from photographs (and film).²² Being historians we enthusiastically decided not to limit ourselves to the last decade or so, which of course opened Pandora's box even further. In addition, for every decade or for different groups, iconic images may contain different symbolic meaning, comparable to *Lieux de mémoire*.²³ To do right by them, one ought to 'follow', as it were, the development of their meaning through time. The recognition of all this of course complicated our selection. So, where to start?

Still, it was obvious that images in the literal sense, i.e., photography, should be included. There is a canon of classics ranging from the Crimean War and the American Civil War to the present day, and it includes work by Roger Fenton, Mathew Brady, Robert Capa, Don McCullin and others.²⁴ Leaving them out was inconceivable. But the same applied to film, documentaries and even cartoons.²⁵ Donald Duck struggling to adjust to living in a fascist state is iconic. When we think of D-Day, we are undoubtedly influenced by the opening scene from *Saving Private Ryan* by Steven Spielberg, whereas our idea of the Vietnam War is influenced by the visualisation of Search and Destroy missions in *La 317ème Section* and *The Anderson Platoon*. For many, *Apocalypse Now* came to encapsulate the essence of the Vietnam War by the sheer madness of surfing under fire with Wagner on the speakers and a lovely smell of napalm in the morning. This masterpiece is stuffed with iconic scenes, whether it is navigating upriver, looking for a Mango Tree, the Bunny-scene or the ultimate confrontation with Colonel Kurz. Though fictitious, it is a visual gateway to the past.²⁶

So photographs, films, and documentaries and cartoons had to be included. However, statues, monuments and places (*lieux de mémoire*) can likewise be understood as images full of comparable visualised signs and associations, only caught in stone.²⁷ Language itself should be discussed as well. We use image-based metaphors and concepts for sense-making, as the brilliant nineteenth-century Dutch author Multatuli already pointed out in an essay on the word "denkbeeld" (concept/idea), which literally means "think-image".²⁸ Indeed, books often use visual metaphors to describe war, such as Ernst Jünger's *Im Stahlgewitter*, or Eisenhower's *Crusade in Europe*. Karl Marlante's novel on the Vietnam War (*Matterhorn*) takes this even further. He essentially reduces the war to the senseless storming of a hill. We soon realised that the intrigue and plot of academic studies on

---

[22] Jansen 2010; Kroes 2007; Von der Dunk 2007; Samuels 2004; Record 2002; Haskell 1993; Lowenthal 1985, 1998.

[23] Jansen 2010; Record 2002; Lowenthal 1985, 1998; Haskell 1993.

[24] On war photography and its classics: Kamber 2013; Tucker et al. 2012; Kroes 2007; Knieper and Müller 2005; Gerhard 2004; Knightley 2003; Cadava 1997; Fabian and Adam 1992.

[25] On war movies: Suid 2015; Bronfen 2012; Slater 2009; Clarke 2006; Westwell 2006; Eberwein 2005; Dolan 1985; Parish 1990.

[26] Taylor 2003; Devine 1999; Bates et al. 1998; Hammond 1998; Wyatt 1995; Walsh and Aulich 1989; Hallin 1989.

[27] Haskell 1993; Lowenthal 1985, 1998.

[28] Multatuli, *Ideeën*.

Fig. 13.2 Objectivism and realism in war photography? Above a 'photograph' of Frank Hurley of the Battle of Zonnebeke in Belgium (left). It was exhibited in London during the First World War, explicitly to capture the war in *one* image. Does it? It turns out to be composed of several different pictures, all stemming from the Battle of Zonnebeke (right). It is not that clear at all where reality stops here and manipulation begins. *Source* https://www.sl.nsw.gov.au/stories/frank-hurleys-world-war-i-photography/exhibiting-war (Accessed 23 May 2019)

war are likewise frequently structured around (visual) metaphors. Take for example the word *Blitzkrieg*, or titles like *A Bright Shining Lie* (Neil Sheehan), *A Savage War of Peace* (Alistair Horne) and *The Face of Battle* (John Keegan).[29] It is images and visual metaphors such as these that shape our understanding of war.[30]

However, to include everything was of course sheer impossible. A selection was necessary, inevitable even. In the end, we settled on a minimum corpus which included examples of all types of imagery (Fig. 13.2).

13.4 The Educational Approach: Contextualised Image Analysis

Nonetheless, it was still far from clear how to go about from there, educationally and didactically. At the centre of the future profession of the officers stands decision-making in complex *contemporary* environments. This understandably leads to a preference for information about recent conflicts and lessons learned from these. Our students, like their operational colleagues, have generally little interest in the more distant past. In addition, their interest is focused on the repetitive, constant and exemplary, and the military 'fundamentals' stemming from it, that may be applied in present-day operations. By organizational culture and personal inclination, they have little patience for the subtleties of each particular historical period.[31]

---

[29] Keegan 1976. On the use of narrative metaphors in historiography: Jansen 2010.
[30] Jansen 2010; Von der Dunk 2007; Samuels 2004; Record 2002.
[31] Klinkert 2008, 2016, 2018; Baudet 2011; Echevarria 2005; Murray and Sinnreich 2006.

Added to that, students at the Netherlands Military Academy, despite growing up in a strongly visualised culture, seem to cling at times to quite naive ways of engaging the vast amount of (war) photos, documentaries, film, television and internet productions that surrounds them. We often encounter an inclination to objectivism and realism in this respect. Images are taken to be precisely what they are *not*: objective and realistic representations of reality.[32]

This not something to be taken lightly. At the same time, it is quite obvious that young cadets' and midshipmen's ideas on war and warfare are influenced to a high degree by war photography, war movies, documentaries and the war games on the internet. The visual codes, professional expectations and traditions they live up to are therefore often those of Hollywood. Many of our students resemble the soldiers in the opening scene of *Jarhead*. They are watching *Apocalypse Now* and confuse the film with things to come. With it comes misplaced romanticism and ill-founded and at times even dangerous notions of what it is like to be a military leader. Unwittingly they echo Michael Herr, who once wrote: *One day at the battalion aid station in Hue a Marine with minor shrapnel wounds in his legs was waiting to get on a helicopter. ... I hate this movie, he said*. In his *Dispatches*, Herr acknowledged his bewilderment about the discrepancy between his expectations and reality in Vietnam, by writing: *This is not the fucking movies about here*.[33]

This added urgency to our endeavour. Based on the idea that the Dutch armed forces in contemporary conflict need thinking soldiers and officer scholars, future officers receive both military *and* academic training. The key role of the Faculty is explicitly to challenge them intellectually, to discard naïve realistic conceptions of reality and to show merit in doubt. While we cannot expect our students to become the new Burckhardt or Ranke, or masters in iconography (image description), iconology (image interpretation) or semiology (sign-interpretation) in the great tradition of Panofsky, Warburg or Gombrich, we believe that even a propaedeutic form of image analysis stimulates critical awareness of messages in (iconic) war imagery, an awareness they will need as military leaders.

At the core of this awareness stands an understanding of the relationship between form, content, and function.[34] It is this triangular analytical toolbox, in combination with the double strategy stemming from the historical method (positioning-the-phenomenon-*in*-time and-*through*-time) that helps our students to engage and understand the puzzling world of images with its wide array of messages and forms of manipulation.

---

[32] On 'imagery' and the interpretation thereof: Mondzain 2010; D'Alleva 2012; Adams 1996; Nelson and Shiff 1996; Berger and Mohr 1995; Mitchell 1994; Johnson 1988.

[33] Herr, *Dispatches*.

[34] On this: Mondzain 2010; D'Alleva 2012; Frazier 1999; Adams 1996; Nelson and Shiff 1996; Berger and Mohr 1995; Mitchell 1994; Johnson 1988.

13.5 (Visual) Education of Thinking Soldiers: Solutions at the Faculty of Military Sciences

It is one thing to argue energetically that one intends to fight visual naiveté and stimulate analytical skills and critical thinking with regard to visual narratives, it is quite another to put it into practice and find the appropriate didactical form for it within the context of a Military Academy. For the last decade or so, the Faculty of Military Sciences in the Netherlands has been experimenting to do just that.

In our experience the key to success is independent individual research on iconic images, based upon the methodological approaches discussed above, and discussions in tutorials. We therefore ask our students to examine certain iconic images. Initially, the focus is on form aspects: frames, lines and perspective; use of colour, ordering, i.e., composition. The analysis of the content(s) thereafter concentrates on subject matter and themes, selection of the image elements, possible (symbolic) meaning and the implied 'story'. Lastly, when studying functional aspects the emphasis lies on the question of how the (iconic) image was published, which audience it was intended for, who paid for it, what there is to say about government interference, what its 'framing' was, how the image was received and how its reception changed its meaning. Naturally, time and again the conclusion is that all three aspects are equally important and that none is dominant. The form determines the content to a large degree, but the choice for content obviously dictates the form, and, naturally, the function of an image can explain much both about form and content alike.[35]

We start doing this quite early in our program. The propaedeutic course on military history (EKO) is deliberately peppered with historical images and historical footage. This is done in order to familiarise our students with the canon of iconic images. By subsequently discussing these, we hope to convey that behind every iconic image there is a fascinating story, and behind that one another, and yet another, and another, and so on and so forth. Our objective is to create a sense of confusion and to provoke the realisation that one hardly ever sees what one thought to see at first glance.[36]

In the second year of the War Studies program, a course on historical methodology (MTO2) is strongly interconnected with a course on Military Historical Analysis (MHA), culminating in a *battlefield tour* to the Normandy beaches.[37] Visual imagery is included in order to illustrate that the very same event can for example result in many different (visual) representations of it. The famous photographs of Robert Capa are of course discussed in detail. We also devote much time to other images, such as those from intelligence agencies or the German

---

[35] Ibidem. Critical is: Rousmanière 2001. See also: Dussel 2013; Cadava 1997.
[36] An important source being: Tucker et al. 2012.
[37] Discussed by W. Klinkert in this volume.

Fig. 13.3 The photographer as artist. Photo of Edward Steichen, on deck of the USS Lexington in the Pacific, in World War Two. It is staged as a scene of a play in a theatre, or a musical. The photographer was evidently driven by aesthetic choices and accents. It takes some time, for students at a military academy, to realise that precisely for these (artistic) reasons some photographs become iconic and others do not. *Source* Steichen: A Life in Photography (Doubleday, New York, 1963)

Kriegsberichter that ended up in the German *Wochenschau*.[38] We also analyse documentaries on Overlord such as *The True Glory, From D-Day to VE Day*, and Hollywood productions like *The Longest Day*, *Saving Private Ryan* and a-typical ones like *The Big Red One*.[39] To perceive subsequent changes in the way students confront imagery and aspects of visual memory from the Second World War is as fascinating as it is rewarding (Fig. 13.3).

From this point on in the curriculum, the study of (iconic) imagery is no longer compulsory. We encourage our students to deepen their knowledge though and offer a number of additional courses, either as an elective or as a minor. The elective on *Media and Defence* (KMD) for example, originally initiated by the Department of Business Studies, deals specifically and more in-depth with the relationship between media, society and armed forces.[40]

A number of inter-active lectures on the history of war photography form an integral part of this course. They propose that (iconic) photographs featuring war and warfare are hardly ever neutral, objective and realistic representations of (military) reality. Particularly in iconic war photographs it is far from clear where realism and objectivism end, and idealisation, manipulation and (self)-censorship

---

[38] Rentschler 1996; Bramsted 1965; Hull 1969.

[39] Wetta and Novelli 2016; Bender 2013; Bronfen 2012; Westwell 2006; Doherty 1993; Black 1987; Basinger 1986; Kane 1982.

[40] On the relationship between media and defence: Carruthers 2011; Osgood and Frank 2010; Gorman 2009; Moorcraft and Taylor 2008; Knieper and Müller 2005.

start, and how technical possibilities and limitations may have dictated this. In so doing we instil awareness that *every* form of visual representation implies 'construction' (through selection, colouring, perspective, aesthetic choices and emplotment) and by necessity also 'distortion'.[41]

Building from this perspective, we then discuss iconic war photography from the Civil War onwards. Classics are discussed, particularly so when they touch on important phenomena such as aesthetisation, or black, white and grey propaganda.[42] This explains our special focus on the images provided by for example the *Kriegsberichter* from the *Propagandakompagnien* for the *Wochenschau* and Allied news agencies such as *Life Magazine* and *Associated Press*.[43]

After this, by far the most important section of the course starts. Groups of students are asked to *iconographically* analyse war photos (using the method described above) and present their conclusions to each other. Famous pictures are selected, but also fairly unknown ones, and comparisons between them are stimulated to strike a balance between canon and counter-canon, typical and a-typical, and by way of this they get acquainted with similarities and differences, and reasons for that. The main questions to be answered are how iconic images are 'constructed' and what role do individuals, authorities, technique and the public play in this? In other words: what is there to be said about the relationship between of form, content and function and how can this be explained by looking to the historical context of the photograph and its place in the history of war photography? Questions derived from this are fairly obvious. Who made it? What else did he/she make? What was his or her background? What kind of composition and aesthetic means are used? What are the subject matter and the message? Why? How is that done? What can be said about the publication, audience and reception?

The possible cases for study are of course innumerable. Student presentations have ranged from Roger Fenton and Lee Miller to German propaganda companies and from Alexander Gardner to Nick Ut. Whatever their choices, after their analyses all students realise that the 'hidden' story behind an iconic image is always different and far more complex than expected, which undeniably stimulates an awareness of the power of iconic images.

The minor *Info at War* (I@W) takes this understanding a step further and addresses contemporary media-ops, strategic communication and information warfare. This is a joint endeavour between intelligence and cyber specialists, and

---

[41] On war photography: Kamber 2013; Tucker et al. 2012 (particularly good); Gerhard 2004; Knightley 2003, 2004; Cadava 1997; Fabian and Adam 1992.

[42] 'White propaganda' employs correct and verifiable information but with slight omissions and specific emphasis. 'Grey propaganda' employs unverifiable information that is not demonstrably incorrect; 'black propaganda' uses falsifications and misleading and incorrect information attributed to sources that are not responsible for it. On propaganda: Stanley 2016; Jowett and O'Donnell 2014; Welch and Fox 2012; Cole 2010; Cull et al. 2003; Randal 2002.

[43] On US propaganda: Axelrod 2009; Casey 2008; Brown 1963. On German propaganda during WWII: Longerich 2015; Verduyn 2010; Möller 2000; Rentschler 1996; Hull 1969; Bramsted 1965.

historians. The historians' contribution centres here on types of (visual) framing and censorship, and the possible psychological and propagandistic effects of imagery.[44] This enables our students to grasp the power of the image by studying different forms of selective representation of facts, relations between the facts, omissions and distortions on the one hand and manipulation, and ultimately demonization, idealisation and stereotyping on the other.[45] Joseph Goebbels and his theories on propaganda are discussed, since he evidently revolutionised modern state-dominated visual languages. In Goebbels' opinion, the best propaganda was the one that was not recognised as such and worked invisibly, an idea that was copied by many democracies.[46] This recognition also offers the opportunity to address the morality of such operations.

Didactically, in *Info at War* the students have again to dissect the visual rhetoric in iconic images, but this time stemming from *moving* images, be they documentaries, newsreel, or, indeed, war movies.[47] Given the advanced phase of their studies, we stimulate our students to select source material themselves and this has satisfying returns. Naturally, there are the 'classics', such as the very early shots from the *Boer War* or the stunning documentary *The Battle of the Somme* (1916). The German *Wochenschau*s and toxic 'documentaries' such as *Triumph des Willens* (1935) and *Jud Süß* (1940) also make for rewarding study material.[48] However, students also analyse the visual rhetoric, (self)censorship and conscious manipulations of images by western democracies. Examples from the Second World War are discussed, whereas the decolonisation era is often represented by Dutch material on Indonesia.[49] The Cold War period is covered by documentaries like *The Anderson Platoon* by Pierre Schoendoerffer (1967) and *The Fog of War: Eleven Lessons from the Life or Robert S. McNamara* (2003), both masterpieces. This also applies to the complex set of films by Joshua Oppenheimer, Christine Cynn and an anonymous film-maker about Indonesia, *The Act of Killing* (2012) and *The Look of Silence* (2014).[50] Serious analysis of our own Defence website and recruitment films can also teach much about the relationship of warfare and media. We therefore

---

[44] Jowett and O'Donnell 2014; Welch and Fox 2012; Brewer 2009.

[45] Stanley 2016; Jowett and O'Donnell 2014; Welch and Fox 2012; Cole 2010; Axelrod 2009; Cull et al. 2003; Visser 2002; Randal 2002; Rentschler 1996; Hale 1973; Hull 1969; Brown 1963.

[46] Longerich 2015; Möller 2000; Bramsted 1965.

[47] For years, our senior students could opt also for a related elective, specifically about fictitious (Hollywood) war movies, its imagery, codes and rhetoric. It was entitled *Battles on Screen* [*Oorlog op het Witte Doek*]. Given the limited space here and the fact that this course is temporarily 'off-screen', we refer to: Wetta and Novelli 2016; Suid 2015; Bender 2013; Bronfen 2012; Eberwein 2005, 2010; Slater 2009; Westwell 2006; Clarke 2006; Neale 2000; Doherty 1993; Black 1987; Basinger 1986; Dolan 1985.

[48] Rentschler 1996; Hale 1973; Hull 1969.

[49] Jansen Hendriks 2014, 2018; Zweers 2013.

[50] Barsam 1992.

Fig. 13.4 Historical reality, documentation and fiction can intertwine in startling ways. Gillo Pontecorvo's brilliant *La Battaglia di Algeri* (1966) about the Algerian War for Independence illustrates this clearly. It features actors *and* veterans. *Source* Still from https://www.youtube.com/watch?v=n3FD874-c2k (Accessed 23 May 2019)

often conclude the historical section of the minor with this funhouse mirror. It leaves our students discussing vehemently on the pros and cons of our own communication strategy and the visual language it employs (Fig. 13.4).

13.6 Conclusion

Young officers enter a disorienting world, full of strategic communication, media-ops, psy-ops, info-ops, embedded journalists, consensus building, propaganda, suggestive historical imagery, politically committed activists and a few critical journalists. Their complex working environment will often manifest itself through visual images, metaphors and narratives. A myriad of concepts and phrases has been used to describe the ways these are instrumentalized. Whatever the terminology, it is obvious that we are talking here about attempts to influence a targeted audience through its value systems, core beliefs, emotions and behaviour. These can be characterised as a form of 'indirect aggression' the effects of which are difficult to measure exactly, but also difficult to combat.

As said, imagery is often at the core of it. Many (political) messages are sold visually in slick convincing images. At the same time iconic images, with their symbolic quality, clearly entail narratives that have the power to change mentalities and value systems. Because of this, it is crucial to study them at military academies.

At the Faculty of Military Sciences of the NLDA (military) students now learn to recognise and understand the rhetoric of visual languages, and judge whether it is visually hostile or friendly fire. We equip them with an intellectual toolbox that we feel will eventually contribute to their situational awareness, which of course is the fundament of all good decision making.

Fortunately, as outlined above, the didactical means to accomplish fundamental changes and improvements in this respect are relatively down-to-earth. It does not require full-grown postmodern semiotics to achieve results. Developing skills in image analysis, and augmenting these with typical assets from the historical method does so too. For time and again we found that this recipe, combined with independent research and group discussions, stimulated fairly sophisticated explorations into the realm of iconic images, and stimulated critical inquiries into the relationship between form, content and function.

Dorothea Lange once wrote: "We see not only with our eyes but with all that we are and all that our culture is."[51] That is the heart of the matter. The modern officer will have to understand how friend and foe intentionally and unintentionally construct meaning by way of the composition, selection, colouring, highlighting, distortion, repeating and framing of images.[52] The (art)historical critical-analytic method provides him with the tools to deconstruct visual propaganda from both sides. It is consequently of great defensive value, since it undermines the messages/lies of potential enemies. But knowledge of the power and construction of visual messages can clearly also undermine our own narrative. Modern officers as 'thinking soldiers' need to come to terms with this. An academically trained officer ought to realise that meticulous and fair image analysis combined with the contextualising historical method puts everything into perspective, including their own (visual) rhetoric.

Within the context of the academic education of officers, the self-critical potential this engenders may even be its most important aspect, although doubt is often unjustly framed as weakness and as a distinctly unmilitary virtue. It importance may be underscored by returning to the very odd way Dutch servicemen portrayed themselves in Mali, as briefly discussed at the start of this chapter. Stunningly, theirs is far from the only example. On July 2, 2018, proud sailors of Zr Ms Holland of the Royal Dutch Navy walked down Times Square in New York in their white uniforms, throwing headgear into the air (Fig. 13.5). An exited crowd applauded them. It was immediately picked up the Royal Dutch Navy and proudly commented upon on their website. Everyone was enthusiastic: the people involved, their military organization, the spectators in New York.

Like its Mali counterpart, this is somewhat puzzling, to say the least. These sailors and their New York audience were recreating an iconic image of the Second World War that had nothing to do with them. Like actors on some sort of

---

[51] Meltzer (2000/1978).

[52] On military history as cultural history: Lynn 2003; Van Creveld 2008; Klinkert 2008; Lee 2011; Black 2012; Dussel 2013.

13 Iconic Images and Military Education: A Delicate Relationship

Fig. 13.5 Crew of the Zr Ms Holland on Times Square New York, July 2 2018, somehow curiously stuck in a self-staged historic iconic image. *Source* Website Royal Netherlands Navy

self-imposed film set they performed the iconic image of VJ-Day by Alfred Eisenstaedt and added the 1944 musical *New York, New York* and the 1949 MGM musical movie *On the Town*. Nobody seems to have noticed this homage was actually a parody or at the very least sent out a confusing message: did these sailors really believe that their recent mission was in any way comparable to fighting the Second World War? Did their audience believe they had won a war? Why model an inconsequential visit in this fashion? Was it meant to display the strength of ties between two nations even in times when trans-Atlantic ties seem weaker than they have been in decades? The example serves (again) to underline the great importance of incorporating the study of iconic imagery in academic military education.

References and Recommended Literature

Aasman S et al. (2010) Kracht van het beeld. Beeld als bron [Power of the image. Image as a source]. Groniek Historisch Tijdschrift. Stichting Groniek, Groningen.
Adams L (1996) The methodologies of art: An introduction. Icon Editions, New York.
Axelrod A (2009) Selling the Great War. The making of American propaganda. St. Martin's Press, New York.
Basinger J (1986) World War II Combat Film: The Anatomy of a Genre, 2003 edn. Columbia University Press, New York.
Bates MJ, Lichty L, Miles P, Spector RH (1998) Reporting Vietnam, Parts 1 & 2: American Journalism. The Library of America, New York.
Barsam RM (1992) Nonfiction Film. A Critical History Revised and Expanded. Indiana University Press, Bloomington.

Baudet F (2011) Ranke and Files: History and the Military. Storia della Storiografia (59–60): 63–83.
Bender S (2013) Film Style and the World War II Combat Genre. Cambridge Scholars Publishing, Newcastle upon Tyne.
Bennet WL, Palatz DI (1994) Taken by Storm. The media, public opinion, and US foreign policy in the Gulf War. University of Chicago Press, Chicago.
Berger J, Mohr J (1995) Appearances. In: Another Way of Telling. Vintage Books, New York: 81–129.
Black J (2004) Rethinking Military History. Routledge, New York.
Black J (2012) War and the Cultural Turn. Polity Press, Cambridge.
Black GD (1987) Hollywood Goes to War: How Politics, Profit and Propaganda Shaped World War II Movies. London.
Bouwmeester H (2017) Lo and Behold: Let the Truth be Told – Russian deception warfare in Crimea and Ukraine and the return of 'Maskirovka' en 'Reflexive Control Theory'. In: Ducheine PAL, Osinga FPB (eds) Winning without killing: The strategic and operational utility of non-kinetic capabilities in crises. TMC Asser Press, The Hague.
Bramsted E (1965). Goebbels and National Socialist Propaganda, 1925–1945. Michigan State University Press, East Lansing, Michigan.
Bredekamp H (2010) Theorie des Bildakts [Theory of the picture act]. Frankfurter Adorno-Vorlesungen 2007, Berlin.
Brewer S (2009) Why America fights. Patriotism and war propaganda from the Philippines to Iraq. Oxford University Press, Oxford.
Bronfen E (2012) Specters of War: Hollywood's Engagement with Military Conflict. Rutgers University Press, New Brunswick NJ.
Brown JAC (1963) Techniques of Persuasion: From Propaganda to Brainwashing. Pelican, Harmondsworth.
Cadava E (1997), Words of Light: Theses on the Photography of History. Princeton University Press, Princeton.
Carruthers SL (2011) The media at war. Palgrave MacMillan, Basingstoke/New York.
Casey S (2008) Selling the Korean War: Propaganda, politics and public opinion 1950–1953. Oxford University Press, Oxford/New York.
Charters DA, Milner M, Wilson JB (eds) (1992) Military History and the Military Profession. Praeger, Westport.
Clarke J (2006) War Films. Virgin Books, London.
Cole R (ed) (2010) Encyclopedia of Propaganda. Routledge, New York.
Cull N, Culbert J, Welch D (eds) (2003) Propaganda and Mass Persuasion: A Historical Encyclopedia, 1500 to the Present. Santa Barbara.
D'Alleva A (2012) Methods & Theories of Art History. Laurence King Publishing, London.
Devine JM (1999) Vietnam at 24 Frames a Second. A Critical and Thematic Analysis of Over 400 Films about the Vietnam War. University of Texas Press, Austin.
Doherty T (1993) Projections of War: Hollywood, American Culture, and World War II. Columbia University Press, New York.
Dolan EF (1985) Hollywood Goes to War. Bison Books, London.
Dussel I (2013) The visual turn in the history of education: Four comments for a historiographical discussion. In: Popkewitz TS (ed) Rethinking the history of education. Springer Press, Heidelberg/Berlin: 29–49.
Eberwein RT (2005) The War Film. Rutgers University Press, Oxford.
Eberwein RT (2010) The Hollywood War Film. Wiley-Blackwell, Chichester/Malden, MA.
Echevarria A (2005) The trouble with history in military education. Historically Speaking 7(1): 11–15.
Fabian R, Adam HC (1992) Bilder vom Krieg: 130 Jahre Kriegsfotografie - eine Anklage. Stern-Bücher im Verlag Gruner.
Fogu C (2003) The Historic Imagery. Politics of History in Fascist Italy. University of Toronto Press, Toronto/Buffalo/London.

Frazier N (1999) The Penguin Concise Dictionary of Art History. Penguin Reference, New York.
Gerhard PG (2004) Bilder des Krieges, Krieg der Bilder. Die Visualisierung des modernen Krieges. [Picture of the war. War of the pictures. The visualization of the modern war]. Wilhelm Fink, Munich.
Gorman M (2009) Media and Society into the 21th Century: A historical introduction. Wiley-Blackwell, Malden, MA (Chapter 10 deals specifically with media and the military).
Hale OJ (1973) The Captive Press in the Third Reich. Princeton University Press, Princeton, NJ.
Hallin DC (1989) The 'Uncensored' War. The media and Vietnam. Oxford University Press, New York/Oxford.
Hammond WM (1998) Reporting Vietnam. Media and military at war. University Press of Kansas, Lawrence.
Hariman R, Lucaites JL (2007) No captions needed: Iconic photographs, public culture, and liberal democracy. University of Chicago Press, Chicago.
Haskell F (1993) History and its Images. Art and the interpretation of the past. Yale University Press, New Haven/London.
Hughes M, Philpott WJ (2006), Modern Military History. Palgrave, New York.
Hull DS (1969) Film in the Third Reich: A Study of the German Cinema, 1933–1945. University of California Press, Berkeley.
Hunt L, Schwartz V (2010) Editorial Capturing the Moment: Images and eyewitnessing in history. Journal of Visual Culture 9(3): 259–271.
Jansen H (2010) Triptiek van de tijd. Geschiedenis in drievoud [Time's triptych. History in triplicate]. Vantilt, Nijmegen.
Jansen Hendriks G (2014) Een voorbeeldige kolonie. Nederlands-Indië in 50 jaar overheidsfilms 1912–1962 [An exemplary colony. 50 years of government-made films on the Dutch East-Indies 1912–1962]. PhD dissertation, Amsterdam University, Amsterdam.
Jansen Hendriks G (2018) Beelden van een oorlog die geen oorlog mocht zijn [Images of a war that couldn't be called a war]. Leidschrift, Historisch Tijdschrift 33(3): 63–80.
Johnson WM (1988) Art history: Its use and abuse. University of Toronto Press, Toronto.
Journal of Visual Culture (2002–present).
Jowett GS, O'Donnell V (2014) Propaganda and Persuasion. A detailed overview of the history, function, and analyses of propaganda. Sage Publications, California.
Kamber M (2013) Bilderkrieger: Von jenen, die ausziehen, uns die Augen zu öffnen – Kriegsfotografen erzählen [Warriors of the image: of those that open your eyes. War photographers speak]. Ankerherz Verlag, Hollenstedt.
Kane KR (1982) Visions of War: Hollywood Combat Films of World War II. UMI Research Press, Ann Arbor, Michigan.
Keegan J (1976) The face of battle. A study of Agincourt, Waterloo and the Somme. Pimlico, London.
Kjeldsen JE (2017) The rhetorical and argumentative potentials of press photography. In: Tseronis A, Forceville (eds) Multimodal Argumentation and Rhetoric in Media Genres. Amsterdam: 51–79.
Klinkert W (2008) Van Waterloo tot Uruzgan: de militaire identiteit van Nederland [From Waterloo to Uruzgan: the military identity of The Netherlands]. Amsterdam University Press, Amsterdam.
Klinkert W (2016) Clio en Mars in opleidingsland: een complexe relatie [Clio and Mars in the land of education: a complex relationship]. In: Brama L (ed) Traditie en vernieuwing [Tradition and innovation]. Mars en Historia, sl, pp 102–115.
Klinkert W (2018) Vorming voor de toekomst: Mars en Clio. Militaire geschiedenis voor thinking soldiers [Education for the future: Mars and Clio. Military history for thinking soldiers]. Netherlands Defence Academy, Breda.
Knieper T, Müller MG (eds) (2005) War Visions. Bildkommunikation und Krieg [War Visions. Communication by imagery and war] Herbert von Halem Verlag, Cologne.
Knightley P (2004) The first casualty. The war correspondent as hero and myth-maker from the Crimea tot Iraq. Johns Hopkins University Press, Baltimore/London.

Knightley P (2003) The Eye of war. Weidenfeld and Nicolson, London.
Kroes R (2007) Photographic memories: private pictures, public images, and the American history. Dartmouth College Press, Hanover NH.
Lee EL (2011) Warfare and culture in world history. New York University Press, New York/London.
Longerich P (2015) Goebbels: A Biography. Random House, New York.
Lowenthal D (1985) The past is a foreign country. Cambridge University Press, Cambridge.
Lowenthal D (1998) The heritage crusade and the spoils of history. Cambridge University Press, Cambridge.
Lynn JA (1997) Rally Once Again: The Embattled Future of Academic Military History. Journal of Military History 61: 777–789.
Lynn JA (2003) Battle. A history of combat and culture. From Ancient Greece to modern America. Westview Press, Cambridge MA.
Mearsheimer JJ (1988) Liddell Hart and the Weight of History. Cornell Studies in Security Affairs, Ithaca NY.
Melching W (2018) Beeldenstorm: iconische foto's en het beeld van de Verenigde Staten [Iconic photos and the image of the United States]. Leidschrift, Historisch Tijdschrift 33(3): 81–99.
Meltzer M (2000/1978) Dorothea Lange: A Photographer's Life. Syracuse University Press, New York.
Mitchell WTJ (1994) Picture Theory: Essays on Visual and Verbal Representation. University of Chicago Press, Chicago/London.
Möller F (2000) The Film Minister: Goebbels and the Cinema in the Third Reich/Der Filmminister: Goebbels und der Film im Dritten Reich. Edition Axel Menges Stuttgart/London.
Mondzain M-J (2010) What does seeing an image mean. Journal of Visual Culture 9(3): 307–315.
Moorcraft PL, Taylor PM (2008) Shooting the Messenger: The political impact of war reporting. Potomac Books, Washington.
Morillo S (2006) What is Military History. Polity Press, Malden MA.
Murray W, Sinnreich RH (eds) (2006) The Past as Prologue: The Importance of History to the Military Profession. Cambridge University Press, Cambridge.
Neale S (2000). War Films. Genre and Hollywood. Psychology Press, London.
Nelson RS, Shiff R (1996) Critical terms for art history. University of Chicago Press, Chicago.
Osgood K, Frank AK (2010) Selling War in a Media Age: The Presidency and Public Opinion in the American Century. University Press of Florida, Gainesville.
Parish JR (1990) The Great Combat Pictures: Twentieth-Century Warfare on the Screen. Scarecrow Press, Methuen, NJ.
Patrikarakos D (2017) War in 140 Characters. How social media is reshaping conflict in the twenty-first century. Basic Books, New York.
Paul C, Kim JJ (2004) Reporters on the battlefield. The Embedded Press System in historical context. RAND Corporation, Santa Monica.
Perlmutter DD (1998) Photojournalism and Foreign Policy: Icons of Outrage in International Crises. Praeger Publishers, Westport, CT.
Perlmutter DD (1999) Visions of War: Picturing Warfare from the Stone Age to the Cyberage. St. Martin's Press, New York.
Perlmutter DD (2008) Blogwars: The New Political Battleground. Oxford University Press, Oxford/New York.
Randal M (2002) Propaganda & The Ethics of Persuasion. Broadview Press, New York.
Record J (2002) Making War, Thinking History. Munich, Vietnam and presidential use of force from Korea tot Kosovo. Naval Institute Press, Annapolis.
Rentschler E (1996) The Ministry of Illusion: Nazi Cinema and Its Afterlife. Harvard University Press, Cambridge.
Rousmanière K (2001) Questioning the visual in the history of education. History of Education 30 (2): 109–116.
Rutherford P (2004) Weapons of Mass Persuasion: Marketing the War Against Iraq. University of Toronto Press, Toronto.

Samuels M (2004) The illustrated history book. History between word and image. In: Schwartz V, Przyblyski J (eds) The Nineteenth-Century Visual Culture Reader. Routledge, New York: 238–248.
Slater J (2009) Under Fire: a century of war movies. Ian Allan Publishing, Hersham UK.
Stanley J (2016) How Propaganda Works. Princeton University Press, Princeton NJ.
Suid, LH (2015) Guts & Glory: The Making of the American Military Image in Film. University Press of Kentucky, Lexington.
Taylor M (2003) The Vietnam War in History, Literature, and Film. University of Alabama Press, Tuscaloosa.
Tosh J, Lang S (2006) The pursuit of history. Aims, methods and new directions in the study of history. Pearson Education Limited, Harlow.
Tucker AW, Michels W, Zelt N (2012) War/Photography. Images of armed conflict and its aftermath. Yale University Press, New Haven/London.
Van Creveld M (2008) The culture of war. Ballantine Books, New York.
Verduyn L (2010) De Tweede Wereldoorlog door de ogen van de Duitsers. De geschiedenis van hetpropagandatijdschrift Signaal [The second World War through the eyes of the Germans. The history of the propaganda magazine Signaal]. Van Halewyck, Leuven.
Von der Dunk HW (2007) In het huis van de herinnering. Een cultuurhistorische verkenning [In the house of memories. A cultural-historical exploration]. Bert Bakker, Amsterdam.
Visser D (2002) Image and identity in military education: a perspective on the South African Military Academy. Society in Transition 1 (33): 173–186.
Walsh J, Aulich J (1989) Vietnam Images: War and Representation. MacMillan Press, London.
Welch D, Fox J (2012) Justifying War: Propaganda, Politics and the Modern Age. Palgrave MacMillan, Basingstoke/New York.
Westwell G (2006) Short Cuts. War Cinema: Hollywood on the Front Line. Wallflower, London/New York.
Wetta F, Novelli M (2016) Last Stands from the Alamo to Benghazi. How Hollywood turns military defeats into moral victories. Routledge, New York.
Wyatt CR (1995) Paper Soldiers. The American Press and Vietnam. University of Chicago Press, Chicago.
Zweers L (2013) De gecensureerde oorlog. Militairen versus de media in Nederlands-Indië 1945–1949. [The censored war. Military against the media in the Dutch East-Indies 1945–1949]. Walburg Pers, Zutphen.

Henk de Jong, MA is assistant professor of Military History at the Faculty of Military Sciences of the Netherlands Defence Academy. His research focusses on cultural aspect of war and warfare.

Dr. Floribert Baudet is associate professor of Strategy at the Faculty of Military Sciences of the Netherlands Defence Academy and serves as its Director of Education. His research mainly focusses on the Cold War and strategic communication.

Chapter 14
Bologna Meets the Battlefield – Using Historical Battlefields in Modern Academic Military Education

Wim Klinkert

Contents

14.1 Introduction 232
14.2 The Battlefield Tour: Terminology 233
14.3 The Emergence of the Battlefield Tour 234
14.4 Development Stagnates 237
14.5 Reintroduction and Growth 238
14.6 Towards the Dutch Military Historical Analysis 240
14.7 Final Remarks 244
References 244

Abstract Traditionally Staff or War Colleges used battlefields from the past as training tools for officers. Analysing and discussing historical military confrontations on the location that these confrontations had taken place, is thought to increase the understanding of officers about the realities of war and improve their decision making in the future. In many ways, it is a very practice-orientated method of education military professionals. Its aim is not to turn the officers into academic military historians. A more reflective or academic approach to educational visits to battlefields seemed, from the military standpoint, unnecessary. But because in recent years, military education has reached the level of its civilian academic counterpart more and more, the battlefield tour has to adjust to that level as well. That is why we need more thorough academic reflection on this didactical tool. This process started about two decades ago, but needs to be developed further. Not only because of the creation of military educational curricula that follow civilian academic standards, but also to find affiliation with cultural historians and historians of

W. Klinkert (✉)
Faculty of Military Sciences, Netherlands Defence Academy, PO Box 90002,
4800 PA Breda, The Netherlands
e-mail: w.klinkert.01@mindef.nl

© T.M.C. ASSER PRESS and the authors 2019
W. Klinkert et al. (eds.), *NL ARMS Netherlands Annual Review of Military Studies 2019*, NL ARMS, https://doi.org/10.1007/978-94-6265-315-3_14

memory, *lieu de mémoire* and tourism, who increase our understanding of the battlefields of the past. This chapter examines the Dutch effort to create a battlefield tour that both meets academic standards on bachelor level as well as gives cadets professional insights into the 'realities of war', which are relevant for their future work as subaltern officers. Based on the philosophy of the 'thinking soldier', but also rooted into the history of military education, this *academic* version of the battlefield tour should help officers in training developing critical thought and skills for academic analysis.

Keywords Officers' Education · Battlefield tour · Staff Ride · Military History · Netherlands Army · Educational Tools · Thinking Soldier

14.1 Introduction

In 1907, an unlikely candidate was appointed as a teacher at the US Staff College in Fort Leavenworth (Kansas): Captain Arthur Conger (1872–1951). He had been in the US Army only since 1898, when he joined voluntarily as a private, and had only seen actual fighting in the Philippines shortly after that. A Harvard graduate in philosophy and theosophy, and a composer, Conger had travelled Europe widely before joining up. The army quickly spotted his pedagogical and academic qualities, which led to his appointment at the Staff College. Within a short period, Conger revolutionized the study of military campaigns at the College by introducing historical source criticism as a fundamental element in the war studies curriculum. He made his students dig deep into a selected number of military campaigns, using original source material and encouraging critical thinking, not hindered by the doctrine of the day. Using maps and original orders and making the students empathize with the generals of the past, Conger encouraged them to think critically for themselves on issues of military command. They were also encouraged to find additional eyewitness accounts and other corroborating source material, all of which they had to assess critically, according to the rules of the historical profession.

Conger realized that the tenure of a military teacher was limited and that his didactic approach was unfamiliar to the army. That made him look for a civilian academic partner: Frederick Fling (1860–1934) of the University of Nebraska, a pioneer in teaching history based mainly on source criticism.[1] During Conger's absence in Germany in 1910–1913, Fling ensured the continuity of the program. On his return, Conger laid even more emphasis on critical analysis of military sources and writing essays. Both were complementary and necessary for officers, according to Conger, in order "to profit from the experience of others" and for "penetrating the

---

[1] Osborne 2003.

fog of war (...) and finding out what is really the tactical and strategical problem confronting him."[2]

When in 1917 the US entered the First Word War, the army schools were suspended, and Conger departed for service in France. Although he remained in the army as an intelligence officer and military attaché in several European capitals until 1928, he did not return to his teaching post. His innovative experiment, combining military operational analysis with historical source criticism according to civilian academic standards came to an end. So did the cooperation with the University of Nebraska. It would take half a century for the US officers' education to repair formal ties with civilian academic institutions in the field of history. Why was the added value that an academic approach could bring not considered relevant for such a long time? But before we look into that question, we should first look at that element of battlefield study that Conger ignored: the battlefield tour.

14.2 The Battlefield Tour: Terminology

The volume of academic literature on the use of battlefield tours as an educational tool is very limited, although those tours have a venerable past and gained a substantial popularity since the 1980s. Maybe they did not attract much academic interest because they are generally seen as either a nice outing with a professional ring to it or because military educational institutes have not fully appreciated the possible academic value of this kind of teaching. Probably it is a combination of these elements. But a more thorough look at this phenomenon is necessary because many present-day institutes for officers' education choose to follow civilian academic standards. This makes the effort to analyse this unique manner of professional teaching and investigate its academic potential more urgent than ever.

Two in-depth studies into the role of battlefields in officers' education exist: Carol Reardon's (1951–) *Soldiers and scholars* from 1990 and Peter Caddick Adams'[3] (1960–) 2007 Ph.D. thesis. They both form excellent introductions to the theme, but fail to address the problem of applying civilian academic standards in the tours. Moreover, Reardon's work only deals with the period 1865–1920. Additionally, the *Society for Military History* in 2001 dedicated a conference on the theme of battlefield tours, which resulted four years later in a special issue of the *Defence Studies Journal*.[4] Although this issue offers valuable new insights and indicates interesting themes for further discussion, a follow-up so far has not materialized. Finally, during the extensive hearings on Professional Military Education (PME) held by the American Congress in 2009, battlefield tours only received a cursory mention.

---

[2] Cited in Reardon 1990.
[3] Caddick Adams 2010.
[4] Also published by the Strategic and Combat Studies Institute at Shrivenham as *Occasional Paper 48.*

Battlefield tourism, on the other hand, has developed into a productive field of scholarly study, but again neglecting the military academic educational element.[5]

The terminology of military visits to historic battle sites is confusing and far from unambiguous. Even between the US and the UK terms differ. In his Ph.D. thesis Caddick Adams has tried to shed some light on the matter, and I will follow it here and expand a bit. According to Adams visits to battlefields can have very distinct characters – from a pleasant day out to promote the *esprit de corps* of the unit to a fully-fledged study trip as an integral part of a military course. When a group just listens to a tour guide, with no obligations before or after, 'battlefield tour' would be, according to Caddick Adams, the proper name. Other types of battlefield visits could be called 'staff rides', when the participants are well prepared as for contents, discusses the topics raised, explains elements of the operation to fellow group members and finishes with a joint reflection in one form or the other.

While this use of terms would ensure a clear and useful distinction, the term 'battlefield tour' is used in daily practice for a wide variety of battlefield visits. To complicate things further, service personnel can also participate in tactical exercises without troops (TEWT), which can deal with a purely fictional scenario, but which can also include historical elements or, alternatively, be completely historical in nature. The TEWT has, mostly, a purely military character, organized either by a staff of some institution of military learning.

The Dutch curriculum for primary officers' education has a relatively long tradition of combining battlefield tours with academic training. Building on this experience, teachers in Breda developed a concept that is both recognized as being academically on a bachelor level while at the same time directly related to the professional work field of (junior) officers: the Military Historical Analysis (MHA) – a course within the War Studies curriculum that combines a site visit with both historical methodology and an academic multidisciplinary approach all in the context of an historical military operation.

14.3 The Emergence of the Battlefield Tour

The first visitor to what is probably the world's most famous battlefield, Waterloo, arrived the day after the battle ended, on 19 June 1815. From that day onwards a steady stream of bereaved relatives and tourists found their way to the site.[6] But these visits had little to do with military education and certainly formed no part of any military educational curriculum.

Visiting sites in the open air for professional educational purposes was first done by the Prussian army. Gerhard von Scharnhorst (1755–1813), one of the most influential reformers and modernisers of the Prussian staff system, included staff

---

[5] Lloyd 1998; Ryan 2007; Bird 2016.
[6] Schoenmaker 2014.

rides into officers' education, which was one of the main tasks of the General Staff. After the resounding German victory over France in 1870–1871, this system became the benchmark for all Western armies. The British army established its General Staff in 1904, one year after the United States. Studies of the German army were translated into English or were written for the purpose. One of the most prominent of those was *The Brain of an Army* published in 1895 by the Oxford historian Spenser Wilkinson (1853–1937). In which he also discussed the so-called 'practice tour' (*Übungsreise*), a TEWT, in which all tasks of staff officers during operations were included and trained. Wilkinson appreciated the importance the German General staff attributed to (recent) military history and the thoroughness with which it was taught. He also grasped that its aim was practical, creating tactically well-trained officers, not academics or critical thinkers. Historical tours did not feature in the German educational system, despite the well-nourished pride in the army's achievements. Only on some occasions were historic sites included into a staff ride and were discussions on decisions made by commanding officers during historical operations included into the field trips.[7]

It was Eben Swift (1854–1938) and John Frederick Maurice (1841–1912), an American and British officer respectively, who brought the historical aspect into the German style staff ride. Swift's predecessor, Arthur Wagner (1853–1905),[8] had made a first attempt to introduce these visits into the curriculum, but had failed, partly because of the alleged costs. In 1906 Swift successfully combined the tactical exercises in the field and the war games in the classroom into an annual trip for both the Staff and War College to the Civil War battlefields. Aware of the possible criticism that it was just an outing, Swift had the participants prepare assignments beforehand and hand in a written professional evaluation of the battle or campaign visited afterwards. Swift used maps of historical campaigns, mostly from the Civil War, and stated his aim was to enhance insight into warfare in practice and to apply theoretical concepts in the fields of strategy and tactics. Particularly however Swift stressed, these tours had to focus on situations the officers were expected to encounter during their career. This practical utility made the trip more acceptable to sceptics, one of whom was no other than Conger himself.

Conger doubted the educational value of visits to historical sites, because the former battlefields were full of misplaced or misleading monuments and explanations of events that were, after a scrutiny of sources, demonstrably incorrect. Swift disagreed; pointing out that seeing the actual terrain would inspire a better judgement on historical decisions and allow new explanations for the course of the battle. This could lead to interesting operational and tactical discussions.

Swift's trips sometimes also included meetings with veterans and with the army brass from Washington, who considered these trips good opportunities to meet

---

[7] On the German Staff and educational system, see Von Moser 1927; Görtitz 1953; Thielo 1964 and Kollmer 2003; in Britain the subject was dealt with by Spenser Wilkinson (1853–1937), Richard Haking (1862–1945) (see Haking 1908) and Arthur Henry Marindin (1868–1947) (see Marindin 1907).

[8] Brereton 2000. See also Duncan 2016.

young colleagues, training for higher rank. Be that as it may, as was the case with Conger's teaching, the period of the war with Mexico and First World War brought the trips to an end.[9]

The British experience began a little earlier than the American one. John Maurice was the innovative initiator of the military history curriculum. With recent battle experience in the British colonies in Africa he arrived at Staff College (Camberley) and organized the first tour in 1885. His inspiration probably came from the German example of the *Stabsreise* but also from the introduction of both the TEWT[10] and the war game by former history teacher and later commandant of Staff College Edward Bruce Hamley (1824–1893). Also the occasional trips to historical sites by another military history teacher at Staff College and famous author, George Henderson (1854–1903) might have influenced Maurice. His initiative struck a chord and the travels to the battlefields of the war of 1870 in France became a yearly event, lasting up to the First World War. The students focused on campaign planning, the interaction between tactics and terrain, and later also on international law in relation to warfare. The trips were called either staff rides or staff tours. Both Swift's and Maurice's tours were not academic in nature. Both organisers were first and foremost active serving officers.

Both the early American and the British visits to historical battlefields were intended for mid-career staff officers only, although from 1902 until 1916 tours to the Civil War battlefields organised for West Point cadets took place.[11] These trips played no major part in primary officers' education however, but they definitely inspired cadets like George Patton and Dwight Eisenhower, who both took part in those tours to study historical campaigns. And as a result both retained a life-long passion for visiting historical battlefields. As far as we know, the British equivalent Sandhurst refrained from organizing such trips.

The Prussian General Staff and military educational system also strongly influenced the Dutch army, especially after 1870. This meant the Dutch army General Staff established a historical department (1891) and introduced strategic map exercises as well as staff rides, both for training staff officers and analysing possible future operations. None of these contained historical analyses, however. Moreover, the Staff College in The Hague did not include historical field trips in its curriculum. In 1905 two teachers of the Dutch Staff School visited the battlefields of the Franco-German war, and similar trips were made during the following years, but there is no evidence that the students were ever invited to join those tours.[12]

---

[9] Reardon 1990.

[10] The term was first used in 1913.

[11] The teacher behind this initiative was Gustave Fieberger.

[12] Klinkert (2016); the early proponents of combining military training with field visits were, in Russia, Nikolai Obruchev (1830–1904), in France Jules Lewal (1823–1908) and, in Canada, Sam Hughes (1853–1921), but all failed to make historical rides permanent elements within the staff course curriculum.

14.4 Development Stagnates

The end of the First World War saw the emergence of an enormous interest in visiting the sites of the recent battles. Former soldiers and family members of those perished made pilgrimages to the former trench lines, but very soon a wider audience of civilian visitors, fascinated by the war they had only known from newspapers and films descended upon the former front lines.

The British Staff College resumed its visits to France in 1923. The staff rides were now a more structured part of the officer training and included assignments to study aspects of modern warfare in greater depth. Also visits to the former fronts in Italy and East Prussia were included. In the United States, on the other hand, these kinds of initiatives remained few and far apart. The relevance of studying the Civil War as part of a modern officers' education was questioned, and recent battlefields were not close at hand. Only the War College organized visits to Civil War battlefields in the 1920s, but they did not seem to be very relevant for the curriculum. As an element in curricula for officers' education the Staff ride with a historical element all but disappeared. The ideas of Swift, Conger and Maurice had evidentially not really taken root.

The same can be said of smaller countries such as The Netherlands. We know Dutch officers visited the former eastern front in Germany, the Alpine front and, of course, many locations on the Western Front. But these study trips were either dedicated trips by officers assigned to write field manuals or a continuation of the visits of teachers at Staff Colleges or Military Academies which had started in 1905.

The Second World War, and the early decades of the Cold War following it, did surprisingly little to revive the former innovative spirit of applying history in military education. Especially the 1950s until the 1970s were 'dark ages' for military history in general. Nuclear war dominated military thinking and the tactics and military operations of the past seemed to have lost all relevance for officers' training. In many military educational institutes military history vanished from the curriculum altogether or remained only a shadow of what it had once been. Military organisations were no longer convinced of the practical use of analysing former battles in depth, let alone visiting the actual sites.

Of course, there were some exceptions worth mentioning. Again it was the British institutes for higher military education that at least kept the flame alive. Visiting Normandy, and the subsequent British campaigns in Western Europe in 1944–1945, became a permanent part of the professional training of British officers. In 1947 the British Army of the Rhine (BAOR) published a number of military guidebooks that have remained in use ever since. Staff College made the Normandy-tour a prominent and permanent element in its course until 1979. Regularly officers who had actually participated in the 1944 campaign explained their wartime decisions on the historical locations, while German officers were invited to share their side of the story. Also, the British army was lucky to have Richard Holmes (1946–2011) among its ranks, who tirelessly promoted military history in general and staff rides in particular. The British Army also was instrumental in keeping the staff ride alive as a form of *education permanente* for officers of other nationalities. They were invited to participate, either as students in a British military college or as colleagues working at one of the NATO-headquarters.

Surprisingly enough, the Dutch Staff College visited Normandy as early as 1948, but this trip was overshadowed by criticism about the costs and found no follow-up at all. The exercises the staff officers conducted abroad, mostly in the Belgian Ardennes, included no military historical elements.

14.5 Reintroduction and Growth

Times began to change during the 1980s. The more or less sudden revival, or sometimes first introduction, of the historical site visit, is really remarkable. Crucial in this re-introduction was William Robertson (1944–),[13] a military history teacher at the Army Command and General Staff College since 1981. In 1983 he organized the first staff ride from Leavenworth to the Civil War battlefields since the First World War. It was part of the curriculum as an elective.

The War College followed suit. Here the well-known military historian Jay Luvaas (1929–2009), like Robertson a prominent author on the Civil War, played an essential part in the revival. Not only did Luvaas teach at the War College,[14] in 1986 he also published the first modern US Army War College battlefield guide to the Civil War.

Simultaneously, visiting historical battle sites also became popular among unit commanders and in army periodicals. In 1987 Derek Miller, for instance, published an article in the American military journal *Infantry* on the relevance of the historic TEWT for the army of today.[15] He based his analysis on his personal experience, developing and commanding a TEWT held in April 1984 based on the fighting in the Hürtgen Forest (Eifel, western Germany) in November 1944 and of other World War II operations later. He stated, "the goal of the entire exercise was learning and professional development" but he also stressed these exercises strengthened the unit's *esprit de corps*.

The Army Historian devoted in October 1988 its entire issue to staff rides, opening with an endorsement by the highest echelons, viz. Carl Vuono (1934–),[16] who described these rides as a valuable analytical learning experience joining practice and theory, helping to improve doctrine and improving insights into leadership and command.

---

[13] Later head of the Combat Studies Institute.
[14] Opened in Washington in 1904, moved to Carlisle in 1951.
[15] Miller 1987.
[16] The Chief of Staff of the United States Army.

In Britain the Joint Services Command and Staff College[17] reintroduced the Normandy battlefield tour in 1988. As the participants now were high-ranking officers from many different countries, the focus shifted from the tactical level to the operational and strategic levels, stressing command in a joint and combined military environment. Seminars were added for discussing the most salient themes for the present and future, using past experiences.

This comeback of the historical staff ride in the 1980s was remarkable. It can be partly explained by the intellectual resurrection of military studies in general after the Vietnam War. After this tragic experience the US Army tried to 'rediscover' the essence of warfare by thoroughly studying the history of conventional warfare. The one-sided focus on nuclear war and strategy had failed to give an answer as to how to actually fight a non-nuclear war. Military history and military thinking quickly found its way into all curricula of military education and into the development of new military doctrines.

The Vietnam conflict also raised academic interest in the complex relationship between war and society and made military history based on that broader perspective a more acceptable civilian academic discipline. Ohio State University was in the front line of this development. Although the military approach to history remained distinctly different from the academic one, some interaction did take place. More than before 'combat experience' from a psychological and sociological perspective entered the staff ride. Moral, juridical, ethical themes became part of the subjects discussed, next to more traditional military themes such as leadership and the elements influencing military decision-making.

This broader, multidisciplinary approach also had British roots, in particular the new approach to military history that was introduced by John Keegan (1934–2012) was important. This civilian teacher of military history at Sandhurst published two seminal studies with a huge impact: *Face of Battle* in 1976 and *The Mask of Command* in 1987. In these books Keegan approached battles from the perspective of both the soldier and the commander: what influenced his physical and mental condition during a battle? How did leadership and command change? How were battles influenced by technology, by the state of medical expertise, by cultural ideas on heroism, sacrifice and responsibility? And, what was the role of the weather, the terrain features, the effect of weapons, etc. Keegan meticulously analysed the historical settings of battles and command decisions using a wide variety of data and insights from several disciplines. Cultural, ethical,[18] social and technical aspects were brought together, be it on the level of the individual soldiers or the decision makers. Slowly this approach found its way into academic military history and into staff rides.

---

[17] Established in 1997 when the staff colleges of the three Services merged. The Normandy tour was part of the Staff College inheritance.

[18] See for instance the work of Martin Cook.

14.6 Towards the Dutch Military Historical Analysis

Before the 1980s the Royal Netherlands Military Academy in Breda had no history of structurally organized visits to historical battlefields. Furthermore, no academically educated military history teacher was appointed until in the mid-1970s, when Jan Schulten (1933–), an army officer with an academic degree in history, a rare phenomenon at the time, acquired the position. He had become familiar with battlefield tours from his posting at the Rheindalen barracks in Germany, where British units were accommodated. In Breda Schulten started to take the cadets to the Arnhem battlefield of September 1944, among others. More importantly, together with colleagues he organized trips, combining elements of military training with military history and military sociology. The most successful and innovative of these was the so-called Peiper tour, following in the footsteps of the *Kampfgruppe Peiper* during the Battle of the Bulge in December 1944. Close to Malmédy in the northern Ardennes, the SS-unit of Jochen Peiper (1915–1976) had massacred over 70 American POWs. This event was the reason to include discussions on the responsibility of military commanders in the tour. Other elements that were added focused on leadership, sleep deprivation and combat motivation. Purely military questions on, among others, fighting with motorized and armoured units in hilly terrain, were added. A generation of Dutch cadets experienced the 'Peiper-tour' in the 1980s and early 1990s, which set a standard for battlefield tours in the Dutch Army.

This initiative 'from below' took root because staff members and cadets appreciated it, but it also profited from the ambition of the Ministry of Defence to raise the level of primary officers' education at the Academy. This meant that step-by-step the scholarly level of the staff improved, but all in all it would take the Academy more than three decades to establish a curriculum comparable to civilian academic institutions. A decisive break through in this process was the Bologna Declaration of 1999, which made an academic bachelor curriculum feasible for the Dutch primary officers' education.[19]

In this long quest for academic status, the opportunity arose to integrate a historical site visit into the curriculum, this time using the case of the Grebbeberg. This small Dutch battlefield of May 1940, the last stand of the Dutch Field Army against the German invader, lent itself perfectly for a more methodological historical approach because the after-action reports are abundant, there are historiographical controversies on the course and interpretation of the battle and the scale permits students to research platoons, groups and even individuals.[20] In a way, the Grebbeberg functions as a microcosm of human behaviour in war: from brave deeds of sacrifice to cowardice, from leading by example to completely dysfunctional leaders and everything in between. Combining these elements of behaviour in combat with tactical questions and the larger political and strategic issues defining

---

[19] Klinkert 2012, 2018.
[20] On the battle: Kamphuis and Amersfoort 2010.

the Dutch defence in May 1940 adds up to a didactically strong combination for explaining to cadets what war actually is. Since the former battlefield is preserved well, it is a protected nature reserve, and because it is the site of the main Dutch war cemetery, the visit really adds to the learning motivation as well as to historical empathy.

More or less simultaneously two other developments created favourable circumstances for further developing this learning tool. First, from the 1980s onwards the Dutch Military Historical Institutes of the three Services evolved into more professional academic historical institutions, staffed by civilian trained historians. They became important military historical think tanks, focussing on the Dutch armed forces. Second, the Staff College in The Hague started to introduce battlefield tours into its curriculum in the early 1990s. The destinations varied from the Belgian Ardennes to Sedan (1940), Ypres (1914–1918) and the area of the Masurian Lakes in North-eastern Poland (1944–1945). These visits formed an integral part of the course on the development of 19th and 20th century military thinking and operational art. Civilian historians from both the Military Academy and the Military History Institute of the Ministry of Defence led the visits. The Staff College did not have its own history department. When the staff courses of the three Services merged, these battlefield tours disappeared from the new Joint Staff College and were taken over by the Army as part of its preliminary course for staff officers, preceding their participation in the joint course. This decision shows that for higher military education the staff ride within the Dutch army is, for the most part, an Army affair and dedicated to acquiring a deeper insight into the operational level of war, with a focus on military decision-making, the role of the commander and on joint cooperation.

In Breda meanwhile, following the opportunities offered by the Bologna Process, a Faculty was established in 2005, providing an academic bachelor education for cadets and midshipmen. War Studies became one of the bachelor programs. Based on the aforementioned experiences, and others,[21] the new War Studies curriculum included a week-long tour for cadets and midshipmen in the second study year. The chair for military history is responsible for its academic quality. This means the tour has to meet the requirements of a civilian academic course on bachelor level. Therefore the name 'Military Historical Analysis' (MHA) was chosen.

On the one hand, MHA has to appeal to concrete elements of military life in order to really activate the students' attention. The story of a battle, of actual events and people in battle is something they can relate to, from which more broad and abstract themes can follow. Moreover, having the students 'make' the tour (they do all presentations, they provide 'commanders of the day') and insisting on the correct use of military terms and of military terrain orientation, creates that military feel

---

[21] For instance, shortly before the new Breda curriculum was designed, the Naval College in Den Helder already organized week-long tours to the WW I trench lines in France, but also to Turkey and Berlin.

part of the trip. In my opinion this contributes positively to the students' conviction that academic study is an integral part of professional military education.

On the other hand, MHA is based on academic considerations:

- It has to be of a multidisciplinary character, reflecting the nature of the War Studies bachelor.
- Training academic skills has to form an important element.
- The course has to be closely connected to the course on research methodology of academic historical research.
- It has to give an insight into the workings of military organisations, especially into the realities of warfare in the broadest sense.

In sum, these considerations must ensure the course reflects the ideal of the thinking soldier. It must encourage critical thinking on an academic level and prepare the students with knowledge and insight into the environment in which they will work. Since 2014 Operation Overlord (Normandy 1944) has been the subject of the course.[22]

How does this work out in practice? The tour is preceded by a number of informative lectures, in which teachers reflect from different perspectives on the operation at hand: the operational aspects of the different Services; the role of military and humanitarian law; the strategic and political considerations that shaped the choices that led to the operation; logistics; the use of intelligence and the civil-military relations within the area of deployment.

Parallel to these lectures the students work, individually or in small groups, on their assignment, resulting in a 45-min presentation held on a historical site. Academic skills are furthered because the students have to find all relevant documentation themselves, assess the value and reliability of their finds and present a coherent analytical exposé, in which the location where it is held provides an added value. The whole process of gathering, assessing and arranging the information is evaluated after the trip. The whole process of working with, sometimes contradictory, information has been introduced in an earlier course on research methodology of historical research. This course, scheduled a few months before the tour, focuses not only on source criticism and historical empathy but also tries to make students aware of historical (dis)continuity, contextualisation, interpretation, the forming of historical 'myths'. The written exercises and most of the examples used all deal with the same historical case as the tour and they make the students aware of the wide variety of (military-historical) source material, the relationship between the main research questions and the sources of information used and on the historiographical discussion as a central element of academic historical work. At the end of the tour, the students must be able to reflect on their own learning process. This self-reflection is presented orally and graded.

---

[22] Earlier tours took place in Belgium (World War I), Alsace-Lorraine (warfare 1870–1945) and Northwestern France (warfare 1650–1945).

In fact, using historical source criticism to stimulate critical thinking brings us back to Conger with whom this article began. He did not believe in the added value of actually visiting the historical sites that were studied. I disagree with him on this issue. Especially for officers, acquiring a 'military eye' for terrain and its influence on military decision-making by actually visiting the site where the historical battle took place is essential. This military dimension is essential for their professional training. Adding historical research techniques and source criticism to the learning goals and making the subjects that are dealt with far more multidisciplinary is essential for their academic development and dealing with a wide variety of issues reflects not only the broader approach to military history which is the standard nowadays in the academic world, it also reflects the wide variety of issues the military have to deal with in modern missions all over the world.

Especially the use of historical methodology has not been undisputed since Conger. In 2005 for instance the prominent military historian Antullio Echevarria pointed out that only when students know how history as an academic discipline really works, they can develop their own critical thinking, instead of just accepting the 'lessons learned' presented to them. Officers in training have to understand the constructivist element in what is presented as reality.[23] This academic critical thinking, Echevarria points out, is not always seen by the military as something that should be encouraged. In fact, Echevarria more or less added to an old criticism of the British officer Ian Hamilton (1853–1947), who remarked that as soon a battle was fought, "the naked truths" and the real "hope and fears" had "put on uniform", meaning they were thrown into the straightjacket of the politically and militarily preferred interpretation, no longer to be put under scrutiny by officers.[24] These criticisms only add to the urgency of including the historian's trade into the curriculum of future officers.[25]

Another essential element of the Military Historical Analysis is its before mentioned multidisciplinarity. An historical single case study is eminently suited for in-depth analysis of the complex and diverse interrelationships that are inherent of modern battle. In the Dutch case, expertise from the different Services is combined with insights from intelligence studies, law, strategic studies and, of course, history. This choice reflects the present War Studies bachelor. Multidisciplinarity in fact is the foundation on which the War Studies bachelor rests. Bringing it into practice is one of our main challenges. Historical analyses with site visits are ideally suited for this. They might even be considered steps to interdisciplinarity, an ideal that works as an inspiration for future didactical developments.

Added to the MHA are the theme of civil-military relations in wartime and of remembrance and memory. Visiting military cemeteries, for instance, offers a unique opportunity for discussing the function, form and relevance of remembering

---

[23] Echevarria 2005.
[24] Hamilton 1905.
[25] Keller 2016. See also Hall 2010.

wars from the (recent) past. This reflection on remembrance can lead to very personal and open discussions with the students who, during their careers, will certainly be involved in remembrance ceremonies.

14.7 Final Remarks

Visits to historical battlefields that are truly embedded into an academic curriculum can stimulate both multidisciplinarity and bring military practice and academic theory closer together in a very stimulating way. Moreover, they give an excellent opportunity to the further development of the students' academic skills and their insight into academic research methodology. Both of these fields are surely in need of didactical methods appealing to young military students. The tours require a substantial investment, both in time and money, but when they significantly help developing critical thinking and eagerness for study, and I am sure they do, it is very much worth the effort.

In the Dutch War Studies bachelor MHA also is one of the prime moments to show how the humanities as a science work, how source criticism works and to make students aware of how their ideas on war and history are influenced by, for instance, images, films and games, and, secondly how science works: by constantly formulating new questions and exchanging ideas. These insights show students the complexity of the world they will enter and can contribute, hopefully, to critical and creative thinking. In end it is these qualities that matter and can make a difference. In the famous words of Michael Howard, we want to "make them wise for ever".[26]

References

Bird G (2016) Managing and interpreting D-Day's sites of memory. Routledge, London.
Brereton T (2000) First Lessons in Modern War. Journal of Military History 64:79–96.
Caddick Adams P (2010) Footsteps Across Time. Cranfield University, Wharley End.
Duncan A G (2016) The military education of junior officers in the Edwardian Army. University of Birmingham, Birmingham.
Echevarria A (2005) The trouble with history in military education. Historically Speaking 7(1):11–15.
Görlitz W (1953) Der deutsche Generalstab [The German General Staff]. Frankfurter Hefte, Frankfurt.
Haking R (1908) Staff Rides and Regimental Tours. Hugh Rees, London.
Hall D (2010) Clio and Mars on Tour, Studies for Military Pedagogy. Military Science and Security Policy 11:215–226.
Hamilton I (1905) A Staff Officer's Scrap Book. Edwards Arnold, London.
Howard M (1962) The Use and Abuse of Military History. RUSI Journal 107:4–10.
Kamphuis P, Amersfoort H (2010) May 1940. Brill, Leiden.

---

[26] Howard 1962.

Keller C (2016) The Civil War Battlefield Staff Ride in the 21st Century. Civil War History 62(2): 201–213.
Klinkert W (2012) Mars naar de wetenschap [Striving for Academic Status]. Netherlands Defence Academy, Breda.
Klinkert W (2016) Clio en Mars in opleidingsland: een complexe relatie [Clio and Mars in the land of education; a complex relationship]. In: Brama L (ed) Traditie en vernieuwing [Tradition and Innovation]. Mars et Historia, sl, pp 102–115.
Klinkert W (2018) Vorming voor de toekomst: Mars en Clio. Militaire geschiedenis voor thinking soldiers [Education for the future: Mars and Clio. Military history for thinking soldiers]. Netherlands Defence Academy, Breda.
Kollmer D (2003) Between past and future. The continuous struggle between humanistic general education and professional training of the German officer. NLARMS, Breda, pp 101–121.
Lloyd D (1998) Battlefield Tourism. Bloomsbury Academic, London.
Marindin A (1907) Staff Rides. Hugo Rees, London.
Miller D (1987) Historical TEWT. Infantry 77(2):22–26.
Osborne K (2003) Fred Morrow Fling. Theory & Research in Social Education 31(4):466–501.
Reardon C (1990) Soldiers and Scholars. University Press of Kansas, Lawrence.
Ryan C (2007) Battlefield Tourism. Elsevier, Oxford.
Schoenmaker B (2014) Waterloo, 200 jaar strijd [Waterloo, 200 years' strife]. Boom, Amsterdam.
Thielo K W (1964) Generalstabsreise [Staff Rides]. Wehrkunde pp 516–520.
Von Moser O (1927) Anlage und Durchfuhrung von Ubungsritten und Ubungsreisen im Gelände [Structure and execution of staff exercises and staff rides in the field]. Belser Verlagsbuchhandlung, Stuttgart.

Prof. Dr. Wim Klinkert holds the chair in Modern Military History at the Netherlands Defence Academy and is professor of military history at the University of Amsterdam. He is specialized in Dutch military history of the 19th–20th century and in the history of Dutch military education. His latest book in English was published in 2013: *Defending neutrality. The Netherlands prepares for War, 1900–1925* (Brill Publishers, Leiden/Boston).

Chapter 15
The Staff Ride as Reflective Practicum – Impressions and Experiences of the Faculty of Military Sciences and Maynooth University

Theo Brinkel, David Murphy and Jörg Noll

Contents

15.1	Introduction	248
15.2	Thinking Soldier and Reflective Practitioner	249
15.3	Staff Ride	252
15.4	No Staff Ride is the Same	254
15.5	Staff Rides – The Irish Perspective	257
15.6	Conclusion	258
References		259

Abstract This chapter will take a close look at the function of battlefield tours, or staff rides, in the academic schooling of aspiring officers. It will apply the concept of the reflective practitioner, as developed by Donald Schön, to military education in general and staff rides in particular. Staff rides should establish a learning environment that allows for maximum student involvement, a non-hierarchical exchange of views and experiences and the positioning of the teacher as coach and enabler. This is the ambition of the staff rides within the bachelor course War Studies in the Faculty of Military Sciences in the Netherlands and in the Irish cadet

Th. Brinkel (✉) · J. Noll
Faculty of Military Sciences, Netherlands Defence Academy,
PO Box 90002, 4800 PA Breda, The Netherlands
e-mail: TBFM.Brinkel@mindef.nl

J. Noll
e-mail: JE.Noll@mindef.nl

D. Murphy
Maynooth University, Maynooth, Ireland
e-mail: david.murphy@mu.ie

© T.M.C. ASSER PRESS and the authors 2019
W. Klinkert et al. (eds.), *NL ARMS Netherlands Annual Review of Military Studies 2019*, NL ARMS, https://doi.org/10.1007/978-94-6265-315-3_15

and officers' courses. The staff rides of the Faculty of Military Sciences are designed to expose students to the military, political, moral, as well as legal questions that arise in highly complex conflicts. The rationale behind the Irish staff rides is that they enhance the classroom experience and allow cadets and officers to gain first-hand experience of specific battlefield conditions. Professional military artistry cannot be learned solely through technical training and learning rules by heart, but it can be experienced in the reflective practicum. With the staff ride, we try to get as close as possible to the highly complex practice of conflict and war by visiting the sites and real contexts in which a conflict took place. The set-up of a good staff ride is a function of the aim to encourage reflection, ethical aspects, questions behind the questions and the confrontation of practice with values and deeply held personal convictions.

Keywords Battlefield tour · staff ride · thinking soldier · reflective practitioner · interactive teaching

15.1 Introduction

Battlefield tours, or staff rides, are an often-used method for learning how relevant theories and insights from strategic studies, security studies, military history and military law can be applied to specific historical and current cases. Students are challenged to reflect on tangible political and security related problems and get an understanding of the complexity of those cases. As this is an integral part of officers' education, in this chapter we intend to have a closer look at the function of battlefield tours, or staff rides in the academic schooling of aspiring officers. The key rationale is that they enhance the classroom experience and allow cadets and officers to gain first-hand experience of specific battlefield conditions. Taking this closer look allows us to see how in particular the staff rides contribute to the education of reflective practitioners. We will focus on the so-called *Integratieproject* [Integration Project] of the third-year students of the War Studies bachelor degree program and on staff rides as part and parcel of officers' education in the Irish Defence Forces.

In line with Melvin, from here on we will use the term "staff ride". On the basis of his experiences with the practice of battlefield tours, he makes a distinction between battlefield tours and staff rides.[1] Melvin sees battlefield tours as "looking at past operations for general interest", where there usually is no systematic preparation in advance. A staff ride, in his opinion, requires an analysis of operations, is part of formal military training and the learning objectives are of direct relevance to the students. A staff ride should include preliminary study of a selected campaign, an extensive visit to the actual sites and "after action review". It involves maximum student involvement through thought, analysis and discussion. Hence our use of the

---

[1] Melvin 2005, pp. 60–61.

term staff ride for the projects at the NLDA and Maynooth University. When in the course of this chapter we refer to students, unless otherwise stated, we mean aspiring officers (military cadets and midshipmen) of all services of the armed forces.

At the Netherlands Defence Academy (NLDA), the Integration Project is part of the bachelor degree program War Studies as offered by the Faculty of Military Sciences (FMS). Students in the Integration Project attend classes on relevant theories as well as on a specific conflict or region of interest. Over the past seven years these were Bosnia-Hercegovina, Turkey, Kosovo, Northern Ireland, the Baltics and Israel/Palestine Territories. Within these broader settings, cases were studied from different academic perspectives in a multidisciplinary context. The related study and field trips were designed to expose students to the military, political, moral, as well as legal questions and dilemma's that arise in highly complex conflicts.

The authors of this chapter have combined Dutch and Irish experiences, because of the long standing and successful cooperation between the NLDA and Maynooth University in the Integration Project and the various exchanges that have taken place. The Irish Defence Forces are small compared to other European forces but, in terms of officers' education, efforts are made to follow best international practices. As a result, staff rides have become an established part of their military education programs. They can also offer an opportunity to interact with local populations and former service personnel, while also visiting key locations in the EU, UN and NATO infrastructure.

For the purposes of this chapter we start with an outline of the relevant educational theories that underlie the courses which include international staff rides. We will first turn to the idea of the reflective practitioner, applying the insights of that concept to military education in general and multidisciplinary education and staff rides as "reflective practicum" in particular. In Sect. 15.3 we will show how this concept is worked out in the so-called Integration Project of the FMS. Section 15.4 will present impressions of staff rides that have taken place up till now that may serve as characteristic elements of a reflective practicum. In Sect. 15.5 the philosophy behind the Irish staff ride practice will be reflected on. With this chapter we intend to show that international staff rides are an indispensable element in officers' education in general and in fostering the reflective military practitioner in particular.

15.2 Thinking Soldier and Reflective Practitioner

In military academic education, students are prepared for their future position as subaltern officers. They will operate in a world that is unpredictable, complex and highly mediatized, with every action by the military under close public and political scrutiny. It is impossible to say in advance against whom, in what region or under which circumstances they will be deployed. As a consequence, education should not only focus on the transfer of existing knowledge, but also on preparing the students to be flexible in fighting and thinking. They need to be educated in such a way that they will be able to solve problems and take decisions in situations that they hardly have learned about and anticipated.

In its Education Quality Manual (EQM), the FMS argues that the combination of professional military education and critical academic education is a meaningful way to prepare students for this future position. Young officers need to be able to design solutions for unpredictable military operational problems and need to be able to reflect on these solutions in order to enhance their experience in combination with their theoretic training. The FMS has called this the characteristic ability of the "thinking soldier".[2] Donald Schön's idea of the "reflective practitioner" forms the basis of this concept.

The idea of the reflective practitioner can be relevant to military officers, just as it can be for other academic professionals such as architects, doctors, musicians or psychological counsellors. The concept of the reflective practitioner originates from Schön's distinction between what he calls technical rationality and reflection in action, or professional artistry. Basically, in Schön's view, technical rationality means that practitioners are used to solving problems by applying the right technical instruments in other to meet determinate and single objectives.[3] The success of this approach is measured in terms of the degree in which the actions lead to the desired outcomes. Its rationality is found in a systematic and scientific way of applying relevant theories and techniques in concrete situations or cases.

Rational problem-solving is about collection of data and the deduction from hypotheses through which the connection can be made between the problem at hand and the whole of professional knowledge and theories.[4] This rational approach is based on a so-called objectivist view of reality. There is supposed to be a reality of facts "out there" that can be taken for what it is and that is measurable and testable.[5] Paperone has applied this way of thinking to the field of the military practitioner. It entails that the problem at hand should be treated as objectively as possible and that a "generalized epistemology of proven tactics, techniques and procedures expected to work again and again" can be applied to all these problems. On the basis of the continuing application of these doctrines and the induction of lessons-learned and best practices, the existing body of theory can be improved or extended.[6]

However, this approach doesn't always work and Schön claims that this is not what practitioners argue they are doing, or what constitutes the core of their work. The professional will also be faced with problems that are characterized by uncertainty, uniqueness and the presence of often conflicting values. According to Schön, these problems cannot be properly tackled by technical rationality, where the right answers and correct procedures seem unavailable and where instruments

---

[2] Faculty of Military Sciences 2016, p. 8.
[3] Schön 1986, p. 3.
[4] Schön 1986, pp. 33–34.
[5] Schön 1986, p. 36.
[6] Paperone 2014, p. 106.

seem to conflict with one another. Paperone argues that this is what the American military have themselves experienced in Afghanistan and Iraq.[7] And this is what future officers may expect in the world they may be deployed in: they will find themselves in situations where traditional (unidimensional) doctrines and ways of thinking are inadequate to understand what is happening and to make sense of the situation. In such cases, rational problem solving does not help. The first thing that they need to deal with is the construction of the problem itself, so that they can make sense of it. Or even: making sense of the problem is constructing it.[8] This is typical of a constructivist or interpretivist view of reality: the role of perception, estimation and beliefs in the interpretation of what we see and accept as reality.[9]

The fundamental critique of those who prefer a constructivist view of problem solving, is that the so-called real facts of the rational approach are just "a collection of socially constructed objectivations that habitually distort reality". Therefore, Paperone argues, sometimes subjective appraisals, or "observer specific narrative interpretations" are vitally important and should inform the way we deal with complex situations, namely where we feel ambiguity, inaccuracy or imprecision.[10] As a consequence, the modern officer needs to be able to understand what is happening, to critically rethink the way of framing problems, action strategies and conventional doctrines and to reformulate problems in order to tackle them. In Schön's words, practitioners have to make sense of "uncertain, unique or conflicted situations" first and invent new rules on the spot. Here, we are dealing not so much with technical or rational problem solving, but reflection in action, or professional artistry.[11]

This professional artistry cannot be learned through technical training and learning rules by heart alone, but it can be experienced in the reflective practicum. In the words of Schön, the practicum can be a prism through which we can see the usefulness of ideas and methods in lessons and it can be a vehicle for reflections of students over the process of framing problems.[12] According to Paperone, the reflective practicum encourages action learning: doing and learning to deal with complexity in indeterminate situations where practitioners try to figure things out in their interaction with the surroundings.

Academic education can be helpful here, because it stresses theory, research methods and critical reflection aiming at the understanding of a broader context than the situation at hand. In the reflective practicum it can be combined with concreteness, specific contexts and situations in order to "come alive". Obviously, reflective military practice cannot be experienced in a laboratory or design studio. There can be no real learning by doing and it that sense the reflective military

---

[7] Paperone 2014, p. 109.
[8] Schön 1986, pp. 6–11.
[9] Schön 1986, p. 36.
[10] Paperone 2014, pp. 107–108.
[11] Schön 1986, p. 35.
[12] Schön 1986, p. 334.

practicum differs from the practicum in the education of architects or psychotherapists. But, apart from training drills and skills, the staff ride, then, comes as close as institutions of military education can get to military practice.

As mentioned above, the typical staff ride includes preparation through study, an actual visit to a historical theatre of operations (in the widest sense of the word) or a critical region, and evaluation, feedback and reflection in the form of further research after the visit has taken place. Furthermore, there should be maximum student involvement. This means that analysis, explanation and discussion should primarily be done by the students themselves. Whereas Melvin sees the role of the teacher as the source of transmission of information, Lloyd prefers an engagement model. In this, the teacher should adopt the role of a coach who fosters dialogue with and between the students. The teacher can offer the possible theoretical tools, but the analysis has to be done by the students. Finally, and this is especially relevant in a military environment, it should be clear that the climate is informal and not hierarchical in order to get a free discussion.[13]

In sum, to prepare military students for their future work, they should not only be experienced in rational problem solving, but in professional artistry as well. The reflective practicum can be an important venue for fostering the latter. For military education, staff rides are as close to a "practicum" as one can safely get. As was seen above, staff rides should establish a learning environment that allows for maximum student involvement, a non-hierarchical exchange of views and experiences and the positioning of the teacher as the enabler of professional artistry. That is what we aim to do in staff rides such as the *Integratieproject* and in the Irish cadet course and officers' promotion courses. In the following section we will have a look at their design and implementation.

15.3 Staff Ride

The staff rides of the FMS are meant to contribute to the realization of the ambitions voiced in the Education Quality Manual and thus help raise students to thinking soldiers. For this reason, much attention is paid to reflection, ethical aspects, questions behind the questions and the confrontation of practice on the one hand and values and deeply held personal convictions on the other. In a comparable, although not similar way, the Irish cadet and officers' courses try to ensure that the students constantly are aware of the following metric: History – Theory – Doctrine – Practice. They are asked to be aware of where they stand within this metric and how this continuum operates.

According to the EQM, it is the ambition of the Faculty of Military Sciences that its students "develop into critical, committed and responsible military. As reflective professionals they are open minded to and aware of differing views, cultures,

---

[13] Lloyd 2009, pp. 180–181.

religions as well as bodies of (military) ethics and law and technologies."[14] Students are educated to be "thinking soldiers", who are able to use state of the art theoretical insights, are informed and critical towards theoretical notions and aware of limitations. They are able to apply theoretical insights creatively to cope with problems in the field. And they are "reflective before action, in action and after action", which means they are able to analyse, abstract and rationalize.[15] The bachelor degree program offers the opportunity to acquire international experience. Battlefield tours and study trips are specifically intended to contribute to just that.[16] The didactic approach preferred by the FMS fosters increasing responsibility of students for their own learning process, for instance through the preparation-feedback model in which students are encouraged to prepare for lectures. Teachers will act as experts, developers, organisers or coaches.[17]

In order for the field trips to comply with this ambition, over the last ten years they have been part of a course called the Integration Project. These two words point at the two main purposes of the course.

The first is that the course is intended to integrate the relevant elements of the War Studies bachelor degree program: military operations, international security studies, military history and military law. Recently two more fields of interest have been added: military intelligence and security and cyber operations. Additional aspects are the ability to communicate in English with relative native and non-native speakers, leadership and the already mentioned ethical aspects of (civil) wars and conflicts, international interventions and military engagement or non-engagement.

The second word is "project" and it relates to the fact that the course is set up as a project: a great amount of independent work, self-study, by the students is taken as a starting point; autonomous, but mentored research that as much as possible is prepared for, executed and evaluated and confronted with practice. We want to get as close as possible to the highly complex practice of conflict and war.

For this the Dutch Integration Project is focused on a time and place that is of political and strategic importance. The staff ride that is part of the course is not just chosen because of the need to understand the conflict itself. The course is about analysing on the basis of a theory, international law, a historic perspective, or of a military doctrine. So far, visits have been organized in Turkey, Bosnia-Hercegovina, Northern Ireland, Kosovo, Israel/Palestine Territories, Berlin and the Baltic States. These are all regions that in recent years have experienced conflict, or are confronted with possible aggression.

All these staff rides are organized according to the same general scheme. During the first weeks of the course, students attend lectures about the region or the country they are going to visit. These classes are intended to give students an understanding of the nature of the conflict area that is studied. They are followed by classes that

---

[14] Faculty of Military Sciences 2016, pp. 7–8.
[15] Faculty of Military Sciences 2016, pp. 8–9.
[16] Faculty of Military Sciences 2016, p. 19.
[17] Faculty of Military Sciences 2016, p. 21.

seek to deepen specific and relevant themes, such as nationalism, genocide, oppression and emancipation, violence as instrument of liberation, counterinsurgency, defence or occupation, reconciliation, reconstruction. Parallel to the lectures, students are expected to choose a specific subject related to the case and analyse this according to one of the perspectives of War Studies, i.e. military history, international relations, etc. This research cumulates in a presentation in the field and a final paper that both count for the grading.

The on the spot presentation in English is not merely a brief version of the paper; it is also supposed to be a presentation that introduces the problem at hand to the audience (class-mates, teachers, guests, visited agencies and governmental bodies) that can stand on its own. The feedback and the impressions during the journey serve as the most important input and reflection for the research. That is why students share their experiences and lessons learned during the trip after the staff ride, in particular if two classes visited different regions. Finally, they have a few weeks to finalize their research and deliver their papers.

15.4 No Staff Ride is the Same

The authors asked former students to testify how they experienced the field trips in this regard. Many students who have visited Kosovo, Turkey, Bosnia, (Northern) Ireland and Israel have contributed to this chapter years after "their" staff ride took place. All of them are still active military, and many of them have been on missions abroad since that time. One of the former students, Marine Captain Xavier Meulenbeek, has even visited Kosovo five times since then. And, while on mission in Iraq, he tried to understand the background and context of the conflict, also in order to put things into perspective. Xavier is not alone in that. The following sections may give some impressions of how the field trips of the Integration Project fostered reflection, attention to ethical aspects and the questioning of existing values and convictions. In the following sections attention will be paid to places, people and presentations (in that order).

Although historical, military and political facts may look the same, each trip will differ from the other. The exists no typical staff ride. While the basic idea is always similar, the dynamics of the conflicts, the development of the peace processes and the organizations and governmental bodies to be visited differ in time and place. So are our hosts and those who are willing to share their experiences and thoughts with us. Each visit, the reflection takes place, may lead to different conclusions or even a different outlook on the conflict itself. As was seen above, practitioners have to make sense of "uncertain, unique or conflicted situations" first and invent new rules on the spot. Here, professional artistry is fostered. Here, as well, action learning – as described above – is encouraged: doing and learning to deal with complexity in indeterminate situations where practitioners try to figure things out in their interaction with the surroundings.

To develop the feeling of what a conflict "was like" or "is like" a visit to a theatre of operations is essential. The place where it happened or still happens plays a crucial role in the staff rides of the Integration Project. One only has to see the small strip of land that was taken and held at ANZAC beach near Gallipoli, Turkey, to understand what problems the Australian and New Zealand forces had to endure. Accompanied by an officer of the Temporary International Presence in Hebron, we walked with our students through the streets of Hebron on the West Bank, where we directly experienced the tensions, insults, and humiliations between Jewish settlers and Palestinians. When in Kosovo, the class visited the bridge in Mitrovica. One of the former students remarks: "Visiting the bridge is my most important memory. The gap between the Kosovars and the Serbs became literally and figuratively visible on this spot and the conflict came very close."[18]

To understand what motivates people in a conflict situation, it can be enriching to learn first-hand from what they went through. In Northern Ireland, tours were organised through the Falls Road (mainly Catholic) and Shankill Road (overwhelmingly Protestant) districts in Belfast and through the Bogside in (London) Derry. The tour guides were former volunteers for the Irish Republican Army and the Ulster Volunteer Force. "Volunteer" is a euphemism for what in continental European understanding would be a terrorist. They usually were very open and happy to answer all questions by our students. The language barrier was minimal, so there was hardly any misunderstanding regarding the message. Students said that by talking to people engaged in the conflict their perspective broadened. "Talking to former terrorists was most exiting. Yet, the political side is thrilling in its own right, too."[19] The encounter with combatants and terrorists places many things into perspective, since they show both sides of the same coin, with their own truths and realities.[20] They reflected the feelings on both sides.[21]

In Kosovo, students walked with Dr. Bujar Gashi in the mountains following the trails of the refugees. Being a former refugee himself, the guide made an ineradicable impression: "In this way, we could get an impression of the horrendous track of the people, although we were young men, and they were a group with elderly and sick people and children. We had just a few things with us, while they had to carry all their most valued possessions. And, above all, we were walking freely, the refugees back then fled for their lives."[22]

Part of any tour is the visit to an official institution, together with the formal meetings and presentations. Apart from the opportunities for reflection these visits offer, they also enable the students to learn about protocol and formality in the international environment. Visiting (Dutch) embassies abroad, ministries of host countries and international organizations are an important part of the trips, all the more because later in their career they are expected to interact with many of those

---

[18] Bram Adrichem.
[19] Robert van Bavel.
[20] Roy Tutert.
[21] Janwillem Mudde.
[22] Peter van den Hurk. Herwin Meerveld and Daniël van Baarsen underscore the importance of this walk.

bodies.[23] During the tours in Bosnia-Herzegovina the students even visited the International Commission for the Missing Persons (ICMP) to see how the remains of those killed in Srebrenica were identified and reassembled. With that, war, conflict, genocide and Dutch (military) history came very close.[24]

The institutions that are visited are not always able to present themselves favourably. One of the students who was asked to reflect on the field trip he had participated in, testified the following: "What we didn't realize during our study prior to the staff ride was that apart from the military there so are many actors and forces actively engaged in 'conflict resolution'. We, as soldiers like to act, while we have to play a passive role and leave the initiative to the diplomats. Organizations such as UNMIK, EULEX, KFOR, UNDOF and all the NGOs, great and small, try to influence the outcome of the peace process. And the higher the number of actors that influence this process, the less effective it gets."[25] On the other hand, students have learned to acknowledge that it takes more than a military solution to end a conflict and that local governance follows its own rules.[26]

Sometimes it is possible to find alternatives for one-sided presentations or to make them more interactive. We had some very good experiences with seminars where the students themselves did the work: we had two presentations by Dutch students and two by students of the country we visited and ensuing discussions. Students can be more open when discussing with their peers. This was most helpful at Queen's University in Belfast, Bahçeşehir University in Istanbul or Bilkent University in Ankara. What was a great stimulus for students to prepare well in advance and make the best of the arguments was the debating competition at the Irish Military College in the Curragh between Dutch and Irish teams. Winning is essential to military students, so there is no lack of motivation.

At Clonard Monastery (the convent of the Redemptorist Order situated right in the heart of the Northern Ireland conflict area, from where some crucial initiatives of peace-making have originated) we organised a *diner pensant*. According to this format, students were divided over four tables where they had dinner with one or more participants in the peace process. They could talk and listen to them in an informal and open setting. We also had a kind of speed dating format during lunch at the Northern Ireland Assembly. Four Members of the Assembly each sat for 15 minutes at a table of five students and had discussions with them. After the time was up, the Assembly Members changed tables. This way, students were able to interact with representatives of four different political parties. It worked much better than the traditional plenary Q&A sessions, because the threshold was so much lower and it was easier to enable each student to make a remark or ask a question.

---

[23] Herwin Meerveld.

[24] We deliberately chose not to visit Srebrenica for the sake of the safe learning environment of the students.

[25] Xavier Meulenbeek.

[26] Daniel van Baarsen.

15.5 Staff Rides – The Irish Perspective

As was said above, the Irish cadets and officers' courses try to ensure that the students constantly are aware of the following metric: History – Theory – Doctrine – Practice. They are asked to be aware of where they stand within this metric and how this continuum operates. It allows them to be aware of the usefulness of classroom activities and the link with staff rides and other military exercises. As the Irish Defence Forces prepares for a level of reorganization across its educational courses, it seems certain that the staff ride will remain a valued feature on future courses.

The organization of the Irish Defence Forces was formalised after the Irish Civil War (1921/23) and today it is an "all arms" force with army, Air Corps and Naval Service elements. Between 1926 and 1927, Irish officers visited the United States as part of a "military mission" with the aim of modelling Irish operational and educational systems on American practices. They undertook staff courses at Fort Leavenworth and also visited West Point (cadet academy), Fort Benning (Infantry School) and Fort Sill (Artillery School). By this time, the staff ride was an established feature on American courses and had been developed to a level of considerable sophistication.[27] As a result of this process, these officers became familiar with the American staff ride system and this became an established part of all curriculum when the Irish Military College (DFTC) was founded in 1930.[28]

Since that date, the staff ride has been a part of all cadets' courses and also officer promotion courses (staff courses). There have been periods when this system was paused and the courses were shortened due to operational necessity. This was particularly true during World War Two when, although neutral, Irish forces were fully mobilised for home defence. Also, during the height of the "Troubles" in Northern Ireland in the 1970s and 1980s, any staff ride type activity focused on the internal security situation.

The normalisation in Ireland since the late 1990s has allowed for an overall expansion and upgrading of educational processes. At present, Maynooth University provides the academic content for three officers' education courses. These are:

- The Cadet Course (Diploma in Leadership, Management and Defence Studies)[29]
- Junior Command & Staff Course (Higher Diploma in Security Studies)
- Senior Command & Staff Course (MA in Leadership, Management and Defence Studies).

---

[27] Robertson 2014, p. 24.
[28] Duggan 1991, pp. 146–147.
[29] It should be noted that the Irish cadet course is a commissioning course of 18 months. It does not entail a degree course. However, all cadets must either have a degree on entry or must undertake one following commissioning.

There are specialised general officers' courses organised as needs demand. There is an established exchange system that sees Irish officers undertake courses at the Command and General Staff College at Fort Leavenworth and also at the UK Defence Academy at Shrivenham. There are also occasional cadet exchanges with St. Cyr in France and Sandhurst in the UK. Due to these exchange systems, Irish cadets and officers can remain conversant with staff ride practices abroad. The recent integration projects organised by the FMS mentioned above, facilitated a highly useful expansion of the Irish cadet program. By regular contact with Dutch cadets, the Irish cadet cohorts gained a valuable insight into the training and educational systems utilised by another European army which is also a NATO member. Furthermore, the input of the Dutch cadets provided a different and external viewpoint on the period of the Troubles.

Staff rides play an important role in all of the Maynooth University courses and are aimed at the level of the specific course. For examples, cadet staff rides focus on platoon-size actions and are intended to immerse the students in the leadership and tactical problems faced by junior officers. In recent years, cadet staff rides have examined ambush sites in Ireland and also locations of Fighting In Built-up Area operations. The JCSC is aimed at captains who are eligible for promotion to commandant (major). These staff rides tend to be carried out overseas and the students are tasked with examining scenarios at the company and battalion level. Recent staff rides for this course have examined WW2 actions in Sicily, Italy, Normandy, the Ardennes and The Netherlands (Market Garden). The Senior Command & Staff Course usually begins with a visit to Brussels to visit UN, EU and NATO locations. Thereafter, battlefield staff rides concentrate on WW1 and WW2 locations at the brigade and divisional level. In this course, students are asked to consider the decision-making process at strategic level. Due to recent WW1 commemorations, classes have also visited locations associated with the Irish regiments that served in the British army on the Western Front.

In general, staff rides are seen as a vital process in linking classroom-based content with the realities of military leadership "on the ground". They are seen as key methods for developing critical thinking. At all levels, students are asked to disassemble decision-making processes while also developing counterfactual scenarios and alternative courses of action. Efforts are made to keep the staff ride processes as realistic as possible and courses are constantly reviewed to refer to emerging military concepts. In this sense, the Irish staff rides share the ambition to foster the concept of the reflective practitioner.

15.6 Conclusion

As was said above, professional artistry cannot be learned through technical training and learning rules by heart, but to a degree it can be experienced in the reflective practicum. With the staff ride, we try to get as close as possible to the highly complex practice of conflict and war. The set-up of a good staff ride is a function of the aim to encourage reflection, ethical aspects, questions behind the questions and the confrontation of practice with values and deeply held personal convictions. We believe that through visits to places of conflict, encounters with war and peace makers, and interactive and safe presentations this objective can be achieved. Activity and interactivity are indispensable ingredients for successful staff rides.

Almost all the students we consulted in the preparation of this chapter refer to their deeper insight into the complexity of a conflict. They realise that in the regions they visited many inhabitants still are affected by power politics. And not only in Kosovo, where Serbs, Russians and Americans still exert their influence. While we are writing this chapter, the border between Northern Ireland and Ireland remains one of the most sensitive issues of the Brexit disaster and Turkey is preparing to scale up the fight against the Kurds. We expect that many of the students will remember the formal wreath-laying ceremony at Atatürk's mausoleum when they see the country transforming into a new kind of authoritarian state.

Looking back at the tours we organized and conducted, reading the comments of our former students, we can only conclude that they turned into thinking soldiers. In that sense the application of the concept of the reflective practicum has proven its value.

References

Duggan JP (1991) A history of the Irish army. Gill and MacMillan, Dublin.
Faculty of Military Sciences (2016) Education Quality Manual. Netherlands Defence Academy, Breda.
Lloyd N (2009) Battlefield tours and staff rides: a useful learning experience? Teaching in Higher Education 14(2):175–184, https://doi.org/10.1080/13562510902757237. Accessed 14 January 2019.
Melvin RAMS (2005) VI. Contemporary Battlefield Tours and Staff Rides: A Military Practitioner's View. Defence Studies 5(1):59–80, https://doi.org/10.1080/14702430500097218. Accessed 14 January 2019.
Paparone C (2014) Two Faces of Critical Thinking for the Reflective Military Practitioner. Military Review 94(6):104–110, http://content.ebscohost.com/ContentServer.asp?T=P&P=AN&K=99646172&S=R&D=a2h&EbscoContent=dGJyMMvl7ESep7I4yNfsOLCmr1Gep65Srq%2B4TbOWxWXS&ContentCustomer=dGJyMPGot1CzrrZLuePfgeyx44Dt6fIA. Accessed 15 January 2019.
Robertson WG (2014) The Staff Ride. United States Army Center of Military History, Washington DC.
Schön DA (1986) Educating the Reflective Practitioner. Jossey-Bass, San Francisco.

Prof. Dr. Theo Brinkel teaches International Security Studies at the Faculty of Military Sciences of the Netherlands Defence Academy and is KVMO professor of Civil-Military Relations at Leiden University. He is currently researching the concept of resilience in relation to hybrid threats.

Dr. David Murphy is a lecturer in Military History and Strategic Studies at Maynooth University in Ireland. He lectures at the Irish Military College and has served as a visiting lecturer at military academies abroad. He is currently an external examiner of the Department of Defence Studies at King's College, London. His recent research has focused on WW1 and the development of the modern Middle East.

Dr. Jörg Noll is associate professor of International Conflict Studies at the Faculty of Military Sciences of the Netherlands Defence Academy. His teaching and research focus on exit strategies, strategic cultures and decision-making in crisis and war. He spent the spring of 2016 in Oxford as Visiting Fellow of the Changing Character of War Programme at Pembroke College.

Chapter 16
Policy for Cadets and Midshipmen – Teaching Dutch Security and Defence Policy at the Netherlands Defence Academy

Georg E. Frerks

Contents

16.1	Introduction	262
	16.1.1 Training of Dutch Cadets and Midshipmen	262
	16.1.2 The Thinking Soldier	263
16.2	Teaching Dutch Security and Defence Policy	264
	16.2.1 Goals of the NVDB Course	264
	16.2.2 Substantive Contents of the NVDB Course	265
	16.2.3 Educational Tools	268
16.3	Challenges	270
16.4	Conclusion	270
References		271

Abstract At the end of their bachelor degree program War Studies and the initial military training Dutch cadets and midshipmen have to learn in which political and policy environment they have to operate in their future professional life. This competence is part of the 'thinking soldier' concept that guides their education at the Faculty of Military Sciences at the Netherlands Defence Academy. The module 'Netherlands Security and Defence Policy', also known under its Dutch abbreviation NVDB, aims to achieve this. This chapter highlights the goals and main contents of this course and elaborates in which manner the complicated substance of this topic is being taught at bachelor level to cadets and midshipmen at the Netherlands Defence Academy by the use of different educational tools.

G. E. Frerks (✉)
Faculty of Military Sciences, Netherlands Defence Academy, PO Box 90002,
4800 PA Breda, The Netherlands
e-mail: GE.Frerks@mindef.nl

© T.M.C. ASSER PRESS and the authors 2019
W. Klinkert et al. (eds.), *NL ARMS Netherlands Annual Review of Military Studies 2019*, NL ARMS, https://doi.org/10.1007/978-94-6265-315-3_16

Keywords Military education · Dutch security and defence policy · policy analysis · educational tools

16.1 Introduction

16.1.1 Training of Dutch Cadets and Midshipmen

Before entering their professional military career Dutch cadets and midshipmen follow an intensive training program that comprises several elements: a military or maritime training and formation of one-year duration and a three-years' interdisciplinary bachelor degree program (BA) War Studies. These educational modules are imparted under the general responsibility of the Netherlands Defence Academy (NLDA), where the Faculty of Military Sciences takes care of the academic BA War Studies. The BA is accredited by the Dutch-Flemish Accreditation Organisation (NVAO) and hence the diploma is officially acknowledged in civilian society, offering further career and educational opportunities for future officers. The BA War Studies offers an academic education focusing on the utility and deployment of military means in a dynamic (inter)national context. Apart from acquiring the relevant academic knowledge *per se* the cadets and midshipmen are also expected to produce new insights and position these in the domain of prevailing knowledge. This requires the acquisition of research skills and a creative and critical mindset. Compared to BA studies taught at regular universities, the BA War Studies at the NLDA is unique in that it provides a strong link with the professional field and the Dutch Ministry of Defence as the cadets' and midshipmen's employer and, indirectly, with security organizations like the United Nations (UN), the North Atlantic Treaty Organization (NATO), the European Union (EU) and the Organization for Security and Cooperation in Europe (OSCE). The NLDA aspires to educate cadets and midshipmen to become a 'thinking soldier' or – further in their career and after the completion of higher studies – the 'officer scholar' – in short, personnel that is able to "structure, delimit, reflect, theorize, analyse, criticize and reason",[1] next to possessing the leadership and military professional competences required from a prospective officer.

One important aspect of this profile is the capability to contextualize and position military operations in the wider societal, political and policy context. This has not only a contemporary relevance, but also needs a historical perspective in order to understand the antecedents of the current state of affairs. This chapter will elaborate how this is achieved by presenting the contents, approach and educational tools used in the course 'Netherlands Security and Defence Policy' (NVDB) that is taught by the FMW as the last module at the end of the bachelor, just before the cadets and midshipmen embark on writing their final thesis.

---

[1] Netherlands Defence Academy 2017, p. 15.

16.1.2 The Thinking Soldier

For a 'thinking soldier' it is of the essence that he or she[2] has an understanding of the political and policy context of his or her actions and decisions. This reflects the Janowitzian side in the well-known Huntington-Janowitz dialogue where the paradigmatic Huntingtonian position revolves around a strict military professionalism as the 'management of violence', functioning autonomously and completely separately from the civilian sphere, yet under political subordination and civilian control.[3] Roennfeldt adds that "Morris Janowitz offers a different view: while officers shall not take an active role in domestic politics, they must be politically sensitive." He calls for a military professional self-conception that includes an "enlarged politico-military responsibility".[4] Roennfeldt continues to say that: "Janowitz sees the military and civilian spheres as integrated and argues that officers should be able to operate in both."[5] He asserted already in 1964 at the height of the Cold War that: "The prescribed career of the future is one that will sensitize the military officer to the political and social consequences of military action."[6] Reviewing the Huntington-Janowitz dialogue Roennfeldt concludes: "Thus, in contrast to Huntington's insistence on an apolitical officer corps, Janowitz requires socio-politically competent officers."[7]

In the current context the need for the Janowitzian approach is even more obvious. More than in the past when soldiers where just supposed to carry out hierarchical orders in a linear and non-critical fashion, current war dynamics and operational contexts require a different attitude and need analysis and reflection by those involved on the spot of the operational action. The concept of the 'thinking soldier' reminds us strongly of the notion of the 'strategic corporal' famously coined in January 1999 by US Marine Commandant General Charles Krulak in the *Marines Magazine*. Krulak argues that: "The inescapable lesson of Somalia and of other recent operations, whether humanitarian assistance, peace-keeping, or traditional war fighting, is that their outcome may hinge on decisions made by small unit leaders, and by actions taken at the lowest level." … "Marines will often operate far "from the flagpole" without the direct supervision of senior leadership." … "these missions will require them to confidently make well-reasoned and independent decisions under extreme stress – decisions that will likely be subject to the harsh scrutiny of both the media and the court of public opinion. In many cases, the individual Marine will be the most conspicuous symbol of American foreign policy and will potentially influence not only the immediate tactical situation, but the operational and strategic levels as well. His actions, therefore, will directly impact the outcome of the larger operation; and he will become, as the title of this article

---

[2] When the words 'cadets' or 'he' are used, both female and male officers are referred to.
[3] See Roennfeldt 2019, pp. 61–62.
[4] Janowitz quoted in Roennfeldt 2019, p. 62.
[5] Roennfeldt 2019, p. 62.
[6] Janowitz 1964, p. 426.
[7] Roennfeldt 2019, p. 63.

suggests – the Strategic Corporal." Krulak also highlights the "ubiquitous media whose presence will mean that all future conflicts will be acted out before an international audience."[8]

Also a flurry of other publications has emphasized the changing role of the military in the contemporary world. They vary from the 'military operations other-than-war' (MOOTW) to the 'postmodern military' as delineated by Moskos et al.,[9] and the Comprehensive or Integrated Approach as championed by the EU[10] and a number of European countries including The Netherlands, that emphasizes the so-called '3-D approach' where diplomacy, defence and development are applied in combination. What all these concepts have in common is the different capabilities required from soldiers and officers, especially with regard to civil-military cooperation and relations and the need to assess and understand the political and policy context, determinants and consequences of their operations.

Though Krulak's observations are nearly two decades old, they are still pertinent today, as are the other dynamics referred to above. Consequently, they have a profound significance for Dutch cadet-officers. It is very important that they learn to recognize both the local and wider societal determinants of military operations and are aware of the political sensitivities and policy aspects of their work. In a way this boils down to what Kalu has called "the soldier-statesman (one who adapts well to the esoteric art of bureaucratic politics, media relations, and in the oft-contested playground of international politics and diplomacy)."[11]

16.2 Teaching Dutch Security and Defence Policy

16.2.1 Goals of the NVDB Course

The section International Security Studies (IVS) of the FMW teaches the NVDB course to Dutch cadets and midshipmen. IVS provides the course director and main faculty, while two other colleagues of the Department of War Studies also give a lecture in the course. The course has four specific interrelated goals:

- The cadets and midshipmen can present and explain the main features of the Dutch security and defence policy;
- The students and midshipmen can identify and apply relevant theoretical angles or approaches with regard to Dutch security and defence policy;
- The cadets and midshipmen can analyze which factors impact upon the Dutch security and defence policy;

---

[8] Krulak 1999.

[9] Moskos et al. 2000.

[10] European Commission & High Representative of the European Union for Foreign Affairs and Security Policy 2013.

[11] Kalu 2008, p. 87.

- The cadets and midshipmen are able to formulate and communicate, in both verbal and written form, a relevant current policy viewpoint in the field of Dutch security and defence policy.[12]

In sum, the NVDB course focuses on the origin and execution of Dutch policy in the realm of international security and defence. The emphasis lies on the contemporary dynamics, but the topic is embedded in a longer historical perspective in order to appreciate the antecedents of the current situation. Similarly, though *Dutch* policy is accentuated in the NVDB course, attention is paid as well to the *international* policy context, mainly because nearly all Dutch operations are carried out in combined NATO or EU operations.

Consequently, the Dutch security and defence policy is analyzed and explained with reference to:

- Developments in the (perception of) the global and national political and security situation over the last two decades;
- The manner in which international organizations like the UN, the EU and NATO are working and have translated these developments into their policies;
- The influence of Dutch internal political, administrative, economic and societal forces;
- The perceptions and interests of the Dutch Ministries of Foreign Affairs (including foreign trade and development cooperation) and Defence.[13]

16.2.2 Substantive Contents of the NVDB Course

The NVDB course is organized in five major components. The first component is introductory in nature and presents the broad background of Dutch history and its international policy over the centuries. It also discusses the presumed existence of a Dutch strategic culture. The second one deals with national and international decision-making. The third one provides a post-9/11 analysis of Dutch defence policy and planning. The fourth component focuses on the details of Dutch foreign, defence and development policy. The last component is practice-oriented and comprises visits to the Dutch Ministries of Foreign Affairs and Defence and also includes simulations or assignments. In this section the contents of each component will be briefly elaborated upon.

---

[12] Cursusbeschrijving Nederlands Veiligheids- en Defensiebeleid (NVDB) 2018 [NVDB Course Guide 2018].

[13] Cursusbeschrijving Nederlands Veiligheids- en Defensiebeleid (NVDB) 2018 [NVDB Course Guide 2018].

16.2.2.1 Historical Background of Dutch International Policy and Dutch Strategic Culture

In order to understand the historical background of Dutch international policy the cadets are required to study relevant chapters of the book 'Nederland in de Wereld' [The Netherlands in the World] by emeritus History of International Relations professor Duco Hellema. One chapter deals with the Dutch foreign policy from the origins of the Republic (1579 and 1581) till the late 19th century. The main question dealt with here is what the past tells us about the present? More specifically, it deals with the issue whether Dutch foreign policy can be characterized by a number of constants or whether a more nuanced analysis based on a contingent constellation of various historical factors is required. The first position is based on the supposed existence of a Dutch tradition comprising, according to former defence minister and emeritus professor Joris Voorhoeve, three elements, i.e. a maritime-commercial, a neutralist and an international-idealist tradition, summarized in the handsome triad 'peace, profits, principles'.[14] This Dutch tradition would especially be reflecting the interests of the Dutch trading bourgeoisie, as also argued earlier by historian Johan Boogman.[15] Hellema argues for the second position and refers to the many historical deviations or exceptions from the peace-profit-principles triad and he proposes to analyse Dutch international policy on the basis of a more differentiated analytical model comprising both external and geographic factors and internal socio-economic and political factors that mutually interact in a more contingent manner than the existence of a Dutch tradition would suggest. The cadets are challenged to reflect on those positions and encouraged to identify the contemporary determinants of Dutch international policy including the relevance of the traditions that Voorhoeve has mentioned. Additionally, in another lecture the notion of 'strategic (defence) culture' is introduced and the question to what degree one can speak of a specific Dutch strategic culture.[16] Strategic culture is defined by Biehl et al. as "a number of shared beliefs, norms and ideas within a given society that generate specific expectations about the respective community's preferences and actions in security and defence policy."[17] The debate on strategic culture has recently gained prominence as the existence of specific national strategic cultures was deemed to be an obstacle for further defence cooperation or integration of defence efforts among European states or in the framework of the EU.[18]

---

[14] Voorhoeve 1985 (peace, profits and principles dates from 1979).
[15] See Hellema 2016, pp. 48–49.
[16] Noll and Moelker 2013, pp. 255–267.
[17] Biehl et al. 2013, p. 12.
[18] Biehl et al. 2013, pp. 7–8.

16.2.2.2 National and International Decision-Making

It is important that the cadets have a basic understanding of the decision-making procedures at national and international levels. They get introductory lectures on how Dutch government administration functions, both in national and international perspective.[19] There is also a lecture on the main institutional and decision-making structures of NATO and the EU with regard to security and defence and how the EU and NATO policies have evolved over the years.[20] They also have to study what the political programs of the main Dutch political parties and of the coalition government have to say about security and defence and make a critical comparison about commonalities and differences. In a role game they have to take two opposing sides with regard to an actual pertinent topic and defend (and attack) their mutual positions. This year they i.a. discussed the political possibility or impossibility of a substantial increase of the Dutch defence budget (moving towards the 2% NATO norm) in view of other urgent societal needs. Another proposition concerned whether Dutch defence should focus more on the EU or NATO.

16.2.2.3 Post-9/11 Analysis of Dutch Defence Policy

Dutch security and defence policy is further introduced in two lectures by respectively the associate professor of History and the professor of Military Operational Sciences of the FMW. The first lecture focuses on the broader chronological developments in Dutch policies since the end of the Cold War embedded in the wider socio-political changes characterizing this era. The second lecture zooms in on the military aspects thereof, focusing on military transformations (technology, doctrines) and the development of Dutch defence policy by analysing a large set of Dutch policy white papers. Also the consequences of the increasingly narrower budgetary margins were analysed in detail. In another lecture, a detailed discussion was devoted to the evolving threat environment. With reference to three influential publications[21] that are also used as a basis for Dutch policy notes and white papers,[22] the cadets are encouraged to reflect on the current threats to Dutch national interests, and critically discuss the analysis (strong and weak points, omissions) in the different publications and white papers.

---

[19] Cadets have to read selected chapters of Breeman et al. 2016.

[20] Cadets have to study articles about recent EU policies Drent et al. 2017 and the development of EU defence capabilities Zandee 2017.

[21] The Hague Centre for Strategic Studies and Clingendael.

[22] Ministerie van Buitenlandse Zaken 2018 [Ministry of Foreign Affairs 2018]; Ministerie van Defensie 2018 [Ministry of Defence 2018].

16.2.2.4 Current Dutch Security and Defence Policy

Partly overlapping with the former topic is the analysis of current security and defence policy. The focus here is on two recent (2018) government white papers: the Integrated Foreign and Security Strategy 2018–2022 and the Defence Note 2018. The course director introduced these in fairly large detail and the cadets had to analyse and discuss these critically with regard to strong and weak points, also in preparation for the visits to the Ministries of Foreign Affairs and Defence discussed below.

16.2.2.5 Security and Defence Policy in Practice

To get a practical feel on how policy is prepared, formulated and implemented the cadets visited the Ministries of Foreign Affairs and Defence at The Hague. At the Ministry of Foreign Affairs they got an introduction into the Integrated Foreign and Security Strategy 2018–2022 and into the dynamics of coordination between Foreign Affairs and Defence by the Directorate of Security Policy. In the Q&A session the transatlantic ties and associated possible developments within NATO were raised as well as the role of the EU vis-à-vis NATO and the current (limited) importance of the OSCE. At the Ministry of Defence different staff members of the Chief Policy Directorate provided short introductions on the Defence Note 2018, developments with regard to NATO and the EU as well as on the National Security and Safety Strategy, which deals with operations within The Netherlands itself. These introductions were followed by lively discussions, where the critical debate by the cadets on the shortcomings and potential future improvements of the Defence Note had a particular saliency.

16.2.3 Educational Tools

The NVDB course has the characteristics of a normal standard academic course in that it comprises lectures and the study of written material and internet sources. One difference with other courses is that the topic is perhaps not immediately part of the direct life-word of the junior military, as the world of high politics, policy formulation and decision-making may initially look beyond their immediate experiences. However, as discussed in Sect. 16.1.2, the thinking soldier needs to be aware of the policy context and policy (and political) determinants and consequences of his work. The formula chosen in the NVDB course aims at bridging this conceptual gap in different ways. A first attempt to do this is to show how Dutch policies have been developed diachronically starting from the times of the Republic and zooming in on the present. This reminds the cadets and midshipmen that policies are the product of struggles and interests, and hence are human constructs that must be understood with reference to those very struggles and interests. In the second place, political decision-making and policy-making are embedded in an analysis of the current Dutch government administration and of the dynamics of Dutch party politics as well as of the international institutions as the UN, the EU and NATO. It is stressed that one can nearly read about such topics daily in the newspapers and on internet. These issues are further enlivened by concrete assignments and role games that enable the cadets and midshipmen to exercise different political and policy roles and positions. Above it was already mentioned that they have to argue and defend positions in a role game with regard to the defence budget and a preference for respectively EU or NATO in terms of future defence cooperation. Third, lectures have apart from the usual Q&A sessions, specific assignments where students have to discuss and present problematic or challenging elements of the lecture. These more active engagements are usually to their liking. Fourth, the well-prepared visits to the Ministries of Foreign Affairs and Defence add an extra flavour to the course and encourage the students to interact with and ask questions to 'real' policy-makers. Fifth, there are two graded assignments/exams that induce the cadets and midshipmen to reflect and critically write on topics of interest to the course. In 2018 one exam dealt with the changing dynamics of European defence cooperation, including ideas to build common defence capabilities, if not a European army. Each student had to write an essay in class of 2–3 pages on the assignment as presented in box 1 below, based on the prior study of a limited number of relevant newspaper cuttings and articles.

> **Box 1: Student assignment NVDB 2018**
>
> *Discuss the advantages and disadvantages of further European defense cooperation and ultimately the formation of a European army. Make on the basis of this a well-founded analysis with reference to the different European political forces at stake. Draw a clear conclusion and formulate an advice to the Dutch government of how to (re)act with regard to these developments.*

For the second assignment, the cadets and midshipmen had to select a topic of their own liking related to the course contents and write an academic paper of between 2250 and 2750 words based on minimally five sources from the course material and at least two other sources of their own choice. Topics selected by the students in 2018 included: A critical analysis of the letter informing Dutch Parliament on a military mission (the so-called article 100 letter); the potential usefulness of a national security council; the Dutch choice for PESCO; the deployment ambitions of The Netherlands; the extension of the European Coast Guard; an advice to the four Dutch coalition parties on defence; the role of Dutch strategic culture in operations; and reliance on the US.

16.3 Challenges

One challenge of this NVDB course is the constantly changing dynamics in the policy field and the wider security environment. This requires regular updates of lectures, literature and course contents. The advantage of this is that one can discuss with the students "what was on the news yesterday". Moreover, the electronic learning environment facilitates the distribution of very recent materials and insights during the course. Second, as indicated above, the material needs to be presented in such a way that the students feel enthused. Making the course contents concrete through assignments, buzz-groups and Q&A sessions can help achieving this. Role games and visits are a good inducement to work and rework the academic and policy stuff. Another good way to raise interest is to formulate issues in a slightly provocative manner as to elicit response and participation. Like all other modules in the BA War studies, the NVDB course is regularly evaluated. If certain bottlenecks appear or useful suggestions are made by the participants, these are taken up in the course set-up of the next year to the degree possible.

16.4 Conclusion

Teaching policy to cadets and midshipmen is the need of the day in view of the transformation of warfare and the concept of the thinking soldier that the FMW promotes. This requires cadets and midshipmen to be cognizant of the policy context, determinants and consequences of military operations. The NVDB course is attempting to reach this goal by learning the Dutch cadets how Dutch international policy evolved over time and to critically read current Dutch policy white papers with special attention to the threat environment and the policies of international institutions with which the Dutch forces cooperate in practice. Bridging the conceptual gap between the cadets' and midshipmen's lifeworld and the world of high politics and policy can best be done by concrete assignments, role games and visits. It is also attempted to relate to their own experiences and ideas, and what prominent issues they have picked up from the daily news. In-class discussions help making the cadets and midshipmen critical and reflective something which they sometimes contrast with the hands-on military approach, though this is only seemingly a contradiction as the above concepts of the thinking soldier or soldier-statesman exemplify. Hence, the NVDB course is a useful final complement to the knowledge already acquired by the cadets and midshipmen in their prior academic and military training.

References

Biehl H, Giegerich B, Jonas A (eds) (2013) Strategic Cultures in Europe. Springer VS, Wiesbaden.
Breeman GE, van Noort WJ, Rutgers MR (2016) De bestuurlijke kaart van Nederland. Het openbaar bestuur en zijn omgeving in nationaal en internationaal perspectief [The administrative map of The Netherlands. Public administration and its environment in national and international perspective]. Coutinho, Bussum.
De Bruijne K, Meijnders M, Héau L (2017) New dots on the security horizon. Results from the Clingendael Expert Survey. Clingendael Report. Institute Clingendael, The Hague.
Drent M, Wilms E, Zandee D (2017) Making sense of European defence. Clingendael Report. Institute Clingendael, The Hague.
European Commission & High Representative of the European Union For Foreign Affairs and Security Policy (2013) Joint Communication to the European Parliament and the Council, The EU's Comprehensive Approach to External Conflict and Crises. JOIN (2013) 30 final, Brussels.
Hague Centre for Strategic Studies and Clingendael Institute (2018) Strategische Monitor 2017–2018, Stilte voor de Storm? [Strategic Monitor 2017–2018. Silence before the Storm?], The Hague.
Hellema D (2016) Nederland in de wereld; de buitenlandse politiek van Nederland [The Netherlands in the world; foreign policy of The Netherlands], 6th edn. Unieboek/Het Spectrum, Houten/Antwerp.
Janowitz M (1964) The professional soldier: A social and political portrait. Free Press, New York, NY.
Kalu KN (2008) Bridging the Divide. An Integrated Model of National Security Education for a New Era of International Governance. The American Review of Public Administration, 38 (1):80–99.
Krulak CC (1999) The Strategic Corporal: Leadership in the Three Block War. Marines Magazine, January 1999.
Ministerie van Buitenlandse Zaken (2018) Wereldwijd voor een veilig Nederland, Geïntegreerde Buitenland- en Veiligheidsstrategie 2018–2022 [Ministry of Foreign Affairs (2018) Working Worldwide for the Security of The Netherlands. An Integrated International Security Strategy 2018–2022]. Ministry of Foreign Affairs, The Hague.
Ministerie van Defensie (2018) Defensienota 2018. Investeren in onze mensen, slagkracht en zichtbaarheid [Ministry of Defence (2018) Defence White Paper 2018. Investing in our people, capabilities and visibility]. Ministry of Defence, The Hague.
Moskos CC, Williams JA, Segal DR (eds) (2000) The postmodern military: Armed forces after the cold war. Oxford University Press, New York.
Nederlandse Defensie Academie, Faculteit Militaire Wetenschappen (2017) Studiegids Bachelor Krijgswetenschappen, Studiejaar 2017–2018 [Netherlands Defence Academy, Faculty of Military Sciences (2017) Study Guide Bachelor degree program War Studies, 2017–2018], Breda.
Noll JE, Moelker R (2013) Netherlands. In: Biehl H et al (eds) Strategic Cultures in Europe. Springer VS, Wiesbaden, pp 255–267.
Roennfeldt CF (2019) Wider Officer Competence: The Importance of Politics and Practical Wisdom. Armed Forces & Society 45(1):59–77.
Voorhoeve JJC (1985) Peace, Profits and Principles. A study of Dutch Foreign Policy. Martinus Nijhoff, Leiden.

WRR (2017) Veiligheid in een wereld van verbindingen, een strategische visie op het defensiebeleid [WRR (2017) Security in an interconnected world, a strategic vision on the defence policy]. The Netherlands Scientific Council for Government Policy, The Hague.

Zandee D (2017) Developing European defence capabilities. Bringing order into disorder. Clingendael Report. Institute Clingendael, The Hague.

Prof. Dr. Georg E. Frerks is professor of International Security Studies at the Faculty of Military Sciences of the Netherlands Defence Academy and professor of Conflict Prevention and Conflict Management at Utrecht University, The Netherlands.

Chapter 17
Legal Education: A Matter of Motivation? An Overview of Aspects of Legal Education for Officers

Kirsten Visser-Schönbeck

Contents

17.1	Introduction	274
17.2	History of Officers' Legal Education	275
17.3	The Legal Obligation to Disseminate	276
17.4	Legal Education for Officers	278
17.5	Legal Education at the Netherlands Defence Academy	279
17.6	Didactical Challenges of Legal Education	281
17.7	Conclusion	282
Reference		283

Abstract Military law covers several branches of law, which implies that an officer has to apply military law in each aspect of his work, either working his day to day office job, applying administrative law or disciplinary law to his subordinates, or being in the field applying humanitarian law or operational law as well. Consequently, law is a subject that must be taught throughout the career of any member of the armed forces, not only during initial education, but also at later stages. Furthermore, it implies that it is of importance to give officers a solid foundation of knowledge in law before they start their careers. Additionally, there is a legal obligation to include law in the program of military instruction, an obligation that is laid down in international treaties. From a didactical point of view, legal education needs a very practical approach, applying the law on cases to clarify the theoretical aspects, whilst at the same time maintaining a strong academic basis. This also has implications for the way legal courses are set up. Using the pyramid of Bloom, the learning objectives can be set on the level of '*applying*' the learned theory on actual situations.

K. A. Visser-Schönbeck (✉)
Royal Netherlands Air Force, PO Box 90004, 3509 AA Utrecht, The Netherlands
e-mail: ka.schonbeck@mindef.nl

© T.M.C. ASSER PRESS and the authors 2019
W. Klinkert et al. (eds.), *NL ARMS Netherlands Annual Review of Military Studies 2019*, NL ARMS, https://doi.org/10.1007/978-94-6265-315-3_17

Keywords Legal education · officers' education · obligation to disseminate · humanitarian law · history of officers' education · legal education for officers · didactical challenges

17.1 Introduction

Military law is embedded in all aspects of the work of any officer. It covers several branches of law, including administrative law, criminal law, disciplinary law, operational law, and branches of international law such as the use of force and human rights law alongside humanitarian law.[1] The wide variety of subjects covered by military law implies that an officer has to apply military law in each aspect of his work, either working his day to day office job, applying administrative law or disciplinary law to his subordinates, or being in the field applying humanitarian law or operational law as well. Consequently, law is a subject that must be taught throughout the career of any member of the armed forces, not only during initial education, but also at later stages. Furthermore, it implies that it is of importance to give officers a solid foundation of knowledge in law before they start their careers. Additionally, there is a legal obligation to include law in the program of military instruction, an obligation that is laid down in international treaties.[2]

However, teaching in general, and law is no exception, also means that the teachers have to face a challenge: how to keep students motivated, whilst giving them all the knowledge they need. Law is often expected to be tiresome, even more so when students expect having to know the laws by heart. From a didactical point of view, legal education is usually based on a practical approach, applying the law on cases to clarify the theoretical aspects, whilst at the same time maintaining a strong academic basis. This also has implications for the way legal courses are taught.

This chapter explores these various aspects of legal education in officers' education. It starts out with a historical overview of legal education at the Royal Military Academy, before it became part of the Netherlands Defence Academy. Then, it looks at the legal obligation to disseminate international humanitarian law, describing the consequences stemming from that obligation. After that, the present legal education at the Netherlands Defence Academy is studied; examining first the current legal educational program during the cadets and midshipmen studies at the Netherlands Defence Academy, and secondly exploring the didactical challenges of legal education. This way a complete picture is drawn of officers' legal education in the Dutch military, at the Netherlands Defence Academy and during an officer's career.

---

[1] Fink 2014.

[2] See for example the First Geneva Convention of 12 August 1949, Article 47, and the Convention on the Safety of United Nations and Associated Personnel, Article 19.

17.2 History of Officers' Legal Education

Legal education has always been part of officers' education. Ever since the Royal Military Academy was founded in 1828, and even before that, military law has been part of the curriculum of officers' education, although the content and number of classes have changed over time. This section examines the historical developments in legal officers' education, in order to see what position legal education has had in officers' education over time and how much importance was attributed to it.

When the Royal Military Academy was founded, military law was from the outset part of the curriculum for cadets.[3] During the 1800s, education in military law mainly consisted of the subjects of criminal and disciplinary law, but it also sometimes included administrative law (then called 'military law' or 'administration').[4] In the academic year 1880-81, for example, military law was taught one hour a week during the third year and the first semester of the fourth year, and two hours a week in the second semester of the fourth year of officers' education (which was the final semester). The main parts of these courses comprised general principles of criminal law and judicial procedures.[5]

It is interesting to see, when looking at the contents of the studies in the academic year 1885–86 in comparison to 1880–81, that the contents of military law in officers' education had slightly changed. An extra course had been added in the fourth year, called 'Customs of War', which included the laws of war, rights of combatants, and rules about occupation.[6] This can be explained by looking at the history of humanitarian law in general: in the late 1800s humanitarian law began its development. In 1864, the first Geneva Convention was adopted, and after that humanitarian law has evolved and expanded to cover more and more categories of war victims.[7,8]

In 1910, education at the Military Academy was revised by law,[9] even though no major changes were made to legal education at that time. This law stated that the study program for the final exam at the Royal Military Academy contained two courses in law: 'Customs of War', which comprised the law and customs of war on

---

[3] Koninklijke Militaire Academie 1911, Bijlage B.

[4] Koninklijke Militaire Academie 1911, Bijlage B.

[5] Koninklijke Militaire Academie 1880, pp. 67–111.

[6] Koninklijke Militaire Academie 1885, p. 113.

[7] Kolb and Hyde 2008, pp. 38–39.

[8] The fact that a course on customs of war was then added to the curriculum is possibly owed to esquire Jacobus Catharinus Cornelis den Beer Poortugael (1832–1913). He wrote a book on war law in 1872, and was governor of the Royal Military Academy from 1883 to 1885. He was also part of the Netherlands delegation to the First and Second Hague Peace conference in 1899 and 1907, and to the International Conference in Geneva on the Amelioration of the Condition of the Wounded in Armies in the Field, in 1864. http://resources.huygens.knaw.nl/bwn1880-2000/lemmata/bwn5/beer.

[9] Wet van 23 mei 1910 (Stbl. No. 138), tot regeling van het Militair Onderwijs bij de Landmacht, voor zoover daarbij de opleiding tot den officiersrang en de hoogere vorming van den officier zijn betrokken.

land and sea and the laws and duties of neutral states, and 'Military Criminal Law', which consisted of military disciplinary law, general principles of common and military criminal law, and jurisdiction and judicial procedures.[10] Military law was taught in every year of officers' education, starting with basic principles in the first year, each year gradually expanding the subjects covered.[11]

In the 1930s, the officers' education program was changed again. Now, military law was no longer taught in every year of education, but centralized in two courses, taking place in the second and third year, being 'War Law' and 'Customs of War', and 'Military Criminal Law'. The course 'Military Criminal Law' covered 68 h, whereas 'War Law' only took 36 h in total.[12]

In study guides from the 1960s, three courses of military law can be found; 'Introduction in Law', 'Military Criminal and Disciplinary Law', and 'Constitutional Law'. 'Criminal and Disciplinary law' is the largest course, being taught in both the second and third year, comprising a total of 48 h.[13] Interesting is that no mention is made of war law or customs of war, whereas in the 1970s and 1980s this subject is included again, albeit as part of the second of two general courses in law, taught in the second year of officers' education.[14] It is unclear why the subject was not included in the 1960s.

What becomes clear from looking at this historical overview, is that the sizes of the courses and the contents of the courses are not set in stone. They change over the course of the years, which could imply that the importance attributed to it also changes over time. This can partially be explained by looking at historical development, the spirit of the times so to say, especially when we look at the introduction of war law or the customs of war at the military academy, which took place just a few years after the very first Geneva Convention was signed.

17.3 The Legal Obligation to Disseminate

An important factor stressing the special position of legal education in officers' education is that there is a legal obligation to educate officers in law, more specifically in international humanitarian law (also known as the Law of Armed

---

[10] Reglement voor de Koninklijke Militaire Academie houdende bepalingen tot uitvoering van artikel 48 der Wet van 21 juli 1890 (Staatsblad No. 126), gewijzigd bij de Wet van 23 mei 1910 (Staatsblad No. 138), – vastgesteld bij Koninklijk Besluit van 7 juni 1912 (Staatsblad No. 186), Article 105 sub d and e.

[11] Voorschrift voor de Koninklijke Militaire Academie, vastgesteld door de Ministers van Oorlog en van Koloniën, onder dagteekening van 29 Juni 1912, IIde Afd. No. 340 en van 26 Juli 1912, Afd. C., 1^e Bureau, no. 8

[12] Koninklijke Militaire Academie 1931, pp. 8–9.

[13] Koninklijke Militaire Academie 1964, p. 23 and p. 32.

[14] Koninklijke Militaire Academie 1973, pp. 38–39 and Koninklijke Militaire Academie 1983, p. 37 and p. 54.

Conflict). This legal obligation is laid down in international treaties, namely the Geneva Conventions of 1949 and the Convention on the Safety of United Nations and Associated Personnel.

Article 47 of the First Geneva Convention of 12 August 1949 states that the

> High Contracting Parties undertake, in time of peace as in time of war, to disseminate the text of the present Convention as widely as possible in their respective countries, and, in particular, to include the study thereof in their programmes of military and, if possible, civil instruction, so that the principles thereof may become known to the entire population, in particular to the armed fighting forces, the medical personnel and the chaplains.

Article 19 of the Convention on the Safety of United Nations and Associated Personnel states in a similar manner that

> the States Parties undertake to disseminate this Convention as widely as possible and, in particular, to include the study thereof, as well as relevant provisions of international humanitarian law, in their programmes of military instruction.

The Netherlands is a State Party to both these treaties. They thus impose upon The Netherlands the obligation to disseminate international humanitarian law.[15] The obligation to disseminate implies not only to spread the word, hand out copies of the text, but it means that the State has to make sure that humanitarian law is understood, and internalized.[16] The fact that this obligation is included in the text is based on "the conviction of the drafters that knowledge of the law is an essential condition for its effective application".[17]

In The Netherlands, the obligation to disseminate is included in the national army military manual (which is being updated at the time of writing this chapter) which states:

> The States which are parties to the conventions on the law of war should take all necessary steps to meet their obligations under those conventions. They should give orders and instructions to ensure compliance and supervise their application. These States should disseminate the conventions on the widest possible scale during peacetime, and include the law of war in military training.[18]

Moreover, the national army military manual imposes the obligation to disseminate upon commanders, stating that "Commanding officers are responsible for ensuring that their subordinates know the humanitarian law of war and act in accordance with that law." This reflects the fact that officers can be held legally responsible for the actions of their subordinates.

More specifically, the manual provides rules about who should give lessons in humanitarian law:

---

[15] ICRC 2005, Rule 142, Instruction in International Humanitarian Law within Armed Forces.
[16] Spijk 2018, p. 5.
[17] ICRC 2016, Article 47: Dissemination of the Convention.
[18] Koninklijke Landmacht 2005 (translation at: https://ihl-databases.icrc.org/customary-ihl/eng/docs/v2_cou_nl_rule142, accessed 01-18-2019).

In view of the subject's importance, lessons should be given by officers, who should themselves have been trained in the subject. The provision of adequate (instruction) material forms part of the commanding officer's responsibility. The commanding officer should, finally, integrate the humanitarian law of war with military courses and exercises, to achieve action which consolidates the standard.

17.4 Legal Education for Officers

A Dutch officer has enormous responsibilities applying the law throughout his or her career. Law is connected to many aspects of an officer's daily work activities. When an officer is working his regular day-job, law applies to himself just like any other person in the military, being subject of administrative, criminal and disciplinary law. But also, as stated above citing the national army military manual, when he is a unit commander, he is the one to apply the law to his subordinates, and he is criminally liable if he knows of any criminal action from his subordinates but does not act upon that knowledge.[19] When an officer is deployed in the context of an armed conflict or a peace operation, an additional responsibility is added, namely the responsibility for the application of international humanitarian law, and all other rules that apply specifically during employment, such as the (national or international) rules concerning the use of force.

Because of these extensive responsibilities under the law, legal education does not only take place during initial education, but also at several moments during an officer's career. An officer can voluntarily enroll in one of the legal courses that are regularly organized by the legal department. Moreover, every member of the armed forces must maintain his or her military basic skills yearly. Military law, covering rules on the use of force and humanitarian law, is considered to be part of those basic skills. In the training program for these basic skills it is indicated that military law should be taught once every three years.[20]

A very important moment when an officer receives legal training is before he or she is deployed. Part of the mission specific training is a legal briefing.[21] The aim of this briefing is to explain the legal aspects concerning their mission, such as the legal basis for their mission (ius ad bellum), the rules of engagement, the status of forces agreement, and international humanitarian law and human rights law. This training can be customized to the job that the officer is going to do while deployed. For example, for a fighter pilot, deploying weapons in an armed conflict in state A, legal training on humanitarian law is more extensive than for someone working on base in state B, where the fighter jets are stationed but where no armed conflict is taking place.

---

[19] Articles 148 and 149 Wetboek van Militair Strafrecht [military criminal law].
[20] CDS Aanwijzing A-700 Gereedstelling, Bijlage B, Annex 2.
[21] CDS Aanwijzing A-700 Gereedstelling, Bijlage B, Annex 4.

The Netherlands uses the Standardization Agreements (STANAG) 2449 and 2597 as parameters for instruction in Law of Armed Conflict and Rules of Engagement.[22] The STANAG 2449 distinguishes between education for non-commissioned officers and officers. For officers states should ensure, inter alia, that they are able to fulfill their command responsibilities relating to law of armed conflict and to be able to take proper action in the face of a breach of law of armed conflict. This means that for officers' education should not only be aimed at making sure that they know the rules themselves but also know how to make others adhere to the rules.

Moreover, a few years ago a set of learning objectives was developed at the Netherlands Ministry of Defence. These learning objectives defined the basic legal knowledge that all members of the armed forces should acquire during their initial education and during their career. Several subsets could then be added to form the required set of knowledge for, for example, either officers or non-commissioned officers, or for initial training or mission-specific training.[23] This set of learning objectives, however, was never actually implemented up until today.

It is interesting to note that there is no evidence found of any discussion about the curriculum of officers or military education. Even the set of learning objectives that was developed did not start any discussion about the contents of military legal education.

17.5 Legal Education at the Netherlands Defence Academy

An officer in The Netherlands receives his initial education at the Netherlands Defence Academy. At the Netherlands Defence Academy (NLDA) law is taught in various courses. Before explaining the current legal training program during initial education, it is important to provide some background information about the educational system at NLDA. For a civilian who wants to become an officer there are several routes to take. This chapter focusses on the two largest branches of officers' education, namely the short program at the Royal Military Academy and the long, academic, program. Other programs, such as for specialists (e.g. doctors or chaplains), medical personnel, and reservists, will not be discussed here.

The short program, which includes cadets from army, air force, and military police comprises one year. Of that year, the first half consists of military training, for basic military skills. After that, the second half consists of theoretical courses, containing subjects like international relations, air power, military operations, and also includes a course in law.

---

[22] Spijk 2018, p. 9.
[23] Spijk 2018, p. 9.

The long program involves cadets from army, air force, and military police and midshipmen from navy. It comprises four years. The first year consists of half a year of training military basic skills, which are after that repeated in each year of the officer's education during a few 'green weeks' (military training). Then academic education starts with a common semester for all cadets and midshipmen, which includes one course in International Humanitarian Law. After the first semester, the group of cadets and midshipmen is split up in three studies: Military Technical Studies, Military Management Studies, and War Studies.

The amount of legal education that is offered to these cadets and midshipmen differs substantially. In Military Technical Studies after the first year there are no more courses in law, which means that the only legal education they get is one course in humanitarian law.[24] In Military Management Studies and War Studies there are more courses, some of which are optional. In Military Management Studies all cadets and midshipmen get, besides the course in International Humanitarian Law, in their first year two courses in law in the final year of their studies: Military Administrative Law, and Military Criminal and Disciplinary Law.[25]

Cadets and midshipmen in the War Studies program have the most extensive possibilities for legal education. They are offered, besides the course International Humanitarian Law in their first year, another course in International Law in their second year and a possibility of choosing a Minor on Military Law in their third year.[26] This Minor covers four main topics of military law, namely military administrative law, military criminal and disciplinary law, legal basis and legal regimes of military operations and military operational law. It measures 20 ECTS (around 560 working hours).

The NLDA does not offer master's degrees in law, but has covenants with two universities in The Netherlands, the University of Amsterdam and Utrecht University, which provide that, when a student has completed the Minor on Military Law and has written a bachelor's thesis in law, he or she is qualified to enter a master's degree course in international law.[27] This implies that the Minor on Military Law has to maintain a certain quality level, in order for these covenants to remain applicable.

Besides their initial education, all officers are also given additional training to specialise them in their specific field of work. For army and air force officers, there is no standard legal course included in this training. For navy officers, however, two courses of law are included in this training, covering all aspects of military law: administrative law, criminal law, disciplinary law, international humanitarian law, human rights law and military operational law. This means that all navy officers,

---

[24] Faculteit Militaire Wetenschappen [Faculty of Military Sciences] 2018a.
[25] Faculteit Militaire Wetenschappen [Faculty of Military Sciences] 2018b, p. 30.
[26] Faculteit Militaire Wetenschappen [Faculty of Military Sciences] 2018c, pp. 126–129.
[27] Faculteit Militaire Wetenschappen [Faculty of Military Sciences] 2018c, pp. 128–129.

regardless of their initial education get two courses that comprise a total of 1, 8 ECTS.

What becomes clear from the analysis above, is that the amount of legal education that aspiring officers are given differs greatly. For military technical studies, the one course in humanitarian law is the only legal course they receive. On the other end of the spectrum, navy officers are educated in all aspects of military law, and cadets and midshipmen in war studies who choose the minor in law, acquire, added up, almost a semester full of legal courses, and if they wish, they have the possibility to obtain even a master's degree in law. Even though this difference would appear to need some justification, no information has been found about why there is such a sharp contrast in the amount of legal education.

17.6 Didactical Challenges of Legal Education

Legal educators, like all educators, face the challenge of motivating and enthusing their students. There are many ways of doing this. A few of these ways are highlighted here.

First of all, it is of great importance to let students know why a certain course is included in the curriculum. Understanding the importance of a course is a first step toward intrinsic motivation. Legal aspects are, as shown above, very important for officers, because law plays an important role in many aspects of an officer's work. Stressing this importance by giving examples of real life situations is a good way of getting students interested in what any (legal) course entails. Most legal teachers have a military background, so they know the practical implications of the law for an officer. Another way of reaching this goal is by showing the students at the beginning of every class how the subject of that class aligns with the rest of the course, or how the course aligns with the rest of their studies.

Making legal education attractive for students can also be established by using interesting examples that capture the imagination of the students. These examples can best be derived from practice, to make sure they are realistic and instructive for the students. However, even though most legal teachers do have a military background, not every teacher has been deployed. A possible challenge here is therefore that not every teacher may have the experience needed to know examples from first hand, but the experience of other colleagues is also an important source of examples.

Looking at the challenge of motivating students from an educational/didactical point of view, it is interesting to take into regard Bloom's (revised) taxonomy. Bloom's revised taxonomy is a system used to classify educational learning objectives.[28] It consists of six levels of objectives, sometimes also called Bloom's pyramid, from low to high being: *Remember, Understand, Apply, Analyze,*

---

[28] Krathwohl 2002, p. 212.

Evaluate, and *Create*.[29] Whereas almost always in education there is from the start a heavy emphasis on the two lowest levels of Bloom's pyramid, to remember and to understand,[30] in legal courses more emphasis is put on a higher level in the taxonomy straight away: the level of application. Most courses usually start with teaching students to remember and understand basic knowledge, fundamental principles of that subject. For law, from the outset courses are aimed at applying the law to cases. Law is, especially at the NLDA, in the end a practical subject, albeit with a strong academic basis. The academic basis can be found in the theoretic vision that legal education is based on, namely that at the NLDA, just like on most other Dutch universities, positive law, or the existing law, is studied.[31] Since students at the NLDA only get taught the basics of law, it would go beyond the scope of officers' education to teach anything but positive law.

The ultimate goal of education at the NLDA is that officers become able to apply the law, so that is what the students should be taught. It does not help an officer in the field to only remember and understand the law; he should know how to apply the law (although there should always be a legal advisor there to advise him). It therefore makes sense to teach students how to apply it. Therefore, in legal education at the NLDA, the objective is often set at *applying* the subject matter. Applying the law means that students should be taught to find the applicable law, know where to find the specific rules, and by using the law solving a case. This implies that a student should not only be able to find the right rules, but also know how to apply those rules. An advantage of using applying as learning objective is that applying the law makes the law come to life, which makes the subject more appealing to students. The learning objective can, at least for legal courses, thus be used as a way of motivating the students.

17.7 Conclusion

This chapter has not tried to explain what military law entails. It is also not an academic study of educational or legal aspects. What this chapter has done is explore many aspects of officers' legal education. First of all, looking at the history of officers' legal education at the Netherlands Defence Academy (and the Royal Military Academy before it became part of the Netherlands Defence Academy) it has become clear that the importance given to legal education changes over time. For example, when the First Geneva Convention was adopted in 1864, legal education gained a more prominent place in officers' education: an extra course in 'Customs of War' was added to the curriculum.

---

[29] Krathwohl 2002, p. 218.
[30] Krathwohl 2002, p. 213.
[31] Hage 2012, p. 1.

An important aspect to keep in mind when talking about legal education for officers is the obligation to disseminate international humanitarian law, which is laid down in international treaties. This obligation has been adopted by the Dutch Government in its national military manual, stating that the law of war should be included in military training. For officers' education this obligation is even more relevant, since officers also have a legal responsibility for the behavior of their subordinates.

Moreover, officers need to apply the law throughout their careers, with enormous responsibilities and great consequences possibly following from it. An officer therefore does not only learn about military law in his or her initial education as an officer, at the NLDA, but also at other times during his or her career, at other institutions, and by other teachers. This means that it is very important that an officer gets a solid basis of legal knowledge. It is especially interesting to notice the differences in the number of legal courses cadets and midshipmen get during their bachelor degree programs. These differ widely, from only one course in international humanitarian law in their first year (for cadets and midshipmen in Military Technical Studies), to a full semester of legal courses (the minor on Military Law), or even beyond their bachelor's degrees they can choose to obtain a master's degree in law. One might wonder whether in all cases officers are given enough legal basis to start their careers.

The main challenge as a teacher is then how to keep students motivated and enthused about law. Students tend to expect that a legal course will be boring. It is up to the teacher to break through this expectation. Using Bloom's pyramid of learning objectives, for legal courses the learning objective is often, sooner than in a general course, set on applying the law instead of just remembering or understanding.

However, the lack of literature regarding this subject, the contents of officers' legal education and didactical challenges for legal education, shows that there has not been much discussion about how officers' legal education should take place. More discussion and research regarding this subject is needed.

Reference

Faculteit Militaire Wetenschappen (2018a) Studiegids Opleiding Militaire Systemen en Technologie Academisch jaar 2018/2019 [Faculty of Military Sciences (2018a) Study guide Bachelor degree program Military Systems and Technology 2018–2019].
Faculteit Militaire Wetenschappen (2018b) Studiegids Opleiding Militaire Bedrijfswetenschappen Academisch jaar 2018–2019 [Faculty of Military Sciences (2018b) Study guide Bachelor degree program Military Management Studies 2018–2019].
Faculteit Militaire Wetenschappen (2018c) Bachelor Krijgswetenschappen Studiejaar 2018–2019 [Faculty of Military Sciences (2018c) Study guide Bachelor degree program War Studies 2018–2019].
Fink MD (2014) Inleiding Militair Recht [Introduction Military Law]. Netherlands Defence Academy, Breda.

Hage J (2012) Hoe moet recht worden onderwezen? [How to teach law studies?] Law and Method, February 2012. https://www.bjutijdschriften.nl/tijdschrift/lawandmethod/2012/2/ReM_2212-2508_2012_002_002_003. Accessed 15 February 2019.

ICRC (2005) Customary International Humanitarian Law Study. https://ihl-databases.icrc.org/customary-ihl/eng/docs/v2_cou_nl_rule142. Accessed 18 January 2019.

ICRC (2016) Convention (I) for the amelioration of the condition of the wounded and sick in armed forces in the field. Geneva, 12 August 1949. ICRC Commentary of 2016.

Kolb R, Hyde R (2008) An Introduction to the International Law of Armed Conflicts. Bloomsbury Publishing, Oxford.

Koninklijke Landmacht (2005) Handleiding Humanitair Oorlogsrecht (VS 27-412) [Royal Netherlands Army (2005) Guidelines Humanitarian Law of Armed Conflicts (VS 27-412)].

Koninklijke Militaire Academie (1880) Programma's der Studiën [Studies guide].

Koninklijke Militaire Academie (1885) Programma's der Studiën [Studies guide].

Koninklijke Militaire Academie (1911) Beknopt overzicht van de geschiedenis van het militair onderwijs sedert 1814 [Concise review of the history of military education since 1814].

Koninklijke Militaire Academie (1931) Programma van Studie aangevende de indeeling van de leerstof voor de verschillende studiejaren, met aanduiding van het aantal uren, maximum voor elk onderwerp uitgetrokken [Study guide Royal Military Academy 1931].

Koninklijke Militaire Academie (1964) Studiegids 1964–1965 [Study guide Royal Military Academy 1964–1965].

Koninklijke Militaire Academie (1973) Studiegids 1973–1974 [Study guide Royal Military Academy 1973–1974].

Koninklijke Militaire Academie (1983) KMA-Gids 1983-1984 [Study guide Royal Military Academy 1983–1984].

Krathwohl DR (2002) A Revision of Bloom's Taxonomy: An Overview. Theory into Practice 41:4:212–218.

Spijk JP (2018) The Obligation to Disseminate IHL, and what Article 47 GCI Entails for the Armed Forces, Militair Rechtelijk Tijdschrift. https://puc.overheid.nl/doc/PUC_217602_11/1. Accessed 18 January 2019.

Kirsten Visser-Schönbeck, LL.M., MSc is a legal advisor with the Royal Netherlands Air Force. She has a master's degree in International Law and in International Relations. At the time of writing the chapter she held a position as lecturer at the Faculty of Military Sciences of the Netherlands Defence Academy, where she taught Military Law.

Chapter 18
Military Engineering – Practice, Education and Research in The Netherlands; the Golden Triangle

Edwin Dado, Alexander Schmets, Rick Krosenbrink and Dennis Krabbenborg

Contents

18.1	Introduction	286
18.2	The Professional Environment of Military Engineering	287
18.3	Current State of Military Engineering Education at the FMS	290
18.4	Current State of Military Engineering Research at the FMS	291
18.5	Interactions Between Education and Research	293
	18.5.1 Research Topics in Military Engineering	293
	18.5.2 Research Topics in Education: Two Cases	294
	18.5.3 Relation of Thesis Research Topics to Military Engineering Curriculum	295
18.6	Interactions Between Professional Environment and Education	296
18.7	Interactions Between Professional Environment and Research	297
18.8	Conclusions	299
References		300

Abstract After the Cold War period, the operational scope of the Dutch Army Engineers has evolved from providing mobility and contra-mobility in a static military setting towards a more integral approach. This approach aims at controlling the military environment, providing safety for military personnel and civilians in a

E. Dado (✉) · A. J. M. Schmets · R. J. J. Krosenbrink · D. Krabbenborg
Faculty of Military Sciences, Netherlands Defence Academy, PO Box 90002, 4800 PA Breda, The Netherlands
e-mail: E.Dado@mindef.nl

A. J. M. Schmets
e-mail: AJM.Schmets@mindef.nl

R. J. J. Krosenbrink
e-mail: RJJ.Krosenbrink@mindef.nl

D. Krabbenborg
e-mail: D.Krabbenborg@mindef.nl

dynamic complex military setting during expeditionary operations. From an organizational point of view, the Engineers Regiment is currently changing to address the needs for a more 'adaptive' military organization. In order to adjust to the changing military operational and organizational context, the Engineers Regiment is adopting new methods and techniques in the areas of military strategy, management, organization and technology. This requires rethinking the desired and required competences of the Regiment's – current and future – employees. Certainly, this change of desired competences of personnel requires similarly fundamental changes at the level of vocational training of personnel as well as the academic education of future officers. Educational and research institutes within or associated with the Dutch Defence organization are challenged to anticipate interactions between military practice, education and research, i.e. the intensify collaboration within the Golden Triangle. This chapter addresses the above-mentioned developments and the required interactions between military practice, education and research within the academic educational and research program provided by the Faculty of Military Sciences in the Netherlands.

Keywords Military Engineering · adaptivity · Competences · Golden Triangle · research · education

18.1 Introduction

In The Netherlands, the educational academic program for army engineer officers is delivered by the Faculty of Military Sciences (FMS) of the Netherlands Defence Academy (NLDA). Traditionally, academic education and research have complemented each other meanwhile strengthening each other synergistically. For students, the research component of higher education is essential in helping them develop academic skills, as well as various other skills they will need to operate successfully in the 21st century. For teachers, the benefits are twofold: (1) the anchoring and deepening of knowledge by research staff through their teaching will constitute a solid foundation for their academic research, and (2) students may contribute to configuring research.[1]

The main challenge that FMS staff faces when it comes to linking teaching and research relates to the small number of research and teaching staff compared to the vast diversity of educational tracks and corresponding work load. In order to obtain additional research capacity, the Military Engineering group of the FMS collaborates closely with the Engineer Centre of Expertise of the Engineer Training Centre (in Dutch: OTCGenie) which – in its turn – works closely with the Netherlands Organization for Applied Research (TNO) and other research institutes. Research

---

[1] Adviesraad voor wetenschap, technologie en innovatie 2015 [Advisory council for science, technology and innovation 2015].

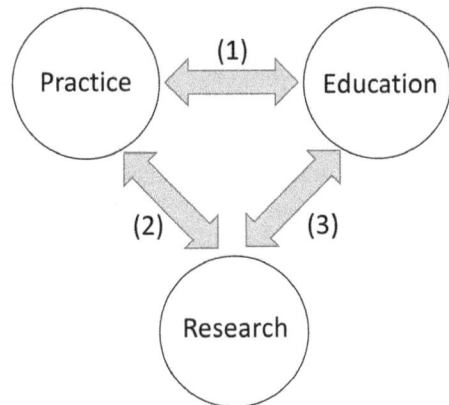

Fig. 18.1 Interactions between practice and education (1), practice and education (2) and education and research (3). *Source* Dado et al. 2019

coordinated by the OTCGenie is often characterized as 'practice-oriented' or applied research, which is research-directed towards solving problems of a 'day-to-day' nature. Therefore, education, research and military practice form together a trinity wherein elements are interrelated. This obviously implies that changes within either one of these components will directly influence the others. In the ever-changing world of military practice, the FMS is obliged to provide education and conduct research that is aligned with the needs of the service man in the field, i.e. the FMS needs to foster and expand the interactions between Practice, Education and Research (see Fig. 18.1).

In this chapter, we will mainly focus on the interactions between the Education and Research delivered and conducted by the FMS and the military practice of the Engineer Regiment in The Netherlands. In the first part of this chapter we will provide a sketch of the professional environment of the Regiment and the current state of Military Engineering education and research at the FMS. In the second part of this chapter we will discuss the current status of activities aimed at supporting the interactions between Practice, Education and Research.

18.2 The Professional Environment of Military Engineering

The Engineer Regiment (ER) has known a number of changes throughout its existence. Often these changes meant a broadening in the scope of the tasks and the field of operations. Since its inception in 1748 the task of the ER consisted of 'mining' (i.e. undermining and destroying enemies' structures) and 'sapping' (i.e. building trenches and field fortifications), in other words: providing mobility as well as counter-mobility. Later, with the advancement of technology, these tasks have expanded considerably.

Since the end of the Cold War, the field of operations has evolved from providing mobility and counter-mobility in a static military setting towards a more integral approach of controlling the military environment providing safety for military personnel and civilians in a dynamic complex military setting during expeditionary operations. This change poses a real challenge for military policy-makers in the further development of Military Engineering in general and the organization of the Engineer Regiment more specific.

In 2009, the Military Committee of NATO published a document titled MC 0560 "Policy for Military Engineering", which acts as the blueprint for national military policymakers of the affiliated member countries. In this document Military Engineering is described as: "That Engineer activities undertaken regardless of component or service, to shape the physical operating environment. Military Engineering incorporates support to manoeuvre (Combat Support Engineering) and the force as a whole (Force Support Engineering), including Military Engineering functions such as Engineer Support to Force Protection, Counter-Improvised Explosive Devices, Environmental Protection, Reconstruction, Engineer Intelligence, and Military Search".[2] According to the most recent Dutch Defence Doctrine publications, six main functions of military actions can be distinguished:

1. Command and control.
2. Military intelligence.
3. Manoeuvre.
4. Fire power.
5. Protection.
6. Sustainment.

The engineer tasks are not directly a function of military action, but are supportive to these functions themselves. Figure 18.2 shows the matrix representing the six main functions of military actions and the related Engineer tasks, as given in the aforementioned doctrine.

In order to cope with the increasing demands from society and government for more safety and security, in 2018[3] the Dutch Ministry of Defence (MoD) presented their long-term vision of the development of the Defence organization as a whole. As a reaction, the Royal Netherlands Army (Dutch: Koninklijke Landmacht) published its own long-term vision, in which it addresses its future role in the field of safety and security. The main focus of the vision is described as: "The human being fights the battle; the technology multiplies the combat power, and with (new) operational concepts combat is organized.

In order to be future proof, the Royal Netherlands Army needs to increase its adaptive capacity by intensifying the cooperation with national and international partners, strengthen the connection of people and technology and invest in both the long-distance battle and the military performance in urban areas".[4] This long-term vision will directly affect the tasks of the Engineer Regiment as presented in

---

[2] NATO 2008.
[3] Ministerie van Defensie 2018 [Ministry of Defence 2018].
[4] Koninklijke Landmacht 2018 [Royal Netherlands Army 2018].

| | \multicolumn{6}{c}{**GOAL OF MILITARY ACTION**} |

	Command & Control	Military Intelligence	Manoeuvre	Fire Power	Protection	Sustainment
ENGINEER TASKS	Technical Advisors	Intelligence physical operating environment	Gap Crossing	Support to S&R	Protective Works	Infra Construction
		Geomatics	Breaching Demolitions	Support to Information OPS	Camouflage Concealment Deception	Operation & Maintenance of Infrastructures
		CBRN Information Management	Area/Route Denial & Clearance		Explosive Threat Management	Real Property Management
		Explosive Ordnance Reconnaissance	Military Search		Conventional Munitions Disposal	Environmental Protection
			(Combat)Road Construction & Improvement		IED Disposal	Utilities (Water&Power)
			Explosive Ordnance Clearance		CBRN Explosives Disposal	Support to Logistics
					Support to CBRN, including Protection, Hazard Management & Monitoring	Underwater Engineering
						Medical Counter Measures
					Fire Fighting	

Fig. 18.2 Matrix representing the six main functions of military actions and the related engineer tasks. *Source* Dado et al. 2019

Fig. 18.2. Some tasks will become obsolete, while others will change or emerge. Also, the individuals behind those tasks need to find a way to adapt themselves to the changing operational environment. This manifest adaptation process places heavy demands on the competences of the Regiment and its employees – a new type of competence that is not the same as it used to be. These types of changes require a change in ways of 'deciding, doing, acting and responding', i.e. it requires a continuous process of change in skills and knowledge of employees working in today's Engineer Regiment. But it also requires the transformation of the Regiment into a learning organization.[5] This poses the real challenges for educational and research institutes, within or associated with the Dutch defence organization; those that are involved in the education of Army Engineers, meanwhile co-developing and expanding the body of knowledge for the Engineer Regiment with respect to the dynamic needs posed by the context at large.

---

[5] Dado et al. 2009.

18.3 Current State of Military Engineering Education at the FMS

In the period 2011–2012 a discussion was started between the representatives of the FMS and the Engineer Regiment about the existing educational collaboration with the University of Twente. The reason for this discussion was the decision to place a fully-fledged Bachelor's degree in Military Engineering as a track within the existing Military Systems and Technology (MS&T) program of the Netherlands Defence Academy. The reason for this decision was – in addition to the imposed cutbacks – the fact that there existed a fair amount of criticism on the existing Civil Engineering program as offered by the University of Twente in collaboration with the FMS.

It should be said that although the Engineer Regiment was satisfied with the Civil Engineering program as a whole, there a 'mismatch' was felt between the desired level of knowledge and skills of the young army engineer officer – making them valuable to their future units – and what they were actually taught during their three-year academic period at the University of Twente. The needs of the Regiment are mostly in the field of technical knowledge and skills related to the tasks that the engineers are expected to fulfil, see Fig. 18.2. Since 2014, the collaboration with the University of Twente is ended and a new Military Engineering curriculum is integrated as one of the three tracks within the technology oriented MS&T program of the NLDA.

Emphasis on design skills in the curriculum gives the Military Engineering track a special position within the MS&T bachelor program, especially because the learning outcomes of the MS&T program explicitly excluded design skills in the past. This fact was also recognized by the visitation committee in 2016, as stated in their final report: "It advises the program to revise its final objectives in such a way that they contain design skills and to describe to what extent the students of the different tracks become proficient in technical and design-oriented methodology".[6]

Comparable (design-oriented) academic educational programs in The Netherlands possess curricula that emphasize problem analysis and design of solutions, with a focus on design and research skills. In addition, (process) management and technical knowledge and skills are developed to support these design and research skills. The extent to which the curriculum pays attention to the different focus areas (i.e. technology, design and management) determines the type of education that is followed by students. This is more or less reflected in the current range of variants within the MS&T Bachelor's program (see Fig. 18.3).

The Higher Education and Scientific Research Act prescribes that if a new track is added to an existing and accredited Bachelor's program, the accreditation will only be transferred to the added track if 60% of the courses in the existing Bachelor's program are part of its curriculum. In addition, the basic principle is that the Military Engineering track as a Bachelor's degree program in its own right

---

[6] QANU 2017.

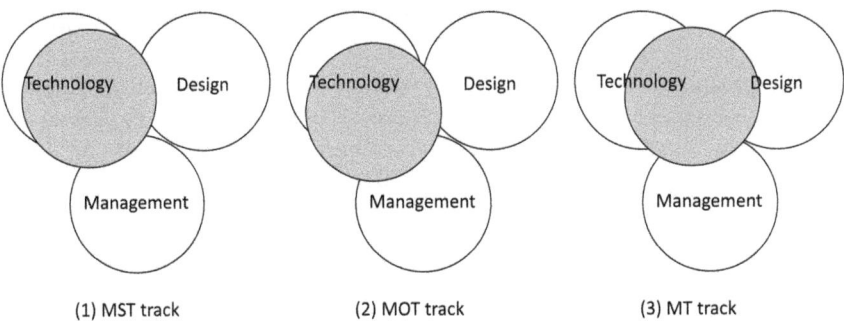

Fig. 18.3 Three tracks within the existing MS&T program: (1) Military Systems and Technology (MST), (2) Military Organization and Technology (MOT) and (3) Military Engineering (ME). *Source* Dado et al. 2019

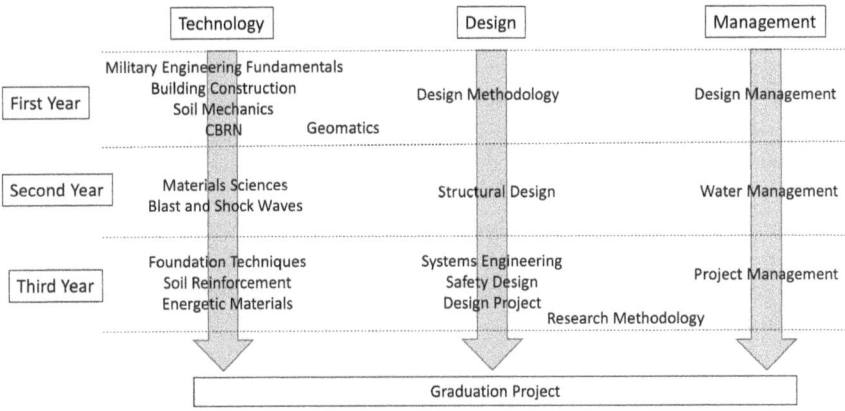

Fig. 18.4 Military engineering curriculum (excluding MS&T courses). *Source* Dado et al. 2019

should provide threshold-free access to at least one Master program. Based on these constraints and the typical profile of a design-oriented academic program, a new Military Engineering curriculum has been designed and developed in 2014 (see Fig. 18.4).

18.4 Current State of Military Engineering Research at the FMS

The main objective of the Military Engineering research at the FMS is to provide solutions for problems that occur in the Military Engineering practice. Therefore, current Military Engineering research at the FMS can be characterized as both 'practical' and 'demand-driven'. Research projects in the past, have taught that addressing demand is a bottom-up approach and responding to research priorities is helpful in achieving research outcomes. Traditionally, the Military Engineering research program at the FMS is in line with the research needs of the Engineer Regiment as defined (and prioritized) by the Engineer Centre of Expertise. The current research program of the FMS still resembles topics related to (and in support of) problems derived from the traditional tasks of the Engineer Regiment:

1. *Mobility*. This topic mainly focuses on different aspects of military (underground) construction including guidelines for ground investigation methods to optimize compound design, improvement of bridge foundation design for ad hoc bridge constructions, ground improvement methods for runway construction and maintenance, underground ammunition storage and possibilities of pile foundations in out-of-area construction.
2. *Counter-mobility*. This entails the design and "construction of obstacles and reinforcements in the field in order to delay, disrupt and destroy the enemy".[7]
3. *Force protection*. This subject focuses on the different aspects of increasing physical force protection of people, equipment, and structures against external threats like war related violence, terrorist attacks, and natural disasters. Current (and past) research includes mass-evacuations in dike ring areas, protection against floods, safety concrete to reduce the effects of spalling and computational modelling of damage development in heterogeneous materials under plane impact load.
4. *General engineering*. This subject focuses on the different aspects of integral design and systems engineering and includes research themes such as process, design and project management, design methodologies, risk management, procurement and construction IT.

Students contribute to configuring research by conducting graduation projects as part of their Bachelor program. But, also within projects as part of courses in the last year of the Bachelor degree program, a research attitude towards the project is being promoted. For more fundamental research, funding has been found for two Ph.D. projects:

1. *BresDefender*. This research focuses on the multifunctional employment of military equipment to mitigate dike-failure emergencies. In this context the usefulness and applicability of the BresDefender concept is scrutinized. BresDefender entails the – alternative – employment of existing pontoon bridge systems as a reinforcement structure for river dikes that are at the verge of breaching. Initially the concept of BresDefender has been subject of an exploratory study in the context of a Bachelor's thesis research project,[8] utilising test set-ups that are available at the Hydraulic Laboratory of the Netherlands Defence Academy at the premises of the Royal Dutch Military Academy in Breda. Real scale experiments on the employment of this concept

---

[7] JP 3-34, Department of the Army 2016.
[8] Elsing 2018.

are envisioned in the context of the Living Lab Hertogin Hedwigepolder. This latter polder has to be given back to the Western Scheldt as part of an agreement between Belgium and The Netherlands, as confirmed by the Supreme Court of the Netherlands.[9]

2. *Expeditionary Planning.* This research focuses on the geography and spatial planning of expeditionary organizations. When deployed, militaries can be considered as expeditionary organizations operating in dynamic complex environments. By studying cases related to recent Dutch experiences in Afghanistan, more insight will be obtained on how militaries organise themselves spatially in operations other than war. Deliverables of this project will help calibrate all planning and engineering activities in future areas of operation in such a way that these activities will not only be about construction but also about stimulating goal achievement within overarching military strategies.

18.5 Interactions Between Education and Research

The Military Engineering domain specific courses are all scheduled within the latter half of the academic education towards the Bachelor of Science in Military Engineering. The topics in this stage of the education are rather advanced, and lean heavily on the fundamentals of science and engineering that has been taught in earlier years, i.e. introductory courses in mathematics, mechanics, physics and engineering.

At this stage of the study program, courses still aim content-wise at a specific scientific or engineering field, e.g. soil mechanics or materials engineering. However, the problems to be solved with the knowledge acquired reach further than the topic of teaching alone. The context of the problems presented is complex, and requires besides topical knowledge also acquaintance with design and systems engineering aspects. Moreover, because several course related projects are group assignments, process and project management skills are developed on the fly. This clearly illustrates the balance between the aspects technology, design and management (see Fig. 18.4), which clearly distinguishes the Military Engineering program from other technology-oriented bachelor programs.

18.5.1 Research Topics in Military Engineering

Research topics in the context of Military Engineering can roughly be divided into three categories:

1. *Work floor – i.e. professional environment – related research.* These research topics originate from the desire for new guidelines, protocols or approaches of

---

[9] Hoge Raad 2018.

day-to-day best practices that require an update, for instance because of a changing environment. These topics will be further elaborated on in Sect. 18.7.
2. *Crisis related research.* These topics relate to large scale crises, at present or in the future. The aforementioned BSc- and Ph.D.-project on the BresDefender is an example of this. But also think about the crisis response to the collision of a – benzene-loaded – transport ship with the weir in Grave, The Netherlands. Or, the knowledge based decision on the location where a large refugee camp can be erected, given the requirements of well-drained – or drainable – soils which allow for optimized sanitary conditions.
3. *(past) Incident related research.* In current society, incidents often dominate public research agendas. Ministers are often called to parliament after the occurrence of incidents or e.g. the disclosure of the previously often unknown adverse effects of certain technologies. Examples of the latter are manifold: the use of hexavalent chromium as corrosion inhibitors,[10] the burn pits in Afghanistan,[11] or the mortar accident in Mali,[12] with two Dutch military casualties.

18.5.2 Research Topics in Education: Two Cases

As an example two case studies from the science and engineering track are provided. The first case is in the context of the course 'Geotechnical Engineering'. In their classes, students are taught a full, technical program on geotechnology and soil mechanics. The formal knowledge is examined in a traditional written exam. Next to this, the students as a team, apply the acquired knowledge to a real-life situation. In the summer of 2017, Geotechnical Engineering (Grondkerende Constructies en Funderingstechniek)[13] course students were given the case to redesign the quay wall at the Royal Naval College in Den Helder, The Netherlands. The project taught the students to learn from engineering projects close to their work/living environments. By examining the offer description of the project towards the market, the students became aware of the necessity of the Ministry of Defence for professional commissioning of projects. This requires at least acquaintance with the subject matter, as provided in the course at hand. The result of the project was a brief report,[14] exposing the problem, and providing some explorative calculations of technical requirements of the quay wall, see Fig. 18.5.

---

[10] RIVM: Rijksinstituut voor Volksgezondheid en Milieu 2018 [National Institute for Public Health and the Environment 2018].
[11] Heilbron 2019.
[12] Onderzoeksraad voor de Veiligheid 2017 [Dutch Safety Board 2017].
[13] Studiegids MS&T 2016 [Study guide MS&T 2016].
[14] Blankestijn et al. 2017.

The second example deals with the aforementioned collision of a ship with the weir in Grave in the context of the autumn 2018 course of Experimental Fluid Mechanics (Onderzoeksontwerp: stromingsleer[15]). Here the students as a team developed a two-way approach. On the one hand they interviewed a couple of stakeholders to learn about the possibilities of a crisis response of the Regiment (which didn't happen), while possible tangible interventions by the Regiment to rapidly stabilise the weir were tested in the NLDA's hydraulic lab, see Fig. 18.5.

18.5.3 Relation of Thesis Research Topics to Military Engineering Curriculum

The main qualification of research topics as presented in Sect. 18.5.1 can be complemented with their scientific and engineering context. Often this context can be related to one of the courses in the specific Military Engineering track of the Bachelor. One may distinguish:

1. *Safety and security*: relating to courses on construction aspects, or safety incident aspects (explosives engineering and CBRN (chemical, biological, radiological and nuclear defence)). But process aspects (decomposition of the problem context) and design aspects (security and safety by design) are inherent and inseparable. An example is a theoretical and simulation study of the test procedure of insensitive munitions, see Fig. 18.5.
2. *Spatial engineering and infrastructures*: the design and construction of infrastructure, including environmental aspects and stakeholder management. For example, in the context of a graduation project the self-building of public spaces in refugee camps was researched, a typical design project with a strong spatial context.[16]
3. *Management and operation of physical assets*: the design of compounds, air strips, but also disaster management, like on the island of St. Maarten in September 2017.

Overall, one may characterise the context of the Military Engineer as the complex, dynamic, and tangible aspects of the physical environment. Currently, ongoing technological development is blending the tangible world and the 'invisible world', e.g. through the Internet-of-Things. This will require a continuous adjustment of the current curriculum in the foreseeable future.

---

[15] Studiegids MS&T 2016 [Study guide MS&T 2016].
[16] Coenen 2016.

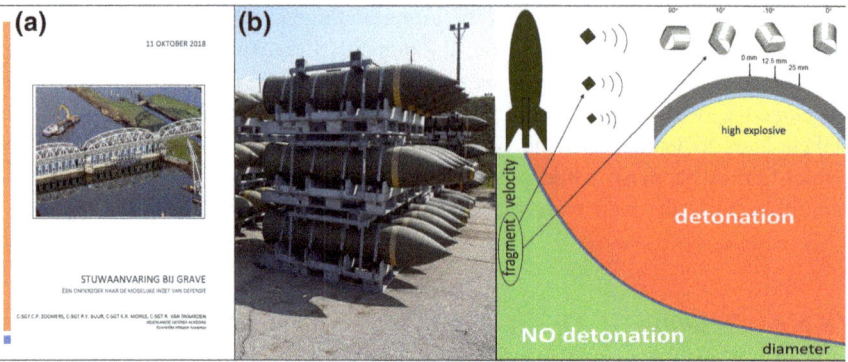

Fig. 18.5 Examples of interaction of research and education: **a** researching the weir accident in Grave. *Source* Netherlands Defence Academy 2018, and **b** infographic of testing the safety of munitions Leibbrandt 2018. *Source* L Koene and AJM Schmets

18.6 Interactions Between Professional Environment and Education

The added value of scientific military education will always be about training officers to become 'thinking soldiers'. Specifically in the field of Military Engineering one needs officers that are familiar with the basic principles of construction, but who are also able to improvise in challenging environments that not always give access to the same technological support as one is used to at home.

It is this need of improvisational ability that makes the Military Engineering track within MS&T unique. The combination of technical and management skills with design thinking competencies is what is asked by the field (Engineer Regiment). Because of the ever-changing reality of areas of operations, education constantly needs to adapt to the specific needs of the field. Therefore, a warm bond between the Military Engineering group of FMS and the Engineer Regiment is indispensable. The Engineer Centre of Expertise serves as an intermediary between both worlds. But how does this interaction take shape?

Every four years the Military Engineering group of the FMS convokes representatives of all units within the Engineer Regiment. During multiple sessions, the demand of these units considering the competencies of their junior officers is collected, recorded and analysed. During brainstorm sessions ideas about future operating environments are combined with the desired operating skills as mentioned above. The result of these sessions are possible new courses within the curriculum or the adaptation of old courses towards new requirements. The last consultation of units dates back to the winter of 2017.

In 2017, all Engineer units gathered at the Engineer Training Center in Vught. After several meetings and even more rounds of discussion, the following changes in the curriculum were proposed:

- The addition of new courses (CBRN, Geographic Information Systems, Safety Sciences).
- The change of already existing courses (i.e. adding qualitative research methods to design projects).
- The removal of irrelevant courses.

This possibility of direct adaptation towards requirements from the field is what characterizes the Military Engineering group in the Faculty of Military Sciences. The curriculum tries to 'breathe' along with the demands of the 'customer' – or so to say, with the challenges that arise during deployment, without losing sight of the rules of accreditation from the Accreditation Organization of The Netherlands and Flanders (Dutch acronym: NVAO) on the hand, and the requirement to contribute to the body of knowledge by conducting scientific research on the other hand.

18.7 Interactions Between Professional Environment and Research

Besides the continuous communication cycle between teaching staff and professionals in the field of education, a same type of checks and balances is applied to research. A central role within research interaction is played by the Engineer Center of Expertise. The center operates as a central hub for knowledge exchange and strives to connect questions to answers; it directs flows of information both inside and outside the Defence organization. Inside the organization one can think of Centers of Expertise of other branches, or of higher level research groups (Army Headquarters, or the Ministry of Defence), or the teaching staff of Military Engineering at the Defence Academy; outside the organization, for example TNO, think tanks, or other universities (for the Military Engineers mostly the technical universities of Delft, Eindhoven, and Twente).

Sometimes, the Military Engineering group of FMS takes the initiative to develop an agenda for future research. In December 2018, the group responded to the release of a new vision for the future of the Royal Netherlands Army, called: "Security through foresight". This vision distinguishes four core strengths for the Netherlands Army and four major trends for the future. The four strengths are:

1. *Size*: The Netherlands is sufficiently small to be agile, yet large enough to create sufficient mass and make a difference.
2. *Technologically advanced*: the Dutch economy and knowledge landscape is geared toward generating high-quality solutions.
3. *Multi- and transdisciplinary*: the Dutch connect relatively easily across different disciplines and institutional stovepipes to create crossover and/or integrated innovations.

4. *Connected*: The Netherlands is one of the most globally connected countries and is widely considered a worthwhile cooperation partner.

The four future trends are:

1. Future conflicts will be complex and unpredictable.
2. Hybrid confrontations: simultaneous efforts on several fronts.
3. Technological superiority is crucial.
4. Sensors and systems: quicker, more precise, deadlier and longer range.

The consequences of these trends force the Royal Netherlands Army to increase its adaptability, intensify cooperation with national and international partners, strengthen the connection between people and technology and invest in both combat over long distances and operations in urban areas.

In order to exploit the core competences of the Army and to cope with recognized trends the following four lines of development were identified:

1. Increase adaptability.
2. Intensify cooperation with national and international partners.
3. Strengthen the connection between humans and technology.
4. Improve combat capability over long distances and in urban areas.

The Military Engineering group used these four lines of development during a brainstorm session at the Engineer Headquarters. An essential part of this session was inviting the right players to the table. Until recently it was a military custom to only invite people from the army's inner-circle, this way no new insights were gathered. With major changes in globalization, informatisation, and the desired work culture in the "Adaptive Armed Forces" it is now more common to invite people from all sorts of backgrounds. In December 2018 the group invited people from several universities, companies, think thanks, and water boards. These people abstracted engineer tasks from the four lines of development using the 'core functions of military operations' (command and control, intelligence, manoeuvre, fire support, protection, and sustainment). An introduction lesson introduced the 'outsiders' in the military way of thinking and invited them to think on new engineer directions of development, with the help of the aforementioned framework.

The results of this session were used both by the Engineer Center of Expertise for more practical research, and by the ME group for fundamental research directions. This exercise yielded many results, the most interesting ones being: exploring the possibilities of mixed civil-military engineer units; starting a field lab for research on demolitions and breaching; research on camouflage and spoofing of digital presence in geo information systems; drone reconnaissance real-time introduced to GIS; measuring the importance of urban planning in post-conflict reconstruction efforts; all towards a more innovation minded engineer organization, catalysed by research of the FMS.

18.8 Conclusions

In this chapter we discussed the interactions between military practice, education and research (i.e. The Golden Triangle) within the academic educational and research Military Engineering program provided by the Faculty of Military Sciences in the Netherlands. As a consequence of the requirements for academic degree courses set by the QANU organization and the evaluation criteria set by the Accreditation Organization of The Netherlands and Flanders (NVAO), the interaction between education and research is traditionally adequately supported by most universities in The Netherlands.

The interactions between the Professional Environment and Education have to deal with the adjustment to the ever-changing military operational and organizational context in which Military Engineers operate. Every four years the ME group of the FMS convokes representatives of all units within the Engineer Regiment. During multiple sessions, the demand of these units considering the competencies of their junior officers is collected, recorded and analysed. Based on these findings the existing curriculum will be adjusted. In 2017, several meetings with the Professional Environment were held, leading to the addition of courses on CBRN, Geomatics and Safety Sciences. It is to be expected that in the future courses related to robotics, cyber, Artificial Intelligence, military aspects of climate change, Underground Warfare, sustainability etc. will be embedded in the curriculum.

For the interactions between the Professional Environment and Research a very similar approach is followed. In December 2018, for example, the Military Engineering group of the FMS responded to the release of a new vision for the future of the Royal Netherlands Army, called: "Security through foresight". The group invited people from several universities, companies, think thanks, and water boards. These people abstracted engineer tasks from the four lines of development using the 'core functions of military operations' (i.e. command and control, intelligence, manoeuvre, fire support, protection, and sustainment) as shown in Fig. 18.2. The results of this session were used both by the Engineer Center of Expertise for more practical research, and by the ME group for fundamental research directions.

Through continuing debate and interactions with peers from the Professional, Education and Research Environments, the curriculum itself will have become an effective instrument fulfilling the needs of the Dutch Defence Organisation for more adaptivity.

References

Adviesraad voor wetenschap technologie en innovatie (2015) Verwevenheid tussen onderzoek en hoger onderwijs – Eenheid in verscheidenheid [The Dutch Advisory Council for Science, Technology and Innovation (2015) Interelation between research and higher education – Unity in diversity]. www.awti.nl.

Blankestijn S, Elsing K, Leibbrandt CG, Van der Wilt CB (2017) Project Kademuur KIM en MARMUS [Project Quay Wall KIM and MARMUS]. Netherlands Defence Academy, Den Helder.

Coenen LEM (2016) A public space for refugees: een analyse naar de zelfbouw van publieke gebouwen in een vluchtelingenkamp [A public space for refugees: an analysis of DIY concepts of public buildings in a refugee camp]. Netherlands Defence Academy, Den Helder.

Dado E, Van der Stoel A, Mevissen S, Borgers J (2009) Supporting Interactions between Education, Research and Practice. In: The Comprehensive Approach: Challenges and Prospects. Royal Danish Defence College Publishing House, Copenhagen.

Department of the Army (2016) Joint Engineer Operations, Joint Publication 3-34.

Elsing KM (2018) BresDefender: een geïmproviseerde beschermingsmaatregel bij mogelijke dijkdoorbraken [BresDefender: an improvised protection measure against possible dyke breaches]. Netherlands Defence Academy, Den Helder.

Faculty of Military Sciences (2016) Studiegids opleiding Militaire Systemen en Technologie (MS&T) [Study guide bachelor degree program Military Systems and Technology (MS&T)]. Netherlands Defence Academy, Den Helder.

Heilbron B (2019) Tientallen militairen ziek door afvalverbranding op missie [Dozens of soldiers ill due to waste incineration on mission]. NRC Handelsblad.

Hoge Raad (2018) [Netherlands Supreme Court (2018)] ECLI:NL:HR:2018:7.

Koninklijke Landmacht (2018) Veiligheid is Vooruitzien. De toekomstvisie van de Koninklijke Landmacht [Royal Netherlands Army (2018) Safety is Foresight. The future vision of the Royal Netherlands Army]. https://www.defensie.nl/downloads/publicaties/2018/11/05/toekomstvisie-koninklijke-landmacht.

Leibbrandt CG (2018) Probabilistic aspects of munition initiation due to fragment impact: a simulation study about implementing tilted and off-centre impact variation in a munitions initiation response model. Netherlands Defence Academy, Den Helder.

Ministerie van Defensie (2018) Defensienota 2018, Investeren in onze mensen, Slagkracht en zichtbaarheid [Ministry of Defence (2018) Defence White Paper 2018, Investing in our people, capabilities and visibility]. www.defensie.nl/downloads/beleidsnota-s/2018/03/26/defensienota-2018.

NATO (2008) MC 0560 Military Committee Policy For Military Engineering.

Onderzoeksraad voor de Veiligheid (2017) Mortierongeval Mali [Dutch Safety Board (2017) Mortar accident Mali].

QANU (2017) Rapport over de Bacheloropleiding Militaire Systemen en Technologie van de Faculteit Militaire Wetenschappen van de Nederlandse Defensie Academie [QANU (2017) Report on the bachelor degree program Military Systems and Technology of the Faculty of Military Sciences, Netherlands Defence Academy].

RIVM (2018) Chroom-6 op de POMS-locaties van Defensie: gezondheidseffecten en verantwoordelijkheden. Bevindingen uit het onderzoek op hoofdlijnen. RIVM Rapport 2018-0061 [Chromium-6 at the Defence POMS locations: health effects and responsibilities. Main findings from research. Report 2018-0061].

Royal Netherlands Army (2018) Security through foresight – The Royal Netherlands Army.

Dr. Edwin Dado is associated professor Military Engineering at the Netherlands Defence Academy, Den Helder, The Netherlands. Edwin holds both a university degree in Civil Engineering (master) and Construction IT (Ph.D.). Among many other activities, Edwin is a member of the Educational Board of the MS&T bachelor and acts as the National Captech Coordinator for the Captech Materials and Structures of the European Defence Agency.

Alexander Schmets, MSc is assistant professor of Military Engineering at the Netherlands Defence Academy in Den Helder, The Netherlands and executive director of the 4TU Centre of Excellence for the Built Environment. He is a nuclear physicist who worked in many areas of theoretical and applied physics. Among many other activities, he co-initiated the emerging field of self-healing materials, and designed the Dutch National Science Agenda (NWA) for the Built Environment and its spin-off, the NWA-route Smart and Liveable Cities.

Rick Krosenbrink, MSc is a major in the Army Engineers and assistant professor of Military Engineering at the Netherlands Defence Academy, Den Helder, The Netherlands. He fulfilled various positions within the Engineer Regiment including several deployments abroad, such as security operations in Afghanistan (2008), development aid in Gabon (2010), and disaster relief in the Caribbean after Hurricane Irma (2017).

Dennis Krabbenborg is lecturer in Military Engineering at the Netherlands Defence Academy, Den Helder, The Netherlands. He started his career with a major construction company, where he was involved in the implementation of large civil engineering projects in The Netherlands. Currently he teaches several military engineering related subjects, and facilitates practical lessons and training and also conducts research in cooperation with other institutions like Delft University and Eindhoven University.

Part IV
International Perspectives

Chapter 19
A European Army of Thinking Soldiers – European Academic Officers' Education: Challenges and Opportunities

Sabine Mengelberg and Riccardo Scalas

Contents

19.1	Introduction	306
19.2	Officers' Training and Education in Europe	308
19.3	Training and Education Within the EU's Security and Defence Domain	309
	19.3.1 Introduction	309
	19.3.2 'Emilyo'; Military Officers' Exchange Program	309
	19.3.3 The European Security and Defence College	310
	19.3.4 The EU Doctoral School	311
	19.3.5 CEPOL; Training and Education in the Law Enforcement Domain	312
	19.3.6 Frontex; Training and Education Regarding EU's Borders	313
19.4	Training and Education Within NATO	314
	19.4.1 Introduction	314
	19.4.2 The NATO Defence College	314
19.5	Officers' Training and Education in Europe; Challenges and Opportunities	315
19.6	Conclusion	318
References		319
Internet Sources		319

Abstract A European army, as recently claimed by French President Macron and German Chancellor Merkel, is not to be expected in the near future due to a varied landscape of national interests of the states involved. The same can be concluded

---

S. N. Mengelberg (✉)
Faculty of Military Sciences, Netherlands Defence Academy, PO Box 90002, 4800 PA Breda, The Netherlands
e-mail: SN.Mengelberg.01@mindef.nl

R. M. Scalas
Netherlands Defence Academy, PO Box 90002, 4800 PA Breda, The Netherlands
e-mail: RM.Scalas.01@mindef.nl

© T.M.C. ASSER PRESS and the authors 2019
W. Klinkert et al. (eds.), *NL ARMS Netherlands Annual Review of Military Studies 2019*, NL ARMS, https://doi.org/10.1007/978-94-6265-315-3_19

with regard to the integration of European training and education or even a European Bachelor's or Master's degree in the European security and defence domain. However, from the end of the Cold War, training and education in the wider Europe broadened in themes and was strengthened by additional institutional structures due to multilateral, organizational and inter-organizational initiatives. Especially with the entrance of the EU into the security and defence domain of the European security architecture. Nevertheless, these initiatives and further strengthening of these initiatives face challenges due to diversified national interests, but likewise offer opportunities. This chapter discusses these developments of training, education and research in the European security and defence domain and addresses the challenges and opportunities.

Keywords European politics · European security and defence cooperation · European security and defence policy · international security studies · training and education in Europe · EU officers' education and training · NATO officers' education and training · multilateral education and training

19.1 Introduction

Cooperation in the European security and defence domain has always aimed for peace and stability. Although European security cooperation strengthened after the end of the Cold War, this past decade security and military challenges accompanied with crises in- and outside Europe have led to a period of insecurity and instability; the solidarity between the member states has been tested numerously. Due to threats compiled of terrorism, cyber threats, migration, an emerging Russian threat claiming its position in the wider Europe, the tension between the United States (US) and the European continent on the direction of NATO and finally Brexit have challenged the European security architecture that was built since the end of the Second World War. For some academics even, this period is entitled as the post-Western global order[1] and agree that the liberal world order as we have known it is under pressure.[2]

In contrast, French President Macron and German Chancellor Merkel have called upon member states of the European Union (EU) several times to strive for the realisation of a European army to enhance solidarity and strengthen the European idea. Macron spoke about the need to create a 'real European army' to handle the Russian threat and to emancipate Europe from its dependence on the US'.[3] One of the reasons behind the creation of a European army, has been the scattering of European capabilities amongst the member states. Up till now most of

---

[1] Kissinger 2014; Mazar 2018.
[2] Heisbourg 2018, p. 214.
[3] Macron 2018.

the 28 different armies in Europe have built their capacities like a Swiss pocket knife: though most of the functions are in place, not one of them can actually 'do the job' solitary and without the help of the US. Within Europe there are more than 29 different battleships, 16 different types of airplanes and 19 different kind of tanks.[4] This is in stark contrast to a so often claimed need for cooperation by US and European leaders to increase European strength and save public spending. For some, a build-up of a European army '…is not an army against NATO, it can be a good complement to NATO…', as stated by Merkel.[5] However, an integrated European army in the classical sense though is not likely to emerge in the near future, if ever.

The issue of scattered and therefore weakened European armed forces, to a certain extent, can be likewise applied to world of education and training in the security and defence domain in the wider Europe.[6] Similar observations can be identified with regard to the multiple possibilities of research and education in the field of security and defence. Though, within the security and defence policy area, EU and NATO have developed broad educational programs on different levels for officers and civil servants functioning in the security and defence domain. Nevertheless, comparable to a desire for strengthening cooperation of European forces, in this day and age of joint exercises, missions and operations, primary, secondary and tertiary education in Europe in general is organised along national lines and, sometimes joint and even combined, usually divided per armed forces.

This chapter provides an insight in the current officers' education within the wider European area and questions the state of art of the current education programs provided.[7] In doing so it reflects on the strengths and weaknesses of these programs and briefly discusses possible future European cooperation in the security and defence domain. First, it briefly elaborates upon the European officers' education in the broader sense. Secondly, it reviews the specific NATO, EU and bi- and multilateral programs that have been initiated. Finally, this chapter reflects on these programs and debates the possibilities of European officers' education as a possible catalyst for the development of strengthened European security capabilities and culture.[8]

---

[4] http://www.eda.europa.eu.

[5] Merkel 2018.

[6] The wider European area concerns cooperation within the EU and NATO area combined with cooperation with states within the OSCE area and sometimes even global cooperation due to the partnership and cooperation programs of both the EU and NATO.

[7] Though the Organization for Security and Cooperation in Europe (OSCE) is an organization that fits within the wider European security area, OSCE training and education is not addressed in this chapter.

[8] The authors wrote this chapter mainly based on primary sources, consisting of treaties, agreements and open sources of the initiatives of the selected security organizations that provide education and training and the authors personal experience acting in the European training and education environment, due to a lack of academic research on the subject of multinational, organizational and inter-organizational cooperation in the wider European training and education area.

19.2 Officers' Training and Education in Europe

Within Europe there are almost 22 European military training and education institutions for the middle and higher staff and command courses and much more institutions for the primary officers' education. In general, these institutions train their national officers based on objectives that are broadly similar.[9]

Nevertheless, international cooperation in the field of military training and education has not been from the recent past. The last decades several cooperation initiatives were initiated by states in an attempt to rationalise and optimize education programs by sharing their knowledge and skills and, in some cases, even integrate their knowledge and skills. International cooperation is usually instigated by top-down political and diplomatic considerations, based on a bilateral agreement and mutual equality. In general, two characteristics can be identified in these bi- and multilateral education programs.

The first characteristic concerns education and training under the umbrella of NATO or EU, like the NATO Defence College (NDC) and the European Security and Defence College (ESDC). In extension to that, some of these multilateral education and training programs are delegated to certain member states, like the Baltic Defence College (BaltDefCol).[10] The difference with the EU or NATO training and education, is that education by these multilateral coalitions, like the BaltDefCol, actually replace national education and simultaneous their curricular remains fit in the education journey of the participating states.

The second characteristic concerns bi- and multilateral attempts to achieve actual common training and education programs which comprise interchangeable curricula. In some cases, this is even performed within the accreditation trajectory of the existing 'Bologna agreements' for the higher education in Europe.[11] This can be illustrated by the Benelux cooperation and the Belgium and Netherlands higher staff and command courses that cooperate since 2014, based on a mutual curriculum, and the training and education programs of the Nordic Defence Collaboration (NORDEFCO) between the Nordic countries.[12]

Hence, cooperation in the field of military training and education between different policies of in- and external security is developed within and between the organizations like the EU and NATO and on a bi- and multilateral scale initiated by the member states. In other words, diversified training and education on a bi-, multilateral and joined international level. Some of these varied initiatives for international officers' education and training in the security and defence domain in Europe will be addressed below.

---

[9] For a systematic, comparative analysis of national military education and training in Europe, see Libel 2016.

[10] http://www.baltdefcol.org/.

[11] http://www.ec.europa.eu/education/policies/higher-education/bologna-process-and-european-higher-education-area_en.

[12] http://www.nordefco.org.

19.3 Training and Education Within the EU's Security and Defence Domain

19.3.1 Introduction

After more than 25 years of cooperation in EU's security and defence domain a European army has not been realised yet. Neither has an overarching European structure of education and training. The European landscape of education and training presents a diverse scheme of national communities.[13] The reason could be the delicate domain of education and training in the sovereign national security and defence domain or because of the power struggles between national military institutions in their fight for survival.

However, education and training programs within the EU have developed since the end of the Cold War on different levels and, encapsulating a broad perspective, including military, police, civil servants, journalists, participants from corporate live and non-EU members and organizations. Amongst the many initiatives, education and training within EU's security and defence domain encapsulates a broad perspective on security and includes in- and external domains of EU's security and defence policy, which will be addressed below.

19.3.2 'Emilyo'; Military Officers' Exchange Program

The civilian students exchange program for the EU is called Erasmus; a highly visible and arguably successful European exchange program that plays a role in bringing young European students together and all over the EU. Inspired by Erasmus an exchange program for military officers (initial phase) was launched under the name 'Emilyo' and found its way under the aegis of the ESDC.[14] Emilio cannot yet replicate Erasmus in full, because Erasmus is supported by the common funds of the EU. However, Emilio does give young military officers an opportunity to exchange and broaden their horizons besides creating an extra venue to develop and expose themselves in an international environment. Emilio remains a work in progress and the program is gaining steady traction and could be supported by the European Defence Fund (EDF) initiative of the EU Commission in the future.[15]

---

[13] http://www.baltdefcol.org/.

[14] http://www.emilyo.eu/.

[15] The EDF was proposed in 2016 and established in 2017 for research, development and acquisition.

19.3.3 The European Security and Defence College

In 2005 the ESDC was established by a so-called Joint Action[16] and was later acknowledged by the EU member states as a premium vehicle for contributing to the development of a European security and defence culture and strategic thinking on a European level.[17] The ESDC has been a growing network of national training institutions, think tanks and other actors identified by member states that has become the main provider of training on the Common Security and Defence Policy (CSDP) in the larger framework of the Common Foreign and Security Policy (CFSP) of the EU.

The ESDC is a training provider on the security and defence topic that acts at the European level and that addresses civilians, diplomats, police officers, military personnel and other civil servants. It relies on the expertise of both the member states, the EU institutions and relevant agencies. The ESDC is academically supported by the EU Institute for Security Studies (EUISS)[18] and the network includes institutions from third countries[19] as well, as they participate under an associate agreement.

The specific set-up of the College was to provide a platform for member states of the EU for training in those areas not covered for on a national basis. This principle continues to be leading, hence there is no perceived competition on the subjects which makes it complementary to training programs by member states.

To avoid duplication with NATO, the College was intentionally set-up as a virtual college, in which EU member states provide the training programs. The ESDC, as stated in the Joint Action, is facilitating this with a small permanent staff of training managers, supplemented by seconded national experts in order to provide expertise coming from the member states. The ESDC is not the only security training provider of the EU, which will be elaborated on below, but as time progressed more and more programs and initiatives have found their way to the College. Examples are training on pre-deployment for EU missions and preparatory courses for Legad and Polad functions.[20] Furthermore, member states regularly offer and execute pilot programs on topics that are deemed necessary to train on a multilateral level (cyber security, piracy, climate change).

---

[16] The legal basis of the ESDC is the Council Decision (CFSP) 2016/2382, amended by a Council Decision (CFSP) 2018/712.

[17] https://eeas.europa.eu/headquarters/headquarters-homepage_en/4369/European%20Security%20and%20Defence%20College%20(ESDC).

[18] http://www.iss.europa.eu/.

[19] Third countries are countries that are not a member of the EU or NATO.

[20] https://eeas.europa.eu/headquarters/headquarters-homepage_en/4369/European%20Security%20and%20Defence%20College%20(ESDC).

More recently the College has become part of EU's External Action Service (EEAS),[21] but retains its necessary academic independence as much as possible in the EU configuration. EU's High Representative is formally the ultimate authority of the College to whom it directly answers, but the member states are involved on both political level directly through the Steering Committee and the various configurations of the Academic Board.

On the practical side, the College facilitates advanced distance learning through the development of Electronic Autonomous Knowledge Units (AKU), modular bases on self-education and testing on specific knowledge accessible from anywhere and comparable to the European Erasmus program.[22] The development of these AKU's are done by national institutions that are members of the ESDC network such as the Belgian Royal Egmont Institute for international relations, the Geneva Centre for Security Policy,[23] EU agencies like the European Defence Agency (EDA)[24] and EU's Law Enforcement Training (CEPOL), which will be elaborated on below, and the multinational European gendarmerie force (EUROGENDFOR).[25] The permanent Secretariat of the college provides continuity by monitoring curricula, facilitating the Academic Board and is manifest in its care for former students and participants through multilevel evaluation and an active Alumni program. The Flagship Course of the ESDC, the 'High Level Course' (usually named after an EU founding person), even has a supported Alumni organization carried by Brussels based Alumni that provides a knowledge and experience base for those coming to Brussels, or going on missions in an EU capacity.

19.3.4 The EU Doctoral School

Another EU initiative, which was created in 2017, has been the European doctoral school on CSDP by the EU and its member states which aims at taking EU education in the field of defence to a higher academic level.[26] The aim is twofold. For one the desire has been to move beyond the level of practical expertise into the level of scientific research after more than two decades of operational experience in the security and defence domain. Second, to provide for academic research in the field of security and defence next to the existing training and education. This initiative has been accompanied by the creation of a joint doctorate training, as a common

---

[21] The EEAS is the diplomatic service and foreign and defence ministry of the EU, established by the Lisbon Treaty of 2009.
[22] https://eeas.europa.eu/topics/eu-global-strategy/52208/sectoral-qualifications-framework-military-officer-profession_en.
[23] http://www.gcsp.ch.
[24] http://www.eda.europa.eu.
[25] Created in 2007 by the Treaty of Velsen, The Netherlands. Participation by seven states: France, Italy, Poland, Portugal, Romania, Spain and The Netherlands.
[26] https://eeas.europa.eu/topics/common-security-and-defence-policy-csdp/4369.

academic training deficit was identified within the area of security and defence matters. Comparable to the other EU initiatives, the doctoral school is provided for by EU's CSDP, the ESDC and the EU's agencies and bodies together with the academic civilian and military institutions of the member states. Hence, the objective is to facilitate a Ph.D. studies on CSDP.[27]

Comparable to the EU CSDP initiatives, the doctoral school does not bear any additional costs as it is based on the principle of 'cost lie where they fall' and in alignment with the resources of the member states. Though, the recent involvement in 2016 of the European Commission in the area of Defence and Security has opened up possibility of supporting through common means, the EDF as was elaborated on above.[28] With the fund, the Commission explicitly budgets €5.5 billion per year to boost Europe's defence in research and development.

19.3.5 CEPOL; Training and Education in the Law Enforcement Domain

The EU, in contrast to NATO, has a task within the EU territory supported by the European Agenda on Security,[29] replacing the former EU internal security strategy, and EU's Global Strategy of 2016.[30] Hence, next to training and education in the defence domain, the EU initiated several other training and education programs capturing the priority areas of this EU internal security task.

One of these initiatives has been EU's Law Enforcement Training (CEPOL), a full EU agency.[31] The focus of CEPOL lies at training of law enforcement officials of the EU Member States[2] and to some extent, from third countries, in particularly in the field of organised crime.[32] Comparable to the ESDC, CEPOL functions on a network of national training institutions for law enforcement officials in EU Member States. Vice versa, CEPOL supports these member states by providing training on security priorities, law enforcement cooperation and information

---

[27] https://eeas.europa.eu/sites/eeas/files/2018-100_docsch_charter_-_final.pdf.

[28] https://cdn3-eeas.fpfis.tech.ec.europa.eu/cdn/farfuture/_5GCkdWcdcnDDwZU5lCgMdw_ ZLMZt6GeYAzLcK3uNXU/mtime:1520243963/sites/eeas/files/defence_fund_factsheet_0_0.pdf.

[29] http://www.ec.europa.eu/home-affairs/sites/homeaffairs/files/e-library/documents/basic-documents/docs/eu_agenda_on_security_en.pdf.

[30] http://www.europa.eu/globalstrategy/en/global-strategy-foreign-and-security-policy-european-union.

[31] http://www.cepol.europa.eu. Since 1 July 2016, when the new legal mandate was created, CEPOL's official name is 'The European Union Agency for Law Enforcement Training'.

[32] Training and education topics: organised crime and counter-terrorism, public order and policing of major events, planning and command of union missions, leadership, language development, train the trainers, law enforcement cooperation and information exchange, specific areas and instruments, fundamental rights and research and prevention at https://www.cepol.europa.eu.

exchange.[33] Next to the support that is given to the member states, development and provision of training for law enforcement officials from third allied countries is provided as well. Here the focus lies on countries that are EU candidates and the countries under the European Neighbourhood Policy (ENP).[34] Furthermore, other countries, apart from the abovementioned, such as Libanon and Tunisia,[35] can be supported in education and training to build their capacity in law enforcement policy areas.

Finally, it has to be mentioned that CEPOL, comparable to the EU doctoral school, disposes over EDF Commission funds.

19.3.6 Frontex; Training and Education Regarding EU's Borders

With regard to EU's internal security responsibility,[36] as a result of EU's internal security strategy and EU's Solidarity Clause, an EU Agency for the Management of Operational Cooperation at the External Borders of the Member States was created. In other words an agency for border and coast guard tasks, known as Frontex.[37] From this agency a European Joint Master's in Strategic Border Management[38] was initiated in 2015 which aims at strengthening knowledge and education on strategic border management.[39] The target audience is gendarmerie, police and comparable European border guard organizations such as the Guardia Civil, Carabinieri and other EU and UN organizations.

Frontex organises courses that are based on a train-the-trainer concept; trainers are trained who can train other border guards in their own country.[40] Comparable to the other EU programs, Frontex builds on EU agencies and capabilities together with expertise and capabilities of the member states and other international organizations. And likewise comparable to other EU training and education initiatives, Frontex education programs are based on a network of 24 member states. Not only

---

[33] https://www.cepol.europa.eu/sites/default/files/CCWP-%20Customs%20Law%20Enforcement%20Training%20Catalogue%202018.pdf.

[34] http://eeas.europa.eu/diplomatic-network/european-neighbourhood-policy-enp_en.

[35] http://www.cepol.europa.eu/who-we-are/partners-and-stakeholders/external-partners.

[36] EU Internal Security strategy from 2008 and the adopted Solidarity Clause, Article 222, of the Lisbon Treaty in 2009.

[37] http://www.frontex.europa.eu.

[38] http://www.ecahe.eu/w/index.php/European_Joint_Master%27s_in_Strategic_Border_Management_(EJMSBM).

[39] The countries are the Baltic States, Spain and The Netherlands.

[40] Education and training for border guards is aligned to the EU Bologna and Copenhagen principles and the European Qualifications Framework for Lifelong Learning (EQF).

does Frontex develop and employ training and education with the EU member states, but likewise with non-EU member states, like the Balkan countries, and international organizations such as the UN and the OSCE.

19.4 Training and Education Within NATO

19.4.1 Introduction

In general NATO training and education is divided between the NATO School,[41] dedicated to training and education on the operational level, and the NATO Defence College (NDC), which will be addressed below.

19.4.2 The NATO Defence College

The NDC provides courses on a senior-level and brings together senior-level military and civilian officials. Its aim is to contribute to the effectiveness and cohesion of NATO by developing training, education and research on transatlantic security issues.[42]

The flagship course of the NDC is the generals' flag officers' and ambassadors' course (GFOAC). GFOAC is a high-level course compiled of officers and civilians from NATO member states and institutions, Partnership for Peace (PfP) countries, countries that are participating in the Mediterranean Dialogue (MD) and the Istanbul Cooperative initiative (ICI), the so-called 'contact countries'[43] and Iraq.

Furthermore, in the line of NATO's cooperation and dialogue priority with non-NATO countries, such as a NATO Regional Cooperation Course (NRCC). This course fits NATO's outreach program entailing the countries of NATO's MD and ICI together with partners from the broader region of the Middle East.

Next to training and education, the NDC includes a research division providing for publications and fellowship programs for NATO members as well as partners. The aim is three folded. For one, to enhance knowledge and analyses about issues within the European security architecture. Second, to strengthen the Trans-Atlantic link. Third, to broaden the knowledge of NATO as a tool for international strategic communication.

Finally, in contrast to the EU, NATO courses are not based on a bachelor or master system and NATO does not support young officers' education until today.

---

[41] http://www.natoschool.nato.int.

[42] http://www.ndc.nato.int.

[43] Also referred to as the 'Other Partners across the Globe', which include Australia, Japan, the Republic of Korea and New Zealand.

19.5 Officers' Training and Education in Europe; Challenges and Opportunities

From the end of the Cold War, training and education in the wider Europe developed as a result of an increase of states as members of the EU and NATO and states as partners of both organizations, broadened in themes as a result of the widening of the security concept and has been strengthened in institutional structure. Especially with the entrance of the EU in the security and defence domain of the European security architecture. However the developments of training and education in the security and defence domain described above face challenges, but likewise offer opportunities. Based on these observed developments some key findings stand out and are addressed below.

First, reflecting on the increase of international cooperation in the security and defence domain, the role of the armed forces has traditionally been defined by the functional imperative of the use or threat of force including defence, deterrence, compliance or intervention. After numerous operations from the nineties, both regional and worldwide, there has been a growing trend of the use of armed forces for a broad range of tasks, from peacekeeping to peace enforcing, to stability, reconstruction and as a means of building cooperative relations with other states and organizations and, what has become a very important tool, training and reforming of foreign militaries. By now, European training and education has fairly developed, as was observed above. Training and education even has become a European export product, which sets a multinational, perhaps global blueprint, as so many other EU activities do. However, for a large part training and education in the security and defence area remains a national effort. To strengthen training and education, for instance because of the complex security environment, operational needs or the multinational nature of conflicts, academic exchange, like Erasmus, and research could be intensified. Intensified because although the above made observations show strengthening of training, education and research programs, there is a lack of joint efforts on an international level.

Second, broadly speaking the EU and NATO are both multilateral training providers that at various points deliver training on similar subjects, certainly when it comes to security and defence. The large military component attached to NATO requires operational and organizational topics in training; NATO has a highly professionalized structure in place through the NATO School and various centres of excellence. Focus is however aimed mainly at the running of and functioning within the military structure. The ESDC on the other hand covers a larger scope of subjects, as the EU in itself covers a much broader spectrum of policy domains. Consequently, there certainly is potential to be complementary to each other, and it would be wrong to consider both organizations as contenders; in the past and sometimes even now it is seen like that, but it is a path that leads nowhere. Both NATO and the EU pose a challenge too to their respective member states; their successful multilateral programs do make it obvious that many member states are by and large trying to train their people to standards that are generally recognized. I.e. in the end the public will ask why so many member states of either the EU, NATO or both are actually doing the same and investing so much resources in what is effectively unnecessary duplication. This can have either reactionary consequences or galvanize people and states into action in order to demand review and change.

Third, from the beginning of 2000 the EU and NATO created several structures for cooperation, such as the Berlin Plus agreements of 2003[44] and strengthened this cooperation in 2016 including a broad palette of security and defence domains to be handled together.[45] With regard to this so-called inter-organizational cooperation in the officers' education programs, cooperation between EU and NATO has likewise been set-up and regular meetings and exchanges are taking place, such as cooperation and exchange between the ESDC and the NDC, a far cry from the early days. However, this cooperation is for now mainly limited to ad-hoc and informal cooperation between these organizations, and some well-known obstacles to intensify cooperation do remain. Obstacles such as the security concerns of different member states in both organizations. However, for academic purposes, there is plenty complementarity to be found in the exchange of experiences, knowledge and lessons learned between the organizations in the inter-organizational setting. Especially with regard to operations, capacity sharing and efficiency, as 22 EU member states are NATO members as well, and most third countries actively participate either through NATO or EU networks or quite often both.

Fourth, reflecting on the wider Europe, both the EU and NATO have opened most of their training and education courses to non-NATO member states in enhancing cooperation with other states and organizations. From the end of the Cold War both organizations have prioritised cooperation and dialogue with countries that were not a member. These partnership programs and dialogues contained multiple aims. On the one hand stability, reform and democratisation. On the other hand, partnership represented the interests of NATO and the EU and its member states. For one because, partners could contribute capabilities for missions and operations that members lacked. Second, partnership, instead of membership and institutionalization, allowed the member states to deepen cooperation in fields of mutual interest, such as peacekeeping and peace enforcing, while denying them the decision-making power and the security guarantees. Third, training and education has always been an important and geostrategic tool in these cooperation and dialogue programs. This resulted in many bi- and multilateral varied cooperation schemes in the security and defence area, for a large part serving strategic interests of national security. These interests vary between interests in specific capabilities of states to the necessity of burden sharing.[46] As such, multilateral education and training can provide a platform for building confidence between nations.

---

[44] Agreements made between NATO and the EU to allow the EU to draw on NATO assets for EU crisis management operations.

[45] Joint Declaration by the President of the European Council, the President of the European Commission and the Secretary General of NATO, Warsaw, 8 July 2016.

[46] Hofland 2017.

Fifth, as was clarified in the introduction of this chapter, Europe faces difficulties with rationalising European capabilities. Nevertheless, one of the solutions to this diversified scheme of European armed forces has been flexible and modular cooperation in numerous forms of bi- and multilateral initiatives between European states, either employable for NATO and/or the EU which do not necessarily have to be competing, but can be supplementary to each other. This can be illustrated by the set-up of EU and NATO member states of numerous bi- and multilateral regional clusters to deepen their defence cooperation, which enriches the network of cooperation and integration. Examples of these bi- and multinational regional clusters are the Visegrad Group Defence Cooperation (V4),[47] NORDEFCO,[48] the Baltic cooperation[49] and the Benelux.[50] Based on the EU principle of subsidiarity, a more flexible form of cooperation could likewise be applied to the world of training and education. Flexible as in cooperation between states and organizations and between organizations. Linking and inter-organizational cooperation benefit both NATO and EU resources and capabilities. For example, in contrast to the EU, NATO training and education is not based or linked to a bachelor, master or post-doc system and NATO does not support young officers' education until today. However, NATO could benefit from the initiatives that were taken in the EU.

Sixth, modern education as we know it in the field of multilateral security and defence domain, be that in a NATO or an EU Framework, faces challenges that a world with less clearly defined borders brings with it; the digital age. Ongoing and intensifying cooperation between states, institutions of both organization and student-participation requires a level of transparency which does not match very well with the classic 'national' domain of security and defence. For most often younger people transcending traditional borders this is the 'new normal' however and a desirable outcome. States will have to find a way to adapt to cater to the needs of a more demanding and dynamic group of people and the increase of globalization and digitalisation. This means that on a multilateral level existing initiatives like the ESDC sectoral qualification framework, and older initiatives aimed to streamline a more transparent education within the Bologna Agreement, must have intensified attention from states involved and both NATO and the EU.[51]

Finally, development of multilateral and international training can be seen as a vehicle for states to 'punch above their weight' as a result of the todays security challenges that states have to meet and for that reason chose for education and training on a strict national or at the most bilateral level. A relative newcomer, as actors on their own, are international organizations that are either providers or

---

[47] Comprising the Czech Republic, Hungary, Poland and Slovakia. See http://www.visegradgroup.eu.

[48] Comprising Denmark, Norway, Sweden, Finland and Iceland. See http://www.nordefco.org.

[49] Comprising Estonia, Latvia and Lithuania. See http://www.baltasam.org.

[50] Comprising Belgium, The Netherlands and Luxemburg. See http://www.benelux.int.

[51] The Bologna Process streamlines the applications for education in the wider Europe, see http://www.ec.europa.eu/education/policies/higher-education/bologna-process-and-european-higher-education-area_en.

require training on the basis of their own mandate, tasks and, more and more, funding. Quite often they provide an area of expertise and capabilities that are not present within the current curricula of states and could support states in their lack of funds and expertise.

19.6 Conclusion

Unless there would be a general retreat into a narrow national interest out of domestic need or otherwise, it is to be expected that multilateral cooperation in training and education will be a continued process. In contrast to the claim by some scholars, who nowadays predict the end of the liberal world order, education and training in the wider Europe might actually be accelerating due to an increase of instability surrounding the wider Europe and simultaneously the availability of cross boundary and distance terminating technology in the field of education. Budgetary pressure and simple availability of organizations such as NATO and the EU, which have their own institutional momentums for evolution, play a role as well in this.

As already concluded, cooperation in the field of training, education and research field can go where other fields, such as policy and operations, cannot. An initiative like EU's Emilyo can be a catalyst for cooperation and positive image building, as we have seen with the successful Erasmus program that aims at getting subjects and matter comparable and compatible and maybe even interoperable. The EU's ESDC Doctoral School initiative can contribute to the particular field of study on (common) security and defence; especially when common funding (the EDF) will be available in the future. Furthermore, the work being done on sectoral qualification cannot be underestimated. While still in its beginning, the potential benefits to (military) education can be huge in terms of transparency and exchange, as it is an 'umbrella' type initiative which are important to the students operating in an international environment. And finally, though on a small-scale base and mostly ad-hoc, the EU and NATO are striving for more cooperation in the security and defence domain of training and education.

In sum, most successful international cooperation in the field of training, education and research we see today remains based on trust. Trust and solidarity have always been the fundamental drivers of international cooperation as laid down in the NATO Washington Treaty (1949) and the Treaty on the European Union (2009). What both NATO and the EU training, education and research programs more specifically are aiming at is to build that trust. When taken a step further, and the BeNeLux cooperation on naval training and education might be exemplary here, real integration can be on the horizon and with it a serious step in efficiency and multilateral (European) synergy in the world of security and defence training, education and research.

Hence, this chapter briefly discussed the developments of training, education and research in the European security and defence domain and observed new venues for additional research into the challenges and opportunities of multilateral, organizational and inter-organizational European training and education.

References

European Commission (2016) European Defence Action Plan: Towards a European Defence Fund, Brussels, 30 November 2016.
Heisbourg F (2018) War and Peace After the Age of Liberal Globalisation. Survival, 60:1.
Hofland HJA (2017) NRC Handelsblad, 18 April 2017.
Kissinger H (2014) World Order. Penguin Press.
Libel T (2016) European Military Culture and Security Governance. Soldiers, Scholars and National | Defence Universities. Routledge.
Macron E (2018) Europe 1 radio station, 6 November 2018.
Mazar MJ (2018) Testing the Value of the Post-war International Order. Rand Corporation, January 2018.
Merkel A (2018) Address to the European Parliament as part of a series of leaders' speeches on the future of Europe, 11 November 2018.
The Global Strategy for the European Union's Foreign and Security Policy; 'Shared Vision, Common Action: A Stronger Europe', adopted by the Council, June 2016.
The North Atlantic Treaty, Washington, D.C., 4 April, 1949.

Internet Sources

http://www.baltasam.org. Accessed 4 January 2019.
http://www.baltdefcol.org/. Accessed 6 January 2019.
http://www.benelux.int. Accessed 4 January 2019.
http://www.cepol.europa.eu/who-we-are/partners-and-stakeholders/external-partners. Accessed 8 February 2019.
http://www.ecahe.eu/w/index.php/European_Joint_Master%27s_in_Strategic_Border_Management_(EJMSBM). Accessed 8 February 2019.
http://www.ec.europa.eu/education/policies/higher-education/bologna-process-and-european-higher-education-area_en. Accessed 8 February 2019.
http://www.ec.europa.eu/home-affairs/sites/homeaffairs/files/e-library/documents/basic-documents/docs/eu_agenda_on_security_en.pdf. Accessed 8 February 2019.
http://www.eda.europa.eu. Accessed 4 January 2019.
http://eeas.europa.eu/diplomatic-network/european-neighbourhood-policy-enp_en. Accessed 8 February 2019.
http://www.emilyo.eu/. Accessed 4 January 2019.
http://www.europa.eu/globalstrategy/en/global-strategy-foreign-and-security-policy-european-union. Accessed 8 February 2019.
http://www.frontex.europa.eu. Accessed 6 January 2019.
http://www.gcsp.ch. Accessed 6 January 2019.
http://www.iss.europa.eu/. Accessed 4 January 2019.
http://www.natoschool.nato.int. Accessed 4 January 2019.
http://www.ndc.nato.int. Accessed 6 January 2019.
http://www.nordefco.org. Accessed 6 January 2019.

http://www.visegradgroup.eu. Accessed 4 January 2019.
https://cdn3-eeas.fpfis.tech.ec.europa.eu/cdn/farfuture/_5GCkdWcdcnDDwZU5lCgMdw_ZLMZt6GeYAzLcK3uNXU/mtime:1520243963/sites/eeas/files/defence_fund_factsheet_0_0.pdf. Accessed 12 February 2019.
https://www.cepol.europa.eu. Accessed 8 February 2019.
https://www.cepol.europa.eu/sites/default/files/CCWP-%20Customs%20Law%20Enforcement%20Training%20Catalogue%202018.pdf. Accessed 12 February 2019.
https://eeas.europa.eu/headquarters/headquarters-homepage_en/4369/European%20Security%20and%20Defence%20College%20(ESDC). Accessed 8 February 2019.
https://eeas.europa.eu/topics/common-security-and-defence-policy-csdp/4369. Accessed 8 February 2019.
https://eeas.europa.eu/sites/eeas/files/2018-100_docsch_charter_-_final.pdf. Accessed 8 February 2019.
https://eeas.europa.eu/topics/eu-global-strategy/52208/sectoral-qualifications-framework-military-officer-profession_en. Accessed 8 February 2019.

Sabine Mengelberg, MA is an assistant professor of the International Security Studies section of the War Studies department of the Netherlands Defence Academy. She holds a master in political science and international public administration. Her research focuses on international cooperation in the security domain and she has nearly finished studying for her Ph.D. at Leiden University. She teaches Bachelor and Master's level at the Dutch staff and command course within the international security domain. Sabine is a representative of the Netherlands Defence Academy to the Academic Board of the European Security and Defence College.

Riccardo Scalas, MA is a senior lecturer at the Netherlands Defence College for the Intermediate and Advanced Staff and Command Officer Courses. His teaching expertise comprises European Union integration and its Common Security and Defence Policy. He is the representative of the Netherlands Defence Academy to the Academic Board of the European Security and Defence College and for the fourth consecutive year Course Director of its flagship High Level Course. The chapter contributed by him is written in a private capacity.

Chapter 20
Lilliputians Divided: How Service Statutes Fragment Lithuanian Security Services

Mantas Bileišis and Svajūnė Ungurytė-Ragauskienė

Contents

20.1 Introduction	322
20.2 Fragmented Officers' Education: The "Ambiguous Lithuanian Officer"	323
20.3 A Historical-Institutionalist Perspective on Lithuanian Security Governance	325
20.3.1 Why Use a Historical-Institutionalist Approach?	325
20.3.2 Context: The Institutional Complexity of Lithuanian Public Governance	327
20.4 Findings	328
20.4.1 Rifts Among the Lilliputians	328
20.4.2 What Stands in the Way of Solutions?	331
20.5 Conclusion: The Worst of Both Worlds?	333
References	334

Abstract From a historical-institutional angle, this chapter focuses on Lithuania's internal security services development. Resulting from both a decades-long period of economic growth as well as demographic decline, the Lithuanian security services are faced with an unfavorable recruitment environment, severely impeding the staffing of military units. In the light of the newly recognized threats from Russia, Lithuania needs to expand its military, which, amongst others, necessitates the expansion of the professional officer corps beyond the number of cadets graduating from the Military Academy. Despite increasing investments in defence and other measures, currently expansion requirements still cannot be met. Changes to the

---

This chapter is written in a private capacity.

M. Bileišis (✉)
Jonas Žemaitis Military Academy of Lithuania, Šilo str. 5A-K7-204A, Vilnius, Lithuania
e-mail: mantas.bileisis@lka.lt

S. Ungurytė-Ragauskienė
Mykolas Romeris University, Didlaukio str. 55-201, Vilnius, Lithuania
e-mail: svajune.unguryte@gmail.com

Interior Service Statute, which regulates the officers' status of uniformed services within the areas of responsibility (AoRs) of the Ministries of Interior, Finance and Justice may offer some room to expand and develop the professional military officer corps. Although under Wartime Law, many of these services would be subjected to military command and considered part of the armed services, until now, defence policy developments have had little effect on the professional development of Interior Service officers. This chapter explores why the security services fail to coordinate the development of professional military competencies amongst themselves. We find three possible reasons. First, the security services fit into the broader Lithuanian governance model, which is characterized by multi-level fragmentation and appears resistant to integration policies, even in instances of great political salience. Furthermore, as the Interior Service Statute covers many agencies and services, some have their civilian functions 'militarized', whilst others have their military functions 'demilitarized'. In doing so, the development of military competences across all services is hampered. Third, and seemingly paradoxically, increased defence spending seems to drive the military and other services in the armed forces apart.

Keywords Lithuanian defence · security governance · uniformed services · interior service · officers' training

20.1 Introduction

Although Jonathan Swift's Lilliputians measured under six inches, they proved able to tie down Gulliver, and, moreover, they managed to persuade him to defeat their enemy's fleet. Next to these exploits, Lilliputians were also known to fight over trivial matters. For Keohane,[1] Lithuania would make for a classic example of Lilliputians. From 2014, in Lithuania, the public policy debate has been defined to a high extent by the behavior of its neighbor Russia, that, feeling threatened by Lithuania's NATO membership, for security reasons, claims a right to an influence sphere beyond its borders, taking military action to realize this logic. However, to date, the debate has not resulted in a coherent Lithuanian security policy, spanning the entire government. Meanwhile military funding and investments increase, whereas, services resorting under the Ministry of Interior (MoI) and other security agencies that, under Lithuanian Wartime Law, would constitute parts of the armed forces seem nearly unaffected. Surely, for Lithuania, a nation dwarfed by its threatening neighbor, security cohesion and capability integration should be high on the agenda.

Geography, demography, and economy alike stack odds against the Baltic States in any military calculation. A combination of flat lands and major Russian standing

---

[1] Keohane 1969.

army units deployed at the borders means that a conflict can be underway on very short notice. Baltic standing forces are small; together the three nations barely reach six million inhabitants to 145 million Russians. Moreover, as the Baltic economies cannot avail of industries to back large standing militaries and defence investments, generally, this means imports will be increased. Although NATO deploys 'tripwire' forces as Enhanced Forward Presence (EfP) for deterrence, the three battalion battle groups and national militaries would have to be able to face off an enemy by themselves for some time. This chapter inquires how officers from services governed by the Interior Service Statute can be better prepared to join military ranks, thereby boosting the national military capability. Moreover, we aim to identify factors that appear to separate the officer corps from the professional military officer corps. The chapter takes a historical-institutionalist approach to study the Lithuanian model of public governance, paying attention to various policy areas along the lines of ministerial responsibility, and taking into account external factors that seem to impact reform across the ministerial lines differently. We contend that the current state of affairs has weakened the Lithuanian state, and, that given the security climate, it is adamant to discuss institutional means to encourage the expansion of the professional officer corps, without burdening the economy or the labor market.

We complement our literature analysis by interviews with officers and policy-makers, who, from the 1990s, have observed developments within both the Military Service and Interior Service. We asked them to assess inter-service relations. Possible solutions are written as they emerged to us, the authors, as a result to problems identified both in the literature analysis and the interviews.

20.2 Fragmented Officers' Education: The "Ambiguous Lithuanian Officer"

The Lithuanian public service is a complex and highly inert system. The Government submitted a new edition of the Law on State Service, over three parliamentary terms, before it was finally adoption, mid-2018, and these changes did not radically alter the system of public service. The Law distinguishes the categories of 'state' (civilian) and 'statutory' (uniformed) services, describing the status of civil servants in detail. The statutory services have their statutes, which describe the status of officials that serve under them. These statutes hold the power of Law, equal to the Law on State Service, and the Law on State Service applies to the 'statutory' officials only insofar as their respective statute does not cover a question at hand. Furthermore, as the Military Service does not fall within the scope of the Law on State Service, this law does not apply to military personnel. Finally, a very sizeable proportion of civilian employees across the public administration institutions are employed as regular employees under the rules of the Labor Code, as are all public service providers (doctors, teachers, etc.).

This system has resulted in a formation of highly fragmented officers' recruitment and education models. There are two main uniformed service statutes: the Military Statute and the Interior Service Statute. Both of these thoroughly regulate service member statuses from the point of view of their recruitment, training, social benefits and the like. The Interior Service Statute covers multiple institutions: Police, VIP protection, Customs, Border Security Service, Penitentiary Service, Public Security Service, Fire and Rescue. Some of these institutions fall under military command in time of war, while others don't (Police, Penitentiary and Customs). The military and these institutions set different requirements for officers' education, and have historically not engaged in co-ordination. In most cases the so-called 'Interior Services' have their own vocational training centers for NCO equivalents, and these provide very limited military competences if any. At the level of officers' enrolment different Interior Service institutions don't set particular requirements for higher education.

University education is required for all officers in Lithuania. The military maintains the Military Academy which offers seven semester academic BA social sciences university degree programs, attended by cadets. In parallel, they follow a vocational military training program. At the beginning of the program cadets undergo a basic military training period. During their semester studies, cadets spend one day a week in vocational training, and have 2–3 weeks of field training. After the 7th semester, and their BA thesis defence, the 8th semester of cadet education is dedicated exclusively to vocational officers' training, including specialization by service of arms. However, over the past decade the Military Academy has consistently failed to enroll enough cadets to meet the demand of the Military, and has relied on a Junior Officer Leader Course, which enrolls graduates of civilian universities to become reserve officers to boost the ranks of the standing officer corps. The Interior Services officers' education is conducted by an exclusive agreement between the Ministry of Interior and Mykolas Romeris University, Faculty of Public Security. This faculty offers law education programs tailored for Police, Border Security, and Customs needs. The majority of the officers in the respective services complete this education, but Law graduates from other universities can join these services as officers by meeting minimum medical and physical requirements. In these instances, a law degree is often not required, and applicants can become officers from a wide variety of educational backgrounds. Other interior services essentially completely rely on civilian education. This situation results in near-absence of military competence among officers of Interior Services.

As we set out to write this chapter, we intended to focus on military officers' education. However, in the case of armed conflict, interior service officers would nearly double the officer corps. Based on the above preliminary overview of regulations, we hold that any standards to be set for Lithuanian officers' training and education need to address common denominators across the military and interior services. Moreover, we wonder why, until now, a discussion on this topic has not taken place.

20.3 A Historical-Institutionalist Perspective on Lithuanian Security Governance

20.3.1 Why Use a Historical-Institutionalist Approach?

At 2.8 million inhabitants, and a nominal GDP of about one third of that of Stockholm, Lithuania is small, even by European standards. The country's system of national governance, including its security system, however, is complex and fragmented at multiple levels.

Until now, little to none research has been conducted on the relations between two entities within Lithuania's national security system – i.e., the military, whose members serve under the Military Service Statute and a series of institutions whose members serve under the Interior Service Statute. Whether and how serving under two separate statutes within one security system affects national defence capabilities has not been researched previously. Before we set out to find some answers to these questions, first, we will offer some institutionalist insights into the founding of Lithuania's contemporary governance system.

From an institutionalist point of view, it is helpful to assess three key periods of post-1990 Lithuania: the formation of the State after independence during the 1990s; accession to the EU and the post-accession period. The literature that covers the first two periods generally has tags of post-communist transition, and EU conditionality attached to them. It is clear that for Lithuania multilateral membership is a key national strategy.[2] However, during the early 1990s, the formation of institutions of the independent state, resulting from internal negotiations amongst political elites, was not burdened by such considerations. The outcome, in 1992, was a semi-presidential constitution, which instated multiple checks and balances on policy-making. In this regard, Lithuania differed from its Baltic neighbors, opting for parliamentary systems. Semi-presidentialism poses risks to democracies in their early formation, but these risks have not materialized in Lithuania.[3] However, there is ample reason to suspect that a semi-presidential system and its accompanying institutional arrangements have a lasting impact on policy coordination from the perspective of policy effectiveness.

From 1992, Lithuania witnessed a return to power of the elites that governed under Soviet occupation. Nonetheless, upon recognition of the prospects, accession to the EU and NATO became the core policy of the 1992–1996 government, and indeed, all governments afterwards. EU, NATO, and the Eurozone were the three international integration policies, based on a broad political consensus. EU accession was the symbolical 'return to Europe', that, within a decade and a half, provided closure to post-communist transformation.[4]

---

[2] Vilpišauskas 2012.
[3] Elgie 2007.
[4] Lauristin 2007.

Fundamentally, the governance model, formed in the 1990s as set by the Constitution, has not been significantly altered by EU integration. It would be incorrect to presume that from 1995–2004, during which period Lithuania applied for EU accession, saw a transition from one governance model to another. That all-encompassing change took place from 1989–1992. In other words, whereas 1990 counted as a revolution, EU accession and NATO membership were adaptations. The governance changes that took place during the accession process, mostly, respected the arrangements already in place. Much recent literature on post-communist transformation supports the assumption that the formation of the Military and Interior Services and the origins of their mutual relations lie further back in history than the most recent edition of their respective Statutes or EU-NATO accession in general.[5]

EU's conditionality greatly impacted relationships between law enforcement and the judiciary, yet from the security policy and internal procedures of law enforcement agencies' point of view changes were fewer. Observations that conditionality does not reshape long-term institutional relationships among government bodies were made before the Eastern enlargement.[6] That seems to be true even in cases where EU reform monitoring remained after accession.[7] Therefore it fair to assume that policy areas, which received less political attention during EU accession must have retained many of their institutional features that were formed in the early 1990s. This assumption of inertia corresponds to the line of reasoning of historical institutionalism, which predicts that radical change of institutional setups is only possible in instances of major upheavals, where inadequacy of existing setups becomes all too evident.[8] Neither EU nor NATO accession, nor the events in Ukraine in 2014 have triggered reforms of uniformed services regulated by the Interior Service Statute. Events that have reshaped military and defence spending seem to have little effect on these institutions; therefore, it seems likely that factors that create inertia lie further back in history.

A preliminary analysis of legal regulations did not lead to any remarkable insights. During the 1990s, Lithuania did not avail of a tradition of its government presenting explanatory notes to parliament. Explanatory notes to the most recent amendments to the Interior Service Statute do not mention inter-relations with the Military Service. In search of data, it has therefore been decided to conduct a series of interviews with senior officers, either acting or retired, who (i) have observed the development of the military and other armed forces institutions since 1990s, (ii) are experienced in planning or exercises involving both sides, (iii) have studied and or educated officers professionally. Selection of interviewees has been based on a snowball principle, asking consecutive officers to identify other potential candidates for interviews. The open interviews were based on an introductory question:

---

[5] Ekiert 2015.
[6] Caparini 2003.
[7] Trauner 2009.
[8] Hall 2010.

"*Multiple uniformed services are regulated by the Interior Service Statute, but under Wartime Law fall under the command of the military. What is your assessment about the current relationship between the military and these services?*" Ten persons have been interviewed, nine of them Lithuanians, and one international. Four out of nine Lithuanians are acting military officers; two are retired officers. Three interviewees have non-military service experiences.[9] Before the interviews, we reviewed both the Statutes of Military- and Interior Service, enabling us to clarify some answers.

20.3.2 Context: The Institutional Complexity of Lithuanian Public Governance

The Lithuanian independence movement, from the late 1980s and early 1990s, has resulted in the 1992 Constitution, which places great emphasis on checks and balances at the level of branches of government.[10] Multiple layers of mutual control characterize this governance model; semi-presidentialism, coupled with a complex election model consistently fails to produce single party governments,[11] and Prime Ministers (PMs) are highly constrained by coalitions.[12]

Key features that produce multiple veto points in policy-making comprise: (i) the presidential appointment of ministers. Due to this arrangement, the PM cannot remove ministers from office without either a presidential decision, or parliamentary vote; (ii) elections consistently produce coalition governments with numerous junior partner ministers; (iii) ministers are personally responsible to parliament for their performance; (iv) prolific and highly autonomous agencies within ministerial areas of responsibility.

During the EU accession process and conditionality, unity amongst the political elites has enabled political stability, even under circumstances in which decision-makers changed rapidly. In this instance, the *acquis* is adhered to more diligently than the democratic conditionality.[13] However, once a member state has become part of the EU, the complexities of this constitutional arrangement and a lack of EU instruments to frame reforms effectively, soon put an end to major reforms. It may be even, that upon EU accession, political consensus, acting both as the driving force of reforms as well as a measure of coordination to Lithuania's

---

[9] We refrain from offering more details on the characteristics of our interviewees in order not to identify them. It is important to point out that these interviews were used as an aid to interpret the development of statutory regulations that we reviewed, and we claim the interpretations presented as our own.

[10] Smalskys et al. 2017.

[11] Mastuzato and Gudžinskas 2006.

[12] Mastuzato 2011.

[13] Schimmelfennig and Sedelmeier 2004.

fragmented governance, became obsolete. During the post-conditionality era, national considerations take precedence.[14]

In the case of Lithuania, coordinating reforms between two or more ministries seems to be hard work for little pay in terms of political dividend. Only few seem willing to do so, even in the face on necessity. Junior coalition-partner Ministers can feel safe in their position as long as they are favored by the President, promoting ministerial budget 'silos' that have a knock-on effect on any reform coordination efforts. Even in instances where budgetary programs combine several areas of ministerial responsibilities, implementation leaves much to be desired.[15] Attempts at introducing inter-institutional cooperation are difficult, and do not offer much in terms of track records. The current Lithuanian government has pursued a strong Center of Government philosophy by establishing the National Bureau of Common Functions that intends to centralize many back-office activities of ministries. It remains to be seen how this initiative will overcome the lack of a horizontal cooperation culture and incrementalist reform attitudes.[16] Moreover, the presence of multiple agencies within the ministries[17] adds to existing doubts regarding the likelihood that inter-institutional policies will become better coordinated. This especially concerns uniformed services, as civilian leaders tend to take a hands-off approach when it comes to regulating them.[18] Agencies can become a liability to effective state performance,[19] and, in Lithuania, no formal agenda exists on agencies and their status.

Policy coordination is well-researched.[20] From the above, it may be gathered that the current state of affairs in public governance policy-making will negatively impact on wartime planning and military capability. As, today's system of national governance does not allow for integration and development of hierarchical defence capabilities, even in a context of recognized existential threats to the state, solutions may lie outside the scope of the MoD.

20.4 Findings

20.4.1 Rifts Among the Lilliputians

Lithuanian officials may be either statutory- or civil servants. Legally, despite the Military Service Statute, the military are not considered a statutory service.

---

[14] Ugur 2013.
[15] Jurkonienė and Karčiauskienė 2017.
[16] Nakrošis 2018.
[17] Nakrošis and Budraitis 2012.
[18] Ungurytė-Ragauskienė and Bileišis 2018.
[19] Randma-Liiv 2008.
[20] Peters 2018.

The Interior Service Statute is applicable to officials from three ministerial AoRs (Interior, Justice, and Finance) and covers border guard service, public security service, the police department, the rescue and fire department, penitentiary and customs department officers; in effect, most of the uniformed people. Moreover, separate statutes are in place, regulating e.g., the national anticorruption agency (Service of Special Investigations) and the national intelligence agency (State Security Department).

During the interviews, three categories emerged to explain, first, the *status quo* of the relationship between the Military- and Interior Service Statutes; second, why the Interior Service Statute has become an 'umbrella' regulation encompassing many agencies, and, last, the implications for Lithuanian military security. Respondents have shared their opinions and assessments on (i) current military threats; (ii) history of formation of the security system, and (iii) how the current institutional security system impacts Lithuania's capacity to counter relevant external threats.

Regarding the assessment of current military threats, the respondents achieve consensus that Russia's political aims in Lithuania are impossible to reconcile with Lithuanian national security interests, and, therefore, countering Russia's military threats is a high national priority. Although we do not rate military risks in various scenarios, the respondents have reached consensus regarding Russia's capability to deploy an overwhelming force on short notice, and, also, that this risk cannot be ruled out from Lithuania's defence planning. Consequentially, the respondents view the expansion of military capabilities, Lithuania actively engages in, as a prudent and meaningful investment. However, opinions about the likeliness of a military conflict range broadly among interviewees. Some suggest opportunities for Russia in Latvia and Estonia to attempt a non-conventional operation to destabilize these countries and NATO without triggering NATO Article 5. In that case, a combined law enforcement and military operation involving Lithuania might be called upon. In such a scenario, a lack of interoperability and capability does exist. Opposed to this suggestion, others describe the likelihood of an armed conflict on Lithuanian soil as very remote, especially in the light of NATO and EU policies, since 2014. The maintenance and strengthening of these multilateral initiatives is seen as sufficient to deter Russia's military threat.

As to the historical background of the development of services regulated by separate statutes, the military, although many officers gained experience during the Soviet period, have built a new administrative structure. NATO accession has affected this structure to a far greater extent than EU accession has done to law enforcement. Furthermore, from 1990 to 1992 the MoI has adhered to staff and organizational structures from the Soviet period. Even when, in the context of EU conditionality, Customs and Penitentiary have been moved to the ministries of Finance and Justice, the officials kept their affiliation with the Interior Service Statute. The ex-communist led government of 1992–1996 also has not pursued major reforms in the MoI's area of responsibility, and neither has it sought to replace leadership or methods of training the agencies. From 1996 to 1999, the government has implemented a very ambitious ministerial structure reform, but, in

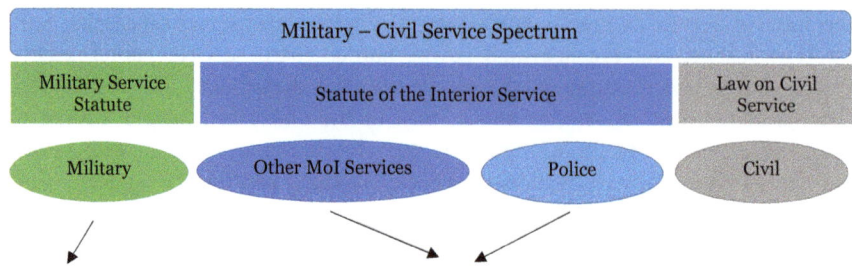

Fig. 20.1 Trends of the development of institutional practices in the military-civil service spectrum of public service. *Source* M. Bileišis and S. Unguryté-Ragauskiené

1999, as a consequence of a political crisis between the President and the PM, the impact of reforms at the executive level of the agencies has remained limited. Especially concerning uniformed services. As EU conditionality took effect in the early 2000s, the system has not been questioned as to its legal status or organization structures. According to interviewees, in the 1990s, the fragmentation of the uniformed services, though not explicitly stated, was based on the political elites' fear that uniformed services might subvert democratic institutions. In other words, tensions between the Military and Interior services is, to some extent, an intended institutional arrangement. Another factor, pointed out by the interviewees, is that MoI including its agencies, in the 1990s, was busy to tackle the rise of organized crime. Whilst the police has militarized (or rather retained some of its repressive character), it nonetheless has moved away from the military, enabled by the regulatory incohesion provided by separate Military and Interior Service Statutes (see Fig. 20.1).

Opinions on how the agencies in the area of responsibility of MoI can be integrated into the development of military security in the current threat environment range broadly, correlating slightly with the previous assessment of the likelihood of the Russian threat. The professional military would nearly double in terms of headcount if non-police Interior Service institutions were integrated into the military. But several respondents point out that in case of a conventional conflict this would be of little importance. Existing military units are mostly light infantry and require significant equipment procurements of force multipliers. In this context, closer cooperation with the MoI services is seen as secondary, to be done by enrolling service members as reserves, especially with the volunteer forces (the Lithuanian equivalent of the national guard) on an individual basis.

It has been noted that a non-conventional armed conflict is highly unlikely on Lithuanian soil. The risks only cover several small localities. Currently, MoD and MoI are engaged in developing interoperability by means of exercises that focus on these particular threats. Continuous cooperation to exercise for such contingencies is already underway, and regarded to be sufficient. However, long-term perspectives on greater Military and Interior Services alignment are mostly fatalistic. Although most interviewees accept that expansion of the officer corps and improved professional mobility across services are necessary on the long-term, the institutional hurdles are perceived as nearly insurmountable. The levels of comprehension, consensus, and long-term commitment of the political elites to instate necessary changes would need to match those of NATO accession, while the threat assessment by the public and representatives of the services themselves does not work in that favor. According to several interviewees, enhancement of joint exercises, training and education, as well as the incorporation of some NATO standards into Interior Service operations may facilitate political decision making on officer corps integration in the long run. However, and compounding the fatalistic attitude among the interviewees, the fragmented landscape of MoI's agencies has led to competition and turf battles to gain the Minister's attention to receive increased funding. It seems, agencies perceive that, when it comes to funding, coordination may result in other agencies standing to benefit more. According to interviewees, across the Interior Service agencies organizational cultures have grown apart and continue to do so. Rotations and officers' mobility across the Interior Service agency is not widely adopted. As a result, re-thinking the institutional setup is expected to cause resistance amongst the officers themselves, especially regarding rotations, the absence of which is currently regarded as a social benefit, rightful because wages are below expectations. Finally, staff retention is problematic within all uniformed services and the agencies focus on the same target groups of potential service members. Respondents point out that an institutional reshuffle will create both winners and losers, and, because neither side of the ministerial divide wants to lose, the status quo is preserved. Finally, some interviewees comment that MoI constantly have their eyes on MoD's funding, but would be unwilling to harmonize the statutes: "they want the military's money, but not its rules".

From the interviews, and regarding the military security area, it can be concluded that the respondents recognize and acknowledge the hurdles described in Sect. 20.2 to a large extent.

20.4.2 What Stands in the Way of Solutions?

The history of the 20th century has caused global fragmentation in an age of nuclear weapons. This fact alone warrants a close study of how small states secure themselves.[21] From the perspective of a citizen of a small state, the knowledge that a century ago small states were few provokes a question if the proliferation of small states wasn't simply a 'glitch' of the international system, far outside of a stable long-term equilibrium. As one observer put it: *"Lithuania's goal is to be free of foreign occupation. But its economy, demography, and geography make it unlikely that Lithuania will ever achieve its goal more than occasionally and*

---

[21] Keohane 1969.

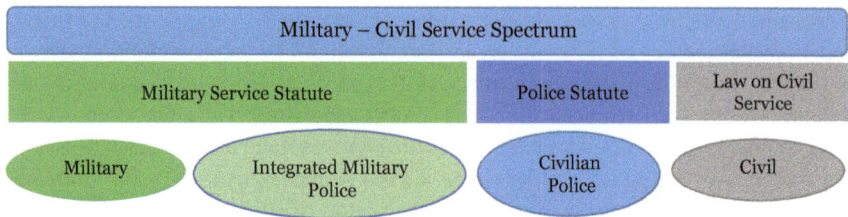

Fig. 20.2 Possible military-civil service spectrum in Lithuania without a statute of the interior service. *Source* M. Bileišis and S. Unguryté-Ragauskienė

temporarily".[22] And there are plenty of reasons to be anxious. The source of primary threat to Lithuanian security, Russia, manages to engage in military conflicts in its neighborhood with little opposition. In order to be on top of their game, security institutions need to be capable to seize every opportunity to improve their security. Therefore, security institutions need to act in concert to render planning and operations coherent. To this end, members of national security agencies are to be highly professional. We contend that there is a body of officers who cannot contribute to military security at the top of their abilities.

Institutionalist literature distinguishes three types of isomorphism to bring governance practices closer together: coercive, normative, and mimetic.[23] Our findings suggest that current Lithuanian governance is unfavorable to either coercive or normative isomorphism. Mimetic isomorphism offers possibilities, but requires changes to the Interior Service Statute. As Pollitt[24] points out convergence does not happen without active pursuit for change, especially if agents who promote reform do not coordinate with each other. According to us, the Napoleonic tradition of military police, a Gendarmerie, would cover many gaps in capability development we identified (see Fig. 20.2). In peacetime, it could complement police, and offer a basis for comparative analysis of policing performance. The civilian police could perform its tasks in an increasingly demilitarized fashion. The status of the military police under a Military Statute would increase substantially career opportunities for prospective officers, besides allowing the expansion of military training and combat organizational structures. We argue that integration of fragmented agencies into a single structure would be beneficial. During the 1990s, when the state was weak, fragmentation served a purpose. Today, we regard this as a liability for Lithuania's national security.

We are aware of the obstacles to this proposed solution. To our knowledge, a Gendarmerie has never been seriously considered. The public security service frames itself as a Gendarmerie, but in fact constitutes an institution of just over 1.000 personnel that currently acts as a redundant force for both the police and the

---

[22] Friedman 2010.

[23] Dimaggio and Power 1991.

[24] Pollitt 2007.

penitentiary service for managing crises. The public security service, moreover, does not have prominence among other Interior Service agencies. We also recognize that even an apparent existential threat from Russia, as well as external pressures resulting from EU and NATO accession have, until today, failed to produce Interior Service agency integration.

20.5 Conclusion: The Worst of Both Worlds?

As Buzan[25] states: "not all states are created equal". There are strong and there are weak states. For him, the key distinction between a strong and a weak state is the weak state's preoccupation with internal security. In the case of Lithuania, the formative years of the nation's security system took place in the 1990s, when the state was clearly weak. What resulted is a system of mutual controls, overlapping jurisdictions, and fragmentation. As Lithuanian society has grown stronger, the state appears to linger on challenges that are no longer there, instead of focusing on the tasks at hand. Our findings lead us to conclude that institutional fragmentation of agencies under the Interior Service Statute hurts both policing and military aspects of the state. Internally, there are no indicators that the Lithuanian security services would under any circumstances challenge democratic institutions to warrant the existing degree of institutional fragmentation. Furthermore, despite the fragmentation there is no comparable institution to the police department. It is the only institution tasked with the full spectrum of public security. Paradoxically the Police is militarized more than necessary, but not militarized enough to be of use militarily. From the point of view of our analysis, the situation is sub-optimal for both public security and national defence. It reflects the pre-occupation with state coercion of security policy-makers to mitigate any internal risks in the 1990s. Somehow this preoccupation has left Lithuania with an internal security model that resembles its Eastern neighbors rather than its Western allies.

This situation in our opinion creates lost opportunities to improve both the quality of public and military security. The existing system does not create a competent officer and NCO corps within the Interior Service, which could contribute to military operations. The agency-based professional development and mobility also reduces incentives for the most talented citizens to join and remain in active service. If they continue on this road, public sector security agencies may find themselves engaged in a lose-lose game on the labor market.

---

[25] Buzan 1991.

References

Buzan B (1991) People, States, and Fear, 2nd edn. An Agenda for International Security Studies in the Post-Cold War Era. Harvester Wheatsheaf.

Caparini M (2003) Security sector reform and NATO and EU enlargement. SIPRI YEARBOOK, pp. 237–260.

DiMaggio PJ, Powell W (1991) The Iron Cage Revisited: Institutional Isomorphism and Collective Rationality. In: Powell WW, DiMaggio PJ (eds) The new institutionalism in organizational analysis, pp. 63–82. The University of Chicago Press, Chicago/London.

Ekiert G (2015) Three Generations of Research on Post-Communist Politics—A Sketch. East European Politics and Societies 29(2):323–337.

Elgie R (2007) Varieties of semi-presidentialism and their impact on nascent democracies. Taiwan Journal of Democracy 3(2):53–71.

Friedman G (2010) The next 100 years: A forecast for the 21st century. Anchor.

Hall PA (2010) Historical institutionalism in rationalist and sociological perspective. Explaining institutional change: Ambiguity, agency, and power, pp. 204–224.

Jurkonienė I, Karčiauskienė R (2017) Lietuvos strateginio planavimo dokumentų sistemos optimizavimo modelis Teminio tyrimo "Kokia yra Lietuvos strateginio planavimo dokumentų sistemos problematika?" ataskaita [Report on the study on the Model of Optimization of Lithuanian Strategic Planning Documentation]. Investuok Lietuvoje.

Keohane RO (1969) Lilliputians' Dilemmas: Small States in International Politics. International Organization 23(2):291–310.

Lauristin M (2007) The European public sphere and the social imaginary of the 'New Europe'. European Journal of Communication 22(4):397–412.

Matsuzato K (2011) Disintegrated semi-presidentialism and parliamentary oligarchy in Post-Orange Ukraine. In: Semi-presidentialism and Democracy, pp. 192–209. Palgrave Macmillan, London.

Matsuzato K, Gudžiskas L (2006) An eternally unfinished parliamentary regime? Semipresidentialism as a prism to view Lithuanian politics. Acta Slavica Iaponica 23:146–170.

Nakrošis V (2018) Public administration characteristics and performance in EU28: Lithuania. European Commission.

Nakrošis V, Budraitis M (2012) Longitudinal Change in Lithuanian Agencies: 1990–2010, International Journal of Public Administration 35(12):820–831.

Peters BG (2018) The challenge of policy coordination. Policy Design and Practice 1(1):1–11.

Pollitt C (2007) Convergence or divergence: what has been happening in Europe? In New public management in Europe, pp. 10–25. Palgrave Macmillan, London.

Randma-Liiv T (2008) New public management versus neo-Weberian state in Central and Eastern Europe. The NISPAcee Journal of Public Administration and Policy 1(2):69–81.

Schimmelfennig F, Sedelmeier U (2004) Governance by conditionality: EU rule transfer to the candidate countries of Central and Eastern Europe. Journal of European Public Policy 11(4):661–679.

Smalskys V et al. (2017) Public Sector in Lithuania since 1990. In: Kovač P, Bileišis M (eds) Public administration reforms in Eastern European Union member states: post-accession convergence and divergence. Mykolas Romeris University and University of Ljubljana.

Trauner F (2009) Post-accession compliance with EU law in Bulgaria and Romania: a comparative perspective.

Ugur M (2013) Europeanization, EU conditionality, and governance quality: Empirical evidence on Central and Eastern European countries. International Studies Quarterly 57(1):41–51.

Ungurytė-Ragauskienė S, Bileišis M (2018) When a Market Runs a Hierarchy: Retrenchment of Bureaucratic Practices in Lithuanian Uniformed Services. Socialiniai Tyrimai 41(1).

Vilpišauskas R (2012) The management of economic interdependencies of a small state: Assessing the effectiveness of Lithuania's European policy since joining the EU.

Dr. Mantas Bileišis is a professor at Jonas Žemaitis Military Academy of Lithuania and chairs study program committees of academic public administrations and public security programs that are taught to officer-cadets and other students of the academy. His research focuses on comparative civil (uniformed) service, institutional conflict and cooperation in the public sector.

Svajūnė Ungurytė-Ragauskienė, MA is a Ph.D. student at Mykolas Romeris University in Vilnius, Lithuania. Her research focuses on the development of the theory of European Administrative Space from the perspective of public services (civilian and uniformed), convergence, and divergence.

Chapter 21
What Sets the Officer Apart? Dutch and Danish Educational Reforms Leading to the Habitus of the Thinking Soldier

Marenne Jansen, Morten Brænder and René Moelker

Contents

21.1	Introduction	338
21.2	Theory: Habitus	340
	21.2.1 Soldier Versus Scholar	340
21.3	Officers' Education	342
	21.3.1 The Netherlands	342
	21.3.2 Denmark	345
21.4	Discussion: Reinventing the Military Profession	347
	21.4.1 Challenges to the Dutch Model: Neither Fish Nor Fowl	348
	21.4.2 Challenges to the Danish Model	348
21.5	Conclusion: Developing the Habitus of the Thinking Soldier	349
	21.5.1 Limitations	350
	21.5.2 Recommendations	351
References		351

Abstract Both The Netherlands and Denmark experienced educational reforms in the last decade. Regarding recruitment and educational model the change in Denmark was more radical than in The Netherlands. Denmark switched to recruiting academics and shortening the educational trajectory whilst the Dutch kept

---

M. Jansen (✉)
Radboud University, PO Box 9108, 6500 HK Nijmegen, The Netherlands
e-mail: marenne.jansen@minbuza.nl

M. Brænder
Aarhus University, Aarhus, Denmark
e-mail: mortenb@ps.au.dk

R. Moelker
Faculty of Military Sciences, Netherlands Defence Academy, Breda, The Netherlands
e-mail: r.moelker.01@mindef.nl

both long (bachelor) and short (applied vocational training and skills and drills) models and mixed their recruiting strategy. Both countries also offer career possibilities for NCOs entering the officer corps. In both countries, however, tensions between the soldier's habitus and the scholar's habitus have not been resolved. We discuss the strengths and weaknesses of both countries educational reforms in terms of "what sets the officer apart?" and recommend possible escapes for the dilemma of a training that on the one hand is too scholarly and academic or one that, on the other hand, emphasises military skills and drills. We suggest that the third way, developing the habitus of the thinking soldier, provides such a way ahead.

Keywords Officers' Training · Officers' Formation · Habitus · Thinking Soldier · Denmark · The Netherlands

21.1 Introduction

The military profession is distinct, but the distinctiveness of the armed forces has been under pressure for decades. Economical, legal, technological, and managerial developments challenge the military organisation, and give reason to critically re-assess whether military officers' education fits today's challenges.

Friedson's[1] classical work on the characteristics of professions neatly fits armed forces: a profession closes its ranks thanks to a distinctive body of knowledge (laid down in certified educational curricula), a code of conduct, (including ethics, norms, and values) and by upholding the authority to select potential new members of the profession. The refinement of this distinctiveness is what Abbott[2] defines as the profession's development of "social closure". According to Collins,[3] closure is obtained by credentialism. Bourdieu[4] adds to that the development of habitus as a way to distinguish "our" sort of people from others. Reform of military education, as we will see, is governed by the same principles of professionalism. Its objective is to set officers apart from civilians, creating a domain of unique knowledge, skills and ethos.

Military education comes in many forms, but two ideals are particularly worthwhile mentioning as they mark the extreme positions, eloquently described by Frederick the Great and General van Scharnhorst. Frederick the Great is supposed to have said "If my soldiers began to think, not one of them would remain in the

---

[1] Freidson 1970.
[2] Abbot 1988.
[3] Collins 1979.
[4] Bourdieu 1984. Bourdieu suggests that the use of economic capital alone (in a capitalist field) falls short of explaining the positions of agents, and states that research should include other capitals such as cultural, social, and symbolic capital.

army".⁵ But, in contrast to Frederick's non-thinking soldiers, technological developments of the 17th and 18th century called for advanced training and education of the officer corps. Artillery and engineering paved the way for formalised officers' training programs, exemplified by the founding of Saint Cyr in France, and the United States Military Academy at West Point. Founded in 1802 both academies started out as technical schools with exact science prominently placed on the curriculum.

Formal training is one way in which the military profession has established social closure. *Informal* education or character formation, ("Bildung"), is another. This leads us to the second view: without brains, armies lose battles. The Prussians found this out at the humiliating defeat at Jena in 1806 where old-fashioned Prussian infantry tactics faced modern French artillery technology on the battlefield. Prussian army reformer, Gerhard von Scharnhorst used that lessons to emphasize the pivotal role of enhancing military educational standards. According to Von Scharnhorst, "ignorance is degrading and dishonouring the military, and often the entire state".⁶ He wanted to create "thinking officers" that could thrive in an intellectual climate: "The man without Bildung is surely a cattle, a cruel beast; in general I have found that only well-educated people sought to alleviate the horrors of war, and that uneducated officers were just as bestial as the rank and file."⁷ This notion of the "thinking soldier" is in line with the famous article 133 of the U.S. Uniform Code of Military Justice: a military leader is expected to act both as "an officer and a gentleman".⁸ Hence, dancing classes and etiquette are still part of military education, because the skills, the knowledge and the character formation are thought to be inseparable. The educational system established by Scharnhorst generated bright scholars such as von Clausewitz, and the Prussian military academy came to serve as an example of the formation of thinking officers.

Recent and concurrent officers' education reforms in The Netherlands and Denmark have enable the recruitment of cadets with a civilian university degree. This is in many ways a new development, and may be seen as a way of meeting the demand formulated by Von Scharnhorst 200 years ago: A well-functioning military requires "thinking soldiers". Nevertheless, this development also causes concern within the armed forces, as it challenges one of the fundamental aspects of military training: the military academy's ability to mould civilians into soldiers. The reason why the introduction of a new kind of cadets, already equipped with academic credentials, is also seen as a matter of concern, is that they signify the potential influx of tensions between a military and an academic way of thinking, or to be more exact, between the soldier's habitus and the scholar's habitus.

Here, we investigate to what extent modern western officers' education, meets the requirements set by the military organisation for modern officers, and focus in

---

[5] Houlding 1981.
[6] Schoy (undated).
[7] Ibid.
[8] This article of the penal code refers to unbecoming conduct.

particular on the recruitment of cadets with civilian university degrees. In this chapter, we will look at two open-ended questions. How are the Dutch and the Danish officers' training programs taking in civilian B.A. cadets organised? And which model seems to be best suited for developing "thinking officers"? Sect. 21.2 introduces the theoretical framework and the concept of habitus that is applied to the two cases. The Dutch and the Danish educational programs are described in Sect. 21.3. In Sect. 21.4, we discuss the strengths and weaknesses of the two models, and in Sect. 21.5 we conclude our findings, identify their limitations and suggest a third way transcending the tension between the soldier's and the scholar's habitus. This concluding section also contains recommendations.

21.2 Theory: Habitus

The notion of habitus is often ascribed to Pierre Bourdieu, but was initially coined by Norbert Elias who defined it as someone's "comfort zone" or "second nature. According to Elias, modern ideals of cultural formation can be seen as a result of the encounter between the "court society" and the "bourgeoisie" in early modern time. These two cultural worlds rested on fundamental different sets of values. Nevertheless, their mutual dependency forced them to refine their norms, and although the bourgeoisie may seem to have won this race for defining the shared values of society, (today, economic strength trumps most things), ideals of the court society remain our golden standard of civility. Habitus is your second, or social, nature. It defines how you are in the world. It is engrained in your mind, in your personal and professional identity. Socialisation can in that respect be seen as the way in which a habitus is acquired. Accordingly, when socialised into a given professional identity, you need to think, act and feel like other members of that profession. For instance, in the process of becoming an officer, one of the harshest reprimands a cadet can face when making a mistake, is that "this is not the officer's way".

21.2.1 Soldier Versus Scholar

What is then the "officer's way" or the soldier's habitus? Observers of the military often point out two aspects in this respect: authority and agility.[9] Given however, that blind obedience to ruling authorities is seldom seen as an uncontested virtue,[10] we will here focus on the second aspect, the officer's agility. Officers are distinguished by their ability to make decisions under time pressure and with a limited

---

[9] Soeters 2018.

[10] Up to the 1960s, societies were more servile, but in the military obedience has always been more extreme, more systematic and it was coerced upon the servicemen. See Osiel 1998.

amount of information available. In that view, the military leader is the leader who can analyse the situation instantly, make a qualified decision, and enable his subordinates to accomplish the goal he has set. In English this is known as the ability to 'command', in German it is known as 'Führung'.[11] This mind-set that is inculcated as second nature is the habitus of the officer that will save his and his company's lives in difficult situations.

The habitus of the scholar is thought to be opposite to swift decision-making and agile action. Scholars learn thorough thinking, critical thinking, analysis and above all systematic doubt. To doubt is the second nature of the scholar.[12] Put like this, one can easily see why the scholar's habitus is seen as incompatible with that of the officer. Thus, from a traditional perspective, it is obvious to fear that taking in more scholars as cadets will make the military ill-prepared for the type of situations that calls for swift decision making. Before jumping to conclusion, we should, however, keep three things in mind.

First, agility is not understood in the same way across the military. There are hierarchical differences, (what counts when you are lying in a foxhole, may not count in the same way when you are sitting behind a desk). Likewise, there are branch and function specific differences (a radar technician may also have to make swift decisions, but the type of information he has to relate to, differs fundamentally from that of his army infantry colleague). That means that this apparent incompatibility may not be equally true everywhere in the military.

Moreover, swift decisions are not decided upon on impulse. They are usually based on training, recognition of patterns and embodied 'savoir faire': Decision-making is something that can be learned. This leads to the second point: Our habitus is a social construction. Therefore, what counts as incompatible aspects between second natures can also be reconstructed. This should not be seen as implying that such aspects can be changed overnight, but serve as a reminder that they may change.

Third, a quick glance at military missions, military action and military technology during the past three decades, clearly tells us that we live in times that call for change, and for a specialised knowledge across different disciplines: The scope of military tasks has developed rapidly (ranging from fighting, to peacekeeping, to reconstruction, policing and to providing humanitarian aid); so has the content of these tasks and the swiftness with which military personnel have to switch between these roles.

And if these purely theoretical claims should not suffice, history shows us how the soldier's habitus has been changing as the role of the military has evolved. Elias' analysis of the development of the Officer's profession in The Royal British Navy provides us with an excellent example of how the military way can be

---

[11] Remarkable is that the German concept of Innere Führung (Von Baudissin 1969) developed along the lines as discussed in this chapter. Instead of demonstrating blind obedience the soldier is expected to think for himself or herself and ultimately take responsibility.

[12] Kramer 2007.

enriched by encountering other ways.[13] In contrast to e.g. the French Navy, where officers were only recruited through traditional channels – i.e. from the nobility – the British Navy recruited its officers both among army commanders (mostly noblemen) and civilians from the merchant fleet. The two groups were opposites. One group was skilled in battle. The other in navigating. And for a very long time, the notion that "opposites attract" had little actual bearing in this case. Nevertheless, following this encounter a shared understanding of what should characterise a Navy officer developed but only by developing the institution of the "midshipmen" as an educational model.

Elias' analysis reveals that the encounter that created the Naval Officer was by no means a smooth process. Likewise, we cannot assume that the encounter between scholars and soldiers at the Dutch and Danish military academies will end harmoniously, nor that it will have outcome intended by the decision makers. Nevertheless, even with the aforementioned provisions in mind, we maintain that instead of regarding the skills mastered by the new cadets (who already acquired academic credentials) as an obstacle, they ought to be perceived as a potential contribution to the modern military. And therefore, we expect that the tensions between these new ideas and the military's own ideals can be productive.

21.3 Officers' Education

This section compares the changes in officers' education in The Netherlands and in Denmark. Table 21.1 gives an overview of the different programs.

21.3.1 The Netherlands

21.3.1.1 Education at The Netherlands Defence Academy

With the suspension of the conscription, changes in warfare, and drastic budget cuts, military organization in The Netherlands had to be rethought and reorganized.[14] Both when operating abroad and in regard to preparation and training, the civilian and the military worlds have grown closer. While these developments may have affected the military habitus, there nevertheless still seems to be a rather fixed image of what military leadership looks like.[15] To develop and train this particular attitude in officers is one of the core-objectives of military academies.

---

[13] Elias 2007.
[14] De Ruiter 2018.
[15] Caforio 2001.

Table 21.1 The structure of the officers' training programs in The Netherlands and Denmark

The Netherlands			Denmark		
Promotion model	Long track	Short track	Promotion model	Civilian B.A. model	Short term employment model (only Army)
High school degree	High school degree	High school degree	High school degree	High school degree	High school degree
Military service and promotion to NCO	High school degree	Civilian B.A. degree	Military service and promotion to NCO	Civilian B.A. degree	Lieutenant training (Army NCO school)
NCO experience and professional degree (equivalent to B.A.)	Enrolment at NLDA	Enrolment at NLDA	NCO experience (24 months) Academy professional degree (equivalent to B.A.)	NCO school & NCO internship	*Commissioned after 6 months*
Enrolment at NLDA			Enrolment at Danish Defence Academy (DDA)		
Commission depends on branch, specialisation and previous career development	*Commissioned after 4 years*	*Commissioned after 18 months*	*Commissioned after 12–24 months, depending on branch and specialisation*		

Source Jansen et al. 2019

The Netherlands Defence Academy (NLDA) has existed for nearly 200 years. Yet, despite all changes[16] the institution's objective still pertains the training of *future military leaders*. This objective is explicated in its mission statement: *"initial officers' training and education and career courses for officers at the intermediate and senior level. By offering an integrated program consisting of military training, personal development and academic education, the NLDA makes an important contribution to professional leadership."* Officers' education in The Netherlands can thus roughly be divided into three categories: military training, academic education and character formation.

The military training is organized and executed by military professionals – officers and non-commissioned officers. Military and civilian staff offer academic education. Character formation is considered extremely important, but has a less

---

[16] Groen and Klinkert 2003.

official character; mostly happens in "between the lines". In this sense, it is considered an essential by-product of military academy training. The motto of the Netherlands Defence Academy is "Knowledge is power, character is more".[17] Numerous activities – organised by and for cadets, compulsory as well as voluntarily – aim at developing skills and an "officer's attitude". This includes initiation rites (including hazing), extracurricular activities and the informal social life at campus. Through such arrangements, cadets start acquiring – embodying – the principles, standards and values to be observed by a true member of the officer corps. Values such as honesty, selfless service, initiative, comradeship, respect, responsibility and decency, are to be observed and practiced through the organized activities, in- and outside of the academy. In principle, this process of embodiment is not a requirement for entering the corps, but social pressure ensures that in practice all cadets acquire these subtle standards.

Thus, whereas strict curricula and end-term demands are in place for the processes of military and academic education, the character formation is only partially defined in evaluating procedures. Yet, the fact that it is not an objective assessment does not imply that it is less important. Actually, the opposite might very well be the case. This is a point, we will return to in the discussion below, where we address the possible consequences of the recent reforms.

21.3.1.2 Officers' Education at the NLDA

As shown in Table 21.1, we can distinguish between three models of officers' education at the NDLA: The promotion model (where cadets are recruited from the NCO corps); The long track model (where cadets are recruited from high school); and the short track model (aimed at applicants with a civilian B.A. degree).

The distinction between these two tracks – initially described by Dalenberg[18] – dates back to the suspension of the draft, but got its present outlook after 2011 when short track officers were required to have obtained a civilian bachelor degree.[19] For both short track and long track cadets, the training at the NLDA is their first encounter with military life and culture, and – in theory – both groups are expected to be able to fulfil the same tasks once they are commissioned. Nevertheless, there are some essential differences: Not only do the two groups enrol with different backgrounds, but on their arrival, they are also assigned to different platoons.

Long track cadets generally spend four years at the NLDA. They are said to follow "the classical" educational program. There is plenty of time for personal development, and the green (military) as well as the white (intellectual) abilities are trained during a longer period. Long-track cadets need to have obtained a high school degree on a preparatory scientific level. Some of them have spent some time

---

[17] Aker 2007.
[18] Dalenberg 2016, p. 20.
[19] Economic conditions however make recruiters relax their standards for entry regularly.

at a civilian university or in a job, but most of them are recruited directly from high school. Ages vary between 17 and 28, but most are 18 years old. Their complete program consists of 48 weeks of military training,[20] three years for the academic bachelor and a final functional training. This is a service specific program, different in content and time for each of the arms of service. For long-track cadets, the Faculty of Military Sciences offers accredited bachelor programs; War Studies, Military Management Studies and Military Systems & Technology. The academic education at the NLDA is underpinned by academic research, relevant for the education and for the defence organization. Generally speaking, cadets can choose which bachelor they prefer. For their academic program, lecturers are required to possess a Ph.D. degree. The majority of the lecturers is (currently) civilian, and have tenured positions. Cadets in the long track program are usually very active in the cadet corps after their first semester. They take up positions in various boards, and organize and participate in many activities.

Short track cadets, already holding an academic degree, are enrolled for 18 months, of which six are placed at a location outside the NLDA. They have a completely different curriculum: unlike the long track cadets, for whom three out of four years are dedicated to academic learning, the focus for short track cadets is on military skills and drills. The first five months of their program consist of military training, after which the general academic education follows, still combined with shorter military trainings. After the first period of military training, short-track cadets follow a selected number of courses, to prepare them intellectually for their commission. The NLDA requires cadets to successfully complete courses in e.g. behavioural sciences, English, mathematics, ethics. Their lecturers do not need academic credentials. Most have a military rank, and work for limited time span at the NLDA. Short track cadets can participate in the corps' activities. Yet, in practice they focus less on such activities and more on the period ahead of them, after the NLDA.

21.3.2 Denmark

21.3.2.1 Changes in the Danish Armed Forces Following the End of the Cold War

As in The Netherlands, the end of the cold war heralded significant changes in the Danish armed forces. The impact of these changes might have been enhanced by the fact that the annulment of the military threat from the East, also altered Denmark's strategic position. Until 1989, the country had profited from its control

---

[20] Without going into all details of the end-terms, competencies and activities, during the military training cadets learn – in general terms – the very basics of the military skills and drills, like ammunition awareness, force protection, fire resistance, marching, hygiene, first aid, map-reading, leadership skills, ethics, physical and mental tenability.

over Greenland and from its position at Russia's only exit from the Baltic Sea to the Atlantic. Accordingly, despite very harsh anti-American rhetoric during the 70s and 80s, the country had remained a key NATO partner throughout the Cold War. With the Fall of the Berlin Wall, Denmark's engagement in US-run operations increased significantly. Like The Netherlands, Denmark had a long tradition of participating in UN peacekeeping missions across the globe. Now, however, Danish troops were deployed to missions involving actual fighting, culminating with the Army's engagement in Helmand, Afghanistan, under British command 2006–2014. Formally, Denmark has not abolished the draft, as this is not possible without changing the Constitution. In reality, however, conscription was suspended during the Afghanistan campaign as the number of volunteers exceeded the military's capacity for preparing men and women for deployment. This is still the case today.

This restricted training capacity was due to the fact that in spite of the country's increased involvement abroad the armed forces went through budget cuts matching those of other West European countries during the past three decades. As part of this process, the Parliamentary Defence Settlement of November 2012, initiated a substantial change of the officers' training program. Traditionally, cadets enrolled in officer training had been recruited either from the NCO corps or directly from high school. In the future, however, at least half the new cadets should be recruited on the basis of their civilian B.A.

The settlement also included a decision to merge he military branches' command centres, to assign core tasks of the Defence Command – such as the financial management of the Armed Forces – to the Ministry of Defence, and to merge the military schools. Although the Army still trains its cadets at the Royal Danish *Military* Academy, both Navy and Air Force cadets are trained at the Royal Danish *Defence* Academy, which is also in charge of the officers' training program in all three branches.

21.3.2.2 Two Tracks, One Officer Corps

Apparently, the reforms of Officers' Education in Denmark and The Netherlands seem to have followed very similar pathways. Both have been initiated concurrently with general budget cuts, signifying defence policies after the end of the Cold War. Both models have been developed to take the volatility of the job market into account, (some may pursue a military career for a couple of years, then leave the armed forces, and perhaps someday return). Both systems open for the enrolment of civilian B.As. And following this, both systems have arranged two different tracks for the officers-to-be to follow, depending on their background. And as in The Netherlands, Danish officers' education can also be divided into three models: a promotion model, a track where cadets are recruited with a civilian B.A., and finally (from 2020), a track where cadets are recruited directly from high school.

This, however, is also as far as the similarities can be stretched. Danish cadets recruited directly from high school will only enter a short track program designed to meet an immediate need for junior officers, and this will be an Army-specific arrangement. Moreover, unlike the program structure developed in The Netherlands, where short track cadets are not expected to pursue a life-long trajectory in the military, Danish cadets from the promotion model and the B.A. model are enrolled in the same program and follow exactly the same career-path once they have entered Officer School.

Danish cadets recruited from the NCO corps need to have at least two years of experience as sergeants and an academy professional degree, which it would usually take them three years to acquire. This means, in practice, that following the Danish promotion model may be more time consuming than being enrolled with a B.A. degree. Accordingly, a number of the cadets recruited from the outside, have served before, but have deliberately taken a civilian B.A. to be able to save time when pursuing an officer's career. When comparing the two groups in the army cohort that started in 2017, those who had not served in the military before were two years younger, on average, than those who had been recruited from the NCO corps.

Cadets recruited from the outside need a civilian B.A., (it can be either a university degree or a professional degree), and to pass a number of tests to be enrolled in the officers' training program. Once accepted, they need to go through boot camp at the branch specific NCO school and serve for a short while as NCOs, before starting at the Officer School. In the Navy, future officers recruited from the outside start their NCO training in August and move on to the officer school in March, 7 months later. In the Army, the preparatory time is 9 months, and in the Air Force it is 17 months.

To sum up, the reasons why both the Danish and the Dutch educational programs underwent reforms may have been similar, but the outcomes of these reforms differ in a number of ways. Two of these are especially worth remarking: First, Denmark no longer has the "long track" model. Instead, all cadets are enrolled on the basis of a B.A. degree (those recruited from the NCO corps have just taken it concurrently with their military service). Second – and perhaps most importantly – Danish cadets in the two main programs follow the same education once they enter Officer School. They literally attend the same classes. And as mentioned above, once they are commissioned as officers, they are expected to follow similar career trajectories. Accordingly, on paper, the Danish model seems to resample the template of the British Navy in the 18th century more than the Dutch model: Danish officers-to-be learn to bridge the gap separating academic and practical skills from the first day at the Officer School. They may have followed different tracks to get there. But once they enter the gates of the academy, they do it as one group.

21.4 Discussion: Reinventing the Military Profession

In the following we will address the benefits and deficits of the Dutch and the Danish models in light of the framework of educating "thinking officers" set out in the theory section above.

21.4.1 Challenges to the Dutch Model: Neither Fish Nor Fowl

The main challenge, facing the Dutch model is that it potentially creates a whole class of "quasi-officers" – academics who have received 18 months of military training, but who have not been acquainted with the "military way". The danger is that they, from the true "military native's" point of view, will be seen as scholars scrounging on the prestige of the uniform, not as true members of the profession. Ironically, this danger is enhanced by the fact that the structure and content of the short-track program is designed to compensate for the academics' lack of proper military training.

Thus, by trying both to accommodate the demand of budget adjustments, and by designing the program to compensate for the deficits the academics, the military runs the risk of getting the worst of two worlds: It will both lose capacity (because of its restrained economic room-to-move), and it will miss an excellent opportunity for re-inventing the military profession, since it appears not to utilise the potential that the influx of cadets with a civilian education represents. Thus seen, it is the very "compensatory" design that constitutes the most immediate problem in the Dutch programmes. If the aim is to merge the scholar's and the officer's habitus, this solution seems to be neither fish nor meat. Compensatory tools might be well-intended, but they also signal the existence of a hierarchy: That some lacks the skills mastered by others.

21.4.2 Challenges to the Danish Model

At the outset, the reform was not received with open arms everywhere in the Danish Armed Forces. Members of the first cohort experienced open resentment from older colleagues, who saw them as second-rate cadets. But in comparison to the Dutch model, its overall – where all cadets, both those with a civilian B.A. and those recruited from the rank and file, enter the academy as one group – seems to meet the demand of creating uniformity much better. And today, military authorities, school leaders, those in charge of training programs, and instructors are positive towards the new model.[21] As one NCO school instructor put it: "They [the B.A. cadets] are so self-dependent. I just wish we'd made this reform 20 years ago."

Although the enrolment of civilian B.A.s was implemented to meet budgetary requirements, the integration of knowledge and skills actually seems to work better, because the cadets are trained together. Nevertheless, the fact that the academy faces difficulties in attracting promotion model cadets constitutes a severe threat to the whole idea of the program. In 2017, 50% of the cohort that started at the Danish

---

[21] Brænder and Holsting 2019.

Military Academy, had been recruited from the NCO corps. In 2018, this was reduced to about 30%. And while the two other branches have succeeded in recruiting future officers from the outside, a negligible minority of Navy and Air Force NCOs chose to pursue an officer's career. These harsh realities imply, that the ideal that new model officers should develop from the interaction between academic knowledge and practical skills may be hard to fulfil.

Furthermore, the Danish program entails one crucial challenge that it shares with the Dutch short track model: Economically seen, reducing actual officers' training to less than two years may be an advantage, but it comes with a price: While the enrolment requirements and the merging of cadets with different backgrounds enable future Danish officers to meet the demands of military training and academic education, the tight time frame makes it highly doubtful that there will also be resources for the character formation. The formal requirements for being commissioned as officer will be retained, but the cost reduction motive also raises fear that neither Dutch nor Danish officers will have acquired the informal skills, the norms and the values, in short, the habitus that makes them a true member of the profession.

21.5 Conclusion: Developing the Habitus of the Thinking Soldier

If you think education is expensive, try ignorance![22]

Creating an officer, who embodies both academic ideals of critical reflexion and military ideals of command, may be difficult, but it is not necessarily impossible. Across the world, in the 18th and 19th centuries, the notion that officers needed both scholarly knowledge and practical skills was one of the objectives for establishing military academies. Here, civilian knowledge met military practice, and the "clash" between the two was thought to be beneficial to the military profession as a whole. In that light, the myth that the scholar's habitus is fundamentally incompatible with that of the military professional, may serve a particular view of some military professionals, but the formation of the military profession thrives on tensions like these.[23] The emerging syntheses of the clashing habitus of the soldier and the scholar would be the habitus of the thinking soldier.

What is seen as an absolutely central feature in the military profession in one context may be regarded as peripheral aspect in another. Likewise, what has been regarded as the absolute opposite of the military mind-set in one context, may be

---

[22] The quote is attributed to many, f.i., Einstein, but the ultimate source is unknown: https://quoteinvestigator.com/2016/05/03/expense/ accessed 16 February 2019.

[23] Elias 2007.

fully incorporated in it and even become a defining aspect of the soldier's habitus. This is why perceiving the academic ideal merely as an obstacle on timely decision making in the military may be a mistake. It makes us disregard the fact that although a swift incorrect decision may be a lot better than no decision at all, a swift and correct decision is what officers' training should, ideally, aim at. Cadets with a civilian education have something important to offer. In other words, given that the armed forces in The Netherlands and Denmark now have to recruit cadets with a civilian B.A., these organisations may in fact profit from this influx of new knowledge into the profession.

From a purely economic point of view, the cost efficiency can be seen as a clear benefit of enrolling cadets with a civilian B.A. degree. Since they already hold an academic degree, their training can be shortened and focused only on the development of military skills. Combining knowledge with skills requires, however, that those entering the military with a civilian background are not asked to leave their knowledge at the door. And following this reasoning, we fear that the path chosen by The Netherlands where military skills and academic knowledge are segregated is not likely to remedy this problem. On the contrary, regarding the differences between cadets enrolled in the two programs as something that should be 'overcome' or 'compensated for' (by training the latter to accommodate to the ideals embodied by the former), is more likely to enhance a perception of the new cadets as second-class officers.

In theory, the Danish model, where cadets recruited from the NCO corps are trained alongside with B.A. cadets, is better suited for integrating knowledge and skills, and creating a shared feeling of belonging among the new officers. In practice, however, it is not unproblematic either. First, difficulties in recruiting from the NCO corps, means that the new model officer will be both inexperienced and less able to embody the military habitus. Second, whereas the new model cadets may be able to meet the formal military and academic demands within the shortened time frame, they may find it more difficult to acquire the nonwritten norms, values and attitude that are also part of the habitus that sets the officer apart.

21.5.1 *Limitations*

Unlike others, who have delved into the specific characteristics of program curricula, practical training, and informal socialization processes,[24] our focus has been on establishing an overall comparative framework for looking at the general strengths and weaknesses of the reformed officers' training programs in The Netherlands and Denmark offers in regard to developing 'thinking soldiers'. Comparative research designs can entail great explanatory power. To fulfil this explanatory potential however, the cadets in both countries should be followed

---

[24] Van Schilt and Moelker 2011; Van den Aker 2007; Groen and Klinkert 2003; Dalenberg 2016.

through their education and afterwards, during their careers, to show whether the fears we have uttered above – in regard to the maintenance of the informal knowledge and skills of future officers – are justified or not.

21.5.2 Recommendations

Above, we stated that the largest potential problem with the Dutch short track was that it failed to establish a framework for embracing both military and scholarly skills. Accordingly, if we should advise local policy makers in The Netherlands, an improved educational model is near at hand and not difficult to implement. Offering the accredited Master of Military Studies as a comprehensive academic training to the cadets of the short model would complete their military training and would contribute to create a thinking soldier. This would lengthen their military training by one year, but it would result in officers that possess at least two credentials, the civilian and the military master. Moreover, the increased length of the program would not only strengthen the competences and prestige of the (not so) short-track program, but also enable these cadets to participate more in the informal character formation of the NLDA.

Our fear in regard to the Danish program concerned less the integration of scholarly and military habitus, and more the cadets' ability of acquiring the informal knowledge and skills that is characteristic of the true member of the military profession. Although Danish B.A. cadets go through NCO school to acquire military skills before actually commencing their training at the academy, the time frame allotted to personal development is very tight. Whether the Danish officers-to-be will lack the personal strengths that traditionally characterize an officer and a gentleman, is – of course – an empirical question that can only be answered by pursuing a research agenda as the one sketched above. Should that be the case, however, it is obvious to suggest that the time frame is expanded, so that the future officers can learn not only to become thinking soldiers, but also thinking soldiers who embody the informal skills and knowledge that have traditionally been the hallmark of the profession.

References

Abbott AD (1988) The System of Professions: Essay on the Division of Expert Labour. University of Chicago Press, Chicago.
Bourdieu P (1984) Distinction: A Social Critique of the Judgement of Taste. Routledge, London, pp. 5 and 41.
Brænder M, Holsting VS (2019) The Power of Experience? Innovative and Authoritative Leadership Values among Army Cadets. Paper presented at the International Sociological Association (ISA), main conference. Toronto.

Caforio G (ed) (2001) The Flexible Officer: Professional Education and Military Operations Other Than War, A Cross-National Analysis. Artistic & Publishing Company, Gaeta.

Collins R (1979) The Credential Society: An Historical Sociology of Education and Stratification. Academic Press, New York.

Dalenberg S (2016) Officer, practise what you preach! Research on effects and interventions in military officer socialization at the Royal Military Academy. Radboud Universiteit Nijmegen, Nijmegen.

De Ruiter RM (2018) Breuklijn 1989: Continuïteit en verandering in het Nederlandse defensiebeleid 1989–1993 [Faultline 1989. Continuity and change in Dutch defence policy 1989–1993]. University of Amsterdam, Amsterdam.

Elias N (2007) The Genesis of the Naval Profession. University College Dublin Press, Dublin.

Freidson E (1970) Profession of Medicine: A Study of the Sociology of Applied Knowledge, University of Chicago Press, Chicago.

Groen PMH, Klinkert W (2003) Studeren in uniform. 175 Jaar Koninklijke Militaire Academie 1828–2003 [Studying in uniform. 175 years Royal Netherlands Military Academy 1828–2003]. Sdu uitgevers, The Hague.

Houlding JA (1981) Fit for Service: The Training of the British Army, 1715–1795. Oxford University Press, Oxford.

Kramer E (2007) Organizing Doubt: Grounded Theory, Army Units, and Dealing with Dynamic Complexity. Copenhagen Business School Press, Copenhagen.

Osiel MJ (1998) Obeying Orders. Transaction Publishers, New Jersey.

Schoy M (undated) General Gehrhard Von Scharnhorst: Mentor of Clausewitz and Father of the Prussian-German General Staff. Toronto. http://www.cfc.forces.gc.ca/259/181/82_schoy.pdf Accessed 13 February 2019.

Soeters J (2018) Organizational Cultures in the Military. In: Caforio G, Nuciari M (eds) Handbook of the Sociology of the Military. Springer, pp. 251–272.

Van den Aker PJEJ (2007) Kennis is macht, karakter is meer! Initiële officiersvorming aan de Nederlandse Defensie Academie [Knowledge is power, character is more! Initial Officer Education at the Royal Netherlands Defence Academy]. Militaire Spectator 176(10):16–425.

Van Schilt J (ed) (2011) Herfsttij van het militaire elitegevoel [Autumn for the military elitist sentiment]. Ridderprint BV, Ridderkerk, pp. 187–224.

Van Schilt J, Moelker R (2011) Vorming, deugden en zelfbeeld vanuit een eigentijds perspectief [Training, virtues and self-image from a contemporary perspective].

Von Baudissin W (1969) Soldat für den Frieden. Entwurf für eine zeitgemäße Bundeswehr. Beiträge 1951–1969. Piper, Munich.

Marenne Jansen, MA works at the Advisory Council for International Affairs, while writing her Ph.D. at the Institute for Management Research of the Radboud University. Her research focuses on military leadership development, and the nexus between development and security. In addition, she is interested in educational philosophy, sustainable development and the role of international organizations. She has taught courses on these topics for bachelor and master students at various Dutch universities, international diplomats, and NGO employees.

Dr. Morten Brænder is Associate Professor in Political Sociology in the Department of Political Science, and Director of the Centre of University Studies in Journalism, Department of Communication & Culture at Aarhus University. His research centres on the sociology of professions, motivation and leadership values, especially with a focus on the military. He is the author of a number of books and several research articles, published in, for instance, Public Administration Review, Armed Forces & Society, and Qualitative Psychology. In cooperation with the Royal Danish Defence Academy he is currently conducting a large-scale study of the cohorts enrolled in the revised Danish officer education programmes.

Dr. René Moelker is an associate professor of sociology at the Netherlands Defence Academy. He holds a doctorate from the Erasmus University, Rotterdam. His work in military sociology concentrates on the sociology of military families, military technology, the military profession, the military sociology of Norbert Elias, military education, the conflict in Chechnya, and the media. His latest projects focus on veterans and military families. His latest edited volume (with M.D. Andres and N. Rones) is entitled *Politics of Military Families* (Routledge 2019).

Epilogue

Military Education Between Alienation and Symbiosis

At the end of this volume, we want to reflect briefly on the position of the Faculty of Military Sciences (FMS) in The Netherlands as an institute that plays a central role in military education. The FMS occupies a complex position in the Ministry of Defence, which is different from other academic institutes. This position is related to the specific character of military education that aims to combine academic education and *Bildung*. Although FMS has academic freedom for its scientific education and research, it is part of the Netherlands Defence Academy (NLDA). Furthermore, its staff and funding rely almost completely on the Ministry of Defence and it is interwoven with regulations of the Ministry of Defence. However, its position is different from other departments in the Ministry of Defence as well. Compared to most other academic institutes, the FMS is much more closely connected to a particular professional environment. This means that it is much more – or at least much more visibly – confronted with demands to remain relevant for its context. At the same time, as an academic institute, it is essential to be able to retain certain critical distance to the military organization. We have seen in this volume that for example developing a particular governance structure is essential in this regard. In this epilogue, we will use the catchphrase "between alienation and symbiosis" in order to sketch the complex position that the FMS occupies.

Today's Relevance of Academic Education and *Bildung* for the Military

Academic education and *Bildung* have traditionally been considered of key importance in officers' education in The Netherlands. We want to argue that this combination continues to be relevant today. Today's military missions increasingly constitute a knowledge intensive environment for the military professional. This in itself justifies a significant investment in military education. While this is not controversial, the question is why academic education is to be preferred over more narrowly focused vocational programs. The reason for this is that – more than vocational training – academic education contributes to the development of critical thinking.

Particularly critical thinking is of key importance in the environments for which military professionals are educated. In this environment, military professionals can be confronted with uncertain and ambiguous threats and intelligent adversaries. What might appear as limited everyday pragmatic challenges potentially correlates with strategic and political controversies. On top of that, military professionals need to be able to ingrate new and often quite sophisticated technology within existing practices in a productive way, also when this new technology requires fundamental transformation of these existing practices. The challenges in the environment of military professionals are not merely cognitive; critical thinking requires more than rational knowledge and sophisticated information processing. It also demands what is often broadly referred to as "character". Challenges for military professionals are also ethical and (social) psychological. Military professionals are trained to apply violent force and are at the same time potentially confronted with violent threat. This confrontation with violence can have significant psychological effects, while it also demands the ability to reflect on moral issues involved. Furthermore, officers may be required to lead a group in difficult circumstances, which demands considerable insight into group dynamics. Critical thinking and character are therefore very much related, particularly in the environments for which future officers are educated, which is, in our view, the main argument why a combination of academic education and *Bildung* continues to be relevant in military education.

Reflective Practice and the Cornerstones of Academic Education

The FMS has embraced the concept of the "thinking soldier" in order to characterize its particular educational ambitions. This concept fits within the broader conception of the "reflective practitioner". As various authors in this volume have discussed, this conception – developed by Donald Schön[1] – aims to characterize the way professionals use knowledge in relation to uncertain, unique and value laden issues with which they are confronted. Also military professionals are confronted with a messy practice that challenges them to apply and tailor existing insights and concepts. While traditionally it was thought that the "scientific method" is the universal road to rational knowledge[2] and consequently practitioners ideally are

---

[1] Schön D (1983) The reflective practitioner. Basic Books, New York.
[2] Toulmin S (2001) Return to Reason, pp. 84–85. Harvard University Press, Cambridge, MA.

instrumental problem solvers that select technical means to practical purposes,[3] the concept of the reflective practitioner incites a different view on the work of practitioners and the nature of the scientific insights they use. If reflection-in-action and reflection-on-action are core challenges for the military professional, critical thinking is crucial for reflective practitioners and should therefore be the basis for military education.

The education of reflective practice requires a particular institute in which critical thinking and *Bildung* are connected. Levin and Greenwood[4] suggest that academic freedom plays a central role in such institutes. In criticizing current trends in public universities, they argue that the connection between academic freedom, *Bildung* and academic integrity is essential for academic education in democratic societies. While according to the traditional Bildung philosophy the notion of (academic) or individual freedom is crucial, Levin and Greenwood understand *Bildung* as "human development". They argue that academic freedom plays a central role in academic institutions, particularly because of its relation to *Bildung*: "without the freedom to speak up and to research issues salient to faculty and students, *Bildung* is not possible and the foundations for academic integrity cannot be built."[5] According to Levin and Greenwood, many contemporary public universities have become alienated from their societal function by becoming overly inwardly orientated. One particular example of this inward orientation is a single-minded focus on publication statistics at the expense of the societal relevance of research.

We can learn from the analysis of Levin and Greenwood that an academic institute occupies a position in relation to a particular biotope. It needs to prove its meaningfulness and relevance in relation to this biotope. In the view of Levin and Greenwood this means avoiding alienation from this biotope. We want to argue that it also requires avoiding the opposite of alienation: symbiosis. An academic institute that identifies too much with the existing values, beliefs and practices of the biotope to which it is related, loses its relevance, because it loses its critical function. As such it loses its ability to constructively contribute to the future development of its biotope, both in research and in education. All in all, a faculty that organizes programs in the service of academic education and *Bildung* should cultivate critical thinking and should look for a productive middle between the undesirable extremes of alienation and symbiosis.

Searching for this productive middle is not straightforward. It requires – for example – *Bildung* of the academic staff itself. On the one hand, a significant part of the academic staff of the FMS has a background in the military organization. Searching for a productive middle between alienation and symbiosis demands that they establish a critical distance from the environment that has intensely socialized

---

[3] Schön D (1987) Educating the reflective practitioner. Jossey-Bas Publishers, San Francisco.
[4] Levin M, Greenwood D (2017) Creating a New Public University and Reviving Democracy. Action Research in Higher Education. Berghahn, New York.
[5] Ibid., p. 56.

them, perhaps even more than they have ever realized. On the other hand, the members of the academic staff with a background in academia should not carry over dysfunctional trends from academia. Doing meaningful research in a military context requires more than taking the shortest route to a publication and educating reflective practitioners demands a thorough understanding of the relevant issues in the military organization.

Controversies That Lead to Challenges

The catchphrase "between alienation and symbiosis" characterizes in our view the complex position of the FMS in relation to its biotope. It signifies that FMS can have a meaningful and productive relation to the military organization through cultivating critical thinking. In this way, it is not only of significance to the military organization, but to society in general. However, when confronted with concrete policy issues, it is not always straightforward what this productive middle is. Obviously, alienation and symbiosis depend on framing and perspective. What some might consider as "relevant" is "symbiotic" according to the perspective of others, and what some might consider "healthy criticism" is "alienation" for others. Nevertheless, we think that the catchphrase can help to reflect on the complex position of FMS. As an example, we want to discuss two particular present day controversies with which FMS is confronted. Our catchphrase will not be able to give definitive answers in relation to these controversies, but we think it helps to characterize the issues that are at stake more clearly.

Shorter and More Focused Educational Programs

An often-heard criticism on the current scientific bachelor degree programs of the FMS is that they take too long and they address issues that are not of direct relevance to the immediate working environment of starting offers. Critics argue that instead, programs should be much more focused on topics relevant to this immediate working environment. Currently, the Netherlands Defence Academy offers several shorter programs. The policy is to recruit people that already have finished a scientific education at a public university, although current conditions on the labor market put this under pressure. This leads to the question of what the extra-value is of the scientific bachelor compared to these quick and tailored programs. The demand for programs that are more directly tailored to immediate working environments is understandable and there is no doubt – as Levin and Greenwood have argued – that an academic institute that cannot prove its meaningfulness to its biotope will eventually become obsolete.

However, in our perspective it is important that the connection to the professional environment is a reflective connection. The risk of programs with a narrower focus is that they perceive existing practice within the military organization as the norm. In that case, education becomes teaching existing practice as "best possible practice". The problem with this is the assumption that existing practice is beyond reasonable criticism. However, good education is never only intended for "now". The officers that are educated now are the ones that will transform the military organization in the future, which is inevitable if a changing world puts new demands on the military organization. A narrow focus in education on existing practice runs the risk of cultivating regressive conservatism: it can perhaps even be explained as a bureaucratic reflex to hide form important developments in the outside world. Such an attitude would stand in stark contrast to espoused beliefs in "innovation". That is specifically the reason why "critical thinking" is of the utmost importance in education. And that is the reason why "an academy" occupies an important position in a generally quite closed institute such as the military organization.

Specialists Instead of Generalists

What is often heard is that contemporary technological development demands more specialization in the officer corps. For example, current developments in the sphere of big data require a mastery of statistics that goes considerably beyond what is offered now. Moreover, developments in the cyber domain, robotics, quantum computing, smart and intelligent networks, biotechnology and space-technology are potentially disruptive, even within a relatively short time frame. At the same time, the exact impacts of such developments on the military organization are essentially impossible to predict. Officers' education – also in the academic realms – is mainly focused on educating generalists. Not incidentally, the bachelor degree programs that are offered at the FMS are multi-disciplinary or interdisciplinary. Some argue therefore that if the military organization requires increasing specialization, the future demands a more specialized officer corps. Such development fits with current developments in academia where increasing specialization has been one of the most important trends in the last decades.[6]

However, the question is if increasing specialization really is the right answer in the face of such developments. Understanding technical details is not the only thing that is important about current technological developments. An important point that is made in a field like Science & Technology studies is that new technology potentially influences existing practice in profound ways.[7] This is not a limited technological issue but brings with it organizational and ethical questions. Such an issue requires reflective practitioners instead of single-minded specialists. At the same time, taking a reflective stance towards technological developments does

---

[6] Toulmin S (2001) Return to Reason. Harvard University Press, Cambridge, MA.

[7] Verbeek P P (2011) Moralizing technology: Understanding and designing the morality of things. University of Chicago Press, Chicago.

require thorough understanding. The challenge for the FMS remains how it can keep track with the many developments in the military domain, while at the same time it can offers a perspective on the integrated implications beyond the specialized focus.

The Vulnerable Location Between Symbiosis and Alienation

This epilogue has attempted to give a perspective on the complex position that the FMS occupies within the military organization. This position is indicated here with the catchphrase "between alienation and symbiosis". The FMS can retain its relevance military practice in particular and the Ministry of Defence and society in general, if it is able to retain a productive middle between these two undesirable extremes. This position between alienation and symbiosis is quite vulnerable. The FMS periodically experiences pressures in the direction of either symbiosis or alienation. Particularly in times of budget cuts such pressures can become significant. After all, not many might be motivated to look beyond immediate relevance and formulate a critical position when the survival of the institute is threatened. Yet, resisting such pressures is essential if the institute is to protect its identity and remain relevant in the first place. If the military organization requires "reflective practitioners" because of the challenges in the contemporary professional environment, it needs to protect the vulnerable position between alienation and symbiosis of the institute in which they are educated.

Netherlands Defence Academy
Breda

Wim Klinkert
Myriame Bollen
Marenne Jansen
Henk de Jong
Eric-Hans Kramer
Lisette Vos

GPSR Compliance

The European Union's (EU) General Product Safety Regulation (GPSR) is a set of rules that requires consumer products to be safe and our obligations to ensure this.

If you have any concerns about our products, you can contact us on

ProductSafety@springernature.com

In case Publisher is established outside the EU, the EU authorized representative is:

Springer Nature Customer Service Center GmbH
Europaplatz 3
69115 Heidelberg, Germany

www.ingramcontent.com/pod-product-compliance
Ingram Content Group UK Ltd.
Pitfield, Milton Keynes, MK11 3LW, UK
UKHW021446190426
11946UKWH00022B/50